THEOLOGIANS AND PHILOSOPHERS USING
SOCIAL MEDIA

Advice, Tips, and Testimonials

Thomas Jay Oord, Ed.

SacraSage Press

SacraSage

SacraSage Press
San Diego, CA 92106

Cover Design: Hammad Khalid

ISBN 978-0-578-19399-1

Printed in the United States of America

Library of Congress Cataloguing-in-Publication Data

Thomas Jay Oord, Editors
Theologians and Philosophers Using Social Media: Advice, Tips, and Testimonials / Oord. Ed.

ISBN: 978-0-578-19399-1

Dedicated to Jay Akkerman, George Lyons, and Mark Maddix

Cutting-Edge Leaders in Creative Scholarship

Table of Contents

THOMAS JAY OORD Editor's Introduction 1

Contributions

1. JAY RICHARD AKKERMAN Pastoral Theology..7

2. KIMBERLY ERVIN ALEXANDER History of Christianity 13

3. BRADLEY SHAVIT ARTSON Rabbinic Studies... 19

4. ARNE BACHMANN, RASMUS NAGEL, HANNA REICHEL,
   THOMAS RENKERT Open Access Theology Journal 23

5. RICHARD BECK Psychology and Theology.. 31

6. COLLEEN BIRCHETT Theology and Technology.. 37

7. FELIPE KOCH BUTTELLI Systematic Theology 41

8. HEIDI A CAMPBELL Religion, Media and Digital Culture 45

9. MICHAEL J. CHRISTENSEN Practical Theology... 49

10. SHANE CLIFTON Theology and Disability 53

11. RON COLE-TURNER Theology and Ethics 59

12. DAVID W. CONGDON Systematic Theology 65

13. GREG COOTSONA Theology and Religious Studies 69

14. BENJAMIN L. COREY Public Theology 75

15. ROBERT D. CORNWALL Historical Theology 79

16. MARC CORTEZ Theological Education 85

17. OLIVER D. CRISP Systematic Theology 91

18. GREGORY CROFFORD Religious Education 95

19. JAMES CROSSLEY Biblical Theology 99

20. DAVID DAULT Theology and Media 103

21. HELEN DE CRUZ Philosophy 109

22. MIGUEL A. DE LA TORRE Social Ethics and Latinx Studies 115

23. JOSEPH DUGGAN Public Theology 121

24. BRUCE EPPERLY Practical Theology 125

25. PATRICIA ADAMS FARMER Practical Theology 129

26. DANIEL FINCKE Philosophy 135

27. JR. FORASTEROS Practical Theology 139

28. DION A. FORSTER Public Theology 143

29. TRIPP FULLER Constructive Theology 147

30. DEANE GALBRAITH Religious Studies 151

31. KARL GIBERSON Science & Religion 155

32. DEIRDRE J. GOOD Biblical Theology 161

33. MICHAEL J. GORMAN Biblical Theology 165

34. ANDREW GRAYSTONE Theology and Media 169

35. CHRIS E. W. GREEN Systematic Theology 175

36. JOEL B. GREEN Biblical Theology 179

37. DAVID P. GUSHEE Christian Ethics 183

38. NATHAN HAMM Theology and Media...187

39. MICHAEL HARDIN Theology and Ethics..191

40. JOHN W. HAWTHORNE Theology and Sociology............................197

41. CHRISTINE HELMER Historical and Constructive Theology..........201

42. ROBYN HENDERSON-ESPINOZA Public Theology...........................207

43. WM. CURTIS HOLTZEN Philosophical Theology 209

44. ZACK HUNT Public Theology 215

45. LARRY W. HURTADO New Testament and Christian Origins 221

46. DARREN IAMMARINO Religious Studies...223

47. THOMAS INGRAM Public Theology...229

48. BRADLEY JERSAK Practical Theology 235

49. DAVID KYLE JOHNSON Philosophy..239

50. CRAIG S. KEENER New Testament 243

51. GRACE JI-SUN KIM Constructive Theology......................................247

52. J. R. DANIEL KIRK Biblical Theology 253

53. ADAM KOTSKO Philosophical Theology...257

54. KWOK PUI-LAN Theology and Spirituality 261

55. JASON LEPOJÄRVI Constructive Theology.......................................265

56. BEX LEWIS Theology and Communications....................................269

57. TODD A. LITTLETON Pastoral Theology 275

58. JAY MCDANIEL Public Theology...279

59. JAMES F. MCGRATH Biblical Studies and Science Fiction............283

60. BRIAN D. MCLAREN Public Theology 289

61. PAUL LOUIS METZGER Theology and Culture 293

62. JORY MICAH Pastoral Theology 297

63. LISA MICHAELS Theology and Ministry...299

64. ROGER HAYDON MITCHELL Political Theology...305

65. BRINT MONTGOMERY Philosophy..313

66. R. T. MULLINS Philosophical Theology 319

67. JOHN C. O'KEEFE Practical Theology 325

68. STEPHEN OKEY Systematic Theology...331

69. KEEGAN OSINSKI Sacramental and Liturgical Theology...................................337

70. ALEXANDER PRUSS Philosophy..341

71. JANEL APPS RAMSEY Pastoral Theology...343

72. TRAVIS REED AND STEVE FROST Theology and Communications 347

73. MONTE LEE RICE Missional Theology 353

74. SARAH LANE RITCHIE Science and Religion 363

75. RICHARD ROHR Practical Theology...367

76. JONATHAN RUSSELL Philosophical Theology..369

77. KATHERINE G. SCHMIDT Theology and Media..373

78. LEA F. SCHWEITZ Science and Religion 377

79. J. AARON SIMMONS Philosophy...381

80. ATLE OTTESEN SØVIK Systematic Theology 389

81. JIM STUMP Science and Religion..393

82. LEONARD SWEET Missional Theology..397

83. JON PAUL SYDNOR Public Theology...401

84. EDWIN WOODRUFF TAIT Historical Theology..405

85. JONATHAN Y. TAN Worship, Music, and Pastoral Ministry 411

86. **KEVIN TIMPE** Philosophy...417

87. **PHILIP TOWNE** Intercultural Theology..421

88. **ALEXIS JAMES WAGGONER** Public Theology 425

89. **NATHANAEL WELCH** Theology and Disability....................................429

90. **KURT WILLEMS** Pastoral Theology..433

91. **AMOS YONG** Intercultural (Not Digitally Adept) Theology...........................439

Index..443

THOMAS JAY OORD

Editor's Introduction

The Medium is the Message?

I will never forget first hearing Marshall McLuhan's famous words, "The medium is the message." I was a first-year undergraduate student thrust into an upper-division communications course. When the professor introduced McLuhan's statement, I was jarred.

I entered college thinking the media used for communication involved simple tools, which were neutral and largely inconsequential. We might prefer some forms of media to others, I thought, but the media didn't influence the message. Whatever medium a communicator chose delivered the desired meaning, without remainder. To hear McLuhan claim the medium was *the* message seemed patently false.

My view today is that McLuhan was partly right. I don't think any medium presents the *entire* message. But neither do I think media are inconsequential to the message they communicate. In my view, the forms of communication shape the content of their messages. Media matter.

I often find it difficult to articulate *precisely* how a medium shapes its message, however. What *exactly* does a video communicate differently than a text, a newspaper differently than a whisper, a billboard differently than a song, etc.? What's going on?

I've come to think the problem of explaining a medium's influence on its message is similar to the problem of explaining art. Just as I cannot articulate well my aesthetic preferences and intuitions, I also cannot explain precisely the influence a medium plays in shaping a message. Language cannot capture art fully. Videos, whispers, billboards, and emails shape messages in unique ways.

The Growing Influence of Social Media and Technology

I began with McLuhan's famous phrase because it rings in my head as I think about contemporary forms of social media and technology. There's little doubt that social media is changing the way most of us live. Most people acknowledge these changes in their personal relationships. But few notice the way social media is changing how scholars do scholarship and religious thought leaders engage followers. This book explores those changes.

I've noticed these changes in my own work. It began in the early 2000s when my academic institution became the first to offer accredited, fully online Masters Degrees in religion. The criticism my colleagues and I received for offering online degrees was intense. Some of that criticism was deserved, but most was based upon naïve assumptions. Now, of course, online education has become common. It has both strengths and weaknesses. But the number of full-throated critics continually declines.

As the internet grew in stature, many theologians, philosophers, and thought leaders considered it simply a new repository for ideas and scholarly materials. And when social media grew, many thought it simply as a means to promote their ideas, projects, or convictions. To reference McLuhan, many scholars and thought leaders initially thought of the internet and social media as means alone and not as affecting their messages.

A good number have since discovered that the internet and social media are more than repositories or marketing tools. Various forms of technology influence the way scholars pursue scholarship, formulate their research, and do tasks related to their disciplines or interests. Activists and religious leaders realized that their choices in social media influence both their message and how they pursue their passions. Media matter for theologians and philosophers.

Today, having an online presence is increasingly necessary for intellectual leaders. Publishing presses want to know about a potential author's "platform," by which they typically mean social media platform. Educational institutions want to know if a potential professorial candidate has experience teaching online courses or engaging the public through social media. The quality of a scholar's or institution's website typically affects the measure of its influence. Most conferences, books, and other intellectual events have some social media footprint. In many ways, scholars and other thought leaders who ignore social media are left behind.

Social media now plays a key role in generating ideas, networking, crowd-sourcing, private or classroom discussions, research, project publicity, personal branding, journaling, event organizing, and more. Some use their presence on social media to generate speaking or writing opportunities. Others do ministry, pursue activism, or create digital content in ways previously unimagined.

Along with the opportunities that social media and technology offer come challenges. Handling online trolls, stalkers, and jerks has become a necessary skill. More of us understand the need to develop a civil, informed, and virtuous online presence. Discerning how to communicate lovingly in the digital age extends the task of discerning how to communicate lovingly in the print or analog ages.

And then there's the issue of time. Nearly every contributor to this book wrestles with how much time to spend online and how best to schedule social media engagement. Many confess to failing. Just about everyone realizes the import of "unplugging" occasionally. We need technology Sabbaths.

Perhaps most interestingly, social media seems to be undermining the view that scholars work in private, "ivory towers." That's never been entirely the case, of course. But social scholarship emphasizes and expands the role communities play for helping scholars, activists, and religious leaders. Social scholarship offers new opportunities to collaborate for the common good.

McLuhan is also known for saying that "we shape our tools and thereafter our tools shape us." Like the first McLuhan quote, I think this quip is partly correct. What we are becoming by using social media is still in process. But like most essayists in this book, I'm convinced social media and technology are shaping scholars and religious leaders in novel ways.

The Nature of this Book

This book explores how theologians and philosophers use social media and technology. I use the phrase "theologians and philosophers" in a broad sense. As the disciplines listed next to contributor names indicate, the labels describing these writers vary widely.

I'm also using the phrase "social media" in a broad sense. It refers to platforms like Facebook, Twitter, YouTube, etc. But it also refers to blogs, podcasts, webinars, etc. Some contributors talk about specific internet sites, such as Academia, Beliefnet, Biblical Studies Online, Patheos, Quora, or ResearchGate. They discuss using digital technology and the internet for book reviews, online journals, or online education, including MOOCs. This diversity adds to the book's usefulness.

I conceived of this book as a way for contributors to reflect on their practices and theories and as a source of advice on how thought leaders use social media and technology effectively. The essays lean more toward the "how to" than toward the "why so." I hope the tips, advice, and testimonials spark ideas or solve problems for readers.

To provide some structure to the essays, I asked contributors to respond to six questions. Most answered the six in the order I asked them. But some contributors took the questions as general guidelines. Readers who keep these six questions in mind will notice patterns in many of the essays.

Here are the questions:

1. What forms of social media/platforms do you use, and which forms are primary?
2. Why did you begin using social media in relation to your scholarly interests, publication, or teaching? Is this the same reason you continue to use social media?
3. What have you been surprised to discover or learn when using social media?
4. What great idea, conceptual breakthrough, or interesting project emerged through or because of social media?
5. How do you manage your time and other obligations in relation to time spent on social media?
6. What three things would you recommend to scholars considering using social media?

Readers should find these essays helpful and informative. Essayists offer valuable insights to those pondering the possibilities of social media and technology. In short, the ideas in this book can really make a difference!

Finally, I express my appreciation to all of the contributors. I thank Kevin Thomas for helping manage the project. I thank Alexa Oord and Andee Oord for their work. And my heartfelt thanks to those who have encouraged me to explore the means of social media and technology to express the messages I believe important.

Contributions

JAY RICHARD AKKERMAN

Pastoral Theology

My first encounter with social media came more than a dozen years ago when my undergraduate teaching assistant told me about something called Facebook, which was still in its infancy. It was 2005, shortly after Thefacebook.com had truncated its name simply to Facebook. Membership at that time was limited only to those with email addresses ending with an "edu" domain, although Facebook dropped this requirement the following year, opening access to everyone.

Initially, my interest in Facebook was as a conservative networking experiment. Rather than using it to search actively for colleagues, family, neighbors, and acquaintances, I simply watched to see how many Facebook "friends" I could acquire by accepting every request I received. Fortunately, this was long before strangers and scammers began inundating Facebook customers with friend requests. So for the first three years or so, most of the 300+ people on my friend list were actually within one degree of separation from me: family, friends, church members, as well as former classmates and students. Around a decade ago, as Facebook grew exponentially, I gave up on my passive "friending experiment." Instead, I became more active in building my social network when I ran across those from my past, as well as other people of interest. Today, Facebook claims 1.86 billion customers and expects that number to crest two billion by year-end (Guynn,

2017). Now I am more selective about the invitations I accept, yet my friend list is nearly 500 percent larger than it was at the end of my initial experiment.

In addition to Facebook, the array of social media platforms available continues to expand. According to the Pew Research Center, Instagram, Pinterest, LinkedIn, and Twitter currently round out the top five platforms. Frequent utilization is high, with 76 percent of users reporting daily Facebook engagement, followed by Instagram at 51 percent, Twitter at 42 percent, Pinterest at 25 percent, and LinkedIn at 18 percent (Pew, 2016). While I have accounts on all of these platforms, Facebook is primary, with usage several times a week, but not daily.

The Apostle Paul offers a confession to the church at Philippi that also rings true for me regarding social media: "Not that I have already obtained all this, or have already arrived at my goal, but I press on" (Philippians 3:12a). I do not claim to be a social media pundit. But I am trying to learn from the mentorship of colleagues and those in other fields who have recognized the blessings and identified the bane of this technology in various circles. Even more, the admonishments of my young adult children are teaching me valuable lessons! So, I "press on" and offer a few of the lessons I'm learning.

For generations, those of us in higher education have understood the value of professional branding. Professors "brand themselves" by the journals and publishers where our work is conveyed, by the leadership roles we accept in our guilds, and by the conferences where we present our scholarship and debate our research. All of these remain true for educators in the information age, yet the various forms of social media available today offer additional opportunities for faculty members to grow their audiences by also branding themselves electronically.

At its most basic level, social media is about sharing with the broader world what we know — or believe, or think, or question — or what we are doing. Very few faculty members worth their salt are short on this type of information. After all, we are in the business of thinking, learning, and sharing. In addition to our work on campus and in our guilds, social media can be useful for professors to share new insights about our disciplines, as well as discoveries in the classroom, in our travels, in our research, and in correlations between what seemed unrelated previously.

Clearly, content matters. Since its invention nearly a half century ago, the phrase "content is king" continues to ring true in the academy (Click & Baird, 1974). Content has long been the coin of the realm for educators. Regardless of academic discipline, strong original content is essential. Typically, interesting original content is found in the interplay between the familiar and the surprising: interesting content either seeks to familiarize the strange; or it addresses a familiar issue in a creative way (Ballard, 2017).These are often at the core of academic research. Fortunately, these interplays are also at the heart of the kind of social media content that is able to gain a larger audience, even "going viral" at times.

Yet for educators in the information age who want to reach beyond classrooms, quarterlies, and conferences, the inherent quality of our content may not be sufficient. In the same way that the music industry is littered with recordings by highly talented artists who mysteriously failed to make the Top 40, sometimes content only takes us so far. Similarly, an insightful blog may gather virtual dust on an unnoticed WordPress site, or a brilliant manuscript may lie fallow thanks to an obscure press. As noted in a recent study on the science of popularity, "Content might be king, but distribution is the kingdom" (Thompson, 2017).

Today, distributing these slices of meaningful content on a regular basis across the social media kingdom provides numerous opportunities for scholars. The following highlights offer some areas for consideration.

First, sharing insightful content informs others about our research. The interconnected nature of social media is particularly adept at linking a dizzying array of people together. Despite a scholar's limited ability to make these connections on our own, powerful logarithms programmed in social media software cull out connections despite the diversity of our networks, while also extending the reach of posted content beyond our direct circle of friends, to the friends of our friends with similar affinities, and so on.

Second, social media offers recruitment potential, reaching prospective students who have similar interests with professors. Furthermore, social media platforms provide dialogic pathways for online engagement with recruiters and faculty members, helping prospects to discern whether a particular institution or program meets her or his needs.

Third, it can bolster the reputation of one's own program or campus. When professors post announcements about receiving significant grants or fellowships, these forms of recognition can enhance the standing of the professor's own institution as well.

Fourth, it makes way for additional points of student engagement as classmates encounter new theories and practices together. For instance, requiring students in a flipped classroom environment to use a designated hashtag on Twitter engages students in fresh ways, while also enabling professors to actually track a student's attention to the content.

Fifth, some social media platforms may be especially adept at keeping stakeholders within an organization informed while also advancing team-based projects using apps like Slack and Asana.

Social media is not a cure-all, and users need to be conscious of both its limitations and boundaries. For professionals with something meaningful to say to an audience, a focused social media strategy can be advantageous. But users should weigh carefully their content, and tone, as well as the scope of their various audiences. Clearly, rants of any kind should be avoided. Educators should also understand any policies or expectations outlined by their institutions. In response, some professors choose to have multiple accounts within a platform (e.g., a personal Facebook account and a professional one), so content and dialogue can be channeled more appropriately to various audiences. Others choose to friend their students, while others do not or cannot. With regard to the former, faculty are wise to stipulate how they intend to use social media. For instance, course syllabi should outline how professors wish to be contacted for official course-related correspondence. For now, the proliferation of social media platforms may still warrant the need for official correspondence via campus-based email, which offers more safeguards and is more universally accessible by students and faculty alike.

Learning which social media platforms are more appropriate for various communication forms is essential. For instance, some regard Facebook, Instagram, and Pinterest as being more naturally geared for personal use, although they can be used professionally, too. While social media is becoming increasingly visual, Instagram and Pinterest made their marks by being much more graphically-oriented than other platforms. LinkedIn and Twitter may be more helpful when building professional connections with colleagues. LinkedIn is unique by empowering users to target others by specific categories (e.g., career titles). Twitter offers users the ability to influence followers directly, while also benefitting users through the influence of Retweets and Mentions (Cha, Haddad, Benevenuto, and Gummadi, 2010).

Social media will continue to morph in the years ahead, which requires ongoing engagement with newly developed platforms, as well as fresh tools offered by existing ones. Fortunately, our students (and our family members) may be our best teachers as these platforms grow into the future, and as we press on together.

References

Ballard, M. (Host). (2017, Feb. 8). *Update-1: The science of going viral* [Audio podcast]. Retrieved from http://itunes.apple.com.

Cha, M., Haddad, H., Benevenuto, F., and Gummadi, K. (2010). Measuring user influence in Twitter: The million follower fallacy. Retrieved from http://snap.stanford.edu/class/cs224w-readings/cha10influence.pdf.

Click, J. W., & Baird, R. N. (1974). *Magazine editing and production*. Dubuque: W. C. Brown.

Guynn, J. (2017, Feb. 2). Facebook on track to hit 2 billion users this year, analyst predicts. *USA Today*. Retrieved from http://www.usatoday.com/story/tech/talkingtech/2017/02/01/facebook-to-hit-2-billion-users-this-year/97363752/.

Pew Research Center. (2016, Nov. 10). Three-quarters of Facebook users and half of Instagram users use each site daily. Retrieved from http://www.pewinternet.org/2016/11/11/social-media-update-2016/pi_2016-11-11_social-media-update_0-07/.

Thompson, D. (2017). *Hit makers: The science of popularity in an age of distraction*. New York: Penguin.

———————

Dr. Jay Richard Akkerman is professor of pastoral theology at Northwest Nazarene University, where he also directs the Graduate School of Theology & Christian Ministries and co-directs the university's popular Wesley Center Conferences. An ordained elder in the Church of the Nazarene, he and his wife Kim live in Nampa, Idaho and have three young adult daughters. Akkerman continues to experiment with social media through a variety of online platforms, including his "Lead With Love" blog (www.nnu.edu/blogs/mdiv/), his God21 Podcast with Thomas Jay Oord (god21.podbean.com/), as well as Facebook (Jay Akkerman), Twitter (@akkerman), and less frequently on LinkedIn (Jay Akkerman), Instagram (@jay.akkerman), and Pinterest (@gtoe).

KIMBERLY ERVIN ALEXANDER

History of Christianity

My relationship with social media is one of the proverbial "love-hate" ones: as a scholar-teacher (and a Wesleyan!), I recognize the value of connections; as an introvert, I am often overwhelmed by it all. I've limited my social presence to Facebook primarily because I find it so difficult to manage it all. I hear that Twitter is a "safer space," but I just like having everything in one location (maybe I'm just not as hip?). I like being able to set up private groups that are task- or project-specific and find it to be a helpful way to connect immediately and to get more conversational input, rather than just individualistic feedback. This is a theologically congruent approach for me because I have a strong commitment to community and prefer to work in conversation with others. The "just send me feedback of my ideas in an email" approach too often culminates to what amounts to manifestos delivered from on high.

I began experimenting with social media back in about 2008. At that time, I was on sabbatical and began blogging. I had a personal blog, where I talked about current events, family-related news, travel, spirituality, etc. Then I set up another blog for things related to Historical Theology. I envisioned it as a site for my current and former students but also for anyone with similar interests. I set up favorite links to helpful sites (archives, other blogs, and digital collections online). There was a photo stream connected to the blog site with favorite historical pics.

I had lists that were era- or theological stream-specific (Medieval, Early Church, Wesley, Pentecostalism, etc.). Finally, I used it for blogging about current studies, reviewing books, WTS and SPS news, etc. It was a moderately successful enterprise.

My next adventure was to set up a *wiki* for use by a class I was teaching at Pentecostal Theological Seminary. The primary function was to allow students to post class notes and to allow others to correct or edit them, giving the class a good set of notes produced by a group. One student was required to post, each week with others making contributions and suggestions. Because of the way I examined the students (mid-term and final essay exams) this was a really helpful way of making sure students were prepared for the exams and it encouraged them to engage with the material and with each other. Students were free to post other items to the site, including interesting links, pictures they found, videos, etc.

But then came Facebook—and it seemed everything else just fell away! My first use for vocational purposes was to set up a private focus group of current and former students who were twenty- and thirty-somethings. I was writing the school's Quality Enhancement Plan for SACS accreditation around the idea of transitioning toward missional leadership training. This space allowed me to hear from students as they engaged with my questions and each other and provided really valuable insight.

I now use Facebook not so much for specific classes (this is discouraged at my institution) but for engagement with groups of students or colleagues. My private group for current and former PhD students in historical studies has been a helpful way of building community among these students and in keeping them informed. The group also includes graduates or even students who've left the program, as well as historians from within our larger orbit. I post varieties of articles on new historical findings or conversations (some new findings in the Georgetown University slave-trading history was posted today). I post book notices or reviews. I also post pieces from higher-ed journals that focus on the vocation of historian or academician, or about how to write well! I think it has been an invaluable tool for me because I consider my role as PhD faculty to include more than just reading their work. I want to mentor them as ministers who are scholars.

I also started a "secret group" for women scholars from similar backgrounds (Holiness and Pentecostal) that functions as a support group. We share prayer needs and concerns as well as give each other space to process the perils of being a woman working in what are, for the most part, fairly conservative, often unfriendly to women in ministry, institutions. A few women, for instance, have shared the pain of having to leave their church because of its lack of inclusion of women in ministry. One recently asked for prayer as she attempted to get a visa for travel to the US because she is working in mission in one of the "hit list" countries. It also serves as a place we can celebrate each other's accomplishments. Starting this group was just one of those spur of the moment whims. I felt the need for it and thought maybe others would as well. I now believe I was led by the Spirit to do it. Recently, one of the members told me it had been a life-line for her.

Well, I guess it isn't a surprise but I'm still taken aback by the hostility present on Facebook. I periodically have to back away from just general Facebook world, focusing only on my private pages. We all have a tendency to want to post what we are thinking about, disturbed by, amused by, but I found out pretty quickly that I can't just say what I'm thinking to everyone! The problem with Facebook in general use is that the audience is so broad that it makes the conversation (if you can call it that) unwieldy. And often the people displaying sincere ignorance or horrible vitriol are people you really love — like family members or former parishioners!

Recently, my pastor posted an informal survey question, I suppose for use in sermon prep. His question was: If you had unlimited funds and ideal circumstances, what is one thing you would do? I responded that I would "Take a Muslim refugee family into my home." One of my lifelong friends, who is theologically educated (D. Min. from a good school) replied "How do you justify that with what Paul says in Galatians 6:10? [Therefore, as we have opportunity, let us do good to all people, especially to those who belong to the family of believers.] Well, that gave me pause because I couldn't see how one admonition to take care of believers precluded me taking care of unbelievers. But it gave me insight into a conversation that is going on in a completely different world than that which I inhabit. I'm in my news and hermeneutical silo and he is in his. We had a conversation that really didn't go anywhere and my pastor kindly asked us to take it elsewhere. My point is that Facebook world is really more like space inhabited by people in lots of different worlds — seriously, from different planets! And we are trying to talk to each other (often, *at* each other) as if we all speak the same language.

Often I just want out of it all but it's just not something one can do responsibly, is it? We need to connect with others and want to connect with others. I think the dilemma for the theologian is that of the prophet: is my word from the Lord for the church, a certain individual or am I supposed to wear sackcloth (or strip off my clothes) in the public square? There is no greater need for discernment than on Facebook and social media.

Finally, I would add one surprise that is a rather personal one. Through Facebook I've been able to connect with former childhood and high school friends, many of whom were certainly not believers in my Holiness understanding of what that meant back in the day. But I've found that some have had *real Christian* conversions, in a Wesleyan sense. Others are living out their faith in the tradition to which they were born in really authentic ways. Many of them have messaged me asking for prayer for various crises or to appreciate things I've said about the current political situation or related issues. So, I find the space of Facebook to be an arena where I can live out my Christian witness within the eyes of many people and I don't want to give that up.

In reading my own reflections, I think I can say that my use of social media doesn't quite fit the role of "public theologian" as much as it does, perhaps, "public pastoral theologian." I'm okay with that now. I sometimes feel the urge to take on the mantle of the former but, for now, in the space I find myself and in the ecclesial circles in which I work, I have to weigh how valuable the latter role is against the former.

Currently, I am part of a discussion that may culminate in the formation of a formal association for Pentecostals who are committed to justice, peace and full participation of women. There is consideration of it becoming an organization that could offer credentials or endorsement for folk who are confessionally Pentecostal but can no longer fit in the classical denominations, as they've become more and more tied to a Fundamentalist hermeneutic and particular political persuasion. Facebook is at least partially responsible for this seed being germinated as many of us have been in conversations with others, some of which haven't gone so well, and we've just become aware of the need for a new place for us to hang our ecclesial hats. We've watched as our like-minded colleagues have been maligned and have rushed to their rescue only to find that the conversation goes nowhere because of those different planets we inhabit. So, the need to find support and confessional identity that is more congruent with our witness and conviction has been recognized.

I've deleted the Facebook app from my phone, keeping only the Messenger app. I try to limit my Facebook time to my mornings, following my quiet start to the day. That isn't, perhaps, the best time because opening the Mac to Facebook can be rather jolting! A few times, when there has been a lot of incivility that was just overwhelming, I've deactivated temporarily but that is difficult because of the groups and contact with folk via messaging. Currently, I'm taking a break from Facebook (other than my groups) for Lent.

This is just good advice for anyone, particularly scholars: filter, filter, filter! Realize that the world is watching and that what you say is out there forever and ever. Most institutions now do deep Facebook searches with regard to hiring faculty. Use discernment.

Use the space strategically. I don't like self-promoters and Facebook is full of them. Still, you can use social media as a way to brand your professional image. Post your professional activities, notices of your new publications, etc.

Observe the Golden Rule. Use the space for the encouragement of other scholars and budding scholars, especially for those working in Christian higher education. Promote the work of others more than your own work. We need each other and we all need affirmation.

Kimberly Ervin Alexander, Ph.D. is Associate Professor of the History of Christianity in the Regent University School of Divinity. Alexander is a past president of the Society for Pentecostal Studies and has been a contributor to numerous ecumenical dialogues and consultations. She is the author of Pentecostal Healing: Models of Theology and Practice, Women in Leadership: A Pentecostal Perspective (with R. Hollis Gause), and What Women Want: Pentecostal Women Ministers Speak for Themselves (with James P. Bowers). Alexander is an avid Facebook user.

BRADLEY SHAVIT ARTSON

Rabbinic Studies

was ordained a Rabbi in 1988, when computers were new, the Internet had yet
to catch on, and we communicated by speaking to each other, by writing letters
on paper, and by publishing articles in magazines, newspapers, and journals. In
a world dominated by the printed page, I know how to build a reputation and to
get one's message out.

But all of that know how has been superseded by the rapid expansion of un-
precedented technology. Journals and magazines have folded in the face of re-
lentless economic pressure, and now one publishes in blogs, online publications,
and the new social media. There are still books, but even they are going electronic. And no one knows what the future holds.

So it was with some trepidation, and a very skeptical agnosticism about the
values of this new social media, that I launched. I did so because it appeared and
appears that if you want to reach a broader audience, if one hopes to participate
and to shape a broader conversation, then there is no escaping the Internet and
its many channels of exposure.

I started, humbly enough, with a Facebook page and a university Web site
where I could post my articles in an archive (www.aju.edu/bradartson). The
Facebook page worked fine, too well in fact. I soon discovered that Facebook limits how many "friends" one can have (5,000), and hitting that limit meant I had to

never make another friend, or else I had to enter the rough-and-tumble world of the public figure page. I did the latter (www.facebook.com/rabbiartson). Now, two and a half years later, I have a bit over 45,000 likes, and use that page to disseminate wisdom rooted in Jewish tradition, to publicize speaking events far and wide, and to post podcasts or videos of my talks. It has succeeded beyond my wildest expectations. I also started a Twitter feed (@rabbiartson) but remain agnostic about its utility. And we host a page for the podcasts of the Rabbinical School (www.zieglertorah.org) where I can post my monthly Lunch & Learn and my monthly Q&A programs. I remain surprised that people in the world want to listen in.

To round off the offerings, I contribute regularly to my very favorite web site, www.jesusjazzbuddhism.org, a rowdy collection of diverse Process-oriented thinkers, artists, writers and theologians, of every faith and of none, but all united in seeking a world in which people can thrive in relationship to each other and the earth. And I contribute articles on the Huffington Post and Times of Israel. Of late, I have started filming short live videos on Facebook and Twitter, which I call "A Moment of Torah." These get anywhere from 1,000 – 5,000 viewers!

What has most surprised me about the response to these various postings is just how thirsty people are for spiritual content that is nuanced, which presents integrated thinking/feeling/spirit, and opens access to ancient wisdom without dogma. We live in an extraordinary age, one in which people are willing to accept helpful wisdom regardless of its source. No longer do people allow themselves to be siloed within one exclusive tradition or stream, instead, people around the world are willing to learn from the tradition with which they identify, and also from select individuals of other streams if the wisdom they offer is affirming for human thriving. Rarely does a few weeks pass without my receiving an electronic message that goes something like this: "Hi, my name is Mohammed and I live in Saudi Arabia. I don't know any Jews, but you are my rabbi." My Saudi correspondent isn't interested in converting; he's interested in living a better life and he's willing to gain insights or tips from anyone who speaks to his heart.

For a long time, I kept waiting to figure what was the benefit of these regular postings on the Internet. It took a while to realize that the kinds of gains I was looking for, rubrics by which to measure a return on the investment of time and money, such as new donors, applicants to the School, invitations to speak, were the wrong kind of return. I was thinking transactionally, as though the worth of the postings was some tangible advance. But I have come to see that the reward for the postings are simply that others are able to see me as one of their teachers. They flock to a place where religion isn't about false certitude or smug supremacy, but instead holds out the possibility of experiencing divine love in one of its many guises, of joining with a diverse band of fellow seekers who insist that the fruit of the spirit must be emotional resilience, relational resonance, and flowing justice.

I must confess that I can't present a schedule of how I allocate time to this project. Somehow, when my schedule presents some open time, I will grab the mobile phone and record a live video for Facebook or Twitter. Or I will find a Scriptural verse that addresses not a ritual concern but an existential opportunity that would pertain to any person. I create a meme using some striking visual image that can reinforce the verse I superimpose on the picture, and then post it with some accompanying comment of my own. As systems go, this is pretty haphazard and chaotic, but it seems to work so far.

My only real recommendation for others seeking to avoid some pitfalls along the way to establishing your own presence would be:

- People are drawn to illustrations, not just words. So use art, colors, photos, and find visually compelling ways to supplement any verbal message
- Speak not to the particulars of dogma, but to the flowing humanity that such dogma clothes. Let people experience a deeper humanity because of exposure to your perspective and insights
- A single or sporadic post is worth no more than not posting at all. It is all about flow — regular, predictable, and ongoing. People will create space to await your gift if they know they can count on its quality and its frequency
- Longer isn't better.
- Don't be afraid to consult with people who know about staging, theatrics, and drama. We are all actors on a cosmic stage.

Rabbi Dr. Bradley Shavit Artson (www.bradartson.com) holds the Abner and Roslyn Goldstine Dean's Chair of the Ziegler School of Rabbinic Studies and is Vice President of American Jewish University in Los Angeles. A member of the Philosophy Department, he is particularly interested in theology, ethics, and the integration of science and religion. He is also dean of the Zacharias Frankel College in Potsdam, Germany, ordaining Conservative rabbis for Europe. A frequent contributor for the Huffington Post, Jesus Jazz and Buddhism, *and for the* Times of Israel, *and a public figure Facebook page with over 45,000 likes, he is the author of 12 books and over*

250 *articles, most recently* Renewing the Process of Creation: A Jewish Integration of Science and Spirit *(Jewish Lights). Married to Elana Artson, they are the proud parents of twins, Jacob and Shira. See Artson's Web site at www.bradartson.com. Feel free to like his public figure Facebook page (www.facebook.com/rabbiartson) and his Twitter page (@rabbiartson). Give yourself a treat by browsing through www.jesusjazzbuddhism.org. And you can listen to a range of his podcasts at www .zieglertorah.org*

ARNE BACHMANN, RASMUS NAGEL, HANNA REICHEL,
THOMAS RENKERT

Open Access Theology Journal

Hanna: We first started thinking about founding a theological open access journal in the summer of 2015. This project eventually became "Cursor_ Zeitschrift für explorative Theologie" and we are about to launch our first issue. Then, all four of us were teaching theology at the university, working on different scholarly projects in our dissertations or second-book projects, and all four of us obviously had different backgrounds and individual habits and experiences when it comes to the use of social media. But we shared the impression that a lot of the academic theological discourse was rather closed in different ways: Scholars tended to think (and talk) within separate schools of thought, without much dialogue between the different camps; scholars tended to publish well-polished arguments that would close discussions rather than open up new venues for them; scholars tended to avoid any impression of questions without ready answers. Furthermore, beyond the academic circles, theology is widely seen as something that is forbidding, censoring, and moralizing on the one hand, while never up to date, especially with technological developments, on the other. I am saying that all of this was our impression, not that this was and is the case everywhere.

Arne: On the other hand, we had the impression that there WAS an interest in theological discussion if one started to look around: The US have a certain type of "theological public" that already existed before the internet, mainly in magazines and through the large book market. There has been some serious discussions going on about topics like "faith and culture", "faith and politics", "faith in a secular post-modern context". This public was relatively successful in its transfer to social media. Some bloggers like Richard Beck (http://experimentaltheology.blogspot.de) have even published "online books" and made their research available in this way.

In Germany, such publics are not equally present. But since the years 2003/4, even here, there has been a vibrant social media culture and theological blogger scene. We found, however, that in the academic theological discussions there was not a huge sensitivity to the cultural shift occurring in connection to digital transformations, so somehow it felt like an academic culture which was considerably closed off from public debate.

I was personally engaged in digital theological discourses before I was involved in academia and I found myself startled by how little German academic theology was even aware of there being new forms of theological discourse in the social web. On the other hand, I found it interesting how little connection the online discourse had to the better sides of academic theology. That's why I participate in Cursor_: in order to create a space where those two forms of theological discourse can meet: to show people in academia what's going on in new forms of theological public and what kinds of questions and sensitivities are emerging from that; and, on the other hand, to help those involved in new forms of theological debate to find the resources they need in order to provide more depth for their discourses.

Surely, there can be an expertocratic snobbism in Academia, but there can also be something C.S. Lewis once called "chronological snobbism" in the social web where people have the feeling that they cannot learn anything new from theological classics. It would be a missed opportunity for academic theology to find a new relevance by communicating to a different public and learning a new vernacular, and it would be a missed opportunity for the more innovative forms of theological discourse to see the established theological discourse in a new light and to profit from "full time theologians".

Rasmus: Another problem is that in the past few years the Christian right (somewhat in parallel to the political right) has turned out to be far more present in social media than "established" theology. It is a worrying discovery for me that there seems to be something in the very structure of online media that makes it very attractive for right wing discourses, both religious and political — and I don't think that this structure has been understood very well so far. Our journal Cursor_ is also an experiment in order to explore if another theological public is possible that avoids both the trap of becoming an isolated bubble of likeminded "progressives" or "academics" and the trap of joining a culture of superficial, non-constructive exchanges of ideological positions.

Thomas: In recent years, the general realization has set in that the same infrastructure once built to enhance dialogue, cooperation, and dissemination of knowledge, can also be used to deliver advertisement and political propaganda, or to construct entire filter bubbles, thereby separating and even isolating its users from reality as experienced by others. The current state of the web has the potential to support communal or even ecumenical conversations, but it can also become a completely solipsistic exercise where users "share" more on social media than ever before, but also have less of a common outlook on reality than ever before.

Arne: However, you have to take into account that the use of social media in Germany differs greatly from that in other Western societies. For instance, Germans tend to share less content in social media and they tend to be more anonymous and passive in the social web. Additionally, higher social media usage correlates with lowers degree of formal education in Germany, while milieus of traditional education are more likely to shy away from social media.

Thomas: Notwithstanding important national differences, we as Cursor_ are aware of these problematic developments within the current state of social media, but we are also excited about the notion of unrestricted and egalitarian exchange of data, ideas, and opinions, which has been fundamentally connected to the internet right from the start.

Currently, there are also new developments happening within different fields of scholarship to include interdisciplinary perspectives as well as the opinions of non-experts under the name of "Citizen Science." In my view, these concerns lie at the heart not only of the humanities, but of Protestant theology itself: The notion of universal priesthood and the egalitarian participation of lay people are theological key issues for the Reformation. To our surprise, despite Protestantism's positive early history of adopting new media, theology so far mostly ignores these current developments. Thus, we found it worthwhile to explore these new possibilities further.

Hanna: When the four of us put our heads together, we wanted to create a space for theological exchange that would see theological inquiry as a tentative, explorative, even experimental process; that would look for progress in knowledge in forms of communal practice. We thought that "open access" could and should mean more than just publishing the same kind of monolithic papers in a pdf rather than print format. We wanted a medium that would be more dynamic and transparent; that would invite and foster participation; and that would open up dialogue between scholars and practitioners of different fields. We wanted to create a space that would take serious recent developments in church and society; search for intersections beyond established discursive borderlines; and develop new venues for a participatory and interactive culture of dialogue and discussion.

So we decided to found a new journal, academic in quality, but broader in its range, and accessible and interactive in its practice. We wanted to embrace the potentials of the online world and the developments in "citizen science" in order to foster our goals and we wanted to create a kind of "inverted classroom" between teachers and learners without necessarily pre-assigned roles.

In this course, we rely on social media and hope to draw on their potential. Within our practice, the employment of social media specifically aims at facilitating quicker and more direct discussion. We cherish the possibility social media provide to opine regardless of formal qualification or academic training. We love its potential to create, develop and harvest fresh ideas. We want to use it to create an easier exchange between writers and readers. Social media also give us the chance to reach a wider audience than just theological scholars or traditional church goers.

Thomas: We intend to engage both readers and authors in a more participatory way. In previous centuries the main challenge may have been to make as much information available to the largest audience as possible. However, the central task today (for us as an academic journal aiming to reach beyond the academic circles) is probably this:

To get the audience's attention and promote its engagement without resorting to click baiting, as well as to create space for inclusive and engaging discourses that experience a high level of egalitarian participation, continual commitment, and thematic quality. This is not a trivial challenge and Cursor_ decided to face it with a double strategy, consisting of a pragmatic-opportunistic use of social media on the one hand, as well as a more idealistic approach to engagement and commitment on the other hand.

First, Cursor_'s use of different social media platforms follows a pragmatic approach: We use Facebook, Twitter and Instagram in order to grab our audience's attention on as many channels as possible, and encourage any first exchanges and discussions. We are fully aware of the short shelf-life of these channels (who remembers Friendster, Second Life and Myspace today?), as well as of certain economic, moral and political ambivalences associated with them.

Most importantly, though, we are convinced that most of the web's promises on egalitarian exchanges of ideas have yet to be fulfilled. But there is a distinct lack of working solutions at the moment. In our view, none of the currently existing social media platforms provide the functionality we are looking for, which incited us to build our own solution, consisting of a combination of different aspects. In order to go beyond the often superficial, banal, or aggressive forms of exchange common on social media, Cursor_ opted for an approach that combines more traditional means with the new collaboration platform PubPub (www .pubpub.org).

We believe that people are more likely to engage with a project whose output can also take on physical forms in "real life." We therefore pay a lot of attention to a well-designed layout and ready-to-print typesetting, we implemented a print-on-demand service, and we regularly organize workshops where authors and readers can interact non-virtually.

On the other hand, Cursor_ uses PubPub, an open-source platform designed for scientific publishing and equipped with extensive functionality for discussions, where anyone can participate free of charge and regardless of academic titles and merits. Our hope is that the specific features of PubPub as a platform will allow for more engagement, commitment, and continuity when it comes to author-reader interaction and general discourse. It is, thus, our primary platform for "social research" or "citizen theology."

Rasmus: Open access online journals commonly employ a structure that is more or less the same as in academic standard print journals. They are organized in volumes and issues, and contain a few peer reviewed articles, sometimes concerning a certain topic. Usually, the articles have only been revised during the review process. After being published their readership is often quite small, — at least in the German humanities. The majority of published work is never again cited in another work.

It was an exciting discovery to see that PubPub works differently. It allows you to use your journal more like a repository for articles that can be commented and constantly revised if necessary. As old-fashioned Europeans we still rely to some degree on the structure of thematic issues, but the technology behind PubPub enables an ongoing discussion and fosters an academic culture that is open to revision and improvement. Non-anonymous and registered online comments can be a low-threshold way for participating in academic debate and providing valuable critique to a very specific issue without getting forced to publish a full article. For this reason, online comments for articles on Cursor_ can get their own Digital Object Identifier (DOI) and are an integral part of the peer review process.

Thomas: Cursor_'s ultimate goal is to encourage and facilitate a kind of exchange of ideas in order to bring experts and non-experts, authors and readers, clergy and laymen together in a communal dialogue in order to advance our theological discourse culture inside and outside of academia. For this, we need a continuous osmosis between two spheres of discourse — social media and PubPub — while still maintaining their independence and autonomy, since they serve different purposes. An open question for us, though, is how to set up a kind of interface, a bridge or a membrane, between these two spheres that lets high quality ideas, attention-grabbing quotes, and especially interesting discussions travel easily in both directions.

What would you recommend to scholars considering using social media?

Arne: Be vulnerable! Use social media as a tool to try out new and unfinished ideas! Don't be afraid to expose your ideas.

Rasmus: Limit yourself. Omnipresence in social media is neither possible nor desirable, and it will end up in having multiple dead or rarely visited accounts with no real use. And use videos and podcasts. Recorded talks, presentations or classes are widely appreciated among students and are often the first way to get familiar with certain topics or scholars.

Hanna: Use social media to reinforce your commitments — they allow you to find many who think alike but who know more or different things than you do. Use their output as a motivation and reinforcement of your own. On the other hand, use social media to also diversify your outlook and commitments. That's harder to do, as social media often foster certain "filter bubbles." But you also have the chance of finding very different opinions — allow them to challenge your own.

Thomas: We'd like to invite you to use and experiment with PubPub. In its current state, most social media is as much a tool for theology as it is an obstacle. The potential of the web for more sophisticated, sustained, and meaningful exchanges needs to be actualized in solutions yet to come. We believe that PubPub could be one such tool that can help theology as a whole to become more open, participatory, egalitarian, and inclusive. Which would, in the end, coincide nicely with what theology is all about. You can test the functionality of PubPub, contribute to our project, and improve this very text by discussing it with us and others on: www.pubpub.org/pub/cursor_-exploring-new-venues-for-theological-discussion.

———————

Arne Bachmann is a theologian, teacher and networker. He teaches Ecumenical Theology at Heidelberg University. He is co-founder of the network Emergent Deutschland and has been an active blogger since 2004. He currently works on a project about community and hospitality.

Rasmus Nagel, M.A., is a theologian and doctoral student. He teaches Systematic Theology at Heidelberg University. His current PhD-work looks at the relationship of universality and particularity in Protestant theology by making use of recent political theory (Laclau, Badiou, Zizek).

Hanna Reichel, Th.D. is a theologian who teaches Systematic Theology at Martin-Luther-University Halle-Wittenberg. She has written one and co-edited several books. Her dissertation on Karl Barth's reception of the Heidelberg Catechism has won several awards. She serves on the executive committees of the Gesellschaft für Evangelische Theologie and the International Leuenberg Conference.

Thomas Renkert, Th.D., is a theologian who teaches Diakonia (Christian Social Services) at Heidelberg University. His dissertation focused on Wolfhart Pannenberg's Eschatology, his current postdoctoral work is on the concept of enacted testimony.

For the latest version of this document and our discussion, please visit: www.pubpub.org/pub/cursor_-exploring-new-venues-for-theological-discussion. See Cursor_'s website, http://journals.ub.uni-heidelberg.de/index.php/cursor/index and PubPub page, https://www.pubpub.org/cursor. Look out for the publication of our first issue in November 2017. Cursor_ also makes use of Facebook (https://www.facebook.com/Cursor_-1443321039013886/?fref=ts), Twitter (@CursorZeth, https://twitter.com/CursorZeth), Google+ (https://plus.google.com/u/3/117436325960188246726), and Instagram (@cursor_zeth, https://www.instagram.com/cursor_zeth/).

RICHARD BECK

Psychology and Theology

've only been a blogger and have avoided Twitter and Facebook. Mainly because I want to do the blog well. I post on the blog every Monday-Friday and that volume of writing limits my ability to be active on other social media platforms. Plus, I think blogging, of all the social media platforms, is the best suited for scholarly reflection done for a popular audience.

I started the blog because I felt I had a few good ideas that could possibly become books. So I created the blog to work through some of this material. To date, three of my four books originated from writing I did on the blog.

I also use the blog to capture and share ideas that are too provisional, innovative or out of the box to move directly into a scholarly outlet, like a journal article or conference paper. Creative and innovative ideas can struggle to get through peer review. Scholarly peer review can be conservative and intolerant of innovation. So the blog became an idea collector for me and a way to publish ideas outside of peer review. That doesn't mean I escape peer review, fellow academics who are readers of the blog kick the tires of these thought balloons. This informal but scholarly feedback is an effective way to gauge if an idea is worth pursuing. Plus, there's the issue of reach. An idea published in a scholarly journal reaches a handful of people. An idea published on a blog reaches thousands.

Finally, I've used the blog to popularize the research I've published in scholarly journals. The blog is a nice way to bridge the academy and the general public, the church especially.

I've been surprised by the scholarly quality of the feedback you get from readers on social media. Yes, the comment sections of many blogs have a horrible reputation. But that's mainly found on blogs that traffic in hot takes of breaking political events and controversies.

Reflective blogging, writing on social media that is working through ideas rather than current events, attracts reflective, intelligent readers, many of whom are academics themselves. Consequently, while a certain style of blogging might not attract huge social media traffic it can create a thoughtful, interdisciplinary community of conversation populated by people working in the academy.

For example, like to blog about academic books I'm reading, using the blog to capture my notes and reflections to be used later for my own purposes. The authors of these books regularly show up in the comments section or send emails. The authors make corrections and add clarifications. This happened when I blogged through Mark Heim's *Saved from Sacrifice* and Douglas Campbell's *The Deliverance of God*. I can't tell you how important it is for a psychologist doing interdisciplinary work to foster relationships and get feedback from theologians and biblical scholars.

One of my areas of interest in psychology is existential psychology, especially the work of Ernest Becker and his seminal book *The Denial of Death*. Becker's work examines how death anxiety sits behind our self-esteem projects (how we seek significance and meaning in the face of death). Later I came across Eastern Orthodox theology and Christus Victor atonement which describe salvation as being less about the forgiveness of sins than about being set free from the tyranny of death. I felt there might be some connections between existential psychology and Eastern Orthodox theology. To explore those connections I started a multipart series on my blog. As I sketched out these connections there was huge enthusiasm from my readers. By the end of the series I had many comments saying "You need to turn this into a book." So I did, publishing my book *The Slavery of Death*. This book represents the most my creative intellectual work I've ever done and the book originated on the blog and was published because of the validation and encouragement of my readers.

I publish every day, Monday-Friday. I'm able to do this because of an accident many years ago, the secret to my ability to blog so frequently.

A few years ago I was going to be on the road for a week on a family summer vacation. I didn't want the blog to sit dormant for a week, so before the trip I sat down and wrote five posts, time-stamping them to appear on the days I was on the road. That got me a week out ahead of the blog. But in the days leading up to the trip I had some more ideas, so I time-stamped those to appear the week after my trip. Soon, being two weeks out ahead of the blog turned into three and eventually I'm now I'm writing 2-3 months out ahead of the blog.

I'll admit that this amount of volume might be unique and not very applicable to others, but getting out ahead of the blog proved to be the secret to sustaining a regular flow of writing given my busy schedule.

Here's why. Trying to sustain a daily blog by writing and posting each day is unsustainable. There are days, weeks even, when I just don't have time to blog. But since I'm out ahead of the blog my posts keep appearing every day. When I do find time to blog, a quiet Saturday morning perhaps, I can knock out multiple posts rather quickly. The key is jotting down ideas while you're not blogging. When you get time to blog you open up your notebook to your list of ideas and crank out a bunch of posts.

The point here is that your time comes in chunks separated by many days or even weeks. You can get a lot of writing done in those chunks, but you have to be out ahead of your blog to bridge between those chunks of time (if you want your writing to appear daily and regularly). If you're able to do this—get enough blogging done and time stamped to create a bridge between your chunks of free time—you can be set free from the tyranny of trying to find time to blog every single day. There are weeks where I can't find any time at all to blog, but since I have time stamped material coming out I don't stress about it. I have created bridge to my next block of free time.

Still, finding material to blog about can be a challenge. But if you're an academic there's a bunch of material you're likely sitting on that you could use to blog. Plus, you can turn your blog into a scholarly aid. So here are some easy blog ideas for academics:

1. If you're an academic you're probably reading a lot. Blog through your observations about the books you're reading. Or simply share a great quote or two.
2. If you're an academic you're probably going to conference. Blog through your impressions of the talks you've heard.
3. If you're an academic you have publications and presentations. Blog through all your old talks and papers, sharing the insights with a popular audience.

4. If you're an academic you're teaching classes. Share material and insights from your lectures.

The point is, academics swim in a sea of ideas and insights. Your own ideas and ideas from books, papers, talks and lectures. Since most of the people reading your blog won't be academic folk take the opportunity to share and popularize even the simple, undergraduate material from your discipline. Write as a scholar but write for the masses, popularizing your discipline. From time to time delve deep into a scholarly post. Mix the academic and the popular.

First, be clear about your motivations for using social media and stay true to those purposes. Many people use social media to build a platform and brand so that they can publicize their work. For example, to either promote a book or help secure a book deal. That's a legitimate goal that will dictate how you use social media. You'll want to be very active on multiple, cross-pollinating forums and be provocative/opinioned enough to gain attention, likes, clicks and shares. There are costs and benefits to this sort of use of social media. With attention comes emotion and controversy.

By contrast, I use my blog as a journal and repository for ideas I'm working on. So I don't need to participate on Twitter or Facebook to promote my blog. Nor do I care about size of audience. I don't write about breaking controversies or issues in the world because I'm apathetic or apolitical. I just don't use my blog for those purposes. So, be clear about what you're trying to accomplish and reconcile your-self with the costs and benefits of your choices.

Second, if you're going to blog as an academic decide if you're writing exclusively for fellow academics of if you're also welcoming in the general reader. Knowing your audience is important. If you're wanting to reach the gen-eral reader you'll need to take care to cover basics and define terms. A theo-logian might define the word "eschatology" and a psychologist might define "superego."

Third, be mindful of your institution and the limits it might place on academic freedom. My institution has a love/hate relationships with my blog. They love having a public intellectual out there, someone on their faculty who has a voice in the game. But from time to time when I take positions that don't align perfectly with the university community or constituency my blog can become a source of worry. We've all seen the problems that have been created when a professor does something on social media that creates a problem for the institution. All that to say, be mindful of your ecosystem. Use social media knowing that what you share will be (potentially) read by administrators, the Board of Trustees, families of prospective students, alumni, and donors.

———————

Richard Beck, Ph.D. is an award winning author, speaker, blogger and professor of psychology at Abilene Christian. Richard's writes everyday Monday-Friday at his blog "Experimental Theology" (experimentaltheology.blogspot.com).

COLLEEN BIRCHETT

Theology and Technology

Although social media such as Facebook has been criticized for its potential to harm personal relationships, I have discovered that Facebook has great potential for doing ministry—both family ministry and family among religious educators. In fact, my experiences of revitalizing my extended family via Facebook have provided me with insights for creating a sense of community and family among Progressive and Postcolonial Educators, both "for such a time as this."

For example, my Uncle Kent passed in December of 2012. His passing was the twelfth of the fourteen members of my mother's immediate family. All of the members of my father's immediate generation had passed. Family members on both sides of the family were mostly out of touch. This signaled crisis mode for an extended family that had been the cardiovascular center that had carried vital nutrients that provided the energy, healed and enhanced the body's agency to block external threats to our overall well-being.

That is, the impact of the loss of an entire generation was one threat to the family system. The other external threat was the decline of Detroit's automobile industry, which had eliminated so many jobs and sent so many others overseas, leaving so many members of our family unemployed. This, in turn had caused family members from Detroit to migrate to other industrial centers throughout the country, eventually disconnecting with the nurturance of the extended family and its churches that had had provided nurturance and renewal for facing life's various challenges.

This had become a personal challenge as I, personally, had relocated several times, eventually situating myself in New York, where I was at the time of my Uncle's death. By then, I had graduated from seminary, and was preparing for ordination in the United Church of Christ. I recall wanting to reach out and touch family members and set up systems of nurturance that would out last the standard brief interactions that accompanied most such occasions.

Spontaneously, I turned to the only source I knew, Facebook. I was aware of the criticisms of social media for its attempt to replace face-to-face communication and its potential to harm rather than strengthen personal relationships. However, during the journey of mourning my uncle's passing, I took the risk of turn long-lost relatives into "Friends". As my grandmother's oldest grandchild, I was in a traditional position of leadership. However, over the course of managing the family Facebook page I created, I awakened to priestly functions of my actions. Webster's online dictionary says the priestly "attends to needs of someone", and serves as a "mediating agent" between humans and God. An agent, then, is "a means by which a guiding intelligence achieves a result."

As such, I consider myself working with God, my Guiding Intelligence, who is guiding me in reviving the Bodily functions that transmit Spiritual nutrients that, even though the members of the Body are spatially separated, they can still gain access to the chemistry of survival such a: affirmation, praise, petitioning God, inspiration, advising each other, celebrating, making and experiencing music together, all accompanied by the catalyst of family photographs.

Affirmation and Praise transmits spiritual energy, to "Keep on, Keepin' On". This was a nutrient that the extended family once provided at graduation ceremonies, birthdays, retirements, and various other achievements. Through Facebook postings, for those who can no longer come into town to attend such events, people receive family postings, along with inspirational Bible passages, or quotes from famous poets, writers and ministers. When someone experiences illness or the loss of a loved one, and we are no longer physically close enough to visit, Facebook postings send encouragement and the assurance that the Family is praying and petitioning God on a given family member's behalf. If someone needs advice, a job referral, or support for a new business venture, postings and other functions of Facebook allow for passing such information along, with the assurance that the Family is praying. Some of these interactions have turned into "pastoral moments' when I have engaged with family members in crisis, via mes-

saging and Chat. Additionally, we keep each other posted concerning achievements of all generations. We also make music together, frequently accompanying
family photographs traditional and contemporary Gospel music.

Spiritual insights from my Family Facebook ministry have carried over into
another area of ministry — the building of family among Progressive, Postcolonial,
African-centered, Womanist, Feminist and Liberationist educators and pastors
into dialogue and resource sharing "for such a time as this". That is, in light of
current political and ethical controversies related to the 2016 elections, there is a
need to call into being a sense of "family", where the nutrients of resource sharing,
affirmation, praise, advising, celebrating and dialogue can equip the Church to
ward off debilitating diseases, while, at the same time, equipping it with catalytic
ideas for change. With that in mind, I developed the "African-centered and
Progressive Educator Forum Facebook Page.

Members are invited to post all kinds of resources and program ideas for
"equipping the saints" for such a time as this. Through this Facebook page, we
affirm, praise God, inspire, advise, celebrate, invite each other to life-affirming
events, all accompanied by the catalysts of "family" photographs. Since January
alone, we have experienced thousands of hits that have made people aware of
Progressive, Womanist, Liberationist, African-centered, Feminist, and Postcolonial
scholarship, films, educational programs, job postings and other resources, along
with the opportunity to engage in conversations, debates and collaborations.

---

*Colleen Birchett, Ph.D., M.Div., M.S. is Assistant Professor and adjunct at New York
City College of Technology. She is a member of the Education Commission of The
Riverside Church, New York. Find her on Facebook https://www.facebook.com/groups
/522803594514355/*

FELIPE KOCH BUTTELLI

Systematic Theology

Facebook, Whatsapp and E-mail. Facebook is mostly used to mobilize some agendas and share information, helping to build up people's opinion with alternative information. Whatsapp is mostly used on specific campaigns to share events and activities and to organize them with groups especially created for this. E-mail is used as a form to address officially institutions, sending documents and lobbying for specific agendas.

I started to see social media as space to live out my activism, especially when I started my activism for Palestine. As the Palestinian struggle is an international struggle, social media was the better way 1 — to receive information and to share agenda with the international groups; 2 — to reach people in their daily life, offering alternative information, critical views and mobilize for activities. My scholar interest is intertwined with my role as activist. So, my participation in social media is informed by my activism and by my role as professor, researcher and intellectual. I still consider that it is the important way to use it.

Something surprising is how it is helpful to establish new connections and to discover new groups that are concerned with same issues as you. New relations developed from the social media that sometime become something "real".

The great project created through social media is the Kairós Palestina Brazil group. It was mobilized in the World Social Forum — Free Palestine, in 2012. That group was described as a platform of ecumenical support to the Palestinian struggle in Brazil. This collective action is voluntary, but the group grew up, and started to become a reference on the discussion.

At certain moment, that not-institutionalized platform was invited to assume form, being members invited to participate in events and workshops. It created a certain need to "give names" and some "responsibilities" to members of the group, even in legal terms, when we got funds for a specific project. This challenge became a clear moment to reflect about the limits and potentialities of such virtual and not-institutionalized organization. There are good and the bad aspects of maintaining it like this, as the society always tends to expect some sort of institutionalization of the movements and groups. Stories and anecdotes always happen when we found time and opportunity to sit down together as group that mostly kept contact through social media.

The activity in social media happens in a natural way, without any specific schedule for that. It becomes also part of the identity — as social activist. It obviously affects people's particular and private life. Stories with families and friends not allowing the use of gadgets not to be stolen from the "real" life to the "virtual" one. As academic, a huge time is dedicated to activities that mostly don't give profit, scholarly feedback — as publishing articles, participating in academic conferences, and so on. The condition of a social activist that works also — not only — on social media, however, gives a public impact for the scholar and academic life. The public changes. On this sense, an academic that is also a social activist gives more amplitude for his and her work. However, not few times this activity might be consider as useless for academic purpose and not part of the job we are payed for. It is a hard decision, but once we assume this kind of way of acting, it is difficult to change the perception. The challenge is to find a balance to be able to be good in both ways of living as academic and as an activist.

The social media can give a huge impact for the academic activity. Living in a world in which the space and time setting has changed considerably, social media allows more people also to learn and to enjoy the local work as academic. It also challenges how we are communicating with the public space, if our scholarly activity is relevant for the society or not. In this sense, I think that the social media as a tool, helps to interconnect our scholar activity with what is happening around. The context of life ethically enquires our academic activity and demands public responsibility of us.

Felipe Koch Buttelli is a Lutheran theologian with a doctorate in Systematic Theology, doing part of it at the University of Stellenbosch, South Africa. He also conducted a Postdoctoral research on the epistemological basis for understanding the role of religion in public space. He is an activist for Palestine. He is currently doing a second post-doctorate and is acting as inviting scholar at the Theology and Development Program of the University of Kwazulu-Natal (UKZN). Contact Felipe Buttelli through Facebook (https://web.facebook.com/felipebuttelli), by e-mail felipebuttelli@yahoo .com.br, and on Academia (https://ukzn.academia.edu/FelipeGustavoKochButtelli)

HEIDI A CAMPBELL

Religion, Media and Digital Culture

have used the Internet as a research and communication tool since 1995, when
I first ventured online to study how people were using email and newsgroups to
discuss their religious beliefs and experiences. Over the past three decades my
research has focused on how communication technology, religious communities
and digital culture intersect. From using early forms of social media such as email,
Bulletin Board Systems (BBSs) and Internet Relay Chat (IRC) to my current activity
on Facebook and Twitter, I have found social media to be a vital space not only
for conducting research interviews and digital ethnographies, but for communicating with my diffuse international network of friends, family, and scholarly
colleagues.

Living overseas from 1996-2005, I quickly learned email, blogs and running
my own web site became important ways for me stay connected with those I
cared about across time and space, and enabled me to keep them easily up-to-
date on my work and life. And since few people were studying the phenomenon of
religion online at that time the Internet proved to be a vital collaborative and
networking space, to meet other scholars and share ideas with those exploring
similar questions of how religion is adapting to digital culture. I met many of my
now key collaborators and research colleagues first online in discussion groups,
often sharing research ideas and discussing our thoughts on the religious and

theological implications of the Internet for years online before ever meeting face-to-face.

Today I primarily use Facebook and the research website I run for digital communication personal and professional purposes. Facebook is the place where I first learned my two nieces and nephew were born, that I had earned Tenure at my institution and is the first place I turned for support when my Mum died. After living overseas and having friends literally all over the world, I find Facebook offers the only way for me to stay in connection with many of the people I care for and to keep up-to-date about what is going on in their lives.

Professionally, I primarily use Facebook and Twitter as a push technologies related to my research, to share relevant information with my scholarly community. I started using these platforms around 2010 as a way to distribute news stories, calls for papers and the latest research on Religion and the Internet, as part of the outreach work of the virtual research center I run, the Network for New Media, Religion & Digital Culture Studies. This is an interactive resource space for scholars, students and others interested in the current scholarship on how religion is being practiced online.

I frequently use blogs as well as Facebook groups as learning spaces for the classes I teach on digital media and religion. These can be used to facilitate conversation and resource-sharing amongst students outside of class time and serve as collaborative research diaries for student research assignments. Facebook groups have also been key in my interdisciplinary work in creating hubs of connection with other like-minded scholars pursuing similar questions about how religion online is changing and merging with religion offline. Through Facebook I have met many people I likely would have never met face-to-face, due to the disciplines they belong to or the far flung places where they live.

I often hear people complain how social media is making people shallow, a waste of time or encourages false relationships. While this may be the case for some, I have found the purposeful and focused use of this technology has been an asset for me helping build community amongst my research colleagues and staying personally connected to dear friends who have journeyed with me online.

I would consider many of the people I primarily communicate and interact with online to be the core of my social and spiritual support network. Some of these interaction, and especially the debates they have generated about the impact of technology on religious practice and communities, has strongly informed my work. Currently I am working on two projects—one on the concept of how to cultivate digital justice through technology use and another on how to read theology in digital culture through Internet memes—that were directly inspired by conversations and challenges I received from friends in the comment sections of personal posts on Facebook.

Social media communication does have its limitations. Yet the possibilities it offers for sustaining relationships and creating new forms of scholarly collaboration are unique opportunities offered by the digital age that are too life-enriching not to take advantage of.

———————

Heidi A Campbell is Associate Professor of Communication at Texas A&M University and affiliate faculty in Religious Studies. She is also director of the Network for New Media, Religion & Digital Culture Studies and author of over 90 articles and author/editor of 9 books on digital religion including Exploring Religious Community Online (Peter Lang, 2005), When Religion Meets New Media (Routledge, 2010),editor of Digital Religion (Routledge, 2013) and co-author of Networked Theology (Baker Academic, 2016). See Campbell's website is The Network for New Media, Religion and Digital Culture Studies at digitalreligion.tamu.edu. She is an avid Facebook (Heidi Campbell and Network for New Media, Religion and Digital Culture Studies) and sometimes Twitter user (@nmrdcnetwork and @heidiacampbell).

MICHAEL J. CHRISTENSEN

Practical Theology

S ocrates allegedly said, "The *undocumented* life is not worth living." I tend to think that my thoughts, ideas, activities, and reflections are worth documenting online, primarily for myself but also for family, friends, fans, colleagues, and any others who care about my life and views.

I use social media to test or promote my ideas and interests, my social vision and mission projects, my travel log and personal news and family celebrations. I use the following platforms regularly: Facebook (personal), Facebook (organization), Public Blogs, Private Groups, Public and Private YouTube accounts, and LinkedIn (in that order of importance). For educational purposes, I use Moodle classroom, Zoom.us, Google Hangouts, and have experimented with Second Life. Occasionally, I've used Twitter but don't make time for it.

I started using social media in 1997 for educational and scholarly purposes, and later for uses that are more personal. I began teaching online for Drew University in 1999, and continue to do so for Drew, Point Loma Nazarene University, Nazarene Theological Seminary, and Northwind Institute. To do so requires that I record micro lectures and publish some of my lectures notes online with appropriate links, images and icons to make them more interesting for students. I upload many of micro lectures on YouTube accounts and provide links to content. I also promote my articles and E-books online, as well as those of others.

I was most surprised to find that I had followers beyond the 'usual suspects' of extended family members and close friends who like to see my pictures. Former students enjoy friending and following their professor, and parishioners like reading posts from their pastor. Constituents of Communities of Shalom and WorldHope Corps (two charitable organizations I direct) benefit from reading my E-newsletters and blogs. It was most surprising to find that friends from long ago, new friends and complete strangers were interesting in reading my blogs and FB posts. It's easy for me to get addicted to reading, liking and posting online, and my family has been helpful in reminding me to limit myself and periodically unplug. My youngest daughter, in particular, reminds me to always ask before posting: what about this particular post is important? Why am I posting it now? What is the intent and message behind each post? There's a significant learning curve to managing your presence on social media.

Long ago, when folks first started publishing online, I had a great idea, a high adventure tale with historical interest, worthy of publication, which I wrote in 1996 during my doctoral studies as a newly minted Ph.D. and instructor. The title of my short story was "The Search for the Lost Cross of St. Euphrosynia" about the apparent supernatural powers embodied by an ornate and jewel-studded altar cross in a famous medieval church in Belarus named after St. Euphrosynia — patron saint of Belarus. The highly valuable cross allegedly was stolen by the Nazis and later sold in an auction allegedly to the Pierpont Morgan Library in NYC. I researched and wrote the story about how the Byelorussians blamed Chernobyl (and other national crises) on the "curse of the Trinity" (inscribed on the foot of the cross) on the land if this cross is ever removed from it church home. And how church and political leaders in Belarus believed that St. Euphrosynia was leading her devotees to find and recover the protective cross from the wealthy Morgan family in New York. I had images to illustrate a lively narrative, interviews, and original research, but could not find a suitable publisher for print media.

Futurist Leonard Sweet, the Dean who hired me at Drew Theological School, loved the story and its historical detail, and suggested that I publish it with accompanying images and links "on the World Wide Web" — a novel idea in the late 1990's! However, faculty peers were negative about the merits of publishing serious research and essays on the Internet. Online articles at this time were not taken seriously, and I mistakenly rejected online scholarly publishing. By 2001 or so, academics were beginning to catch on that online teaching; publishing and sharing scholarship was an acceptable alternative to standard, conventional publication. Millennial scholars and students have a difficult time understanding and relating to these early days of trying to use social media for educational and scholarly purposes.

Leonard Sweet believes (and practices) John Wesley's stated expectations for Methodist preachers: to spend at least 5 hours a day reading secular resources, seeking to understand the common man's cultural world, ideas and values—what we would refer to today as understanding popular culture. Wesley also strove to understand the contemporary scientific world and rational thought of his emerging enlightenment time. Though he was a "man of one book"—the Bible—he read many books and was culturally literate. I also value the five-hours-a-day rule—of reading news and current events, relating popular songs and films to public theology, exegeting popular culture, and engaging in social media with a spiritual and scholarly purpose. With the Bible in one hand, and social media in the other, so to speak, I seek to share the gospel and Christian scholarship within my spheres of influence, 'so that by all possible means I might influence some.' (I Corinthians 9:22).

Let me conclude by offering three bits of advice to scholars considering using social media:

1. General advice: **Lead, follow and get over it**. Become a *Leader* in using social media to engage peers, collaborate for learning, publish your scholarship, and/or further your good ideas in wider circles. Or *follow* others (like Len Sweet or Tom Oord) who have creatively and successfully created a following for their bold ideas and reflections. And *get over* your objections and fears about diluting or giving away your scholarship in online venues and formats. If you can't get over it, at least get out the way to let other scholars do this important work in for a postmodern age.

2. **Choose your audience.** Decide whether you want to blog, post and promote your ideas and scholarship for other scholars only (plenty of scholarly and peer-juried sites out there); or use more popular sites and formats (like Facebook and LinkedIn) to promote and publish your ideas. Some manage to do both.

3. **Teach by doing.** Show students, colleagues and followers how to select, vet, and footnote online resources; find the best Internet sites and search engines for scholarly content, and how to properly document sources. We all learn by doing, and we can model good online research and publishing in audio, visual and digital typeface formats.

Michael J. Christensen (M.A., Yale, Ph.D., Drew) is an author, speaker, practical theologian, and professor affiliated with Drew University, Point Loma Nazarene

University, Nazarene Theological Seminary, and Northwind Institute. He teaches courses on Spirituality, Christian History, Leadership Development and Theology and Practice of Shalom. He has published eleven books and many articles on various topics of practical theology, including: Equipping the Saints: Mobilizing Laity for Ministry; Children of Chernobyl: Raising Hope form the Ashes; The World After Chernobyl; City Streets, City People; C. S. Lewis on Scripture; Partakers of the Divine Nature: Deification in the Christian Traditions; and (with Rebecca Laird) three post-humous books by Henri Nouwen known as The Nouwen Trilogy: Spiritual Direction, Spiritual Formation and Discernment. Dr. Christensen also is Founder/CEO of WorldHope Corps, USA and WorldHope Malawi — which drills village wells, provides educational scholarships, sponsors community health initiatives, and conducts leadership training in Malawi, Uganda and elsewhere. Christensen blogs at http:// michael-christensen.blogspot.com/ and http://fluidfaith.blogspot.com Visit the web-sites that feature Dr. Christensen's international ministry: www.worldhopecorps.org and www.communitiesofshalom.org Christensen is active on Facebook (Michael J. Christensen, San Diego). His bio and books are featured on Amazon.com author pages: https://www.amazon.com/Michael-J.-Christensen/e/B001IGNLTW

SHANE CLIFTON

Theology and Disability

I retain a profile in many different social media platforms; WordPress, Facebook, YouTube, Twitter, Google+, and LinkedIn. While some are little more than placeholders, I write a blog on WordPress and add the occasional video to YouTube, and then use Facebook and Twitter to share material and engage in conservation.

I began blogging more than a decade ago as a means of sharing scholarly work with a broader audience. My first attempt was a blog entitled "Pentecostal discussions," which was a shared effort with the faculty at the college in which I work. The content remains online, but we only managed to keep it going for a little over a year. The challenge was getting meaningful participation from a wide group of people, all of whom had other more pressing concerns.

I began blogging again under my own name (shaneclifton.com) in 2010, with the intention of theological engagement with contemporary issues. But only a few months later, in September 2010, I had a serious accident that left me a quadriplegic. The blog went silent until I'd made sufficient progress in my rehabilitation to use voice recognition software, after which I took it up again as a way of processing my experiences. For me at least, writing proved to be cathartic. From that point on, the blog became a very personal sharing of my struggles and achievements, as well as addressing philosophical and theological questions that emerged from them. I've wondered along the way whether this open sharing of my life was a useful way of helping people understand what it's like to live with a spinal cord injury, or if it was otherwise driven by ego and pride. A little bit of both, most likely.

I have surprised myself, at times, by the things I've been prepared to share. I've spoken on my blog about incontinence, catheter changes, disabled sex, dummy spits, and so forth. I once described a visit to a clinic investigating the erectile dysfunction that often attends to spinal-cord injury. Many years down the track I can still recall the panic after having hit "post" on that blog entry, and wondering "what have I done!" Yet it is the personal connections that emerge from social media that turn out to be most rewarding. Especially important to me is the times when it generated contact with other quadriplegics from around the globe, who have found that my writing resonated with their own experiences.

I've learned over the years the types of posts that attract the most attention. I'm almost certain to get high view counts if I criticise controversial people; taking on John Piper and Mark Driscoll for their sexism, and Joseph Prince for his hyper-faith treatment of healing for physical and mental illnesses. For the most part, though, I've tried to avoid going down that path, doing so only when extremely aroused. My goal is not to be a witch hunter, but to get people thinking about the physical and social complications that go with disability, dependency, and fragility.

In this light, of more importance to me is the traction I've had with some of my disability critiques of pop culture. My most popular entry was a review of JoJo Moyes' quadriplegic snuff book (and subsequent film), *Me Before You.* The review gave me an opportunity to inform a public, otherwise taken up by the apparent romance of the narrative, about Moyes' abhorrent and prejudicial treatment of disability; her promoting of the idea that life with quadriplegia is not worth living. The post was widely shared and discussed, and had circulation that lasted beyond the usually short shelf life of the average social media posting.

In terms of interaction, I have found that Facebook stimulates the most active engagement. When I publish a blog entry and post it to Facebook, the blog might be widely read yet receive few comments, while the Facebook thread will be the prime site of community discussion. Internal Facebook commentary is likewise often hot and heavy, if not fleeting. I've had a video on Facebook that had more than 65,000 views, but some months later is very hard to find. By way of contrast, I get comments on blog posts that were published years ago.

One of my key goals in blogging has been to develop my writing skills. Academic writing tends to be dense and obtuse, and after years of writing theses, journal articles, and theology tomes, I turned to blogging to learn to express myself in a more engaging and creative manner. Ultimately, this effort set me up for the publication of my memoir, *Husbands Should Not Break*. I'd also like to think that it has had an impact upon the way I write my academic work. Theology is too often a turgid discipline, but I hope to produce work that is both academically substantive and enjoyable to read.

Writing about my own story also connected me with others, and opened doors for me to conduct research drawing on the insight of the stories of people that have lived with quadriplegia over the long term. Initially, I interviewed John Trefry, who had defied expectations at the time of his injury that his life was essentially over, by living as a quadriplegic for more than 50 years. During that time, John married, raised a family, and ingested his life in service to others with a spinal-cord injury. John died not long after I recorded and published his story, so his priceless narrative, which might otherwise have been lost, has been able to live on in my blog. I met with John only two years after my own injury, at a time when I was struggling with the magnitude of my loss and was unable to envision a positive future. Working with his incredible story gave me hope, and stimulated the thought that there were other profound and insightful stories of people flourishing with similar injuries, which were waiting to be told and published.

Since then, I have interviewed six other quadriplegics who had lived long and well their disability, and these narratives became the core of a study conducted under the auspices of Sydney University, "quadriplegia and the good life." Another of the participants, Sheree Hurley, died not long after I recorded her story, and her parents were immensely grateful for the record of her life (I didn't tell them that participants in my study seemed to be dying off, although fortunately the others are doing well). My forthcoming book, *Crippled Grace: Disability, Virtue Ethics, and the Good Life* (Baylor University Press), is the fruit of thinking that began with the writing of my blog.

In respect to other social media platforms, Facebook is a medium that facilitates much shallower conversations, but it has proved useful as a means of gathering opinion. For example, I've asked Facebook friends what they thought of the proposed title of my books, and their ideas proved stimulating. It is also capable of generating raw and ready debate, if you like that sort of thing.

As is now well attested, social media is a terrible time waster, and I've not been immune from its distractions. Like too many of us, I spend too much time on Facebook, a habit I have repeatedly resolved to break, largely unsuccessfully.

Over the years, I've been more intentional about building the content on my blog. Writing a post takes longer than one might imagine, especially when you are seeking to do so regularly—consistent posting helps to maintain and grow a blog audience, and to that end I've tried to set aside some time each week for the task. Even so, if social media is to be your servant rather than your master, it needs to be kept in its proper place. During the course of last year, for example, I took a sabbatical to write an academic manuscript, and decided that I had more import-ant things to do than to blog. So I set it aside, and since that time have blogged only occasionally—when the mood takes me. My numbers have suffered, but it was never about that anyway.

I am increasingly disillusioned about the tenor and tone of conversations on the various social media platforms. Globally, we seem to have arrived at a point in history when civil and respectful conversation is no longer possible. In my earlier online engagement, I was generally of the view that social media was an efficient and effective means of disseminating ideas, engaging in constructive conversa-tion, and opening our minds to fresh insights and new ways of thinking. Today, however, we seem to have lost the ability to weigh and judge sources and argu-ments, and instead come at most issues with ideological and predetermined cer-tainties, looking to attack rather than converse and learn. And as I have faced up to this new reality, I've also come to see that I have too often been part of the problem. There are few people as certain as academics in the rightness of their own views, and as insistent that others should agree.

The last few months I've largely retreated from social media conversations, watching but not participating in debates about fake news, and marveling at the frenzied viral reactions to those caught out in airing unorthodox opinions (from the right and the left). As I contemplate re-engagement, I'm determined to do what I can to change the nature of my interactions with others. It's time to restore virtue to our public conversation, to model the fruits of the Spirit; love, joy, peace, patience, kindness, goodness, faithfulness, gentleness and self-control. The man-ner of our public witness is as or more important than its content or, rather, the latter depends on the former.

The forgotten virtue of humility might be the place to begin for scholars. You'd better know before working to 'build your profile' that your scholarship and opinions are unlikely to change the world, that you are one voice in a crowd, and that social media fame, if by some faux-miracle you go viral, is fleeting and skin deep. Humility will keep you writing for the right reasons; to express yourself, participate in public conversation, develop new skills, and model virtue. It will also help you to hold your public profile loosely, so that it can be set aside as cir-cumstances dictate.

Shane Clifton, PhD, Is Professor of Theology at Alphacrucis College in Sydney, and an Honorary Associate, Centre for Disability Research and Policy, the Faculty of Health Sciences, at the University of Sydney. Shane is editor of The Australasian Pentecostal Studies *journal, and has published in the fields of Pentecostal studies, ecclesiology, and disability. His latest book is* Crippled Grace: Disability, Virtue Ethics, and the Good Life *(BUP).*

RON COLE-TURNER

Theology and Ethics

M y main social media platforms are Twitter and Facebook. I also use two platforms that are designed especially for scholars. These are ResearchGate and Academia. I depend on them for access to science journal articles that would otherwise be inaccessible to me. In fairness to these platforms and to other scholars who depend on them, I need to spend more time there in order to upload more of my own publications.

I also blog frequently. I use the "author page" feature at Amazon, and part of my digital presence includes several eBook titles available through several online channels.

I came slowly to social media, resisting it at every step. The story of my conversion, however, takes us back to 2001, long before today's Twitter and Facebook were invented. Thanks to a small grant from the John Templeton Foundation, a friend and I launched a project we called the "Science and Religion Information Service" or SRIS. In some ways, SRIS functioned like a news outlet. My job was to monitor embargoed press releases summarizing new research in science, sometimes 20 or more each day.

When I saw something that I thought would generate public interest and have an interesting ethics/religion angle, I contacted two or three acquaintances for their comment on how religion might respond to the new discoveries. I bundled these comments into our own press release, which I distributed to the media through the very same channel they used to get their science news in the first place. All this happened quickly and under terms of a strict news embargo that hid the news and our commentary from the general public. When the embargo broke, science journalist around the world would publish their news stories. Frequently they used our material to explain the social or religious impact of the research. One day I opened the *New York Times* and saw a news story that used several paragraphs of our material — text that was on my little laptop before the *Times* shared it with the world.

Like all good things, the grant ran out. I didn't want to let this effort die entirely, so I continued to write my own responses to breaking news in science research. That led to my first efforts at blogging. No more *New York Times*, but at least the world could see a religious response to breaking science news. They could, that is, if they bothered to look for it, which they usually didn't. So I began to ask how I could promote my blog. That is the main reason why I turned to Twitter and finally to Facebook. Quite simply, I wanted to create a network of people interested in what I was writing about in my blog — how to think religiously or theologically about scientific research as it unfolds in front of us.

All the while, the technology platforms were evolving. More precisely, they were co-evolving with society. Each technology advance triggered changes in human social interaction, and shifting human social patterns prompted new technologies. When I first heard of Twitter, I said to myself, "now that's something I'll never use." But then I began to tweet my blogs to my two or three unsuspecting followers. One day someone retweeted my stuff. I still remember the feeling of tweeting to my handful of followers, one of who retweeted to hundreds. Not quite like getting in the *New York Times*, but pretty cool.

Without being aware of it at the time, Twitter was changing the way I did my work. First I thought of tweets as tiny blogposts. Then I came to think of a tweet as something more like the first sentence of a typical blog post. If I hook readers in the tweet, they may be willing to follow a link to a full post or maybe a journal article.

A bigger surprise for me was how much Twitter helped me keep up with my research, especially in those areas of science that I follow most closely. My most recent book is a theological response to the science of human origins research. So I try very hard to keep up with that field, which is exploding with new discoveries and mostly with new techniques of analysis. My Google news alerts are set for things like "Australopithecus" and "Neandertals."

Odd for theologian, I know. But that's the point. How else can I know what leading researchers in paleoanthropology are thinking except through something like Twitter? So I use Twitter to follow all the key people I can find. It's really helpful to hear their comments on *other people's work*. Most valuable, of course, is when they link to original articles, especially to the ones just published. More often than I can count, I have learned about key references this way. I didn't expect the close interplay between Twitter and science journals. Twitter has gone from "something I'll never use" to something I can't work without.

Another group of people I follow are scholars and thought leaders dealing with challenges posed by human enhancement technologies. These include secular transhumanist sources and also members of the Christian Transhumanism Association. Others are experts in bioethics debates about things like human germline gene editing with new techniques like CRISPR. I depend on Twitter to keep me current on this discussion.

I also follow scientists who study the effects of psychedelic drugs like LSD or psilocybin, along with organizations who support this research. I have actually published a few articles on this topic, and I expect to publish more.

An odd mix, to be sure, spanning paleoanthropology to transhumanism to mystical experience connected to "sacred" mushrooms. But that's why I have come to like Twitter. When I check my feed, I find out very quickly if there is breaking news from any of these areas.

Some of my colleagues use social media for teaching. I don't. In fact, I tell my students that I am not likely to "friend" them on Facebook. They may follow me on Twitter, but I won't follow them in return. I am not quite sure why I have these rules. I think it's mostly fear on my part of boundary complexities I don't want to have to deal with. What that means is that I use Twitter and Facebook for roughly half of my professional or academic life . . . never for teaching, but constantly for research.

Social media platforms can offer a space or a meeting point for geographically dispersed individuals who share common interests. So far, however, I haven't seen much evidence that existing networks of scholars have taken their conversations online.

Sometimes I compare the potential of social media for scholars with the conversation that occurs at an academic meeting. During the discussion, the floor is open to various points of view. Insight is shared, publications mentioned, and the positions held by key contributors to the field become evident. At the best conferences, the conversation continues during breaks, at receptions, or over meals, sometimes resulting in shared research projects after the conference is over. Good conferences are a real boost to scholarly work, not just because they generate new insight but because they create a sense of a scholarly community made up of geographically isolated individuals who care about each other's work.

Wouldn't it be great if social media let this sort of scholarly interaction continue when we are no longer in the same room? Social media technology can do this, of course. The question is whether people will use it for that purpose. In my experience and in spite of all our good intentions, this has not happened. Will that change? It may out of necessity, at least if the trend toward fewer face-to-face meetings is real and continues or if social media platforms continue to offer improved visual contact. Still, I remain doubtful that established scholars will ever take their conversations online.

What is happening, however, is that new movements and social configurations of like-minded intellectuals are emerging on social media. One example I can point to is the "Christian Transhumanist Association" or CTA, a loose network of mostly young and somewhat techie Christians who sense that there must be a deep, theological connection between the technology that saturates their lives and the creative love of God. So far, CTA is not much more than a couple of groups on Facebook and a network of people who follow each other on Twitter. But there they are, connected at least in their own minds. Search for "Christian Transhumanist," and CTA comes up immediately. If you insist on thinking in terms of the old ontologies of buildings, budgets, and endowed lectureships, CTA does not exist. But if you can think in terms of new ontologies of technologically-mediated nodes of connection, CTA is real. Invoking Alfred North Whitehead once again and recalling his warning about the "fallacy of misplaced concreteness," I am wondering anew about what, after all, is "real." Because of social media, I am coming to see the world differently.

Don't get me wrong. I am truly grateful to have a "real" job in a real institution with a real budget. But something new is happening, and sometimes I get the sense that the old is passing away, or at least fading into irrelevance. Whether CTA is a long-term winner in the new ontology is beside the point. New, technologically-mediated social realities are emerging all the time. Will these new realities or the old institutions command our attention in the future?

Social media is also showing me something about myself that is really quite surprising. For most of my academic life, I have valued institutional networks. My job, my membership in the American Academy of Religion or in the International Society for Science and Religion, for example, define who I am, at least in terms of my professional identity. But then I consider the list of people and organizations I follow on Twitter. My list is unique. No one else shares my interests. They do not match those of any organization, traditional or emerging.

So I have to ask: Are my interests connected? They are, I think, at least in my own mind and in my work of trying to make sense of the world. I follow theologians, paleoanthropologists, transhumanists, science journalists, leaders in science and religion, neuroscientists who study the effects of psychedelic drugs on the brain, a few former students who are shaking things up, and (of course) my employer and my denomination. I am pretty sure no one else on the planet follows the same list of people I follow.

Why is that important? In a very real sense, it tells me who I am and what I am called to be in this world. Sometimes when I go to speak, say, before a group of scientists, I wonder what on earth I am doing. They know more about the science than I ever will. But then I realize that I am the only one in the room who knows at least a little about their science and who also ponders deep, traditional questions of Christian theology, such as humanity in the image of God or Christ's incarnation in our humanity. On any given day, I might be thinking about the incarnation and about the genetic modification of our humanity using new gene editing technologies. And then it hits me that someone, somewhere, should be trying to bridge these fields and to think about both at the same time.

Now add to that the additional fields that have a serious academic claim on my attention. If it is a unique list, and if *someone somewhere* should be living intellectually in the tenuous spaces between these fields of inquiry, then maybe what I am doing is not totally nutty and my Twitter feed not completely incoherent.

Anyone who knows me well knows that I am really not very social. So I tend not to have a problem with spending too much time on social media. If I find useful information or insights on social media, I am happy to read on. But when I see political commentary or a photo of someone's lunch, I am out of there.

My usual pattern is to look quickly at Twitter and Facebook at transition points throughout the day, but reserve any serious engagement for later in the evening. It is clear to me that if anything, I need to spend more time on social media in generating content. My best hours are kept for writing articles or book chapters, and I think that is the way it should be. But I know I need to connect my social media work more directly with my conventional academic pursuits. Only in the past year or so have I begun to tweet my own scholarly publications or blog posts. I also use Twitter and Facebook to call attention to publications or speaking appearances by others. I also blog and tweet about new research in science or technological that corresponds to my interests. Finally, I try to be a good colleague and friend by retweeting news that is important to others.

Let me conclude with three things I would recommend to scholars considering using social media. First, I strongly recommend that scholars today use Twitter and perhaps Facebook to supplement their scholarly work. One of the first things to do is to create your scholarly network. Who are the people whose work you already follow? Are they on Twitter? Follow them if possible, but don't stop there. Who do they follow? Gradually build out your network of people and organizations that you follow. Depending on your interests, following journalists can be very helpful. Facebook is valuable, I think, mainly in terms of groups. Use the search function on Facebook to look for groups that match your interests, and then try to join. This can be especially valuable if you are interested in two or more academic disciplines or even sub-disciplines.

A second suggestion has two parts. Start by recognizing how information and communications technology is redefining social and cultural reality. As much as you can, become critically aware of your new environment. Then get into the habit of asking yourself again and again what this new situation means for you in terms of your identity and calling. Given who you are, and given these new platforms, what are you being called upon to do and to say? The privilege of being a scholar or an intellectual, especially a Christian scholar, has always come with a heavy burden of public responsibility, even if only to the church. For me today, part of that burden is to be present and accounted for on social media.

Third, be yourself on social media even as you let social media help you discover more fully who you are, at least professionally speaking. What is your distinct compilation of interests, your unique intellectual or scholarly niche in the world? What is the small but critically important nexus of novel connections that no one else occupies or even understands? This is something like "creating your brand," but it goes much deeper than that in its theological significance. In the end, the important thing is not you or the technology. The important thing is what new and unique connections come into existence in you and through you, and how you offer them to others.

Ron Cole-Turner teaches theology and ethics at Pittsburgh Theological Seminary. He is on the Executive Committee of the International Society for Science and Religion and the steering committee of the American Academy of Religion's Human Enhancement and Transhumanism Unit. His theological research focuses on questions posed by human origins and by human enhancement technologies . . . in other words, where have we come from, and where are we going? He is ordained in the United Church of Christ. Ron's blog can be found at http://www.theologyplus.org. He is active on Twitter (@RonColeTurner) and on Facebook (Ron Cole-Turner). He also uses academia.org and researchgate.net. His author page on Amazon can be found at https://amazon.com/author/roncoleturner.

DAVID W. CONGDON

Systematic Theology

A s an older millennial, I witnessed the early years of the digital revolution first-hand, which left me with a cautious openness to new technology. I tended to adopt new media and platforms about a year or two after they became sufficiently widespread that they seemed safe and legitimate, but not so widespread that they were the latest fad. I began blogging in early 2005, joined Facebook in early 2006, and Twitter in early 2009. My participation in social media coincided with the start of my seminary program, and thus I associated social media from the start with my theological work.

Through my blogging I developed a fairly sizable readership in what is sometimes called the "theoblogosphere." This was a fruitful and important experience. Blogging gave me a space to test out my inchoate ideas and develop my own voice without being constrained by space limitations or the expectations of professors and peer reviewers. The blogosphere connected me to scholars around the world in a way that proved crucial for my later scholarly and professional activities.

That period came to an end for me, however, when I left Princeton to take up a position as an academic editor. Blogging took up too much of my time, and I needed to devote every hour outside of work to my own book projects. Twitter eventually came to fill that void. The brevity of a tweet removed the pressure of producing hundreds of well-crafted words for a blog post. And unlike a blog,

Twitter made it easy to build a network of followers. I might only receive a comment or two on a blog post, but on Twitter I could guarantee a sizable number of likes, replies, and retweets.

Today I primarily use Twitter as the platform for my social media scholarship. While I have been using Facebook longer, I keep those posts private and tend to use that platform for more personal updates related to family.

Initially I did not fully recognize the potential for Twitter as a medium for scholarly discourse—as opposed simply to sharing news stories and political observations. That changed for me when I began to see the widespread use of Twitter "threads" (series of tweets connected to each other by way of reply to the previous tweet) as a way of developing a sustained train of thought. More recently Twitter has created a feature called "moments" that allows one to display these threads in a more readable format with a unique URL.

In an age where academic publications can take years to see the light of day—often generating little to no response—the use of Twitter for scholarly discourse allows one to engage in real-time dialogue about immediate concerns with people both inside and outside of the academy, as well as outside of one's discipline. Twitter allows for genuinely interdisciplinary interaction. It is not ideal for nuanced discourse, but what it lacks in complexity and sophistication it more than makes up for in relevance, immediacy, readership, and analytics.

I am constantly surprised by how concise I am able to convey an idea. The arbitrary limit of Twitter can initially seem like a great burden to academics prone to prolixity, but ultimately it forces one to trim everything superfluous and find shorter ways to say the same thing. This is a lesson more scholars should take to heart outside of social media.

The use of threads and "moments" to communicate extended strings of thoughts has made it possible to engage in serious academic discourse on Twitter. I have recently mobilized this feature to launch what I call #TwitterSeminary, in which I post a long thread of tweets—social media lectures, so to speak—on a particular topic. Since I have been unable to find a teaching post, this social media feature has allowed me to "lecture" digitally on topics that are important to me but may not warrant the effort to produce an article or book. Or they may be topics I have already discussed in formal academic publications but want to promote to a wider audience. I am able to reach significantly more people through a tweet than I am through an academic book or article. #TwitterSeminary has thus allowed me to communicate my theological ideas and proposals to new readers.

For those scholars interested in using Twitter for academic discourse, I would recommend the following three things:

1. Don't let the ability to create lengthy threads relieve you of the responsibility to adhere as much as possible to the character limit. I have friends who write a long paragraph of text, chop it up every 140 characters, and then post it as a Twitter thread. This fails to take advantage of the medium. It also misses the challenge—and the opportunity!—that Twitter poses to academics.

2. Practice online generosity, humility, and hospitality. The anonymity and immediacy of social media easily generates a culture of "trolling," in which people make snap judgments, post insensitive statements, and even spew abusive and offensive comments. Some argue that social media, and Twitter in particular, inherently produces this behavior. There may be some truth in that, but we can also learn to cultivate social media virtues. When it comes to scholarly dialogue, these virtues are especially important. We have to remember that a tweet cannot convey the depth of research and thought someone has put into an idea. A hermeneutic of charity is absolutely essential. The following rule is worth remembering: assume the best about a tweet before responding.

3. Don't reply to people on Twitter by using a quote-retweet. It comes off as rude and self-aggrandizing. Post a personal reply first, and only do a quote-retweet if you actually have something to say to a wider audience.

David W. Congdon, Ph.D., is an acquisitions editor at University Press of Kansas, editing books in political science and law. He is also a systematic theologian and scholar of modern Protestant theology and hermeneutics. He is the author of The Mission of Demythologizing: Rudolf Bultmann's Dialectical Theology, Rudolf Bultmann: A Companion to His Theology, *and* The God Who Saves: A Dogmatic Sketch. *See his website at dwcongdon.com and follow him on Twitter @dwcongdon.*

GREG COOTSONA

Theology and Religious Studies

Social media increasingly defines our cultural worlds. It certainly influences how I communicate. To that end, I primarily use Twitter and Facebook. I also post, at more or less regular intervals, on my personal blog and on the *Huffington Post*. I should add that, in addition to my personal Facebook account, I currently manage two other public pages on science and faith (Scientists in Congregations and Talk of God, Talk of Science), and these have offered me the opportunity to interact with others and to put my ideas and questions out to the public. Incidentally, I've enjoyed more success with followers on Facebook than on Twitter for reasons that escape me. Finally, I'm told that it's a great idea to create an email list, but I have not succeeded at that, and thus my use of email as social media is spotty.

Let me begin by affirming that I love old, fashioned, "Dead Tree Books" (DTBs). I love smelling the paper, the feel of the actual cover of a DTB in my hands, and seeing the place where I've made marks with an old school pencil. Similarly, I have also enjoyed those moments when I've done a book tour, when I've been able to speak to a room about the process of writing or why I chose particular style for a particular book. All this adds up to a delight in the way we used to disseminate scholarly ideas. As a scholar in the old days — at least as I like to imagine them — we essentially wrote the best book or article we could and found a publisher who then *published* (by which I mean distributed them to *the public*) our DTBs through various channels. All that strikes me now as exceedingly well-behaved and a bit quaint.

Today's environment is more chaotic and dynamic. And I've found that the need to move to new media for getting my ideas out (i.e., published). There are two particular experiences that transformed my attitudes on the use of social media.

First of all, I was able to study the culture of emerging adults (age 18-30) for eighteen months through a planning grant from the John Templeton Foundation, which we named Science for Students and Emerging, Young Adults (or SEYA). The guiding question was this: How do emerging adults form their attitudes on religion and science and how do these attitudes change? I convened a group of twelve thought leaders in emerging adulthood. A SEYA team taught on the integration of science and religion with 638 emerging adult participants and had informal discussions about relating science and religion. Finally, I conducted in-depth qualitative interviews with thirty college students and post-college emerging adults. Through this process, the SEYA team discovered a number of things, particularly that, in order to reach this demographic, we need to engage the internet and social media. The importance of social media is that websites seem static unless new information is presented or "pushed" toward the users through email, Facebook, Twitter et al. And sadly, were learned that DTBs are, to some degree, dead.

Secondly, I had a very specific experience with "old school" media promotion versus new media with a trade publication "self-help" book, *Say Yes to No: Using the Power of No to Create the Best in Life, Work and Love* I wrote for Random House in 2009 and then a subsequent book, *C. S. Lewis and the Crisis of a Christian* for Westminster John Knox in 2014. On *Say Yes to No*, I spent a considerable amount of money on truly great publicists (like tens of thousands of dollars) whose job it was to connect me with podcasters, radio broadcasters and print media editors. I found myself on international news, and ultimately I was interviewed about the book's ideas by Kathie Lee and Hoda on the *Today* Show. It was really exhilarating—and I learned a great deal—but it didn't produce significant book sales, which is one key measure of impact. For the C. S. Lewis book, I did almost all the publicizing myself, primarily with Facebook and some Twitter ads for under a couple thousand dollars. It's almost impossible to draw direct causation, but I do know that C. S. Lewis book promotion through new media correlated with better sales.

As a result, for my next books, whether they're scholarly or more popular, I'm heading toward social media. And of course, I'll get my non-book ideas out through those channels as well.

Social media also brings with it several surprises. The first is a shocking level of incivility. This has recurred in the various ways I publish my ideas through social media. One common question I hear from friends on Facebook is "Greg, how do you put up with those snarky and mean comments?" (I have some techniques I'll cover below.) As several studies have demonstrated (for example, Sherry Turkle's *Reclaiming Conversation*), empathy is lacking in social media interchanges. In fact, the use of social media seems to produce a decrease in empathy. I can attest to that. Over the past couple decades, I've had the experience of speaking in a variety of contexts, in other states and countries, and what people write on Facebook or in a blog comment—and how they say it—they have never uttered to my face. What's a bit subtler is that, once these arrows are shot your way in social media, it's easy to become engaged in a war of insults. I've learned the importance keeping your head in the heat of battle. Or never warring in the first place.

The second is how much I have to learn about how it is truly the way we communicate today, and yet, how much I have to learn in effectively employing social media. And that's why it's good to read all the ideas you'll find in this book!

Just to repeat: when I managed the SEYA project, I realized that I'd need to engage social media for the sake of emerging adults. And that is a particularly important demographic for me as I seek, among other things, to integrate mainstream science with mere Christianity. In addition, if we're going to utilize social media, the audience will skew toward emerging adults.

One conceptual breakthrough: the people you affect may not be those that comment. Let me relay one story of an emerging adult, Emma, who read my posts on Facebook (in this case on the 2016 election) while living in Thailand. She was depressed by the Christian voices in the United States, and was grateful for an alternative and especially for how I engaged in debate and discussion without rancor. She commented in a private message, "I'm glad you're presenting these ideas, and I'm really thankful for your voice. Please keep at it." Hearing from Emma taught me that there are many more people listening in than directly commenting. This implies that the way we comment may be more important the content of our initial posts.

As to successes (which I was asked to address in this piece), I have experienced some success with social media, but many more failures! (I wish, for example, I had more Twitter followers.) Generally, I simply try to address the social media once a day (Facebook posting, tweeting) and then write a longer piece/s during the week and post blogs once every two weeks (although of course I wish it were more frequent). I can't always stick with this rhythm, but with this practice has gradually become a habit, and therefore it does happen most weeks.

I also really try to be sure that, when there are comments on my social media posts, that I don't respond out of anger or despondency or whatever. Sometimes taking a breath and regrouping is more important than an urgent response. But here, it seems, I've already moved into my suggestions.

I conclude with three things I would recommend to scholars considering using social media:

1. Create a strategy and goals. In this respect, you may find talking with a social media pro or consultant helpful. Whenever I've talked with John, a friend in Silicon Valley who specializes in marketing and internet optimization, it's been amazingly helpful. John's also helped me to be realistic about how many people I can reach. I would add that we need to be pragmatic about how often we can post. Sure, it's great to blog four times a week, but how will that fit around taking kids to school, making dinner, spending time with your spouse, let alone—if you're an academic—preparing classes, teaching, and attending committee meetings? Moreover, even with goals and strategy, be flexible. The world of social changes rapidly. (And so do our lives.) We don't even know today what tomorrow's most important social medium will be. I'll never forget when I heard about Twitter in 2009—it sounded like a weird curiosity, and I was skeptical that it would last.

2. In light of my previous answers, be careful of your angle of approach and avoid polarizing language. I know we can gain followers if our opinions are "high contrast," as a marketer might say, but that really means we're acting like jerks or taking on the role of shock jocks. I can't recommend that approach as a Christian specifically, or as a human being more generally. We don't need more polarizing discourse! Minimally, make sure the way you promote your work is consistent with the type of work you do, who you are, or at least the nature of your public voice. Consider that this post might have a longer shelf life than you'd anticipate. So do yourself a favor: don't post out of anger or despair (and now I realize I'm repeating myself).

3. Finally, social media should fit into a larger strategy of whom you want to communicate with—age, theological approach, etc.—and what you want

to say. In other words, always publish out of your mission and identity. (And yes, it's critical to have a mission or personal branding statement. For the latter, see http://cootsona.blogspot.com/2012/08/an-exercise-in -personal-branding.html). Post in the service of what *you* are convinced the listening public needs to hear. To paraphrase a book by my speech coach, Nick Morgan, *Tell your story, change the world*. Social media helps us do exactly that.

――――――――

Greg Cootsona is a theologian and writer. He also teaches at Cal State Chico and directs a three-year grant project at Fuller Seminary that assists emerging adult ministries in integrating Christian faith with mainstream science. Greg served for eighteen years as associate pastor for discipleship in New York City and Chico, California. He has written seven books and just finished Emerging Adults, Christian Faith, and Science. *He and his wife, Laura, have two college-age daughters. Cootsona blogs on Huffington Post, http://www.huffingtonpost.com/author/greg-696 and on http://cootsona.blogspot.com. He's also on Facebook (Greg Cootsona), Twitter (@GregCootsona).*

BENJAMIN L. COREY

Public Theology

O ver the years I have grown passionate about the use of social media to influence theological viewpoints and public opinion on a variety of issues. To that means, I use Facebook, Twitter, and Instagram, each as a specific tool to engage the public. With Instagram I invite readers/followers into my personal life through photos and to connect with me on a more personal level, Facebook I use to disseminate my own work and other articles that are relevant to topics I frequently discuss, and Twitter is where I will directly engage readers and critics alike, along with using their 140 character platform to offer short sound bites and commentary at critical "trending" moments.

I made a very deliberate decision to approach my work in theology and missiology from the angle of using blogs and social media to influence others. I knew that I had two choices- work within the confines of the academy and write for peers and students — where my work *might* be read by a few hundred or at most, few thousand people — or, I could try to utilize modern social media as a public scholar. Choosing the latter, I have been able to write on concepts of theology and missiology at a popular, bite-sized level with the possibility the information would be accessed, comprehended, and applied by a much larger audience — with the potential and hope for more real-life impact. For me, what I wanted more than anything was for my work to actually change hearts and minds, and to actually have a real-world impact, so public theology became the only choice for me.

As I reflect on my experience thus far, I've learned that it's possible to change lives of people you've never met, and that someone behind an anonymous avatar can unexpectedly change your life. Some of my most rewarding moments have been in response to my theological work on Christian nonviolence and enemy love. In the American setting these ideas are routinely met with dismissal and even outrage, but over the years I have received countless messages and emails from people who have found their hearts changing as a result of following my work on that topic. From people who wrote and apologized for mocking me, and who told me that they ended up getting rid of their guns so they were better prepared to love their enemies, to the time I put out a call on Twitter for gun donations so that we could melt them down into garden tools — and got eight guns donated by followers in 24 hours — seeing people grow and respond to a theology of radical enemy love has been one of the most rewarding experiences of my life.

However, more than moments when my ideas influenced others, my most favorite moment has been my unlikely friendship with the "Irish Atheist" — an anonymous commenter who presented on my blog as an angry troll who hated all religious people. At first he would critique my positions, other times he would directly articulate that we were enemies — let's just say, he wasn't a fan.

At first my instinct was to ban him from commenting on my blog, but I instead opted to attempt to dialogue with him- not to convince him of anything, but for the sake of honest discussion. As that played out, we realized that we truly had more in common than we had in difference. Trading blog comments eventually gave way to direct messages, and those conversations helped us both to see the humanity and decency in the other. After a few years, we found ourselves having beers together in Chicago while I was in town speaking, and we've been good friends ever since — each having a deeper appreciation for why the other believes what they believe.

I've also learned that all tribes, whether liberal or conservative, have "Twitter Police" who will quickly find you if you say something they don't like. Experiencing the full force of Christian tribalism through doing theology publicly and always having *someone* upset with you, actually gave birth to some concepts on how Christian tribalism is impacting the church in America. I went on to express these thoughts in my book, *Unafraid: Moving Beyond Fear-Based Faith* (HarperOne).

However, one of the beautiful aspects of working out philosophy and theology with social media versus by only writing in the academy, is that you don't have to have it all figured out when you hit the "publish" button. Instead, social media and blogging offers a platform to wrestle with and work out concepts that you're trying on for size — every major theme I've covered in books is first test-driven on my blog, and then refined. The feedback one gets in this context is broad and helpful, offering the opportunity to hear from voices from all walks of life, instead of only hearing feedback from voices within the academy or your own theological/ contextual bubble. This exposes your thought process to a far more diverse audience than I have ever experienced in academia, and I think my ideas have grown stronger because of it.

In fact, I can't think of a single idea that has not been shaped in some way by the feedback I get in the public realm. Most often I find this in regard to praxis, and how a given theology would impact someone, depending on their circumstances. I think the reality is that we are often teaching and preaching to people like ourselves, and that this limits our ideas because our understanding of how these ideas potentially *impact* others within a different context, or life experience, is limited. Some of the most important questions about any given theology are, "What does this mean for people, contextually? How does it grow and take new shape and expressions when in one context versus another? What does it look like to apply this in one context verses another?"

The only real way to explore the answers to those questions is for the original idea itself to be explored and critiqued by a variety of voices from a variety of contexts, and to allow your idea to grow and morph and take new shape as result.

While I have no regrets in my decision to take the path of a public theologian, it certainly is a bit of work to utilize social media in a way that is actually effective. I have a certain slot in my daily schedule set aside specifically for social media, and this is usually right after my daily writing time. This slot gives me a chance to share what I have written, but also to pre-schedule other social media posts throughout that day or weekend (pre-scheduling a post ahead of time is your *friend*). Being active on social media doesn't mean one has to constantly be *on* social media — by scheduling posts, your social media handles can be active with the public even when you're busy doing other things.

Let me conclude with three things I would recommend to scholars considering using social media:

1. If you want your ideas to be widely read, you'll have to adjust your writing style for a broader, more public audience. Dry, academic language may work within the academy, but that's not what will get your ideas accessed by a broader audience. Instead, learn how to adjust your style so that lay-

people feel as if you're trying to dialogue with them, and not just a select group of academics. Essentially, you can either show off your advanced vocabulary or you can make your ideas accessible to an average reader, but you'll often have to pick one or the other. For me, I'm far more concerned with sharing my ideas and making them accessible than anything else.

2. To be widely read means to be widely criticized, so if you're not keen on your name and ideas being used for blog fodder or heresy hunting websites, social media may not be the route for you.

3. If you're going to use social media to do theology or philosophy, learn to do it well. Read up on social media best practices and do your best to follow at least some of those recommendations.

————————

Benjamin L. Corey is a two-time graduate of Gordon-Conwell Theological Seminary (Theology & Missiology) and received his doctorate from Fuller Theological Seminary. He is the author of Undiluted: Rediscovering the Radical Message of Jesus *and,* Unafraid: Moving Beyond Fear-Based Faith. *Corey is also the managing editor at Patheos Progressive Christian.*

ROBERT D. CORNWALL

Historical Theology

We live in the social media age, as demonstrated by the President's use of Twitter to "communicate" with the masses. I put communicate in quote marks, because there are questions as to the veracity of much that the President shares via Twitter. However, what his tweets illustrate is that in this new age, communication can be immediate and unfiltered. Not only that, but everyone seems to be getting on board the train. Where once scholars could share their ideas in monographs, lengthy articles, and conference papers (all of this still happens, of course), the lure of social media has begun to entice scholars to share their wares more broadly than their immediate colleagues. I count myself among those who have adopted a social media persona.

I engage this social media world as one who is by education and scholarly endeavor a historical theologian and church historian. I have published widely in my field of expertise, which is eighteenth century Anglicanism. I also serve as a pastor of a local congregation, which makes me a practical theologian as well as a historical theologian/church historian. Due to my position in the church, I face a different set of concerns and issues than I would if I were a tenure-track academic. I do not have to publish or perish. As a pastor, I must be a generalist, which may make my engagement with social media easier. After all, on Sunday morning my congregation isn't interested in an in-depth analysis of Henry Dodwell's rejection of the legacy of the English Reformation. However, I can bring to a wider audience insights I've learned from my scholarly work (even if not in a sermon). With this introduction, I will try to address the connection of scholarship and social media.

When it comes to Social Media, I am, first and foremost, a blogger. I started blogging in 2006, using the Blogger format provided by Google. I'm not sure why I chose the somewhat unwieldy title of *Pondering on a Faith Journey*, but it is the title that emerged, and I've kept it as my moniker to this day. From this platform, I have written on a wide variety of topics, ranging from politics to church life to church history and theology. I review books and write brief essays (1500 words, which is long for a blog post) on matters of concern to me, the church, and the world at large. Having written my share of academic articles and books, I believe I have made a mark in the academic world. If one focuses on the academic community, then my audience is rather small and very specialized. As noted earlier, I am by discipline a historical theologian/church historian, who has focused on eighteenth-century high church Anglicans, with special attention to a rather small community of high churchmen known as the Nonjurors. The Nonjurors draw the interest of an even smaller community of scholars than those interested in High Church Anglicanism. While I did create a Facebook page for the Nonjurors, giving this group of churchmen wider exposure, it hasn't been one of the bigger draws on Facebook.

The academic audience is small and specialized. Unless the topic has a degree of controversy attached, it's quite likely that a session on eighteenth century English church history will draw a rather small crowd at an American Society of Church History meeting. On the other hand, as a blogger I can reach out to a much broader constituency. I can also be more of a generalist, and write on topics of interest, but also topics that are further afield from my academic specialty. Thus, my blog essays and reviews might not be peer reviewed (or copy edited), they do offer immediacy. Philip Clayton noted in his book *Transforming Christian Theology for Church and Society* (Fortress, 2010), that I had posted the very first review of his book *Adventures in the Spirit*. My review appeared long before any reviews appeared in an academic journal (p. 1). That remains true to this day. As soon as I read the book and write the review, I can post it for all to see. I've discovered that publishers are very willing to provide review copies of their books to bloggers who are known to write thorough reviews.

While I have used my blog as the primary means to share my views on things I consider important, I have partnered the blog with other social media efforts. I make regular use of Twitter, Facebook, Goodreads, Google+, and even Amazon to make known my posts to an even larger audience. In addition to my personal Facebook page, I have an author page, a page for the blog, and separate pages that relate to several of my books (the more popular/general books. Of these, my Facebook page stands out, not only as a means to publicize blog posts but to share other, shorter messages, along with sharing posts from others. There is another level of communication that I make use of. These venues, which include Hootsuite, Scoop, Bible Gateway Bloggers Grid, and Network Blogs, can be used to schedule and share posts across platforms. There are often paid services available to us, but to this point, I have used the free versions.

Back in the day, when I was engaged in teaching, the only readily available social media entity was email and email-based list-serves. I joined one that related to my scholarly interests in British church history and another focused on Disciples of Christ theology and practice. Those forms of social media may still exist, but they no longer serve as a primary vehicle for sharing. Most of these conversations have moved from list-serves to Facebook groups, or similar venues. Email is still of use, but it no longer functions in the same way it did in the recent past. Yes, we still send information and updates via email, but it doesn't serve as a means of fomenting conversation. Over past decade I have used social media, predominantly my blog, to stay in the conversation about matters of church history, theology, and ministry. I would say that the book reviews I post on my blog make the largest scholarly contribution. I do write other pieces, often briefer, that are rooted in scholarship, but they are not scholarly per se. That is, they're not peer-reviewed essays and articles. Nonetheless they allow me the opportunity to keep engaged in the scholarly world.

Like many who use social media, especially Facebook and Twitter, I have found that social media allows for a more unfiltered engagement with an audience, which is much larger than one would have if one is solely engaged in academic writing. With regard to my personal blog, I try to update it at least five times a week (usually Sunday through Thursday). I began posting on my blog almost daily after reading a post written by Scot McKnight on his *Jesus Creed* blog. Scot opined that if one wanted to cultivate an audience, one should post regularly (indeed, daily if possible). That has been my general practice ever since.

As a pastor, I'm not under pressure to write for a scholarly audience, but I have tried to keep engaged in my fields of study and interest. Though, I will admit that my scholarly output has diminished in recent years, even as I put more focus on communicating to a broader audience. I have found that social media keeps me in conversation with colleagues in the academic/scholarly world, though that world is much broader as a result. I should say that my blog posts focus more on theology, preaching, worship, ministry, than on church history, which is my specialty.

Regarding other forms of social media, I have used Facebook, Google+, and Twitter to extend the reach of my blog. Facebook has proven valuable in connecting with other scholars, especially those persons whose books I have reviewed. Because I write rather lengthy book reviews on my blog, I'm able to communicate with authors and publishers through Facebook and Twitter, letting them know when a review is published. This often allows them to forward in one form another the reviews. This in turn drives people to the blog. My time on social media has another benefit. It allows me to keep abreast of what other scholars are doing. Even as I share on social media, so do many others. In essence, social media provides a valuable form of intellectual community.

Academic institutions tend to reward engagement in highly technical scholarship, which generally has a relatively small audience. As a historian of eighteenth century British church history, with a focus on the Nonjurors, I know that the audience is small. I contributed twenty-five articles to the *Oxford Dictionary of National Biography*. I had the opportunity to contribute a rather large number of articles due to the fact that there are very few Nonjuror scholars in the world, and there were sufficient numbers of individuals in the original DNB that needed their entries revised or replaced to require my expertise. I'm proud of that work, and it might prove helpful to a handful of scholars, but it doesn't have the reach of social media. So, even if institutions do not reward engagement with social media, it does allow for the sharing of scholarship to an audience that doesn't read academic journals or scholarly monographs. I rarely write about the Nonjurors, but I do write a great deal about theology on my blog and that work is enhanced by my scholarly preparation.

I'm not sure this is a surprise, but I do think that social media has tended to democratize scholarship. As a historian, I've found the work of John Fea especially interesting. John is a historian of American religion and culture. His blog brings his expertise on American history into conversation with contemporary issues. Since he has focused on the question of whether the United States is or was a Christian nation, his blog posts have provided a response to people like David Barton that is rooted in deep scholarship. His writing is enriched by his scholarship, but it is also accessible. That's important.

One of the criticisms of academic theology and biblical studies is that theologians and biblical scholars only write for the guild. Blogs, together with Facebook, allows those willing to enter the fray, an opportunity to speak to an audience that is receptive but may not have the specialized vocabulary. This format allows scholars to reformulate their message in a way that reaches this audience. That is important!

Several years ago, I participated in a conference put together by Philip Clayton and Tripp Fuller. It was called *Theology after Google*. The title of my presentation was "Brick and Mortar Meets Google: Bridging the Ages of Spirituality." In that presentation, I noted my appreciation of social media—being that I was a blogger—but I also wanted to make clear that to embrace social media didn't mean throwing out brick and mortar. As a "brick and mortar" pastor, I serve folks who fully embrace social media (some of whom are old enough to be my parents), while others haven't even embraced email. As a person who engages rather fully social media, I also know that there is more to life than Facebook and Twitter. I closed my presentation with these words:

Our task, it would seem to me, is not to throw out everything. We don't have to tear down the seminaries and universities. We don't have to toss out our theological libraries. But, we need to carefully figure out how to bridge these two ages—the age of brick and mortar and the age of *Google*. Even as the codex (ink on paper books) that we've been reading for centuries won't disappear overnight, neither will brick and mortar churches.

What is my conceptual breakthrough? Nearly a decade later, I would have to agree with what I shared at the conference. Brick and mortar isn't going away quite so soon—even Amazon is setting up its own Brick and Mortar stores.

Social media is addictive. I know I spend more time on Facebook and Twitter than I should. I learn a lot about the world, with more immediacy, as I scan my Twitter feed, but if I'm not careful I can be drawn into what has come to be known as "fake news." I know that if I didn't spend so much time on social media I might get more reading and writing done. I might even spend more time outdoors or with my wife. But, even when I'm away from my computer, my phone is always at my side.

Since I serve a congregation as its pastor, I have to make sure that I'm attending to my pastoral responsibilities (though social media has proven helpful even here). I believe that I am able to take care of my obligations to the church, so social media hasn't interfered there. Of course, as I noted it might cut into time I could spend reading, writing, or even walking through the neighborhood. One thing I can say is that apart from a computerized version of solitaire that I play each evening while watching TV, I am not a gamer. That probably is my saving grace!

I conclude with three things would you recommend to scholars considering using social media:

1. The first word of wisdom has to do with remembering one's audience. One can assume that the readers of an essay written for a peer-reviewed academic journal will have some expertise in the field. An essay published on a blog will reach a much wider audience, so the purpose will be to pitch the essay to a more generalized audience. That doesn't mean dumbing down the work, but it may require more explanation. Remember also that a lengthy blog post will be 1500 words, while a typical essay for an academic journal will be several times as long.

2. My second word also has to do with remembering the audience. Take seriously their interest in the topic and respect it. Provide good information that will encourage further study. In other words, give as much attention to what is shared in popular media forms as you would in an academic journal. This will be increasingly important in the coming years as people are faced with reams of information, much of it sketchy at best, if not completely false. Remember that audience that is open to good information, but may not know how to discern fact from fiction.

3. I suppose I can say this with impunity since I'm not employed by an academic institution. In the years to come, scholars will need to give as much attention to the popular media as they do to scholarly production. Tenure committees may not agree, but perhaps this needs to change. So, institutions might want to reconsider the way in which they reward scholarly over popular exposition. This is especially true for biblical studies and theology. Blogs and other forms of social media allows scholars to speak directly to "people in the pew." The church needs this expertise, but it needs it in forms that are understandable and digestible, there is no better way of delivering it than in a format like a blog (and whatever follows blogging).

––––––––––

Robert D. Cornwall, Ph.D., is a pastor, theologian, historian, ecumenist. He serves as pastor of Central Woodward Christian Church (Disciples of Christ) in Troy, MI. He has written or edited more than fifteen books, numerous articles, and edits the journal Sharing the Practice *(Academy of Parish Clergy). He has been a leader of local interfaith and community organizing efforts, regional commissions for the Disciples, and is a Chaplain for the Troy Police Department. See Cornwall's blog* Pondering on a Faith journey *at bobcornwall.com. You may sign up to receive blog updates. He is a regular user of Facebook (Robert D. Cornwall), and Twitter (@drbobcwcc), and occasional user of LinkedIn, Google+, Academia.edu, and Pinterest. You may follow him on his author pages at Goodreads and Amazon.com.*

MARC CORTEZ

Theological Education

The only social media platforms I use with any regularity are my blog, Facebook, Twitter, and Academia. I keep my LinkedIn profile fairly up to date, but I don't use the service for anything beyond that. And although I have Instagram and Pinterest accounts, they almost never get used.

I initially got involved with social media because of my academic interests. In other words, it's not that I was already active on social media and only then decided to use my online presence for academic purposes. Other than a largely inactive Facebook account, I had almost no social media presence before I started blogging in 2008. At that time, I began to see the value of social media as a way of supporting and promoting the Th.M. program I had begun directing at Western Seminary (Portland, OR). Initially the blog was a forum for interacting with my students outside of class, but I quickly saw its value for expanding the reach and visibility of the program by promoting our classes and highlighting our students' accomplishments. This led to an increased use of Facebook and Twitter, primarily to maintain and develop the online relationships established through the blog.

Within a few years, though, my use of social media shifted from a more exclusive focus on promoting a particular degree program to using that platform as a way of promoting my school as a whole. This required a shift in direction. Up to this point, I used social media primarily as a vehicle for more academically oriented theological discussions. This was appropriate for the kind of degree program I was promoting, but it was not a good style for promoting an entire school. This is when I began writing for more of a general audience, focusing on articulating theological discussions in a way that would be beneficial to the average Christian leader. This is also when I began using my Facebook and Twitter accounts to connect with a broader audience rather than just interacting with people I had already gotten to know through other venues.

Engaging a broader Christian audience remains central to how I use social media today. Although I enjoy academic theological discussions, I have continued to keep my online presence focused primarily on providing theological resources to the evangelical community as a whole. Indeed, this latter emphasis marks the real difference in my current use of social media. Although I continue to think that my online presence is a valuable way of serving my academic institution, what really keeps me going is the thought that I am providing a tangible benefit to the broader community.

The thing that has surprised me the most along the way is that you really can create and maintain meaningful relationships online. Before I got started, I was one of those who disparaged online relationships, which explains my limited use of social media for personal reasons. Yet over the years, I have established quality relationships with people all over the world, some of whom I will probably never meet in person. In many instances, we have had the opportunity to discuss difficult theological issues they have faced in life and ministry, some involving situations that might have been far more difficult for them to share with me in a face-to-face conversation. I am not saying that these relationships can or should replace our offline relationships, especially since I am well aware that online relationships come with their own limitations. Nonetheless, I learned that these relationships can be far more valuable than I realized beforehand. Indeed, one of the more enjoyable aspects of almost every conference I attend is meeting one of my online friends for the first time, something made possible by the meaningful relationships we developed through our online interactions.

A second lesson is that it is entirely possible to have meaningful and productive theological discussions online. This has been, and continues to be, surprising to me because of how many online discussions go so badly wrong. It's easy to conclude from this that the problem is with the medium itself and that we should simply avoid online theological discussions. I think that's tragic given the potential of online forums for resourcing the broader Christian community, and I was pleasantly surprised to discover that it really is possible to have good discussions about important issues that involve meaningful and constructive disagreement.

Finally, although I have always known that the best books on writing all emphasize the value and importance of writing on a daily basis, I did not experience that for myself until I began using social media regularly. What really made the difference for me was that writing online is so different from the kinds of academic writing I had done previously. Engaging social media well requires you to think and write regularly about a much broader range of issues than is typically the case in academic writing. And given that your audience can be almost anyone, the comments and questions you receive in response to your writing are almost certain to be more diverse than those you will encounter in other contexts. All of this means that engaging social media required me to expand my intellectual and theological "range" in helpful ways.

Along with these unexpected benefits, my use of social media has also contributed in more direct ways to my academic work. Probably the most obvious example of this is that I am currently co-editing a reader in theological anthropology with someone I only know through online interactions. That is an opportunity I simply would not have if it were not for my involvement with social media. I have also received numerous invitations to present papers at conferences or speak on issues that arose as a direct consequence of my online presence. So my online work has played a direct role in shaping my academic projects.

I have also used my blog on numerous occasions to test ideas I am developing. For instance, I once ran a series of posts on the nature of "heresy," which I wrote specifically so I could get a better handle on the issue before I dealt with it in an elective course I was preparing. Given the nature of my online writing, those blog posts do not reflect all of the academic work I was doing on the subject. But they did give me the opportunity to think about how I would communicate that information to a more general audience, which is precisely what I needed to be able to do for my class. Similarly, I have used my blog to develop thoughts on things like the *imago Dei*, the value of studying medieval Christianity, and the problem of evil. The real "breakthrough" experience on these things was not so much *what* I thought about these topics, which I tend to develop more in connection with my teaching and academic writing. Yet each involved a breakthrough with respect to *how* I could best communicate these ideas to a broader audience. Since clarity of communication often contributes to clarity of understanding, though, I walked away from each of these experiences with a deeper knowledge of important issues.

Anyone who engages social media regularly knows that one of the biggest challenges involved has to do with managing the time demands. When I'm doing it well, I confine my online activity to specific times of the day that I set aside for that purpose. The reality, though, is that I have always struggled to restrict my social media use in this way. It's far too easy to convince yourself that you're just going to "check" on something and that it will "only take a minute." I have also found that this temptation is particularly difficult to resist if you view your social media engagement as a service of some kind, whether to your institution or to the broader Christian community. That gives you a kind of missional justification for slipping in some extra online time, which is difficult to resist in the face of unattractive alternatives like grading or email.

Regardless of my own struggles with time and social media, I do think the best way to do this is to be intentional and strategic with your time allotment. For me, this works best if I know three things: (1) how many hours a week, (2) how many days a week, and (3) what time(s) of day. For me, the first one is important because it helps me put my online work in perspective. It's one thing to think that I am going to spend two hours a day on social media, it's something else to realize that this means investing 10-14 hours a week. The second one requires me to be intentional about how I want to use each day. For example, I try not to engage social media to any great extent on Fridays or Sundays. The reasons for the latter might be obvious since I try to focus that day on worship, ministry, and family. On Fridays, though, I work from home and write/research most of the day. So some might think that Fridays would be a perfect day for maintaining my online presence. Yet I have found it almost impossible to engage social media on Fridays and not allow it to consume more time that it should. The meetings and classes that fill the other days of the week require me to be more disciplined and stick with the amount of time I've allotted for that day. Since my Friday schedule is far more flexible, which is what makes it a good day for writing, it is far too easy to allow one hour to turn into two or more. Consequently, I find it best just to protect Fridays entirely.

For anyone interested in using social media as a resource for their academic work, my first recommendation is to be clear about why you are doing it and what you hope to accomplish. Although I think social media can be a powerful tool for an academic, I have already noted that it can consume a fair amount of time. Before you begin, then, be certain that it is worth the investment. I recommend having purposes and goals that you can evaluate. Be prepared to ask yourself at the end of the year what your online activities accomplished and whether those accomplishments were worth the time you invested. Having said that, I should also caution against under-estimating how long it takes to create a meaningful online platform. Do some research so that your goals will be realistic; but do set goals.

My second recommendation relates to what I said earlier about time management: be intentional and strategic with your time. Done well, social media can be a lot of fun, which means that it can also be quite tempting.

Finally, if you're going to write online, use it as an opportunity to become a better writer. Many of us have already developed an effective academic style of writing that serves us well for our books, journal articles, and conference papers. But I recommend approaching online writing as its own genre, one that requires us to develop new skills. There are a number of excellent books and online resources about writing for general audiences and the specific skills needed to write online. Grab some of those and allow them to help you develop new ways of using words to interact with the people around you.

Marc Cortez (Ph.D.) is a theologian, youth worker, father of teenage daughters, and frequent worrier about teenage daughters. He teaches in the graduate and doctoral programs at Wheaton College, focusing primarily on Christology, theological anthropology, and theological figures like Karl Barth and Jonathan Edwards. A former youth pastor, he remains active in youth ministry and is a frequent viewer of superhero movies. Marc blogs somewhat infrequently at Everyday Theology (marccortez .com). Feel free to sign up for email updates on the site. Marc is also a regular user of Facebook (Marc Cortez) and Twitter (@_MarcCortez), and he sporadically (i.e. almost never) checks in with his LinkedIn, Pinterest, and Instagram accounts.

OLIVER D. CRISP

Systematic Theology

P eople of my era—the so-called "Generation X"—are often the butt of jokes about their social media usage. This is particularly true when it comes to the withering criticism of Millennials. We use it badly, or inconsistently, or don't know what we're doing . . . and so on. There may be a grain of truth to some of these suggestions as there are in many caricatures, though I don't put a lot of store in such pop psychology factoids about generational differences. I understand that Gen Xers do use certain sorts of social media and not others; and younger scholars may use it differently according to the mores of their own generation. That much may be accurate. Also, I it is probably true to say that my own use of virtual platforms, as they are sometimes called, is probably fairly typical of someone of my age and stage of life who is at work in an academic context.

My main social media presence is on Facebook. I don't have a professional page at present, only my "personal" page. (I used to have a beard and some smart-Alec created a Facebook page for it as well, so you can "friend" Oliver Crisp's beard. I've never found out who did that . . .) I've got a page on LinkedIn and academia.edu as well, though I use them much less. I also blog a bit as a guest in various places (such as Zondervan's Commonplaces blog, located at: http:// zondervanacademic.com/blog/series/common-places/) as well as on the website for a grant I'm involved with at Fuller Seminary where I work (see more below). The grant is called "Analytic Theology for Theological Formation," and we write about stuff related to the talks we have and books we're reading. It also has a Twitter presence and a Facebook page as well. I've also done podcasts for Onscript, Homebrewed Christianity related to my research, and The Tentative Apologist, as well as some lectures and talks on You Tube, which my kids think are hilariously bad. I think that represents fair usage by someone who (according to my kids) started his life back before the internet ever existed, in the Digital Dark Ages, the thought of which sends shivers down teenage spines around our dinner table.

I began using social media because it is such a helpful tool for staying in touch with a range of people scattered across the globe. It's immediate, it's fun, and it can be informative. I often post information about conferences, books, papers, people and their research — but hopefully in a light-hearted way. I don't engage in serious intellectual conversation on social media. I don't think it is a very good platform for such interactions. And I try to keep a light touch. But I do think it is a good way of connecting with people, of staying abreast of developments, and of developing "virtual" relationships as well. I also post things about my own work, but I am very wary of too much narcissism, which is the bane of social media. (Well, perhaps note *very* wary; but wary nonetheless. I do post things other than selfies with celebrity academics at conferences.) A lot of people in my field use social media or these sorts of things. Partly that's because we're nerds who like to write, and may be a bit socially awkward in the "real" world (wherever that is located). Social media helps with that for sure!

I've been surprised to find just how helpful things like "crowd-sourcing" can be. If you ask the "hive mind" for a response to a research issue, it is amazing how often that turns up useful material. Also, it is helpful for the purposes of discovering things going on that might otherwise pass me by, such as conferences, fellowships, research opportunities, and so on that I am able to pass on to relevant people, or even apply for myself.

I don't have a story about a major breakthrough that happened through social media (at least, not one I'm about to share in the context of this particular project!). However, I do think that social media has made a significant impact on how I do theology. To take one example (already mentioned in response to previous questions), I'm currently leading a major $2 million dollar research project on Analytic Theology at Fuller Theological Seminary. It has a website (http://analytictheology.fuller.edu) and a Facebook page, as well as recordings of talks and videos available on the Fuller Studios website (https://fullerstudio.fuller.edu /analytic-theology/). The website includes a blog that deals with current issues in the field related to the project, and reports on activities of the project such as weekly research seminars we have been running. It also has resources for those working in the field or interested in learning more, as well as material about the grant and personnel. None of this would have been feasible until very recently, but it is now expected that big research projects have this kind of virtual presence. That is a significant change in how we do theology and how we make the results of our theologizing widely known. Similarly, the annual LA Theology Conference that I co-organize with Professor Fred Sanders of Biola University has a website and video resources that are invaluable, in addition to the published proceedings of the conference (http://latheology.com) that come out in the Fall each year.

YouTube alone has made a significant impact on the way in which I teach, and now online teaching is part of academic life, finding new and interesting ways of presenting what is often conceptually dense material is something in which I have had to take a professional interest. (And, yes, dear reader, this includes video posts by your intrepid correspondent.) Alongside this I have had to navigate online classrooms, and although they are not publicly available, they do include social media aspects such as forums and posts that are shared within the classroom community. Now I am reading material from students across the globe who have logged in asynchronously and left me comments on a video or on some reading that the whole class can access. It isn't the same as a conventional classroom (whatever the tech-people at my institution tell me) but it is an important and significant change to academic life and one that provides new vistas for learning. Of course, it also presents new challenges for professors trying to help students engage with complex subjects in ways that are accessible — yet without reducing that complexity to a mere bit-size review, or blog-post size chunk of information. But that is true of any novelty in professional life. The difference in this context is the *nature* of that novelty: the fact that it involves getting one's head around more of one's academic life being on a computer and less in the physical classroom space with which I began my career.

When it comes to handling my time in relation to social media, my success varies, to be honest. Sometimes I'm great at time-management and do just enough on social media to stay connected, but at other times it takes up too much time and I have to rein it in. But on balance I think that it is a medium that can be very useful, as long as it is "slave not master" of one's life! My wife often tells me to get off social media when she thinks I'm doing too much of it, which is also a help.

These days, I think that if you're starting out in the Humanities involvement in some sort of social media is pretty much expected. It certainly helps with making contacts and hearing about what is going on in the field in an informal way. But as to recommendations aside from actually using social media I'd make the following suggestions. First, don't let it take over your life. Manage it. Use it; but remember it is a tool, and interactions online shouldn't be a substitute for interactions in the "real" world! Second, realize its limitations. Social media does certain things very well; but it does other things badly. So, for example, I don't engage in serious intellectual argument on social media because in my experience it is a bad medium for such discourse. It is good as an informal research tool (e.g., crowdsourcing), and as a mean of getting informally informed (so to speak) about the profession if you "friend" and interact with those in your scholarly field.

Oliver D. Crisp, Ph.D., D.Litt., is professor of systematic theology at Fuller Theological Seminary, and a professorial fellow of the Institute for Analytic and Exegetical Theology, University of St Andrews, Scotland. Crisp has written or edited more than 22 books. He serves as an editor of the Journal of Analytic Theology, *co-organizes the annual Los Angeles Theology Conference with Fred Sanders, and is currently the Principle Investigator for the $2 Million Templeton-funded grant, "Analytic Theology for Theological Formation" at Fuller Seminary (2016-2018). Crisp is a Facebook user and occasional LinkedIn, Academia.edu, YouTube, Google+ user as well. He has been a BioLogos Theology Fellow, blogging for them, and also at the Analytic Theology website associated with the Templeton-funded grant, "Analytic Theology for Theological Formation": http://analytictheology.fuller.edu.*

GREGORY CROFFORD

Religious Education

My main online presence is my theology blog, "Theology in Overalls: Where Theology Meets Everyday Life." WordPress hosts this at: gregory-crofford.com. This year, I celebrate five years of blogging with a new post going up almost every week. I also have a Facebook account under my more informal name (Greg Crofford) as well as a Twitter account (@africasojourner). Often, I'll paste the link to my blog posts at LinkedIn. Finally, when I write a blog post, I frequently will create a thread around it on NazNet.com, where I'm an active participant.

Social media — especially Facebook — is a way for me to process ideas that I come across when reading. For example, this trimester I taught the bachelor's level course, "History of Christianity from 1500 AD." It struck me while reading the textbook from Justo González that some of the "troubles" going on in the U.S. right now, particularly politically — and especially as they interface with the public face of Christianity — are nothing new. So, I would post up a paragraph or two from González as my FB status and received almost immediate response from friends who agreed that the parallel was striking.

Including images that fit the theme of your post is helpful when blogging. Since I like photography, I can often use a nature photo or something general from my archives. Other times I will use an image from the internet, but one must be careful about rights to the photo. Wikimedia Commons has a wealth of images that are in the public domain but they do require the user to give credit.

Reaction from readers is unpredictable. The blog posts that I think will resonate the best often get minimal response. Others that I compose with little expectation of feedback can generate greater impact than I thought they would. In one instance, our denominational magazine editor contacted me, asking permission to print a post that had seemed to produce negligible interest. You never know who is reading!

Blogging can help a writer work through thorny theological issues. The traditional formulation of the doctrine of Hell had bothered me for years. Something about it didn't seem to square with Scripture, and appeared offensive to God's character. Since I had started my blog about that time (2012), I decided to write a series of posts on the topic. About five posts in, I realized that I had the start of a small book. Two years later, Wipf & Stock published *The Dark Side of Destiny: Hell Re-Examined* (2013). I hammered out my more recent book, *Mere Ecclesiology: Finding Your Place in the Church's Mission* (Wipf & Stock, 2016) as a series of blog essays. The blogging format allows for instant feedback (often via a Facebook link) and encourages me to keep writing.

Facebook is an intergenerational platform. While in recent years many younger users have fled for other providers, there still are a good number of twenty-somethings among my FB friends, as well (of course) as older users. Because my writing can appeal to all ages and avoids trendy language, Mark Zuckerberg's invention suits me well.

Researchers have studied internet addiction, and surely social media is part of that phenomenon. But in my experience, social media is the opposite of the isolation that often characterizes addiction; instead, it connects me to the broader world of ideas. Usually, it is not a distraction but helpful to my academic work, especially as it provokes ideas. For example, reading a status from a friend can spark my thinking or can point me to a book that can be included in a future class. In turn, I can share some of the fruit of my study via Facebook or my WordPress blog. For me, social media is more synergy than distraction. However, if I find it getting in the way of other pressing tasks, I will take a 7-14 day social media "fast" to refocus on what is most important.

In conclusion, I would recommend the following three things to scholars considering using social media:

1) *Participate in Facebook theological forums.* These can help provide informal peer review of your ideas, especially if you're one who frequently likes to

try out new ideas. Positive response and additional perspectives from others help incubate ideas that may evolve into full-blown blog posts. Also, as long as it is an open group, you can sometimes include some of the better insights from others in your essay as quotations in the same way that news outlets will often include Tweets reacting to current stories.

2) *Use standard English, proper grammar, spelling, and tone.* You're creating a public image through the overall effect of what you say online. People are more likely to purchase your books if they already have an expectation of quality that you've created through the caliber of your social media interactions. Use standard English instead of words that—while cutting-edge today—quickly grow stale. When was the last time you heard someone say something was "groovy" or "far out"?

3) *Resist the temptation to be crude.* As an ordained minister, I know that people expect me to be wholesome, including in how I use language. From my perspective, vulgarity deducts 10 points from a person's I.Q. It shows that they've failed to master the nuances of their own mother tongue and so must resort to the low hanging fruit of coarse language.

———————

Gregory Crofford, Ph.D. (University of Manchester) is an ordained elder in the church, ministering with the Church of the Nazarene. He is a Senior Lecturer and the Coordinator for the Ph.D. (Religion) program in the Department of Religion at Africa Nazarene University (Nairobi, Kenya). Formerly, he served as Coordinator of Education and Clergy Development for the Africa Region (Church of the Nazarene). Areas of academic interest include Wesleyan theology, early Methodism, missional ecclesiology, and ecotheology. See Crofford's general theology blog, "Theology in Overalls" at: gregorycrofford.com. Greg is a frequent Facebooker ("Greg Crofford") and NazNetter (NazNet.com) and less often will send a tweet out into the great beyond (@africasojourner).

JAMES CROSSLEY

Biblical Theology

mostly use Facebook, Twitter, WordPress, and probably in that order, though I (obviously) reserve longer pieces for blogging. I began using social media for scholarly interests in 2005 because I thought 'biblioblogging' (i.e. academic blogging related to biblical studies) was too beholden to the political mainstream and some of this needed to be challenged. By this I mean that it would typically follow the traditional media on issues like foreign policy (at the time such blogging was dominated by the fallout from the Iraq War), irrespective of the personal politics of the blogger. I wanted to see what would happen if some of these tendencies were challenged.

I'm not sure much did change and similar patterns would continue on Facebook (which almost replaced Below the Line blog debates), though bizarreness of the Trump phenomenon has thrown things up in the air. But this is probably connected to the reasons why I continue because most of my posts remain political, though I am not as reflexive as I once was and I tend to look at different political groups rather than overtly promote my own particular line.

But another reason why I have continued to use social media is because of the rise of a certain kind of open access scholarship, particularly that which does not involve too many hidden fees. For this reason, I have also become involved with Biblical Studies Online (https://biblicalstudiesonline.wordpress.com/) in collaboration with Deane Galbraith where we (or, rather, mostly Deane) collect as much online open access scholarship as possible for anyone to use. My personal blog, Harnessing Chaos, also reflects such open access interests, particularly when I write early, pre-publication summaries of parts of chapters and articles. Not only are they then publicly available but I also get some helpful feedback for when I develop the ideas further.

Despite some things being roughly the same on issues relating to academic discussions of foreign policy (e.g. tacit acceptance of a coup in Honduras or a drone killing wedding guests), I have been surprised at just how some things have changed in terms of what we might call scholarly social attitudes. According to another blogger's much discussed five-point religio-political scale of bibliob-logger convictions, which we can apply to social media users more generally, I would say that most scholarly users of social media a decade ago would have been categorised as 'Fairly Conservative' but that this has now decisively shifted to 'Conservative Liberal'. I would never have predicted that in 2005.

Put another way, biblical scholars on social media are more likely to talk about the fluidity of identity in scriptural passages, problems with theology, favoured liberal scholars, scepticism towards historical accuracy of biblical texts, the importance of (limited) inclusion, and promoting responsible academic hierarchy and 'leadership', rather than fixed textual meaning, good theology, favoured con-servative scholars, a trusting attitude towards the historical accuracy of biblical texts, the importance of (limited) exclusion, and promoting of responsible aca-demic hierarchy and 'leadership'.

I was also surprised to learn how open prominent academics felt compelled to be in certain situations in our post-2008 crises. In the UK, as readers will know, Brexit has been a divisive national debate. As we wrestled with the questions of Remain or Leave, it was striking that even some of the normally reserved public figures were openly discussing their heartfelt difficulties . . . and doing so on aca-demic blogs. The Vice-Chancellor of the University of Sheffield, Sir Keith Burnett, was gracious enough to make his thoughts (originally published in an intellectual venue) available for all on his official blog (https://www.sheffield.ac.uk/news/nr /comment-keith-burnett-patriotic-1.665626). It may be difficult for those living outside the UK to appreciate but I don't think that I will ever forget his emotional words:

It is ironic that in a country which claims to prize free speech, and worries about its erosion on campus, speaking truth to power may prove so worrying to some. But before I tell you why I think these make our country stronger, let me take a long hard look in the mirror and ask myself: "Do you really love England, Keith?"

"Yes I do!" I answer. "How can you prove it?" I ask back.

I'm tempted to spit back at that.

Would his grappling have inspired others involved in their own heated debates, such as with close friends and family? That's difficult to know. But for a public figure of the standing of Sir Keith to publish such personal words takes a certain kind of courage, irrespective of whether his mirror story 'really happened' or is meant to function as a fictional story with a higher poetic truth.

I think blogging pre-publication versions of my work has helped me. This was initially unintentional (i.e. I simply thought that it would be a useful blog post on a given topic) but I then found that it helped me use ideas that I had actually forgotten, at least in detail, as well as keeping an online archive of sorts. I have found this especially useful when dealing with receptions of the Bible, particularly in English political discourse at Christmas and Easter when politicians are obliged to comment. The main discussions typically take place on Facebook but it requires the more conventional space of the blog to make the extended points. But presumably because of the festive timing, such blog posts bring new readers and new interactions for me and I have found myself discussing ideas with people who work in or close to mainstream English and British politics. Such interactions are much easier now that I work in London but when I was not then I am not sure that I would have made such connections without social media.

Through Biblical Studies Online, I also started doing interviews and podcasts. I never thought that this would interest me but since I have interviewed a range of people (some published, some not) which in turn got me into soft ethnographic work. This has turned out to be one of my favourite means of research and it was completely unexpected.

I will often go days and weeks without engaging on social media, at least in terms of academic activity. I don't exactly plan this but it works because I will most likely be focusing on other obligations. Sometimes I'll post regularly and at length, especially when I'm starting to work on something. I also travel on trains a lot which means writing a blog post or reading, hate-reading, or commenting people's tweets and Facebook updates are much better ways of passing the time than looking out into the darkness, engulfed in the terror of existence while half asleep.

I also combine research and social media. This is increasingly easy with the number of academics now present online but it can also provide masses of untapped data for someone like myself who is into the critical study of religion and politics. I often find myself looking at certain Facebook groups to get an idea of the kinds of issues and debates happening, as well as links to external discussions and events. This can lead to all sorts of new ideas for research that I don't think would have happened (to me) if it wasn't for social media.

Finally, I offer the following three recommendations to scholars considering using social media:

1. If you blog, you might want to use a blog post to write substantive posts relating to your academic views. They can serve as an archive for both yourself and for others to find, as well as a gateway to the harder books and articles. In my experience, blog posts have been a vital means of disseminating ideas freely that might otherwise go ignored.
2. Think about using Facebook or the like to discuss ideas. People tend to be far more open to discussion than they ever were in comments sections on blogs. Plus, they aren't anonymous so the likelihood of trolling is greatly diminished.
3. Try not to get too wound up. No matter how much humble bragging you read, most people aren't that happy.

———

James Crossley, PhD, is Professor of Bible, Culture and Politics in the Centre for the Social-Scientific Study of the Bible, St Mary's University, Twickenham, London. He has published numerous books and articles on the historical Jesus, Christian origins, contemporary receptions of the Bible, and assumption about religion in English political discourse. See Crossley's blog, Harnessing Chaos (www.harnessingchaos. wordpress.com), as well as the site he runs with Deane Galbraith, Biblical Studies Online (www.biblicalstudiesonline.wordpress.com). Crossley is on Facebook and Twitter (@jgcrossley)

DAVID DAULT

Theology and Media

My social media usage has a primary and a secondary stage. Primary is Facebook; that is the anchor point around which everything else orbits. I engage with Facebook much more often than I check email these days. It is often the first platform I check in the morning, and the last thing I will check at night. It also serves as the "norm" by which I think about all other social media platforms.

I was a graduate student at Vanderbilt when access to Facebook first became available. I had used Myspace and other sites, so Facebook was the natural next migration. Looking back, the contrast is striking. Myspace was anarchy. Everybody tweaked their profiles so much that the platform was hideous. By contrast, Facebook was clean and uniform.

Over the years, that uniformity waxed tyrannical. There were periods when a new rollout of a function, or a major change in the "look and feel" of Facebook would upend me. For a while, I was an avid user of third party programs that would hack the Facebook interface. I was trying to fight the changes, and restore what I saw as a more familiar environment.

Over time, I have given up on trying to control the interface. I have made my peace with the platform, in just about every way possible. I will have more to say about this.

As to the secondary platforms: I am becoming more active on Twitter, but this took a long time. Facebook allows for long form digression; Twitter is the complete opposite. I got started using Twitter as a business practice. My use of it the first two years I was on the platform was completely instrumental. As a result, my engagements went nowhere. In the past few months, I have become more comfortable with the platform.

I am on LinkedIn and Academia.edu, but to be honest, these are still instrumental for me. I have done very little social engagement, or even messaging, across these platforms.

The other platforms, like Snapchat and Instagram, are completely off my radar. I know they exist, but I have found no use for them.

My mother passed away in 2009. At the time, I had just begun a tenure-track position. I had secured a book contract, and was working on a second one. From the outside, everything looked to be on its proper trajectory.

In reality, grief was causing me to unravel. Within a few months, I was spiraling down into depression. This condition, in part, manifested as a steadily growing writers block.

In various forms, that writers block lasted for almost six years. On the worst days, it wasn't that I lacked inspiration; I could not type. I could not write longhand. It was devastating, and it was terrifying.

A student who became a family friend once asked me what the writer's block was like. I explained that it was like I had lost an arm. The analogy was that writing was a cup of coffee: no matter how much I loved coffee, I lacked the capacity to drink it. I could remember picking up the cup, and I wanted to pick it up, but I did not have the physical capacity.

It was the same with my writing. I could remember doing it. I wanted to do it. I could not do it.

At the suggestion of some friends, I began to use a parallel set of strategies during this time. The first was to record interviews with colleagues at me school and in the guild. This practice led me to my work in radio.

I also began to use Facebook as a strategy for recovery. A friend observed that, even when all other writing and typing seemed beyond me, I could engage with Facebook. So I began to invite folks into theological conversations on the platform. I would also join discussions that were already happening.

In these cases, I could manage to get words typed, and even form whole paragraphs. After the engagement, I would then go back and copy-and-paste the paragraphs into a Word file or (later) a Google doc. Over the past few years, these collected snippets have become the bulk and basis of what I have managed to write and publish in my field. As my ability to write in native environments has returned, I still find the practice useful. I will gather and save these snippets along the way, for future use.

Facebook has also served a therapeutic function for me during this time. When I realized how deep the writer's block had gripped me, I did not know how to speak about it to my colleagues. Facebook became a forum of support as I discerned when and how to "out" my condition. The platform continues to function for me as a genuine community. On both good and bad days, I share my struggles, and find much needed empathy and affirmation.

Like many, I entered graduate studies with a tendency to be combative. I was not simply strident in my argumentation; I was a smart aleck, or worse.

This approach has consequences. The most immediate consequences were with my colleagues in the program. I developed a reputation, and some even came to avoid me altogether.

These misadventures in graduate study were happening at the same time that I began using Facebook. As you might imagine, the same bad habits I developed with my colleagues bled over into my online life. I had both a rapier wit and a rapacious need to offer correctives whenever I thought, "someone is wrong on the internet."

What I discovered was that burning down folks on Facebook left me with a terrible feeling. It was the same terrible feeling I had come to expect and dread in my interactions face to face with my colleagues. They shared a common source in my reflex to be a jerk and a know-it-all.

My rehabilitation was slow, and occurred in the opposite order that common sense would dictate. Instead of learning to be a kinder soul first face to face, I learned these skills on Facebook.

Over time, I learned to engage in conversations online that led to edification rather than elimination. My interactions became kinder, and more kindhearted in their intention. I learned how to listen for the points of commonality in arguments, rather than points of attack.

These are lessons I am still learning, but they have affected my face-to-face relationships. First, I learned to avoid the "hangover feeling" that came from bad online interactions. This helped me to spot similar tendencies in my "real world" interactions.

I am pleased to report that after some years practicing these skills, my relationships have become better. My interactions with colleagues are improved and improving. I credit the change to Facebook.

One of the notable aspects of social media is the use of algorithms to drive user experience. While this has been a developing mechanism, and algorithms have improved over time, the practice has led to some unwanted effects.

In particular, these algorithms have created a series of "silo" effects. Over time, the system tracks the things you "like," and reinforces your experience with similar items. This creates an ideological echo chamber.

As I increased my capacity to have civil conversations on Facebook, I began to study these algorithms to see if there were ways I could un-silo myself. My first goal was to increase my engagements with folks with whom I had ideological disagreements. My second goal was to use long-form, irenic disagreement as a model for others on the platforms. In other words, I wanted the feeds on which I posted to become laboratories and teaching tools for "deep reasoning."

The model is one I learned from Peter Ochs, and his many colleagues and students who practice "Scriptural Reasoning." This is a trialogue between Jews, Christians, and Muslims. Each Abrahamic tradition comes to a "tent of engagement" to reason together around common texts.

The goal is relationship, not conversion. The deepening relationships allow them to venture together into greater disagreement. Over time, as my friend and colleague Nicholas Adams would say, they learn to "disagree better," and to "make these deep reasonings public."

I have a large number of Facebook friends. I knew anecdotally that a good number were on the opposite side of the political and ideological spectrum. But I was also aware that I did not see their posts. I knew they were there, but I could not "see" them or their activities.

So I began to practice a version of this engagement across difference on Facebook. To do this, however, I had to find ways to work against the algorithm. The system's desire was to present me with similar views to my own. I needed to find a way to get it to present me with difference. The solution was nonsense. Dadaism.

For the past three years, my Facebook strategy has been in two parts. One-half of my wall is spent in long, multi-paragraph conversations around political and moral topics. The other half is a steady stream of short, weird, and obtuse random statements.

The purpose of these Dadaist posts is to create a steady bed of "neutral space." These posts are devoid of political content, and they "provoke" only insofar as they cause readers to scratch their heads and wonder. As a result, these posts tend to attract "likes" and engagement across the full spectrum of my Facebook friends.

Remember, "Likes" drive the algorithm. Hence, as my "opposites" continue to like these neutral posts, the algorithm brings more of my posts into their feed and theirs into mine.

This increases the possibility that we will see a post with political or moral substance. When this occurs, a practice of deep reasoning can begin.

It is not a perfect system, granted. But I have found that the inclusion of regular randomness on my wall has lessened the silo effect in my feeds. My political discussions online have continued and have grown in overall quality.

Those who visit my walls have also commented often about the quality of discourse in my feeds. Those who have continued to "show up" for these discussions have deepened relationships with each other. They have learned over time to listen better to each other. The experiment is ongoing, but I have been pleased so far with its success.

I will admit I have never been very good at managing my productive time. Unlike some of my colleagues, I do not block out or log off from Twitter and Facebook. They are "always on," and I check them throughout the day.

So the rhythms of my work and time on social media are in constant oscillation. It is true that this does not make for rapid productivity. However, my productivity is no faster when I don't work in this oscillating manner. So I have chosen to keep at it, despite appearances.

The misconception about social media is that it is somehow "ad extra" to one's work and participation in the guild. This view misses the point that social media is social.

As musician, Amanda Palmer writes in *The Art of Asking*, her various managers kept telling her to "stop Twittering and get back to work." Palmer's response is a byword to anyone who wishes to be considered a public scholar in the 21st century: "They didn't understand. That *was* the work."

The basis of social media is relationships. And relationships take time. They take investment and continued risk. Relationships demand vulnerability. These are not traits in which we scholars excel. But this also might be the reason that scholars, as a whole, have been so ineffectual in public discourse.

Social media presents an opportunity to rethink the self-imposed limitations of our guild. I, for one, am pleased at the prospect.

Let me conclude with three recommendations I have for scholars considering social media. First, on a purely practical level, you must recognize that the game has fundamentally changed. If you are any sort of track that expects you to publish, you will need to consider and cultivate a presence on social media. Publishers today expect their authors to know how to build a following and create a buzz with that following. That skillset cannot be bought, and it can only be rented for a very brief period. So your best bet is to start—now—at whatever level feels comfortable. Continue finding your level as time goes by.

This means (second) that you should not jump willy-nilly into every platform. It took me years to find my comfort level with Twitter, and even now, I move with deliberation in that environment. Find the platforms where you feel a genuine sense of community, and where you find your voice is most authentic.

Which leads us to the third observation: social media is an amplifier. Whatever your strengths (and weaknesses) in "real life," social media can exacerbate them. This is why, for a season, I got so caught up in being combative online. The platform was amplifying my area of growth and struggle. But patient attention within the platform can also lead to tremendous growth over time.

A final point: scholars are stereotyped as socially reluctant. Face to face, interaction is not our first choice for interactions. For this reason, social media actually works to our advantage. As avid readers, many of us form our deepest relationships with and through words. Social media thus allows us to forge relationships with others in the forum of our strengths—reading, writing, and carefully chosen words. Far from being a trivial distraction, these relationships can become a significant cornerstone in our public scholarship.

––––––––

David Dault, Ph.D. is an award-winning radio and Emmy-nominated television producer and media consultant. He is the host of the weekly radio program, Things Not Seen: Conversations about Culture and Faith, distributed nationally by the Public Radio Exchange. He teaches at Garrett-Evangelical Theological Seminary and at the Institute for Pastoral Studies at Loyola University. Dault is also the authorized biographer of Old Testament theologian Walter Brueggemann. He lives with his family in Hyde Park, on the south side of Chicago. See Dault's website, ThingsNotSeenRadio.com. Please sign up for his newsletter at the site. Dault lives on Facebook (David Dault, Things Not Seen Radio, and Material Scripture) and is often on Twitter (@DaultRadio, @NotSeenRadio, @DividesAside). He has accounts on LinkedIn and Academia.edu.

HELEN DE CRUZ

Philosophy

I have a fairly active social media presence on the following social media platforms: Facebook, Twitter, and blogs including Tumblr and Medium. I particularly like the format of Facebook. It has a certain intimacy to it, and the length of a typical FB post suits me well to write and to engage with. Twitter is good to get some engagement with people outside of my immediate circle and to step out of the echo chamber, but it is more liable to abusive language — I've been called a snowflake, social justice warrior, leftie fool, and things not fit for print.

I have accounts with LinkedIn, Google+, Quora, Pinterest, and Reddit, but I am only a consumer, not a producer, of content on these platforms. I also have accounts with two research-specific social media platforms: academia.edu and ResearchGate, which I mainly use to put final versions of papers, and a bit for getting comments for papers in draft form.

I began using social media to explore my scholarly interests in 2011, when I started blogging with NewApps, a group blog devoted to art, politics, philosophy and science (hence Apps). It was a spirited, diverse group of people, and the blog was lively and controversial. We (not me personally!) had a few public meltdowns that gripped the public philosophy sphere. My writing for NewApps consisted mainly of short philosophical ideas (about 800 words or so) in the philosophy of religion and the philosophy of cognitive science. Soon thereafter, I began to write for Prosblogion, a group blog devoted to the philosophy of religion. Topics included the problem of evil, religious disagreement, the philosophy of perception. Usually a post would address a controversial idea, such as Dawkins' proposal that giving your child a religious education is child abuse, and I'd formulate my ideas on the problem. There was a lot of engagement; it was not uncommon to have 50 comments per blogpost. Responding to comments was intensive — it would take several days before a discussion dwindled.

For reasons I'm not entirely sure about, the philosophical engagement in the blogosphere became less and less active. I noticed there was a decrease of comments, especially quality comments; some blogs have since closed down so it was not just a problem that ailed our blogs. Blogs now still seem to be fruitful places to discuss issues in the profession (e.g., Daily Nous, where I hosted a discussion on Brexit), but not to do philosophy per se. One of the newer mediums to engage with each other in a relaxed scholarly context is Facebook. I like Facebook to float philosophical ideas or to ask about teaching.

Specifically, Facebook has made me a better teacher. I have learned lots of ideas for classroom engagement, suitable readings, and assignments. I also use Facebook for exchanging philosophical ideas and for trying out new ideas. There is a risk to this (you can be scooped) but ultimately the reward is far greater, as I believe philosophy is a thoroughly social enterprise, which benefits from discussion at every level of the creative process, not just the fairly advanced level where you present your work at a conference or submit it to a journal.

I also use social media to socialize with other people, including other scholars. Facebook makes me feel part of a larger community, a community where I have a place. As many other academics, I have been an itinerant — in the past decade, I have lived in three different countries, moved employer five times, and moved house more times than I can remember. As a result, it's difficult to build local support networks, which makes the digital ones all the more precious. The enduring connection social media offers makes it easier to reconnect and meet up in real life. I noticed this especially when I left Oxford in 2014, and returned in 2016. I could pick up my life pretty much immediately, even having a friend offering to take care of our children while we waited for the movers to bring our furniture and boxes.

In general, one thing I found in frank conversations on Facebook and to some lesser extent also in exchanges in blogs, is that everyone's winging it. Philosophers, and academics in general, tend to suffer from impostor syndrome, from feeling guilty for not being the perfect parent or partner, from being overwhelmed with the demands of work, and from missing deadlines. I now know that such feelings are not uncommon. Indeed, very successful scholars deal with the same mundane problems as I do.

Although people sometimes fault social media for putting up pictures of perfect lives, and to some extent this is the case, I frequently see stories of how other academics struggle with combining, for instance, a full-time demanding academic career with being a mother, especially given gendered expectations. I feel a lot less guilty for not baking cakes, not being part of the PTA and not sewing my children's costumes. Thanks to social media I can see how people can successfully live different styles of parenting. I'm a member of several secret Facebook groups and one thing I find interesting there is how our background makes a large difference to who we are, as academics and philosophers. For example, women of color (I self-identify as such) face unique challenges in the professional work sphere that I have been able to identify better by being part of a dedicated Facebook group.

There are three aspects of my work that could not have been done without social media. First, I've conducted several interview series, for instance with people who have philosophy PhDs and who are employed outside of academia. It was hard to find these people without reliance on snowball sampling (basically, asking the few people I knew who were in this situation to contact their contacts, and so forth). This series was very successful; it first appeared on the NewApps blog, later in the Philosophers' Magazine in abridged form, and it was also translated in several languages, including Chinese. As a follow-up to this project, I have a Tumblr blog "Doing things with philosophy", which features profiles of alt-ac philosophers. I also interviewed 20 philosophers who are engaged in religious practices including a female Orthodox rabbi, various religious atheists, two Shi'a Muslims, and Christians of various stripe including Eastern Orthodox, Catholic, Calvinist and Pentecostal Christians. Currently, I am doing a series on philosophers and their passions outside of philosophy, including baking bread, hunting down and preparing fossils, cycling, writing fiction, sewing their own clothes. Social media has also allowed me to start, together with Marcus Arvan, a mentoring program for job candidates in philosophy.

I've done several experimental philosophical studies, where social media are a good place to find willing participants. Surprisingly few experimental philosophical have examined what philosophers think, and how other aspects of our lives interact with our philosophical work. This is one of my long-term research projects, and social media helps me to accomplish it.

I am not the best time manager — that being said, I do get stuff done. I have the Pomodoro system to help me get over the tendency to procrastinate (I've always had problems with procrastination, long before engaging with social media). The technique works as follows: I put a timer for 25 minutes and dedicate this time to doing just one task, usually research or grading. If successfully completed without interruption, I've then completed a "pomodoro". I then take a short break and then complete another. If I can do 5-7 pomodoros of writing or grading a day, that is a good day.

My usual time for social media (chatting, posting, and responding to messages on Facebook) is between about 9.30 and 10.30 PM. One danger of social media is the urge to feel connected all the time, which is partly why I do not have a smartphone. I have an old Samsung that has Internet (not even 3G) but it is so unwieldy to use the Internet on it that I don't bother—I just use the thing for texting and phoning. That way, I'm reachable for my closest family but not connected all the time.

The following are three recommendations I have for scholars considering using social media:

1. Social media is a great tool to help you develop and network as an academic, but try to have fun and don't overthink it: A few months ago, I went to an impact training day, organized by my faculty. They had hired a guy who was great at promoting his research to a wider public, outside of academia — this is called "impact" and it is important for British academics to have impact. He explained how to carefully groom your social media presence, for instance when it is best to tweet. If some of your reach is in Australia, you might tweet in the early mornings, sometimes (that would be late evening in Australia). He also explained how you could get more followers on Twitter by following and unfollowing people who are likely to be interested in your research. Many of us found this unsavory (people follow you back in good faith and then unfollow you), and I think that if you're timing your tweets and following people so you can unfollow them, is quite disingenuous. Keep the fun in it.

2. Be aware of dangers associated with social media. There are dangers to being visible on social media. You need to be mindful about what you write. I've stopped posting pictures of my family ever since my Facebook circle extended beyond personal friends. You need to show restraint, both in commenting and when responding to potentially abusive comments (this is especially difficult on Twitter due to character limitations). A few of my Facebook friends have had problems with friends taking screenshots of things they said on their FB walls out of context and posting it in a public

forum. There are blogs, all with anonymous or pseudonymous bloggers of course, dedicated to abusing and hurting other philosophers. One person I know even got into trouble with their university administration, following controversial comments they made that were made public in this way. Several others got death threats and rape threats, all on anonymous blogs that do not log IP addresses. Thus a social media presence brings problems of privacy invasion, harassment and abuse. The advice I give about this is just not to read those blogs. I have stopped looking at them and feel better for it.

3. Do not be afraid to apologize — eventually, even the most careful and restrained person will make a faux pas. For instance, you can inadvertently share something that was supposed to remain confidential. It is best, in that case, to unconditionally and with no "buts" apologize and say it won't happen again. A sincere apology goes a long way in mending damaged relationships, and social media is no different.

Helen De Cruz, Ph.D., is a philosopher of cognitive science and a philosopher of religion. Next to her PhD in philosophy (2011, Groningen), she also holds a PhD in archaeology and art sciences (2007, Free University of Brussels). She is currently a senior lecturer (associate professor) in philosophy at Oxford Brookes University. She has co-written A Natural History of Natural Theology *(MIT Press, 2015), and is currently writing a monograph on religious disagreement, to appear with CUP in 2018. See Helen De Cruz' personal website, http://helendecruz.net, see also Facebook (Helen De Cruz), Twitter (@HelenDeCruz), Medium (@helenldecruz), occasionally also LinkedIn, Google+ and Pinterest.*

MIGUEL A. DE LA TORRE

Social Ethics and Latinx Studies

am a scholar-activist, not an activist-scholar. The emphasis is on my scholarship, informed by my activism. If not for my activism, my scholarship would be
stale and limp. Scholar-activists endeavor to make their complex, nuance analysis accessible to a more general audience for the purpose of raising consciousness. And while academic theses and rigorous articles in scholarly journals are
crucial for contributing to the overall discourse; so too are short op-eds, blogs
postings, and other social media which garners a larger audience. For this reason,
just as important as the thirty-three books I have published are the blogs and
articles I write which avoids lofty ideals and insider jargons. To that end, I engage
in several social media platforms. On my website (www.drmigueldelatorre.com), I
list articles published on my blog (https://ourlucha.wordpress.com/), op-ed published by different news sources, and videos of lectures, sermons, and presentations I have given.

I began using social media in relation to my scholarly interests because of my
commitment to liberative ethics. Although it remains important to understand
the world as it is; it is just as important to contribute our analytical skills to change
the world by seeking a more just alternative. As important as my books are, I realize the general public would be more incline to read my six-hundred-word blog
rather than my sixty-thousand-word book. Some of my blogs have received as

many as 50 thousand hits while other barely had 50 hits. I have been surprised to discover that most who are familiar with my scholarship were first introduced to my writings through my social media contributions.

The ideas and concepts expressed in social media are usually the earliest formulations of concepts I am in the midst of understanding. Eventually, these preliminary explorations develop into articles and/or books. I would say all of the conceptual breakthroughs experience, and the interesting projects in which I have engaged emerged from something I originally posted on social media. For example, my first forays into the immigration debate appeared as op-eds. With time, these concepts developed into two separate books: *Trails of Hope and Terror* (Orbis Books, 2009) and *The Immigration Crises* (Cascade Press, 2016). And while the books may, in my opinion, contribute to the discourse, developing new media forms of disseminating my analytical contributions potentially have a greater impact.

As of last year, we released a documentary for which I wrote the screenplay and co-produced. Titled *Trails of Hope and Terror* (https://vimeo.com/79285280), this international award-winning film has been shown in multiple festivals. Soon it will be available for mass distribution. What the film accomplishes, which my books on the topic falls short in capturing, is the raw trials and tribulations faced by the undocumented. The use of film enfleshed the concepts described solely through words, allowing the viewer to see through a new lens. More people have now seen this film then have read anything I ever wrote on this topic.

Engaging in a new form of expressing ideas is always risky, if not daring. Not long ago I was asked to deliver the charge to the graduating class of my institution. Rather than simply reciting some encouraging words, I chose to write and recite Slam Poetry (https://www.youtube.com/watch?v=9LJz4KykImo). This was my first foray into this form of communication. I wanted to introduce a different scholarly methodology. The predominant Eurocentric method of focusing on the rational written word downplays passion, emotions, and the soul. And while there is not a simple dichotomy, an either/or between the mind and the heart; nevertheless, the latter has consistently been minimized in favor of the former. From the margins of scholarship, some — specifically those from disenfranchised communities — have turn to the arts by which to communicate theoretical arguments and analysis. Too that end, reciting poetry became, for me, a new way of conducting scholarship.

All too often, the Academy specializes in sustaining and maintaining a way of conducting scholarship which at best ignores its complicity with advancing the neoliberal goals of Empire, and at worst, justifies Empire. The consistent call for

objectivity normalizes and legitimizes the oppression and repression of disenfranchised communities—mainly communities of color. An uncritical acceptance
of current methodologies in the construction and dissimulation of knowledge
creates and reinforces oppressive structures as Eurocentric scholarship is fused
and confused with academic excellence. Eurocentric epistemology, unconscious
to how the discipline has been racialized, exemplifies a so-called "color-blind"
excellence in creating comprehensive scholastic paradigms for all of humanity. By
its very nature, Eurocentric thought and methodologies of dissimulation maintains universal normativity which is achievable independent of place, time, context, or people group. Such normativity created by Eurocentric scholars are
accepted as being both universal and objective, and thus applicable to all Others.
To seek other forms of distributing knowledge contrary to the means dictated by
the academy is to have one's scholarship questioned, if not dismissed.

The subjectivity of Eurocentric thought and the acceptable methods of disseminating said scholarship can be lifted by the Academy to universal objectivity
because the Academy retains the power to define a reality securing and protect-
ing their scholastic privilege, a privilege which more often than not benefits
Eurocentrism. This traditional understanding of scholarship, along with its nor-
mative dissimulation becomes complicit with global structures of oppression
which maintains a partially masked attempt to incorrectly understand the world
rather than correctly initiate transformation.

Scholars from disenfranchised communities are all forced to exhibit academic rigor through the use and application of dissemination paradigms—read as
the most prestigious peer-review journals—more often than not lacking any connection to the space where the vast majority of humanity dwells. Consequently,
the particularity and presentation of scholarship emanating from spaces rejected
by the gatekeepers of the Academy poses a risk and danger in the minds of these
same academics that our work constructed with and for the least of these will
negatively impact the gatekeepers' prevailing so-called rigor.

I argue that the failure to engage in public scholarship through the means by
which the public dissimulates information, simply makes the classroom a place
where like-minded individuals of a certain class gather to feel good about themselves, no better than a social club. I am reminded of my dissertation chair, John
Raines, who constantly articulated the classroom is adequately named—for it is
truly a room-of-class where participants learn their class and what society expects from the class to which they belong. If this is true, the classroom room
nestled in one of the Ivy League schools serves a very different function from the
classroom located at the local community college. The fact some students are

able to pay sufficient money to attend particular rooms-of-class located on prestigious campuses indicates they will have certain opportunities which are denied to those of lower economic class, those who are more often than not students of color residing on the margins of society. Far from being an objective neutral educational system, students who attend (class)rooms can either be conditioned for domestication by, or liberation from, the existing social structures. All too often, the educational system serves to normalize these power structures as legitimate. For me, dissimulating scholarship through social media, where anyone with a Wi-Fi connection can access, becomes a subversive methodology challenging the gatekeepers of academic rigor.

The difficulty, of course, is managing one's time with the other obligations, especially in relation to time spent on social media. I thus have priorities. Please don't confuse priorities with either/or paradigms. And while all are crucial in becoming a well-rounded liberationist thinker, there are only so many hours in the day forcing me to prioritize my time. First and foremost is my scholarship in the traditional form of books and articles. These modes of academic production establish my academic credentials, earning me the right to be heard and taken seriously.

Second, but just as important, is translating my academic production to a more general audience. Engaging in research to accomplish my first priority of traditional forms of scholarship does provide ample material to engage in social media. As previously stated, these productions are more often than not the earliest formulation of ideas and concepts which will find a fuller expression in my more traditional scholarship production. Last, but not least, time must be carved out to dream; to try to think outside the academic box. Such dreaming is what lead to co-producing a documentary. My current dreaming is leading me to the possible production of a YouTube channel focusing on liberative religious thought.

For those interested in engaging in social media, I would suggest we are mistaken if our understanding of social media is relegated to simple opinions. Blogs from academics, while accessible, requires the same scholastic rigor as all of our other works. Anyone can hide behind obtuse jargon. It takes a true intellectual to communicate complex concepts so the uneducated can understand.

I have learned to craft complex and critical arguments and recite slam poetry. I script articles for peer review journals and film scripts for documentaries. I defend my ideas on national and international cable news programs and on internet podcasts. I take students on journeys through the imagination of the written word and through existential experience of immersion classes. My ideas appear in encyclopedia entries and on opinion pages in newspapers. I engage in all means necessary so as to reach all peoples in all places in the modest hope of influencing and impacting the discourse. This has made me a better scholar, a more relevant scholar, a more rigorous scholar. I invite you to join revolutionizing what the Academy has normalized over the past several centuries.

Miguel A. De La Torre authored several hundred articles and over thirty-three books. He presently serves as Professor of Social Ethics and Latinx Studies at Iliff School of Theology. He is a past-director to the American Academy of Religion, President of the Society of Christian Ethics, and the current Executive Officer of the Society of Race, Ethnicity and Religion. De La Torre is the founding editor of the "Journal of Race, Ethnicity, and Religion." A Fulbright Scholar, he has taught in Indonesia, South Africa, Mexico, and Mainz, Germany. He recently received a Louisville Institute Grant allowing for research in Cuba. See De La Torre's website, at www.drmigueldelatorre.com and/or his blog https://ourlucha.wordpress.com/. He is also a monthly contributor to Baptist News Global (https://baptistnews.com /?s=de+la+torre). De La Torre is an avid Facebook (https://www.facebook.com /miguel.delatorre.1238) and Twitter user (@DrDeLaTorre).

JOSEPH DUGGAN

Public Theology

Facebook is my primary social media platform. I have been using Facebook since May 2008. At Postcolonial Networks we attempted to use LinkedIn groups but that platform never took off. We also use Academia.Edu, but their platform has recently changed and not for the better. Academia.Edu has monetized the site and taken away some of the more productive networking features. Previously Academia. Edu was even better than Facebook as it exclusively draws scholars and has drawn many more scholars from Africa, Asia and Latin America. Indeed, I have received feedback from scholars in Asia that many have no regard for Facebook, but find Academia.Edu much better. Again, these comments were before the Academia.Edu site became monetized.

We began using Facebook after the first Postcolonial Networks meeting even before Postcolonial Networks formally began as a nonprofit. Our first scholarly meeting at the University of Manchester in Manchester, UK was so successful that we turned to Facebook to continue the conversation among meeting delegates. We never expected that a group established to keep in touch with 30 meeting delegates would lead to these scholars introducing their friends to the group. As the group expanded in the hundreds in the first year, so also did the topics of conversation. The first participants were concerned about the intersections of colonial Anglicanism and faith identities in the postcolonial period. As the group expanded so did the topics of conversation.

While a member of Facebook since 2008 and with many years of wonderful conversations and networking, the group and Facebook is now of far less value. Facebook began for friends and continues to excel for friends. In his February 16, 2017 "Building Global Community" post, Mark Zuckerberg, the founder and CEO wants Facebook to be instrumental in building global community. Facebook however lacks the social ethical principles to make Zuckerberg's vision a reality. For some time Facebook has demonized members through time-outs and threatening membership to Facebook group leaders who attempt to invite "strangers" into conversation. Facebook fears "others"! To build global community it must move beyond these very basic impediments.

Social media especially Facebook should be a powerful tool for building multi-racial, multi-ethnic, multi-religious online cultures, but it is really the opposite. Facebook is a bubble of ideas and culture that tends to reward dominant culture and silence Majority World voices. When the Postcolonial Theology Network group members were able to post without group administrator approval, the posts that dominated was about content in North America and Europe. White males often dominated and reframed initially more expansive conversations producing a very narrow thread. At various times throughout our history, Group Administrator approval was not without risk or criticism of our members. Postcolonial Theology Network and its group administrator were criticized as colonial administrators for censuring poor behavior, language and careless use of others' ideas without citations.

Greatest success of Facebook for Postcolonial Networks was when we were leading postcolonial conferences throughout the Majority World and building call for papers. Now Facebook is of limited value at this time.

Social media is like breathing and all the normal activities of my day. Social media does not control my time or reduce my productivity, so I am not challenged to move from curating content on Facebook or participating in a conversation to my other offline responsibilities. I have learned those who are hooked to Facebook or other social media tend to be less effective group participants either because they lack the freedom to manage their aggressive instincts and thus to responsibly participate in complex conversations. Those who are controlled by social media tend to be also controlling in their conversations and less effective in fostering scholarly conversations that are meaningful.

My three suggestions to scholars considering social media involves encouraging them . . .

1. To find groups with compelling content and conversation and require their students to read, evaluate and practice building effective groups through contributions that are prophetic and change culture.
2. To bring their curiosity to social media rather than their desire to win arguments. Members of groups should seek to be changed rather than to find sources of agreement or need to change others.
3. To bring their discerning mind to social media conversations and not lose their center in complex conversations

Scholars in every social media conversation should always raise the bar of participation not lower the bar by ineffectual ways of engaging people, norms generally accepted by our culture but with no place at an academic meeting.

Joseph Duggan, Ph.D. is a knowledge activist, founder of: Postcolonial Networks, Borderless Press and the founding editor of Palgrave Macmillan's series, Postcolonialism and Religions. He is also an Episcopal priest who serves in California. See Postcolonial Networks and Borderless Press websites: http://postcolonialnetworks .com/ https://borderlesspress.com/ the Postcolonial Theology Network on Facebook and Postcolonial Networks page where we now post knowledge activism content.

BRUCE EPPERLY

Practical Theology

My primary platform is Facebook, although I do have a website. Also, I regularly publish short pieces in Process and Faith, Jesus, Jazz, and Buddhism, and also weekly lectionary commentaries for Patheos, read by several hundred pastors weekly.

I had a number of reasons to begin using social media. First, I wanted to get the word out and share the work I was doing in theology, spirituality, and lectionary commentaries. Second, to comment on theological and spiritual trends in the larger culture, especially the impact of theological reflection on values and politics. Third, to publicize my work. Given the modest promotional budgets of many presses, an author has a responsibility to promote their own work and to make it known to persons who might benefit from her or his work. Fourth, to provide a series to fellow pastors in need of creative progressive approaches to preaching the lectionary.

I have been surprised to discover the contentiousness that often emerges over innocuous concepts. We are in a culture in which people go to the mat over small disagreements or must drown out any oppositional thinking, usually without giving serious consideration to the point being made.

I have also found that people report life-changing experiences as a result of materials I have posted, not to mention the hundreds of pastors who depend on my "Living a Holy Adventure" lectionary commentaries on Patheos. I also receive kind affirmations, such as "I would be lost without your lectionary commentaries" or "you're commentary helped me look at the lectionary readings in a new way."

I often crowd source. That is, I will put out a question on an issue I am thinking about—for example, "what themes in progressive theology would be most helpful for me to address" or "where is the most important issue theologians or the church should address in our time?" I usually get ten to twenty responses to such questions.

I regularly ask for books in certain areas. I am planning an upcoming study on Proverbs and asked what texts were important or insightful and received responses describing a couple academic sources.

I like to explore the broader wisdom of folks on Facebook, especially since these days I live on Cape Cod, seventy five miles from the Boston seminaries and do not have regular face-to-face interactions with scholarly colleagues.

In this political cycle, it is easy to become engrossed in the back and forth of political positions. I tend to make occasional theological comments related to politics and culture, and often a firestorm emerges, despite the broadly ecumenical and irenic nature of the comments. I try not to set the record straight without intellectual bullying, recognizing that often those who object have minimal theological or political experience or even information. I do not want to use Facebook as a tool of divisiveness although setting the record straight or being clear of my intent is important. I probably take a look at Facebook a couple times each day for a few minutes, posting an affirmation from one of my books, a link to an article I have written, a photo of my neighborhood (usually the beach or a pond), or a narrative of an event in my life or the larger culture.

If I were advising scholars about social media, I'd recommend they write things of quality. Despite the casual nature of Facebook, you leave a permanent record. Be clear in your submissions and responses: if you are making a political or social comment, ensure that it is factual. Do not involve yourself in character assassination, even of persons you deem unfit for higher office. Address everyone in the spirit of the Golden Rule, respecting the personhood of those with whom you disagree.

Feel comfortable in promoting your good ideas, a book you've read, or an essay/book from a colleague. I regularly promote other peoples' work, knowing that they face the same challenges in getting the word out as I do.

Finally, always follow your "better angels" and think twice about entering controversial conversations, knowing that few people are persuaded to change their positions by what they read on Facebook. Be courteous, kind, respectful and—erudite!

Bruce Epperly is Pastor and Teacher at South Congregational Church, United Church of Christ, Centerville, MA. He has written 40 books in theology, spirituality, scripture, and ministerial spirituality and wellness. He regularly writes book reviews, articles, and lectionary commentaries for the on-line religious platform Patheos.com. His Tending to the Holy: The Practice of the Presence of God in Ministry was chosen the Book of the Year by the Academy of Parish Clergy (2009). He teaches theology, ministry, and spirituality courses at Wesley Theological Seminary.

PATRICIA ADAMS FARMER

Practical Theology

Social media works for practical theologians — at least for me. I began reluctantly, only because I was told that social media was a form of marketing for my books and blog posts. As an introvert, I looked upon "marketing" with horror and "social media" with suspicion. But I realized that, if I were serious about being a writer, I had to stretch my personality and give it a try.

Now, I am glad I took the risk. Otherwise, no one — or very few — would be reading my books and blogs. I realized that this form of social contact is, in fact, a boon for introverts like me. I actually find it invigorating! By reaching like-minded people around the world, I now have fans and friends in places like China, Brazil, Sweden, the UK, Canada, and Norway. I have also crossed generational lines with social media. One of my essays, "Help! I'm an Introvert in an Extrovert World," was picked up by a well-known millennial site, proving that introverts of all ages love social media. I found my "tribe"!

Currently, I use Facebook, Twitter, and YouTube. On Facebook, I can organize my personal, professional, and group interests better than on any other form of social media. Twitter is short, sweet, and easy. Both are important to me. YouTube is the most challenging and creative: Besides the usual slide show and videos, I employ "Powtoon" for animated shorts, all of which highlight my theological ideas, creative work, and books. In all these areas, social media has served me well.

Still, using social media to highlight one's work as a theologian and writer entails risk and vulnerability. Such courage does not come easily to me. Born in the late Fifties in small-town America, I was ingrained with traditional ideas about women: Always be self-effacing; don't be assertive. Coupled with an INFP personality type in which "self-promotion" feels like torture, it's a wonder I ever created a Facebook profile. Even after I grew up to be a progressive feminist, I still harbor those fears of "putting myself out there."

With social media, however, boldness comes a bit easier, and this sometimes surprises me. It must be like the person who cannot imagine speaking in front of a crowd, but can host a radio show with ease. The "unseen" voice gives one a mysterious sense of psychological freedom. And so, I have chosen to share my ideas and my work, regardless of the outcome. And the outcome is, more often than not, surprisingly good.

However, this mysterious sense of boldness to share things on social media that you might not be able to share as easily in person works two ways. Sadly, the psychology of social media also emboldens bullies. So, as with every new advance in technology, the possibilities for good and evil rise in equal proportion. If social media can help some of us share ideas that add beauty and goodness to the world, then we need to embrace that. Otherwise it will be left to the bullies alone!

The most surprising feature of social media for a theologian—sometimes called "digital theology"—is wrapped in yet another mystery: the sense of connection, enrichment, and belonging in an authentic global community. As a writer of narrative theology—a rather small slice of the theological community, finding like-minded folks in my actual geographical location would be rare. But discovering "soul friends" across the world through social media offers the lavish gift of connection and belonging. This feels like a miracle. It is more than "networking," which sounds like a sterile business project for selling something. True relational moments happen in the global community of social media. These newfound relationships, or what Thomas Jay Oord calls "relational extensions," have transformed me and my work. As a process-relational thinker, I have found a community in which I can thrive. No longer do I feel like I am "marketing," but rather sharing and receiving. I am enriching my own soul at least as much as I hope to enrich others.

This spiritual quality of relating to people of diverse cultural backgrounds feels a bit like church. Instead of being locked into clear-cut homogenous groups, the field of relations crosses borders, offering insights outside of my narrow focus. My work as a writer grows richer with the cross-pollination of ideas. In this context of spiritual and relational sharing, fresh possibilities present themselves at every turn. Perhaps this is the most surprising aspect of social media: it actually fosters creativity.

Because of this creative dynamic, one of the most intriguing aspects of social media is how a single idea, which would normally stay within the narrow confines of a small group, can take flight around the world. I've had that happen. I wrote a couple of theological novels that used the term "fat soul"—a term that popped into my head while working with my characters. This term represented a theological concept expressed in a slightly different manner by one of my favorite process philosophers, Bernard Loomer. But the concept of "fat soul" suddenly grew exponentially—gaining girth—through Facebook. My colleague Jay McDaniel formed a Fat Soul Band in his hometown. Fat Soul International was born with interfaith events popping up in churches. Dr. McDaniel and I ended up writing a Fat Soul International Manifesto, creating a Fat Soul website (fatsoul.org) and hosting an active group on Facebook called the Fat Soul Café. The term "fat soul" is now showing up in spiritual texts by some of my colleagues, with fresh interpretations and meaning beyond anything I could imagine. As the concept grew, I compiled a collection of my own essays called *Fat Soul: A Philosophy of S-I-Z-E* and I promoted the book exclusively on Facebook. It has been sold in the US, Canada, and in the UK. None of this could have happened without the mysterious power of social media connection.

Of course, this takes time, focus, and commitment. I find that self-discipline is vital, or the entire day could be swallowed up with Facebook. This shows how far I have come from my initial reluctance to venture into the world of social media. I try to turn to social media at particular times during the day that do not affect my sleep, my time with family, or my work. I've found that the best time for social media is that "in-between" state when the mind is not ready for heavy thinking or writing, but rather relaxed and open to new ideas. Thankfully, social media is not normally demanding. It can even be energizing to the mind and spirit.

Now, if I were giving advice to those considering using social media, I'd begin by saying practice the "social" part of social media, i.e., use good social skills. I have learned that if one lacks good social skills in person, it often shows up glaringly on social media. I would particularly encourage scholars, who sometimes lack social skills, to stretch themselves a bit on social media. Dare to interact, encourage others, and "like" posts other than your own. Take time to support one another as much as possible. Do not come across as being in competition with others, but rather a part of a relational whole, each supporting the other. If a comment begs for attention, give it. Learn to say, "thank you." Try posting someone else's work every now and then. Affirm others; encourage others. Practice the same social skills you would in person. And if you need help with social skills, social media can help you grow in this area. Yes, it takes a few more minutes of my time, but as a relational theologian, I believe it's a way of living out my theology. So remember to "like" others as you would have others "like" you.

Second, practice moderation. Facebook can be addicting. We are all busy professionals, and it's good to find that sense of moderation, always keeping our priorities in line. It is also easy for the curious of mind — and we theologians are among the most curious! — to stop and read every last tantalizing article as we scroll through Facebook. Social media is an opportunity to practice not only social skills, but the golden mean.

Finally, do not engage bullies! In particular, learn to spot those with emotionally-laced reasoning — or what is sometimes called "motivated reasoning." Rational arguments about honest questions can be productive, but not those tinged with obvious bias or anger. These people will never be persuaded by logic or facts. They work out of emotion and create their own realities, even to the point of creating "alternative facts." We see motivated reasoning most fully in political discourse today, but it affects religious discourse as well. I have never seen one of these arguments come to a good end; no one convinces anyone of anything, and the person practicing motivated reasoning becomes even more defensive and entrenched in his/her own views. For those whose arguments are motivated by emotion, one needs to practice empathy, find something on which both can agree, and call it a day. Sometimes it's simply best to ignore — or even delete — negative or spiteful comments, even while offering a prayer on his/her behalf. Social media needs more light and less darkness. So, may we who seek to bring light into darkness practice compassion, always, even on social media.

––––––––––––

Patricia Adams Farmer is a pastor, process theologian, and author of several books, including Embracing a Beautiful God *and* Fat Soul: A Philosophy of S-I-Z-E. *She writes for* Jesus, Jazz, and Buddhism *and serves on the advisory board of Process and Faith. Recently, she returned from a five-year adventure in Ecuador. Her experience as a writer in South America influenced her desire — and need — to discover "digital theology." Visit Farmer's website at www.patriciaadamsfarmer.com and sign up for future blog posts. Besides her personal page on Facebook (Patricia Adams Farmer), she also has an author's page (Patricia Adams Farmer, author). She enjoys producing animated videos on YouTube (Ronald Farmer) and creating memes for Facebook and Twitter (@pafarmerecuador). She co-hosts the Facebook group, "Fat Soul Café, in which she invites inspiring posts from people of all faiths.*

DANIEL FINCKE

Philosophy

have a blog that uses WordPress software and is hosted on the Patheos blogging network, on the Atheism Non-Religious channel. I found myself naturally absorbed into social media because I have the type of gregarious personality that wants to be able to connect with people all throughout the day, combined with the sort of hermetic personality that wants to stay at home all the time working on my reading and writing and doing other sedentary activities. So, social media created that balance for me. I could be around people whenever I wanted but also focus on my work whenever I wanted, with no commitments.

Getting so active posting on Facebook, I organically wound up just commenting on a lot of the issues of the day and getting into lengthy debates with people. Colleagues suggested I should consider blogging since I apparently had so much to say about daily events.

I found the medium was perfect for me. I am a perfectionist who is shy to publish anything imperfect as Official Scholarship. But I am also a fast and opinionated writer who is comfortable whipping out a few thousand words a day about whatever I'm thinking about—so long as we're not calling it Official Scholarship. So, the informality and low expectations of the medium were huge positives to me. It was a perfect, low-pressure way to draft my philosophical ideas where I would have incentive to write them out because they would be read immediately.

When I started my blog, I was also in my sixth year of writing my dissertation and after spending so much time writing this long, long document that no one except my adviser and one of my readers was reading and that likely no one beyond my dissertation committee would *ever* read, it was extremely freeing to write off the top of my head, instantly publish, and get instant readers and feedback and be part of conversations. I had also learned a lot of philosophy in 9 years of graduate school and loved having an outlet to put it all together for myself in a way that wouldn't be new or rigorous enough to count as scholarship but which would be personally beneficial and thought provoking to others.

My philosophical interests were deeply shaped by my devoutly religious high school and college years and by my response to my subsequent deconversion. Consequently, the blog gave me an outlet to work out my philosophy in the context of how it related to my own personal journey with respect to religion. I had a lot of pent up things to say publicly and to work out as I went. And I wanted to engage in the street level discourse about atheism and religion.

Probably in no small part due to the fact that I was raised and deeply socialized as an evangelical Christian, I have a visceral belief that people's views on the ultimate questions of metaphysics and ethics and epistemology and meaning in life have deep and important significance to people. I think of philosophy, and in particular philosophy of religion, as a matter of vital importance for individuals and society.

I want my philosophizing to be done in a style and a place where it will be accessible to the whole of society and contribute to the public discussion rather than just the scholarly ones. And over time, blogging as part of the atheist community, I came to have a sense of mission to be part of the atheist movement and humanist community and the philosophical discussions it has. I especially have developed a sense of mission to help fulfill a vital and all too often neglected role of providing resources for people who have recently left religion and need philosophical help.

I see blogging as a medium in which to do philosophy for a community, much like the apostles of the New Testament who did their theology by writing letters occasioned by the concerns of churches. I love the idea of scholars developing their ideas in the contexts of current debates, letting their questions and their answers develop in response to the contours of practical problems. Philosophy's relevance to everyday life becomes clearest to people when they have problems that philosophy can give unique insight into, so doing one's philosophy in response to pressing controversies makes it something people will read and see the importance of.

Because of the popularity of my blog, I had people telling me that I had inspired them to take philosophy classes. I realized that these were potential students for me. Eventually my blog network started using Google Hangouts to create videos of us talking to each other which we broadcast live and then reposted on our blogs. This got me comfortable with Google Hangout to the point where one day as I set out on my 2 and a half hour commute to New Jersey for my adjuncting gig, I grumbled to myself, I wish I could just meet my students on Google instead of having to do all this travelling. And the light bulb went off. I realized that I could offer my blog readers and large network of Facebook friends classes over Google Hangout.

Realizing I had nothing to lose in asking my Facebook friends what they thought, I threw up a post on Facebook and *voilà*, three months later I had a private online teaching business. And a year later I was able to make it my full time job. Four years later, I'm still in business, making more money each year and achieving more stability as each year I accumulate more students who remain studying with me year round, providing me some job security.

I would recommend to scholars considering using social media the following three things:

1. Find online communities that have a natural interest in the kind of work you're doing and join them. Interact with them as a full community member, not just as someone dropping by with promotional materials. Develop credibility among them. This is an incredible way to build an audience for your work.

2. Make your work, or at least accessible summaries of your ideas, available on any social media platforms you can. Look for current events stories that you can comment on from your area of expertise and leverage your scholarly knowledge to make a meaningful contribution to the discourse on whatever social media platforms you can create. Don't just use your social media presence to put up notices about publications or speaking engagements. Be engaging.

3. Be a full human being in public. Let people in your social networks get a sense for your personality. Talk about more than your work. Intrigue people by being an interesting person and they will take more of an interest in what you write.

————————

Daniel Fincke, PhD is a philosopher and entrepreneur who spent 11 years teaching at universities and since 2013 has been in business for himself teaching live, interactive private philosophy classes online. He mixes philosophy popularization and creative philosophical thinking on his blog Camels With Hammers, *which is hosted on the Patheos blog network's "Non-Religious" channel. He has a teaching award, has appeared on numerous podcasts, and has been profiled in* Inside Higher Ed.

JR. FORASTEROS

Practical Theology

S ocial media is all about communicating and storytelling. And since theology
means 'words about God', it follows that social media offers plenty of new
opportunities — and pitfalls — for talking about God.

I'm an early adopter, so I try basically everything. I had FourSquare, Periscope
and Snapchat accounts. The main platforms I use are blogs, podcasting, Facebook,
Twitter and Instagram. I have just started using a weekly email newsletter.

I began blogging in college, and quickly found it was a way to meditate publicly on new ideas, getting feedback from a larger community. While I blogged as
a youth pastor (and also got Facebook then), teens had not quite started using
social media by the time I left youth ministry.

In my role as a teaching pastor, I used social media from day one — especially
blogging, Facebook and Twitter. The main reason was access: rather than the one
hour on Sunday morning (and possibly again on a Wednesday night) I could connect with people, the social media allowed me to engage them throughout the
week. I could extend the preaching event throughout the week by posting preview or follow-up blog posts. I could engage pastorally and theologically in real
life events multiple times per day.

Today, I have several goals in using social media. The main one is to communicate more content. My sermons are 25 minutes, and we have no other teaching

opportunities throughout the week. Podcasting and microblogging (on FB and Instagram) are two easy ways to explore more content. My StoryMen and In All Things Charity podcasts do theology and pop culture engagement that doesn't fit into sermons, necessarily. My Bible Bites podcast functions as "Sunday School for the 21st Century". We use it to communicate densely packed, high-quality information that people can consume on-demand, or in small groups. Don't Split Up! is a horror film review podcast I use to talk about the social ills horror examines— I can engage subjects there that simply aren't accessible in a worship context.

Microblogging has become an excellent way to offer quick devotional thoughts throughout the week. Since they are also on-demand, I can offer thoughts that may never make it into a sermon but are germane to my day or to my immediate context. They can be less polished, more off-the cuff (and therefore more authentic /vulnerable).

More importantly, I have found Social Media to be an invaluable opportunity to listen. It's easy to forget, when our work is turned to face God, the pain that exists in the world. Social Media give us windows into the lives of basically everyone in the world. Theologians often occupy a precarious position between God and the world, and Social media make it much, much easier to listen to the world around us. Insight into what my congregation thinks about Sunday afternoon through Saturday has helped my preaching stay grounded, rather than abstract.

Social Media also gives me access to voices that are not in my normal circles. With the rise of the #BlackLivesMatter movement, I realized that, though I had considered myself an ally of persons of color, I listened to very few persons of color on a daily basis. I immediately went to Facebook and Twitter and searched out voices of color and followed them. I committed to listen only, not to engage. I've gained incomparable insight into conversations to which I am a cultural outsider—for free—by using social media.

Social Media has made me a better teacher. I learned that facts and figures rarely persuade people. For a long time, I engaged in debate and argument on blogs or social media. But while I won quite a few arguments (at least in my own mind!), I seldom convinced anyone.

I've learned that images and stories persuade far more effectively than facts and figures. Social media is perfectly situated to deliver stories and images.

I have learned to take care in engaging arguments on social media. I mostly ask questions, share stories, and use images. For instance, when addressing the refugee crisis, I have shared pictures of refugee children to humanize the refugee stories.

I have to manage my Social Media on a schedule. On Sundays, I post the sermon podcast from that morning. Monday morning, I create a sharable image from the sermon and share it on personal and church accounts. Every morning, I reserve time to share a reflection from morning devotional readings if I have one. Other podcast recordings are Tuesday-Thursday afternoons, along with editing and posting. Newsletters are also on Wednesday and Thursday afternoons. If I blog, it's typically a film review I saw over the weekend, and I write that review over the weekend.

I offer these three general principles to those considering social media:

First, no matter what you do, social media must be authentic. If people feel like you're just trying to sell to them, they'll tune out. If you're not willing to be honest and vulnerable on social media, then you may as well not use it. A good rule to follow has to do with how much you ask: for every one thing you ask from your audience, make sure you're giving them ten things. In other words, the age-old adage holds true: listen a lot more than you speak.

Second, be intentional. What platform are you using? What are the specific strengths of that platform? Why is this the best platform for you to use? If you're going to use Facebook and not Twitter, why? If you're going to blog, why? What's the strength of a podcast instead? The limitations? Make sure you understand the platform you're using. Otherwise, you'll just be noise.

Finally, be consistent. If you're going to do something every day, do it every day. If you're going to post on Tuesdays and Thursdays, do it every Tuesday and Thursday. Once a week? Twice monthly? It's fine. Just do it consistently. People need to know when and what to expect from you.

JR. Forasteros is an author, pastor and podcaster in Dallas, TX. His wife, Amanda, skates as the notorious derby girl Mother Terrorista. Together, they love to cook, travel and explore new places. His book, Empathy for the Devil, *is available from InterVarsity Press. JR. blogs at NorvilleRoges.com (sign up for his newsletter there too). His podcasts are at StoryMen.us and NorvilleRogers.com/podcasts. Follow him on Facebook and Twitter @jrforasteros.*

DION A. FORSTER

Public Theology

I make use of most of the larger platforms (Twitter and Instagram @digitaldion, Facebook (Dion Foster), and YouTube (dionforster). I also make use of some other social networking platforms that are more business oriented (LinkedIn — Dion Forster; Academia.edu — Dion Forster; Researchgate — Dion Forster). I also use Tumblr — digitaldion.tumblr.com which is a conduit for many of my ideas and smaller posts.

All of my social media sites are set up in a loop. At the very start are Instagram and Tumblr, they repost automatically to Twitter, which reposts automatically to Facebook (which is where just about everything ends up).

My primary platforms are Facebook for engagement and conversation, YouTube and Twitter for 'broadcasting' ideas and information (I seldom engage in conversation or created community in these spaces, most often the engagement, or conversation, moves to Facebook), and Instagram for more personal / family stuff.

I also have a longstanding website that goes back to 2007. For some years it has been in the top 1 to 5 rankings for websites in the 'religion' category in South Africa. I use 'long form' writing a lot less these days, but for many years that was my primary communication tool — my website is reachable via www.dionforster.com or www.spirituality.org.za

I started using social media to share ideas, create conversation and begin to 'showcase' some of my work as a very young scholar. Now that I am a little more established it is a place where I announce new publications, solicit input on research processes, and keep my students and friends up to date (particularly Facebook, Twitter and YouTube are used in this way). I still have a number of 'die hard' website / blog followers who comment whenever I post stuff there. But I have a sense that the current popular tools are much more transient — I post stuff, it has a shelf life of a day or two, and then I need to produce new content or new forms of engagement. I enjoy the feedback loop and conversational nature of Facebook most, but I find making my VLOG's for YouTube most rewarding and helpful (I speak easily, so can capture an idea, or share a moment, and then edit it and upload it). The fact that YouTube keeps the content makes it a lot like my web page i.e., people 'find' posts from months or even years ago and comment on them and engage. That is super.

My reasons for using online tools today remain pretty much the same (generate content, seek to showcase my thoughts and work, create community and learn). However, the tools I use to do that have changed over the years. It started with my website, then moved on Facebook, now it is most commonly YouTube, and Facebook / Twitter, and for academic stuff academia.edu and researchgate.net

I am constantly amazed at how social media democratizes information creation and sharing. Some years ago. If I wanted to share something I had to write a scholarly article, or get a contract for a monograph / book. Of course I still do that (but that is more for the sake of academic credibility than 'reach'). I would say that I am equally well known for my online / social media engagements as for my books and academic publications (of course the audiences and engagements in those spaces differ). I will confess that colleagues in the academy don't always understand (or appreciate) the social media reach. However, as a 'Public Theologian' I have had to think about how I engage the different 'publics' of public opinion (see my YouTube videos on bilingualism, language and public theology, and the other video on Habermas and discourse theory called 'Is Facebook making us dumb'.) My work has got a much larger reach, and I have even received funding and invitations to speak, collaborate in research, or teach, because of my online 'presence'.

I recognize that it is not everyone's cup of tea. But I have certainly benefitted a great deal (and my ideas have too) from social media engagement.

I have had a number of invitations to speak at various events because of people seeing videos I've made, or articles I have written. Some years ago I wrote a book faith and work. A video interview I did on the book reached the CEO of one of Malaysia's largest IT companies (a telecom and cellular company). The CEO bought copies of the book for all of her senior executives, and I ended up visiting Malaysia to speak at various events over a period of 3 years. The relationships established during those trips became important for later projects that I ran (particularly the faith based anti-corruption campaign that we initiated with the United Nations, World Evangelical Alliance, Micah Challenge, Unashamedly Ethical, International Bible Societies and Salvation Army). This campaign ended up impacting the policy of the G20 and the G8 consultations in 2014—which is quite remarkable. As a result of this effort I was invited to become an 'expert' on religion and development for the World Economic Forum (I attended the WEF meeting in Cape Town in June 2015 and have been an active participant on the expert panel since).

Furthermore, an interesting aspect of the EXPOSED campaign was that we ran it around the world using social media. It was relatively effective (although we found we still had to aggregate our efforts with traditional advocacy networks and processes). I published an article on this with a colleague: Bowers-Du Toit, N.F. & Forster, D. 2015. Activating moral imagination: EXPOSED 2013 as a fourth generation faith-based campaign? STJ | Stellenbosch Theological Journal. 1(1):19–40.

Time management is challenging. Of course there are times where I simply cannot maintain my social media presence as I should. The traditional expectations of the academy (teaching, research, supervision) must come first! The University is happy for the additional exposure, but my performance appraisal is still based on traditional criteria. I find it particularly challenging to find the time to edit my videos (it can take 1-3 hours, depending on how complicated the shots are and whether I filmed in multiple locations, on multiple devices etc.)

That being said, I have found that having a digital presence is becoming much easier! I can do almost everything that I need to (including filming, editing and uploading my VLOG) from my iPhone 7. Frequently when I am traveling that is how I record and upload new content. It is quite remarkable.

My advice to those considering using social media is this: work out what you want to achieve with an online presence. For me it is a mix of giving a 'voice' to my ideas and research, and building a community of engagement and interest. Once that choice has been made one is able to decide what medium (or platform) is best to achieve that aim, and also how to present yourself or your work online. For example, Instagram is generally not an easy space to present theological concepts and ideas (unless one is recording short videos, or you're engaged in simple 'news briefs' about events that are happening. Longer form, and conversational, platforms, tend to be better for my discipline — points can be made, argued, justified, reasoned and engaged).

So, I guess that is one point. The second would be that ongoing content creation is crucial to growing and sustaining an online presence. The internet is rather fickle — it has a short attention span. Persons will move on from dormant website and channels that become outdated.

Lastly, I would say don't be obsessed with 'gear' and perfection! Part of the 'appeal' of the kind of content I produce is that it is 'off the cuff'. Most of the consumers of my VLOG and posts engage it because it is NOT perfect, it does not emulate a million dollar seminar, or a high production value documentary. It feels a bit like 'reality TV' for theologians! In order to do that very basic equipment (such as a smartphone) is perfectly adequate. People are often more interested in the content than in the production value. That being said, be careful not to devalue your content by producing poor quality online material (sound and picture quality / video stability / framed shots) do matter a little. But that is easily learnt.

Dion A Forster, Ph.D. is the Head of Department of Systematic Theology and Ecclesiology at Stellenbosch University. He is the director of the Beyers Naudé Centre for Public Theology. His research focusses on Public Theologies and Theological ethics. He has authored and edited numerous books and scholarly articles. He has a Public Theology VLOG on YouTube and a website and blog at www. dionforster.com. His YouTube Public Theology VLOG series is entitled, 'It's not a lecture, just a thought' at http://www.youtube.com/dionforster. You can also connect with him on Facebook and @digitaldion on Twitter and Instagram. For academic publications please see his Academia.edu and Researchgate.net accounts.

TRIPP FULLER

Constructive Theology

use a variety of social media forms and technology, including blogs, podcasting, Twitter, Facebook, and Tumblr. I have probably tried all of them at some point, Periscope, like Instagram, the order of use; my favorite is Twitter and then, alright, my favorite is Twitter, the most useful for platform building with Homebrewed has been Facebook.

I started the podcast when I was working at First Christian Church in Winston-Salem. I needed a way to deliver content before our pub group met. No one read the books before arriving. So I started interviewing amazing theologians like Thomas J Oord. When the group members listen to the interview online, we can talk about it. That's how it started.

It wasn't a podcast a first. But it turned into a podcast and I kept doing it. I got free books and I talked to people I wanted to talk to. But it really started as a minister doing Christian education.

I have been surprised to discover that the church is full of people who think critically and want to do it faithfully. They've had experiences, but they don't know they have permission to acknowledge those experiences. And they want to find the language.

Many church people are into visions towards kind of more beautiful living, greater justice and they actually have lots of practices they don't know are theological. Having extremely heady, nerdy podcasts gives just enough critical distance from your living. It has given people permission to acknowledge something, to step into something, to start to embody something. Ironically, the more things change practically, the more I try to avoid practical things in the podcast.

Strangely, my podcast numbers are better on a theologian whom no one has heard of but that wrote a cool book than a podcast with Rob Bell. I guess most people are like, "Rob has been on a million podcasts, but this scholar is talking about something unusual. So I am going to share it." And when they share it, the three people at every church get to hear the ideas. These people wish they had 100 people at their church, so they could have a theologian come and speak. But they don't. And the podcast allows them to hear that theologian anyway. When we network those people, they have a kind of enlivening role in their congregations.

Theology beer camp is one of the most gratifying events I've organized. One hundred people dropped $250, flew to LA, and spent three days together. Everyone's highlight was the day John Cobb showed up. An overwhelming majority of them were from denominations where ministers where not encouraged to John Cobb. But people present knew of Cobb from the podcast, and it was like "Oh, this is John Cobb!" The Pentecostal were saying, "We love John Cobb: he likes the Bible, has missionary parents, and prays!"

We are trying to connect the podcast to the academy. We do a podcast live at AAR, for instance. We even have sponsors who help pay the costs. We had Jürgen Moltmann, for instance, on the anniversary of the publishing of his famous book, *The Crucified God*. Fortress Press helped pay for that event.

When it goes to time management, the biggest insight is learning to say no to the right things so you can say yes to the best things. I had to learn tons of stuff as I went along. I sometimes hear people in the academy say, "I don't have time to do that stuff." I think there are two reasons they say this. First, they don't really want to. They are insecure and worry that people could assess them in public without having to peer reviewed. They may feel like an imposter.

But professional theologians have less time than ever to spend with students. Institutions hire adjuncts, and the full-time professors spend more and more time in administration. The same is true in churches. I've tried to learn efficiency and productivity tactics so I can have more time to invest in what matters most: the people, my family, my community. And I have more time for my passions, the podcast, and stuff.

A lot of people don't realize it takes sacrifice to give the attention to create content that matters. When you create that content, you need to give just as much attention to the people you are connecting in the distribution of it.

The three pieces of advice I have for those considering using social media are these . . .

First, learn to communicate what you care about. Then engage in social media platform building. You have to decide you want to do it. One reason a lot of people don't engage in social media is that they see their role as an educator not as a vocation but just a job. But you must focus on your passions and use social media in that.

Second, when you want to build a platform and connect with people using social media, you need to get to know the audience already present. So, join the Facebook groups or start listening to podcasts connected to it. If suddenly start posting in 10 groups and don't engage, the community will ignore you. But if you listen and you get to know the community, they will value you. You can create your own content. It's about making friends.

Third, professors should require the class assignments to be done in public. Instead of writing a paper, create an audio track and explain the ideas to others. Or pick some other medium. Let your students teach you by modelling what communicating these ideas look like in whatever medium they want. Then you try to do it along with them. And you end up learning a lot.

Remember that social media allows everyone to change their minds. You have permission to be wrong. Most major figures on social media have been repeatedly called out by their people. They learn to change their minds and learn from it.

───────────────

Tripp Fuller and his wife are both ordained ministers, followers of Jesus. They have two sons and a daughter. They intentionally see family and vocation as a larger process of figuring out to create community at home. He is also a professor, minister, and podcaster on Homebrewed Christianity. Find Tripp on Twitter at @trippfuller, Theology Nerd or Homebrewed Christianity.

DEANE GALBRAITH

Religious Studies

I use Facebook primarily, Twitter regularly, and LinkedIn and Instagram occasionally. When I first joined Facebook in 2007, the decision had very little to do with scholarship. If you remember it back then, every status update had to begin with "[Name] is . . . ," and my Facebook friends consisted almost entirely of family and non-academic friends. So lengthy posts about the latest German Pentateuchal scholarship wouldn't have gone down well. But as the platform became more flexible in what could be posted, it also became much more amenable to academic discussion. In fact, this use quickly dominated, and there was a dramatic increase at this time in the number of Facebook users who were academics.

I later started a *Relegere* Twitter account (@relegere1) and Facebook page to notify of new issues and articles published in the journal *Relegere: Studies in Religion and Reception*, a journal specialising in Reception History. Also, I have a Twitter account (@BiblicalStud) to provide updates for *Biblical Studies Online* (https://biblicalstudiesonline.wordpress.com/). That site and Twitter account were set up after James Crossley and I discussed — originally via Facebook — our shared concern that good quality biblical scholarship should be freely available and accessible online. So *Biblical Studies Online* collates hundreds of free or open-access resources in biblical studies: videos of talks by leading scholars, online courses, and a host of primary sources, on subjects as broad ranging as the history of ancient Israel, the historical Jesus, or Beyoncé and the Bible. The site gets regularly updated with new resources (so please subscribe to updates on Twitter!).

The social media sites connected with the journal *Relegere* are very much prompted by this same concern: to make quality scholarship available online, free and open-access. If you subscribe to @Relegere1 on Twitter, for example, you would have read about our recent free online (and print) book published on the Israel-Palestine situation (*The Bible, Zionism, and Palestine*). You could also read a very timely analysis of what people in the North of England make of the Bible after Brexit. And most importantly, you could read John Lyons' innovative proposals about the future of biblical studies.

One of my abiding, if admittedly peculiar, interests is in the Giants mentioned in the Hebrew Bible (e.g., Rephaim, Nephilim, Anakim, King Og, Goliath, etc.), and in their reception in later texts and popular culture. I have a blog, *Remnant of Giants* (https://remnantofgiants.wordpress.com/), and associated Twitter account (@gigantologist) which notify of the latest developments in the specialist subfield of Biblical Gigantology. (Perhaps surprisingly, biblical giants are frequently mentioned in news stories and in popular culture more generally.) While this might seem like a niche area, one site ranked *Remnant of Giants* as the most popular Old Testament / Hebrew Bible blog in the world. It's huge. Literally.

What have I been most surprised to learn, on social media? The most surprising thing I ever learned on Facebook — while viewing a holiday photo — was that John Dominic Crossan wears a speedo!

More seriously, though, social media has often been an invaluable resource for my academic work. I live in one of the remote corners of the academic world (Dunedin, New Zealand). So one of the great benefits of social media from my perspective is that it helps to reduce the distance which separates me from most other academics — the majority of whom are based on the other side of the world. There have been many times that I have had the beginnings of an idea, usually less than fully formed, and posted it on Facebook and waited to see what others made of it. As well as hopefully generating some discussion, it has the benefit of forcing me to formulate my thoughts in at least a preliminary way.

Here's a really good example of how social media has helped my scholarship. For a long time I had been puzzled by the narrative of Jesus' resurrection in the non-canonical Gospel of Peter. If you haven't read this resurrection narrative, to say it is weird would be a gross understatement. First, Jesus comes out of his tomb supported by two angels; then Jesus and the two angels grow until they reach gigantic proportions, stretching from earth to the heavens; and — as if that weren't odd enough — Jesus' own cross follows him out of his tomb and converses with God, having apparently developed the ability to walk and talk! Commentators have struggled to explain this unusual resurrection account adequately, ever since the Gospel of Peter was discovered just over a century ago.

Back in 2011, when I had been researching the giants in the Hebrew Bible/Old Testament (Nephilim, Anakim, etc.), I came across references to Jesus being described as a 'giant' in ancient Christian interpretations of LXX Psalm 19 (Psalm 18 in the MT and English numbering). I thought this might be the key to the Gospel of Peter's strange resurrection narrative, so posted a quick summary of my proposal on Facebook and on *Remnant of Giants*, and soon received very helpful comments and encouragement from a number of scholars who had worked on the gospel or related areas. In particular, I received invaluable replies from Gospels scholar Mark Goodacre and Coptic scholar Alin Suciu — followed up generously by further messages and emails.

Following these discussions, and after some further research, I developed what had been a short online post into a full paper, which I gave at the 2014 ANZABS annual meeting, New Zealand's major annual conference for biblical studies. This culminated in an article in the July 2017 issue of the journal *New Testament Studies* ("Whence the Giant Jesus and his Talking Cross?"). It all started, though, with a post on social media, and interacting with the comments of other scholars.

The contributions go both ways, of course, and sometimes I get to offer comments on other scholars' posts. Just recently, I noticed a tweet by New Testament scholar Larry Hurtado (https://twitter.com/LarryWHurtado/status /840512190327185408) which linked to his review of J. R. Daniel Kirk's recent book, *A Man Attested by God: The Human Jesus of the Synoptic Gospels* (Grand Rapids: Eerdmans, 2016). The review contained some pointed criticisms. I then read a developing conversation on Kirk's Facebook page about the review. One thing that had raised an eyebrow when I read Hurtado's review was his insistence that he had never, to his knowledge, alluded to the Chalcedonian confession of the divinity of Jesus in relation to his discussions of early (first-century) Christian understandings of Jesus. As it so happened, the previous day I had been reading a journal article by Hurtado in which he alluded (quite explicitly) to the Chalcedonian Creed of 451 AD, claiming that it was consistent with the "binitarian" beliefs about and devotion to Jesus "within the first 20 years of the Christian movement." I thought this might be helpful for Daniel and for the academic discussion generally. So I made a quick post on Daniel's wall, notifying him of the relevant quotation. Within twelve hours, Daniel had included it in a response to Hurtado (http://www.patheos.com/blogs/storiedtheology/2017/03/14/man-attested-by-god-response-hurtado/), and I am sure even Hurtado was grateful for the correction, in the spirit of open scholarship. Admittedly, mine was a small contribution, but an illustration of one way in which Facebook can facilitate knowledge-sharing within the scholarly community — recalling Sathya Sai Baba's injunction to "Love all, serve all."

In order to manage my time on social media, I tend to check in on updates early in the morning or later on in the evening. That leaves quite a bit of time for doing other things.

The three things that I would recommend to scholars who are considering using social media are these:

1. Enjoy yourself.
2. Don't be boring. It is far, far worse to be boring than wrong.
3. Be generous in your contributions if you have something useful to share.

———————

Deane Galbraith is a lecturer in Judaism and Paganism at the University of Otago, New Zealand. He is a founding editor of what has become the leading journal in Reception History in the areas of religious studies and biblical studies, Relegere. He is also series editor for Relegere Academic Press, which publishes open-access print and free online books, as a site of resistance to the extortionate pricing which is prevalent in the academic-publishing oligopoly. See Deane Galbraith's Biblical Studies Online *(co-edited with James Crossley) at biblicalstudiesonline.wordpress. com (Twitter updates @BiblicalStud) and* Remnant of Giants *at remnantofgiants. wordpress.com (Twitter updates @gigantologist). See also* Relegere: Studies in Religion and Reception, *the online, open-access journal in reception history at relegere.org/relegere and Relegere Academic Press's open-access online books at rap.relegere.org/rap/index (Twitter updates @relegere1). Galbraith is regularly on Facebook (facebook.com/deane.galbraith), and from time to time on Twitter (@dorhamidbar), less so on Instagram and LinkedIn.*

KARL GIBERSON

Science & Religion

O n Facebook I have a personal page where I post ordinary things—family pictures, and negative commentary about Republicans, especially Donald Trump. I also have a professional page where I post things related to science and religion. Every time I publish something I put a notice there.

I don't use Twitter in a formal sense very often, but I have my FB pages set up so that my posts go out automatically as Tweets. I have a personal website, www.karlgiberson.com, where I have blogged and posted various other promotional things. I used my personal site to promote my most recent book, *Abraham's Dice*.

I started my own website while I was at Eastern Nazarene College. My work there was apparently so controversial that the administration essentially prohibited the promotion of anything I did, even when it was fully supportive of the college mission and portrayed students in a positive light. My book, *Saving Darwin*, for example won a major literary award from the *Washington Post Book World*—a "Best Book of 2008" recognition—and the college would not even mention it in any of their outlets. In contrast, another professor might give a lecture on wetlands at a local high school, or be invited to speak to a Sunday school class, and that would be widely promoted as college news. Once I realized that the college leadership considered my work "toxic" I started my own website where I could do whatever I wanted.

I find social media to be "fun" for the most part. I am on FB a lot and sometimes I spend too much time there, but most days I just give it a few minutes every so often. But the overall growth of social media has made it much easier to see where people stand on issues of common interest.

My primary discovery on FB has been dramatic. In my conversations with former students and college classmates I have realized that the evangelical community is actually far more right wing and conservative than I had realized. Because Eastern Nazarene was a moderately liberal evangelical school, I had mistakenly assumed that it was more politically liberal than it really was. The ascendancy of Donald Trump brought me into all kinds of FB conversations that I frankly found disturbing. The fact that people self-identifying as "evangelical Christian" were so supportive of Trump—who I consider held explicitly anti-Christian views — and so hostile to Bernie Sanders — who held traditional Christian views was startling. The extent of irrational "Hillary hate" was also disturbing.

This is a bit of a political digression, but it was these conversations—all enabled by social media—that brought me to the unwelcome conclusion that "Evangelical Christianity" is little more than a political label and no more connected to the teachings of Jesus than "Red Sox Fans" or "Residents of New Hampshire." In fact, I consider many of the policies of the GOP to be contrary to the teachings of Jesus, such as Paul Ryan's embrace of the philosophy of Ayn Rand, arguably the most explicitly anti-Christian philosopher in history. So because evangelicals are so supportive of the GOP I came to think the group "Red Sox Fans" would actually be more likely to take the teachings of Jesus seriously than "evangelicals." These were all positions to which I came via social media. This contributed to my growing alienation from evangelical Christianity.

In similar fashion, my work in science and religion over the years convinced me that evangelicalism in America was infected with powerful strains of anti-intellectualism. I encountered many students — and even some administrators — at Eastern Nazarene, for example, who somehow thought that populist pseudo-intellectuals like Ken Ham, Ravi Zacharias, or David Barton were important authority figures who could be used to refute the consensus of scholars, or who at least deserved a place in the classroom as an option. My experience on FB, where I would encounter these same people commenting about politics, climate change, economics, etc. helped me understand that the evangelical culture is consistently anti-intellectual in the sense that "everything has two sides" and flakey fringe thinkers like David Barton or Ken Ham on the right wing were a reasonable juxtaposition to scholars like Francis Collins or Mark Noll on the educated wing of evangelicalism. These realizations led to me to reject the label "evangelical" because of its negative cultural connotations. The question of labels became increasingly important as I evolved slowly into a more public role.

Social media helped me to understand what it means to be a "public intellectual." On social media I would often find discussions of me that I could read as though "Karl Giberson" were some other person than me. And, in fact, the "Karl Giberson of Social Media" was often, in fact, a different person!

Let me share some interesting anecdotes about this. A few years back I reviewed, for *Books & Culture* (a high-brow evangelical journal) an "Anthology of Great Science Writing" that had been assembled, edited, and annotated by Richard Dawkins. Dawkins, of course, has long been the boogeyman of evangelicals, as our generation's most famous atheist. Over the past few years every book on science and religion by an evangelical, including mine, contained an obligatory bashing of Dawkins and his merry band of anti-religious New Atheists. For this review, rather than simply exploiting yet another opportunity to bash "Dawkins the enemy of religion", I focused on "Dawkins the lover of science." This was actually a more faithful stance to take for this review since the entire volume, with countless introductions by Dawkins to its many pieces, contained none of his typical critiques of religion.

My positive review was reposted on Dawkins' liberal website and generated a long discussion among his fans who could not quite comprehend that "Giberson the infamous critic of Dawkins" had written such a complimentary review. A few posters tried to parse my comments to make them seem negative, but these were strained and indefensible. It was entertaining. It was also sobering however, as it made me realize that *science versus religion* was such a standard trope that everyone in the conversation was assumed to be on one side or the other.

On the other end of the spectrum, extended discussions of "Karl Giberson the infamous critic of fundamentalism" have appeared on the conservative website "Naznet." These discussions, dominated by conservative Nazarenes, were actually much less charitable than the conversations on Dawkins' website. On this website, I read highly fictional accounts of my work, my beliefs, and eventually my departure from Eastern Nazarene College. One commenter assured readers that I had left the college in a huff because they wouldn't give me a smaller teaching load than all the other faculty. (This was complete fiction.)

Experiences like this helped me understand that a public intellectual needs to have a thick skin; people who disagree with you will say all kinds of negative things and you just have to live with that. The Reformed Nazarene site published an article titled "Karl Giberson Needs God in his Life," which contained this interesting comment: "Karl Giberson despises Ken Ham, who I consider an honorary Nazarene for all the reporting he has done about Giberson and other false teachers in the Nazarene denomination." The Discovery Institute posted a piece titled "The Sad Decline of Karl Giberson." (Both of these are still available on the web.)

I actually found it easy and often entertaining to read about this guy "Karl Giberson" who somehow managed to make enemies of both the religious right and the secular left!

Social media can be time-consuming, of course, and managing a public persona takes time, thought and energy. I don't think I am adept at it, largely because I have typically had so many things going on — teaching, writing, speaking, running projects — and growing a public persona was never of great interest to me. In contrast, I think Rachel Held Evans has done a superb job of building a public persona through social media. She is a great model for how to do this well.

Some things I have found helpful, however, include: 1) getting a designer to make a site for me so my public page looks professional; 2) setting my FB so that posts go out as tweets; 3) reposting pieces on the Huffington Post that I have published elsewhere, in less public places.

My advice to those considering increased use of social media is the following:

1. Decide if you want to do it. Lots of people want to be "a well-known blogger" or a "tweeter with lots of followers." But they don't want to "write a lot of blogs" or "compose thoughtful tweets." If you don't like the work required, don't try to become a public figure with followers. (On the other hand, sometimes becoming a public figure happens on its own, as was the case with me.)

2. Don't engage individuals or small groups, unless you want to for fun. Individuals will say all kinds of things and you can spend hours wasting your time on a tiny audience. When I was at BioLogos I had a colleague who felt the need to respond to everything that needed correction. Just because something is posted in a public setting does not mean anyone is paying attention to it. You should always have a sense for the size of your audience.

———————

Karl Giberson is Stonehill College's first Professor of Science and Religion. He holds a Ph.D. in Physics from Rice University and taught Physics and Science & Religion at Eastern Nazarene College for over 25 years. He is an accomplished writer and has written, co-written, or edited eleven books, several with major presses like Harvard, Oxford, and HarperOne. He is a regular contributor to the popular conversation on science and religion and has written for the NY Times, *the* Guardian, USA Today, *the* Daily Beast, Salon.com *and many other publications. He has spoken at numerous venues including the Vatican, Oxford University, London's Thomas More Center, the Venice Institute, Sicily's Ettore Majorana center, as well as many American colleges and universities. He can be found on the web at karlgiberson.com, followed on Twitter at @gibersok, and has a professional Facebook page.*

DEIRDRE J. GOOD

Biblical Theology

Social media has changed our world. In terms of scholarship and teaching, we are limited only by what can imagine would enhance pedagogy or what we can actually bring about. I've used blog posts and discussions to develop course materials. I use Facebook and Twitter regularly and I blog infrequently. I'm presently co-editing a volume on theological education and I use Google chat for regular consultations with authors writing for the volume. For teaching online I presently use Moodle and Zoom.

I began to use the web & bible software in classroom teaching in the 80's as an early adopter at the seminary where I taught. I was the first member of the Faculty to exploit online technology, even before the communications infrastructure was fully able to support timely delivery of course materials. One course I taught offered resources in how to teach the Bible in congregational settings. In this course, students prepare and are videotaped conducting parish Lenten programs using learner-based teaching techniques. When I began to teach online with Blackboard and then Moodle, I either made my own podcasts to accompany written materials or commissioned professional file makers to film short segments on course materials supplying course content.

Teaching an *Introduction to Koine Greek* course online was one of the most challenging courses I've developed and probably not one of the most successful.

In this regard, a seminary with limited technological resources is very different from a large research university. In 2010 I successfully applied for an Online Course for Theological Faculty Teaching Online from the Wabash Center for Teaching and Learning in Theology and Religion to adapt introductory courses for online delivery and to learn more about online delivery methods.

We used social media to promote and report on a hybrid course on Matthew's Gospel I taught with a colleague in the fall of 2016. With a nearby church as a community of accountability, the weekly class brought together parishioners and seminarians from all degree programs. Classes blended online discussions between the two communities as a way of deepening and expanding learning and formation. Questions from congregants often drove discussions: "Who is Jesus in Matthew?" asked a parishioner in a class on Matthew's birth narrative. Classroom and church were a two-way street. We explored and recorded embodiment as part of the fabric of acted biblical interpretative methods and as productive of meaning. The parable of Matthew's wheat and tares came alive in new ways as embodiment produced congeniality and connection among the younger students and the older parishioners. We understood the interconnectedness of opposites, the commonalities and differentials in seemingly distinctive destinies — and we enjoyed being together. By abandoning the value judgments implicit in the parable, we can joyfully say that the joint class itself was such an enactment.

For class assignments later in the semester, students visited parishioners and taught Matthew through interpretative dialogue to parishioners as engaged participants. Students also participated in worship at the parish church using an Advent passage from Matthew. Three days later both groups reprised that experience in the seminary Chapel which involved a recorded "mannequin challenge" to embody the message of the selected passage. In these ways the class also explored and developed understandings of oral pedagogies, oral interpretative methods, and the diversity of expressiveness that oral communication allows. Altogether, these were experiences that knit a community of learners and secured an environment of shared production of knowledge and meaning.

We studied Matthew as literature, theology, and the addressing of a marginalized, emergent community, straddling an old story even as it began its own version of that story, and all in an imperial context. Our interpretative maneuvers moved between Matthew's ancient historical and literary contexts and its analytical relevance to issues today. Conjoining the biblical studies classroom with a congregation added unaccustomed dimensions for both groups. The adventurousness of the academy was offered reality checks in translatability and relevance by the presence of a community of accountability. Parishioner study participants found themselves stretched and their understandings enhanced by classroom conversations. Studying Matthew in this way enables us to enact its past as though present and unfolding. We straddled an old story, perceived its new versions, and created pathways for ongoing exploration.

Elizabeth Drescher claimed prematurely in 2014 that social media saved General Theological Seminary (https://medium.com/the-narthex/did-social-media-just-save-general-seminary). Although the majority of the faculty including me departed from that institution within the year, her point was well taken. While we had no exceptional social media skills, we were able to use social media to inform interested parties about the evolving 2014-15 seminary controversy primarily because we believed that our issues needed to be aired in public. In addition, faculty colleagues at other institutions started a petition to support us that thousands of faculty across the world signed, whilst other colleagues and friends started a fund to support us financially when the Board accepted our (untended) resignations. Others stepped forward to help, for example in creating a website preserving information about and documents relating to events of that year (see http://www.safeseminary.net/).

Although we left the seminary, use of social media helped to create, explain and publicize issues at stake in our particular situation that we have come to see now as part of far broader and ongoing crises in theological schools and seminary education across the country. We are considering publishing materials on crises in seminary education that will bring the most benefit to everyone who has gone or is going through particular theological school and seminary catastrophes across the country.

I am presently on the advisory committee of American Values, Religious Voices (valuesandvoices.com). "American Values Religious Voices: 100 Days. 100 Letters" is a national nonpartisan campaign that brings together scholars from a diverse range of religious traditions to articulate core American values that have grounded our nation in the past and should guide us forward at this time of transition. For the first 100 days of the new administration, we will send a one-page letter to President Trump, Vice President Pence, Cabinet Secretaries, and Members of the House and the Senate. The letters offer insight and inspiration drawn from the collective wisdom of our faith communities and their sacred texts." Prof Andrea Weiss conceived the project. There are now over 2,000 subscribers. The campaign is on Facebook, Twitter and Instagram @ValuesandVoices and will be published as a book.

I spend several hours each day searching for and improving online course materials even as courses are underway and this time includes use of social media. In a recent temporary position, I was able to draw on skills of reference librarians in the excellent university library that helped to educate me and expand teaching resources and my online publications.

If I were to recommend three things to scholars considering using social media, they would be the following:

1. Get training from your IT department, your local library, and your local Apple store to expand your awareness of online research, social media resources, and other technological possibilities.
2. Do not hesitate to ask for help and information from younger colleagues.
3. Go regularly to conferences on technology & social media.
4. Apply for workshops and funding to develop your technological and social media skills.

Deirdre J. Good is Theologian in Residence at Trinity Wall Street and was Academic Dean at General Theological Seminary. In 2016-7 she was Interim Associate Academic Dean at Drew Theological School. She was Professor of New Testament at General from 1986-2015, and prior to that served as the chair of the religion department at Agnes Scott College, as well as on the religious studies faculty at Valparaiso University. She is a graduate of The University of St Andrews, Cambridge University, Union Theological Seminary, and Harvard University Divinity School, where she completed her doctoral studies. She is the author of many scholarly articles and the author and co-author of numerous books, including Jesus' Family Values, Jesus the Meek King and Mariam, the Magdalen, and the Mother. While she is an American citizen, she grew up in Kenya where her parents were missionaries. Deirdre Good blogs occasionally at notbeingasausage.blogspot.com, is an avid Facebook and Twitter user (@good_deirdre), and occasional Instagram, LinkedIn, YouTube, and Google+ user.

MICHAEL J. GORMAN

Biblical Theology

T he social media I have used include both a web/blog site, with the platform WordPress, and Facebook. The web site used to be primary for me, but now Facebook is. I also have a Twitter account but seldom use it.

General Reflections

I began using the web site in 2007 for four reasons: (1) to have a space for some theological, biblical, and spiritual-pastoral musings that were serious but not publication-length; (2) to test or preview articles or books that were in preparation — to whet people's appetites; (3) to publicize publications, lectures, courses, study trips, etc.; and (4) to review, critique, or advertise the work of colleagues and friends.

Today I use Facebook for the same sorts of things, though I use my web site much less. (At the same time, naturally, I use Facebook for more personal things — photos, family news, political commentary, etc.)

Additionally, I also find Facebook to be helpful in other ways because it is more interactive than one's own web site/blog. For instance, I depend on Facebook for learning about the publication of new books that matter to some of my friends and colleagues. (Of course, I use many other resources for such information.) I also occasionally use Facebook for "crowd-sourcing" about such things as recommended texts for courses or resources for research. Facebook is also useful for learning about conferences and, in the case of scholarly pages that one "likes" or to which one is invited, for learning about new publications, discoveries, etc.

I depend on Facebook for the various kinds of information provided by colleagues: links to news, book reviews, and book announcements; discussions about scholarly issues; and ruminations about their own research in which they may be soliciting input.

Both Facebook and my web site have been useful for alerting people to conferences, professional meetings, and the like in which I am involved. For instance, I often give recommendations about sessions of the SBL (Society of Biblical Literature) annual meeting to attend. They have proven similarly useful for notifying people about lectures I give and study tours I lead. Just in the last year, dozens of people have told me that they heard about, and then attended, one of my lectures at a university, seminary, or church near them because of a blog or Facebook post. Although I have sometimes hesitated to "advertise" such events, the results are beneficial from both me and (I hope) the attendees.

Similarly, as I was writing this essay, I was also preparing to lead a study tour, called "The Cities of John and Paul," to Turkey, Greece, and Italy. Two people joined that tour because of Facebook and blog posts. One woman from Alaska heard about the trip from a mutual friend, Scot McKnight, who saw the trip notice on Facebook. Another woman, from London, "googled" something like "footsteps of Paul study tour," and the first hit was a link to an announcement on my website. Both women, it turned out, were writers who were working on projects related to Paul—one a spiritual work, the other a novel. Each benefited immensely from the trip and also contributed much to the journey and all participants.

Specifically Academic Uses

On the more academic side of things, I have been surprised at what a serious kind of platform social media can be for scholarship and for theological conversation. That was true for the web site and is still true for Facebook.

Especially important is the give-and-take atmosphere of a blog or Facebook post. Of course, the comments and exchanges are generally not long, but starting a conversation that brings in voices from everywhere (literally, sometimes) is extremely valuable and almost impossible to replicate in any other forum, even academic conferences. Naturally, the depth of a book-review panel or in-depth discussion of a topic for hours is not present, but what is present—variety, speed, links to other resources, etc.—can be rather amazing.

I have been rather constantly amazed at how in-depth and perceptive many of the comments are on my blog posts and even my Facebook posts. Similarly, I have been surprised at the quality of many of the online blog-site reviews of my published work. Unfortunately, some of these comments and all reviews come in response to already published work, which does not allow me to change what I have written. But they do provide avenues for new thoughts and even for new projects.

In 2009, for instance, an astute reader of my work and my blog raised a really interesting question about my recently published book—a question I had not at all addressed. This provoked me to do some serious reflection and then online writing in response to the question.

One blog-site review seriously challenged something fundamental about the same book. That led to a new book, on that exact subject, by 2015.

Especially enjoyable for me has been posting excerpts from work in progress. Seldom does this result in new projects or major breakthroughs, but often it results in the kind of fine-tuning that one expects from peers whom one asks them to read one's work. But these reactions come, not from the "usual suspects," so to speak—which is refreshing.

I have greatly profited from the fact that social media constitute an international forum. I regularly hear from or about scholars from India, Myanmar, and various countries in Africa. This not only informs me but also enriches my own perspectives and work.

In effect, then, I see the various forms of social media as extensions of my informal theological discussion group, on the one hand, and of my classroom/ seminar room/lecture hall, on the other. It is the latter dimension of social media that I hope to utilize more in the future. I have posted, and will continue to post even more, links to videos of my public lectures, overviews of selected topics, summaries of my thoughts on various biblical and theological issues, and so on.

Some Practicalities

Since I do not have a smart phone (flip phone only!), I am not constantly bombarded by email, Facebook posts, and the like except when I am at my computer. I look at social media at the beginning and end of each day; at the start and end of other computer sessions during the day; and then occasionally during long computer sessions (i.e., writing projects)—as a sort of "reward" or break. I refuse to let

Facebook take more than a few minutes at a time, however, and I try to scan quickly to look for posts by people on whom I rely for up-do-date book notices and other interesting posts.

If I were giving advice to scholars considering social media, I'd first of all definitely encourage using it, both for getting one's own thoughts, publications, and news out there and also for hearing about and from other scholars. Second, I would keep my list of "friends," or at least the friends I follow, on Facebook relatively small and relevant. Build a network of scholars who regularly post reviews, links, book and conference notices, and the like. Third, I would be cautious about what I post, both in terms of whom I criticize and how, and in terms of what I reveal about current projects and the like. Facebook material is not copyrighted, to the best of my knowledge. And a fourth: keep in mind that Facebook is generally for short posts and for links, including links to one's own web site. The use of both together can be profitable.

———————

Michael J. Gorman is a United Methodist layperson and holds the Raymond E. Brown Chair in Biblical Studies and Theology at St. Mary's Seminary & University in Baltimore, Maryland, where he previously served as dean of St. Mary's Ecumenical Institute. He has published numerous articles and is the author or editor of a dozen books on the apostle Paul, the book of Revelation, Christian ethics, and biblical interpretation. Gorman is on Facebook (https://www.facebook.com/michael.gorman.587) and has a web site, "Cross Talk ~ crux probat omnia / Life through the lens of the cross / Biblical and theological reflections by Michael J. Gorman" (www.michaeljgorman.net).

ANDREW GRAYSTONE

Theology and Media

In the digital environment I have many names. I create and control different personas—all of them expressing aspects of the whole "me." But what is the impact of living with multiple identities? For instance, am I *more* or *less* honest online? Would using a pseudonym help me to be more myself? What is the relationship between the digital "Andrew" and the Andrew I see in the mirror?

There's a story in Mark's gospel in which Jesus encounters a man who is described as being demon-possessed. Uniquely in the gospels, Jesus asks him his name. And he receives a very strange answer. "My name is Legion," the man says, "for we are many." It's an extraordinary phrase. After all, in common usage we assume that every human body is in possession of a single self. If one body has multiple or competing personas we tend to say that person is mentally ill—perhaps schizophrenic.

Lots of Bible commentators have said that the story of Legion is the story of Jesus healing someone who was mentally ill. I'm not so sure. Maybe, in his meeting with Legion, Jesus is signifying a wider truth about the need for us to have an integrity between the embodied person we are and the personalities we express. Maybe this healing is a pattern of how God can heal *dis*-integrated personalities. Maybe this poor man has been the subject of what today we might call identity theft. Aspects of his personality have been stolen by malevolent forces, and he needs to be restored to singularity. Through meeting with Jesus, Legion regains "his right mind". And the integrity he finds is so remarkable that it is actually frightening to the crowds who see it.

Well, *my* name is Legion too, for there are many of me. There are my four email addresses for a start, all a bit like my real name but not quite. Then there's the name I use on Twitter. To the members of my online church I'm called Radioman—that's my screen name. And my internet bank said my real name had already been taken, so I had to make up a new one. I could go on.

In a Multi-User Domain like *Second Life* I can create and control multiple personas. According to my choices they can be male or female, human, animal or some entirely fictitious species. They can have any conceivable form of sexuality or personality. They can even interact with each other whilst under my control. I can take them into situations and behaviors that I wouldn't dream of going to in the off-line world. But crucially, all of these personae are generated by the one embodied form that is essential to who I am—the bloke typing these words right now.

When my physical heart stops beating, almost all of those online personas I have created will end with me. So they could be considered as cultural expressions of my self—like animated works of art expressing fragments of my personality. But some of these creations have such an independence from me that—like Frankenstein's monster—they are no longer under my direct control. My email account continues to scan for mail on my behalf and send messages in my name when I am "out of office". If I create a "bot" in a Multi-User Domain it will continue to interact with other avatars even when my computer is switched off. A friend's *Facebook* account continues to be active five years after his death. Like *The Picture of Dorian Grey* his online self seems to have a life of its own.

I've been interested to see how different digital platforms bring out different aspects of my personality. Twitter has a way of bringing out the cheeky side of me. When I use email I tend to be quite efficient—it's a place for doing business. I think I'm funnier at St Pixels (my online church) than I am at home, because the context brings out a type of humor that my wife and kids just don't get. There's nothing wrong with that, though it does cause me problems sometimes. The other day I thought of a joke and I immediately thought it would go down well on Twitter. But then I remembered that lots of people who follow me on Twitter do so because they've met me in a work context—and I decided the joke was just a bit too raunchy for some of them.

There's nothing exclusively digital about this. In off-line life I express different aspects of my personality in different contexts. I use one sort of language when I'm talking to my children, and a slightly different language set when I'm talking to my pastor. But each of these personas relates directly back to the physical "me" who is writing these words—the me that is five feet six, balding and a bit overweight. Christian holiness requires that I don't behave in one way in private and another in public—or behave online in ways that I wouldn't behave off-line. In other words, Christians believe in the sacredness and the singularity of the embodied person. The integrity of personality is a goal in human wellness. It's fine to express yourself in many different ways in many different places, as long as they all connect back to the real, embodied, off-line you. But if the digital environment leads us into contradictions or compromises, we're in trouble. If I say to my wife "I love you in an off-line kind of way" she has every right to get a bit worried. If my Second Life avatar starts sharing stuff with someone else's Second Life avatar that I wouldn't want my pastor to see, that's a problem.

And that's where Legion had got himself confused. He was afflicted by a muddle of conflicting personalities. To use Sherry Turkle's phrase, he was asking "Who am we?" That's why it's so significant that Jesus asked him his name—the only time he does this with anybody. Maybe Jesus looks at me joking away on Twitter, working away on email, preaching away at church, loving away in my family, and says "Andrew, who are you?"

Legion's problems before meeting Jesus weren't just psychological but also social dis-integration. The crowd didn't know him—they were scared of him, and they kicked him out. Crowds can do that. That's why bullying is so rife in the online world—and I don't just mean the obvious schoolboy name-calling. There are much more subtle forms of bullying. "I've got more followers than you have." "Share this link or you're not really a good friend." "Me and my friends share jokes that you don't even understand."

The psychologist Erik Erikson said that for a person to be mentally healthy they had to have a clear understanding of who they are, and that has to match with who other people think they are. So if I think I'm Brad Pitt's better-looking cousin, but you think I'm an idiot, I have a problem. Or if I think I'm a great church leader, but you don't, I have a problem. Erikson called that "an identity crisis." This distinction becomes important in the digital context. Being known consistently and corporeally by others is essential to the way we understand ourselves as Christians.

Consider my household electricity bill. Some years ago a meter reader would visit my house four times a year with a torch and read the meter in the cupboard under the stairs. He would write the reading beside my name and address, and take it back to an office, where a clerk would calculate my bill and post it to me. There may have been some mechanization in the calculation, and I may never have met the clerk, but the process was essentially human-to-human. In the digital environment the entire contract is mechanized. My digital meter is read remotely by a computer, which attaches the serial number of the meter to my account number. The computer calculates the bill and generates an invoice. Since I have a standing order with the bank to pay the bill, the electricity company's computer automatically exchanges my account number with my bank's computer and the money is transferred. The transaction is notified to me by email, but unfortunately it goes into my "junk" folder and is automatically deleted! There are human beings working at the electricity company who are eventually paid for their work, and there are human beings in my family who are warmed by the electricity. But everything about the transaction between the two is automated and pseudonymous. The process is convenient and cheap, but the possibility of personal transaction — from offering a cup of tea to the meter reader to pleading for an extension on the payments — is all but lost.

Much of the rhetoric of the internet has suggested that this is a good thing. We are advised to treat cyberspace as a dangerous place, and to protect ourselves by carefully guarding our pseudonymity. This is unfortunate on several counts. First, as Nancy Baym's research has demonstrated, in most cases people are more, not less honest online than they are in person. Second, in spite of the absence of non-verbal clues on which much human interaction depends, and however hard one might try to disguise one's identity online, in many cases the individual gives away far more about themselves than they could possibly control. And third, it is naïve to suppose that just because you use a screen name in conversation with other users, there isn't a massive collation of meta-information by the owners of websites and ISPs.

An alternative and more holistic approach might be to encourage users clearly to "sign" their digital presence; to identify themselves unmistakably by reference to their embodied self in all expressions in the digital engagement. The creation of digital stuff (blogs, tweets, avatars, texts or whatever) that can't be linked to an embodied individual diminishes the personhood of the creator, and also of the consumer of that stuff. Just think how you feel when you get a text that has an opaque message, and you can't for the life of you work out who it's from. So I always use my real name on Twitter and Facebook. I use a screenname at my online church because there isn't an option to use my own name, but I make sure that my avatar can easily be linked to my given name. And I will never respond to a blog or an email that is written anonymously. As Jesus demonstrated in his encounter with Legion, naming is fundamental to human dignity and to holiness in relationship.

Perhaps we need to institute the digital equivalent of the Fair Trade movement. The Fair Trade movement has humanized the two ends of the production chain. The farmer who produces my coffee knows that it will eventually be drunk by a real individual human being with rights and dignity; and the one who drinks it knows that it was produced by a real human being with the same rights and dignity. This recognition of the sacred individuality of the human being is the beginning of justice. Similarly in the digital environment, we need to make every effort to retain the humanity of the one who produces content and the one who consumes it.

I'm sure we need to hang on to the singularity of personality as a goal in Christian holiness. And we should assert that those with whom we meet in embodied personhood — with whom we share houses, streets, or bread and wine — will always remain our primary community. Perhaps the answer to the question "Who am we?" is, "I am many things, but they are all me."

Andrew Graystone was a TV producer for BBC Religion and broadcasts frequently on religion and politics. He teaches communications and Christian ethics at the Nazarene Theological College in Manchester, where he is also a governor. His MA explored models of regulation in the digital environment. He is currently working on a doctorate looking at ways in which digital culture impacts theological notions of embodiment. He is a visiting Fellow of St John's College, Durham. Andrew is a member of a messy multi-cultural Nazarene church in Manchester, where runs the crèche. Andrew tweets @AndrewGraystone. Most of his tweets are either jokes or snarky comments about left-wing politics and the nonsense of church life. He regrets approximately one in every three tweets. He uses Facebook intermittently as Andrew Graystone, and also manages accounts for a pre-school nursery (Charnwood Trust) and an evangelistic project (One Friday.) He maintains a blog at www .mediafutures.info, mostly as a way for people to get in touch with him, or as a place to publish random bits of journalism or commentary.

CHRIS E. W. GREEN

Systematic Theology

use Facebook, Instagram, Medium, and Twitter—the last by far the most. And since many of my followers are the same across the various media, I try most of the time to use them differently toward distinct ends. As a rule, I find Facebook and Instagram work best for personal matters, while Twitter and Medium work best for my scholarship and ministry. Hence, I tend to post family updates and pictures of my wife and kids on Facebook or Instagram during my "down time," and to use Twitter during the workday while I'm writing and doing research, often to share quotes from or reflections on the texts I'm reading at the time. I have been known to break my own rules, however—fairly often, in fact. So, from time to time I share my art or findings from my studies on Facebook and post family-related updates or throw out other personal anecdotes on Twitter.

In the beginning, I didn't engage online with anything like a plan or agenda. And I gave no thought either to the gains or to the losses that might be involved. I simply stumbled into using the various platforms, and found myself trying out various modes of engaging along the way. I quickly discovered, however, that social media (rightly engaged) have a unique gift to offer scholars and ministers: they put us in touch with a great number of people we could not have met otherwise and from whom we have a great deal to learn. Through the peculiar engagements which social media make possible, we are positioned to see, hear, and read beyond the orbit of our day-to-day lives and the ordinary limits of our experience and expertise — which for obvious reasons opens us to incredible possibility even while it puts us at unanticipated risks.

I might say, using Augustinian terms, that I both *use* and *enjoy* social media; they are, in different ways and at different times, for me both means and ends. Certainly, much of the benefit as well as much of the enjoyment come by simply "eavesdropping" on the conversations of others. Other uses and joys come from the responses I receive to my work, and from the response that I am able to give to others. Occasionally, I'll post thoughts of my own — sometimes in the form of a "tweet storm," although usually in much shorter form — , inviting constructive engagement from those who read it. More often than not, I get responses that do in fact prove helpful.

Much of the time, I simply lurk — and learn. To cite but one example of many: thanks to social media, I, like so many others during and after the killing of Michael Brown in Ferguson, MO, have been able to see a bit more clearly the depth and complexity of the racism endemic to our society. Of course, I had been aware of that racism for a long time. And I had tried to combat it personally, ministerially, and professionally. But the relationships that have been made possible for me through social media have given me the chance to see the abuses from perspectives I never would have found on my own. Precisely in that way, it has called me to deeper and wider awareness of the racist tendencies still at work in my own affections and imagination, as well as my responsibility to my neighbors, black and white.

Surprisingly often, my engagement online raises questions and concerns that become fuel for my research, writing, and/or preaching. For example, a few years ago, one of the pastors whom I follow on Twitter asked how Christians ought to think about disagreement in theological terms (and not just in pastoral, ethical, or sociological terms, as it is often couched). I was intrigued, and so started reading and reflecting. Eventually, I wrote a paper putting forward a proposed theology of disagreement rooted in the possibility of God surprising God, which I presented at a conference. Later, I published a revision of the paper as an article in a peer-review academic journal. A few other examples also come to mind. Right now, I'm finishing up a paper on the Trinity and divine agency for a collected volume edited by a friend I met on Twitter. A few weeks before Lent, a couple of pastors asked me to share my thoughts on the lectionary readings for the season, and so each week through the season, I posted those reflections on Medium. Besides all that, I'm also using Medium for a long-term project offering theological commentary on difficult passages in scripture, beginning with the epistle of Jude. I consider this open-access theologizing a way of putting my scholarly work to use beyond the academy for the sake of various churches and ministers I can't serve in other more direct ways.

It is easy to waste time online, of course. And it is easy to over-share, to press too deeply into someone else's business, or to get overwrought in the heat of back-and-forth debates. But these challenges and temptations notwithstanding, the relationships that social media make possible are very much worth the trouble of facing those challenges and temptations. We can and should take the time needed to learn to navigate online engagements wisely. And while I would not want to downplay the unique interpersonal, psychosocial, and spiritual dynamics that social media bring into play, I also do not want to lose sight of the fact that they provide us the possibility of engaging one another humanely and so transformatively.

Needless to say, I would not want to insist that every scholar and every minister should be present online or make use of social media. But I would say that I find the platforms a remarkably helpful way of doing and sharing work that matters for the church. For example, as a theologian, I believe that I am called to work toward the visible uniting of the church, and social media provide a unique and remarkably expansive "space" for the necessary conversations to take place. I could turn away from that space only if I were convinced that what was taking place there were detrimental to that end. But Lord knows that more good happens more often in that informal space than typically takes place in formal dialogues.

With that in mind, I might make the following recommendations to those scholars and ministers who are considering using social media for the first time or considering changing the way they have been using them until now. First, as should be expected given what I have already said, I'd recommend using social media as a way of eavesdropping on conversations we would never hear otherwise, and meeting people we'd never meet "in real life." There are so many good and wise people who can help us live more truthfully and lovingly; we stand to gain by giving our attention to them. Second, I'd recommend regularly asking followers to provide suggestions for new lines of research and study (books to read; themes to research; scholars to follow, etc.). Feedback of this kind is invaluable for teachers and researchers; especially those who like me can get locked into their own circles of thought. Third, I'd recommend using social media to share updates about one's own work or to share some of what seem the most important parts of that work. It can be good to share more personally, as well. As I said, I use these various media to share my artwork and snippets from books and papers I'm reading or writing. If done in the right spirit and at the right time (if not done too often!), this kind of sharing becomes an invitation for others to engage in formative and enriching conversation. Fourth, I'd recommend using social media to help "spread the word" about other scholars whose work needs to be noticed and appreciated. This is especially true, I think, for young scholars who are trying to find their place in the academy, and of scholars whose work has been unfortunately or unjustly neglected.

Chris E.W. Green is Associate Professor of Theology at Pentecostal Theological Seminary in Cleveland, TN, and Teaching Pastor at Sanctuary Church in Tulsa, Oklahoma. He is award-winning teacher, and the author or editor of four books and a number of academic articles and essays. His research interests include systematic theology, philosophical hermeneutics and epistemology, and the intersection of theology, aesthetics, and culture. Find Chris at Twitter: @cewgreen; Instagram: @cewgreen; Medium: @cewgreen; and Facebook: Chris Green

JOEL B. GREEN

Biblical Theology

I use Academia.edu, Mendeley, Twitter, and Facebook. I maintain two Twitter accounts and two Facebook accounts, with the second related to my editing a website for seminarians and pastors (catalystresources.org). For closed groups, I also use programs like Slack, Trello, and Asana for project-related communication, tracking, and document sharing.

My interests have shifted over time, so that different platforms have been primary at different times. For example, because of its "circles" feature, for several years I used Google+ to pass along research tips and job possibilities to my PhD students. This worked early on, when more of my students used Google+; with waning participation on their part, though, I've shifted to an email list.

I first joined Facebook because my social-media savvy daughter informed me about ten years ago of a page called "Joel B. Green Is My Homeboy." The page had been created by a former student, and I wanted to see the page and participate in the discussion. Changes with Facebook mean that this page disappeared years ago, but I've remained on Facebook and expanded my social media footprint.

Today, I use social media for a range of reasons—e.g., to encourage awareness of research into human origins or neuroscience of interest to biblical scholars and theologians, to direct traffic to my own or others' online materials (podcasts, reviews, blogs, essays, interviews), to highlight my print publications (or print publications with which I am associated as editor), to draw attention to my speaking calendar, and to manage projects within a group. From time to time, I also use Twitter or Facebook to publicize events at my institution, especially those related to the Fuller Faith and Science Group or the School of Theology.

Since my email address is readily available online, I'm often surprised by how people use social media to contact me. Prospective students ask questions about programs at Fuller Seminary or graduate students at other institutions ask research-oriented questions — using Facebook's messenger feature or Twitter's direct message feature. From time to time, Twitter users ask me New Testament translation issues, for book recommendations, or to address a theological question that really can't be answered in 140 characters!

Some of my former students have been tweeting through the Bible, one tweet for each chapter each day. When they reached the Gospel of Luke and the Acts of the Apostles, they invited me to participate. Writing such short "commentaries" on each chapter in Luke-Acts was a lot of fun for me, and I was shocked by the amount of attention those tweets attracted. One of the media guys at Fuller Seminary even gave them an afterlife by collecting them into two "Twitter commentaries."

I'm not as much of a consumer of social media as I am a supplier. Even so, I've found various social media, as well as a news aggregator like Feedly, indispensable for alerting me to what my colleagues are thinking or writing.

I'm an early riser, and part of my daily, early-morning workflow is to check various media. Throughout the day, I will return to one or another application once or twice. For posting my own materials, I tend to depend on Buffer, which shares my content at strategic times rather than when I happen to be online.

I'd recommend the following three things to scholars considering social media:

(1) Decide what you want social media to do for you, and stick to that agenda.
(2) Protect your public persona by thinking carefully about what and where to post.
(3) Set a time, whether internal or external, to ensure that social media doesn't claim too much time. Talking about work isn't the same as getting the work done.

Joel B. Green, PhD, is a biblical scholar and theologian with cross-disciplinary interests in theological interpretation of Scripture and the interface of neuroscience and theological anthropology. He is the provost, dean of the school of theology, and professor of New Testament interpretation at Fuller Theological Seminary. He has written or edited more than 45 books. Green maintains a personal website at JoelBGreen.com. His Twitter handle is @JoelBGreen, and he can also be found on Facebook (Joel B. Green) and Academia.edu (fuller.academia.edu/JoelBGreen). He still thinks Google+ was a good idea (+JoelBGreen).

DAVID P. GUSHEE

Christian Ethics

I use a personal Twitter, Facebook ("public figure" and personal), Instagram, and website, and blog exclusively at Religion News Service, the latest of multiple different blog platforms I have used over the past three decades. I also have professional social media platforms for my Center for Theology and Public Life, Society of Christian Ethics, and for the church I am pastoring. So it all adds up to something like ten different social media platforms. I am most personally active on my personal Twitter account: @dpgushee. I have others manage all the rest of them.

In terms of the genealogy of my social media work, it precedes social media. There was a time when scholars and regular people wrote articles. They were called "opinion pieces." (I was trained in a social ethics tradition where this work was seen as very important.) They were typed on typewriters or computers and then sent to newspapers. Then they were printed on newsprint and mailed. Hard to believe, but true. I began doing that in the mid-1980s.

With each change in media environment, I have adapted. Print articles gave way to online articles, in various sites, some of which no longer exist. Eventually Facebook came along and became a place to write. Then Twitter followed and became a place to tweet a thought briefly or, of course, to link to a longer piece. Then we learned there is an art to getting people's attention, and that desirable platforms changed. So I have rolled along with the changes for 30 years, all with the same purpose—to get my ideas out to the church and to the world. I do now increasingly feel like social media is getting "beyond me" or sometimes "beneath me." That is, I am having trouble keeping up with the latest technical and strategic innovations, and I am having trouble stomaching the increasing negativity and division. I vacillate between wanting to get better at social media and wanting to abandon it.

I have been surprised at virality. When my book called *Changing Our Mind* came out in November 2014, it was my first full experience of social-media virality. Jonathan Merritt of Religion News Service did an exclusive feature article and interview with me on the book, and then a few days later I spoke at the Reformation Project meeting, in an address that was called "historic" by some. The Friday afternoon that the Merritt article came out, it bounced around the world on social media to such an extent that I was astonished. After a while it seemed as if no one in Christendom or in the gay community had not heard about the book. Then something similar happened with the YouTube of my Reformation Project speech. What I notice is that content matters less than before; what matters is the ability to make a tweet, link, or article go viral.

Of course the other meaning of virality is "like a virus," and social media is a virus or, better, carries viruses, in the sense of pathogens. I have been surprised at the viciousness of social media; at the way in which friendships break up almost daily based on, say, Facebook posts, and at the experience of being Twitter-stalked and Twitter-bombed by swarms of viral enemies.

When I was very actively on Facebook, and used a personal page exclusively, I found it eating up both my time and my energy. I was so constantly distressed by my own arguments with (former) friends, or by my friends' arguments with one another, that it cost me sleep and happiness. In the summer of 2016 I gave up, unplugging my personal page and retaining only the "public figure" page, to be managed by staff.

Finally, in early May 2017, I decided I needed and wanted to get back on a personal Facebook page, but with a smarter approach. My personal page will only be for personal stuff. I will not post or repost articles there, or engage in arguments. We will see how this new method goes.

I now think of social media mainly as advertising—as almost literally a 'platform' for lifting up my ideas and causes and getting them some attention. I have also concluded that it is best for others to manage my online presence.

I recommend several things to those considering using social media. First, don't forget that social media is not the same as academic publishing. Don't get distracted from the publishing that academia still requires. Second, don't forget the invaluable concept of peer review, which is entirely lost or skewed in the land of social media. Third, don't forget that academic freedom protections may not apply to what you say on social media. Fourth, don't forget that people can be vicious on social media, and it is a great place to lose friends. And finally, don't forget that social media skews young. Those of us who are not young but try to keep up youthful appearances can end up looking pretty foolish.

———————————

Rev. Dr. David P. Gushee is Distinguished University Professor of Christian Ethics and Director of the Center for Theology and Public Life at Mercer University. One of the premier ethical thinkers in American Christianity, he is the author of 21 books. He serves as President-Elect of the American Academy of Religion and President of the Society of Christian Ethics. He is the pastor of the 1400-member First Baptist Church of Decatur, Georgia. Find David Gushee on Facebook (https://www.facebook .com/dpgushee/), Twitter (https://twitter.com/dpgushee), and Instagram (https:// www.instagram.com/dpgushee/) . See also his work at http://religionnews.com /columns/david-gushee/ and the Center for Theology and Public Life: https:// twitter.com/ctplmercer

NATHAN HAMM

Theology and Media

'm not a theologian, but I play one on social media. And I do mean play. If you want to do social media theology in a creative and compelling way, it's crucial to learn to take your work seriously without taking yourself too seriously.

`For as long as I can remember, I've loved making things and sharing them with other people. Stories, poems, songs, photos, videos. I began using social media so I could make things and share them online. I wanted to create new things, to connect with new people, and to communicate in new ways without needing any kind of outside permission or approval. On social media, there are no gate-keepers. For good or for ill, you can share almost anything, anytime, anywhere. That's both the promise and the peril of social media.

Although I wasn't exactly an early adopter of social media, once I ventured online, I recognized its immense potential for creativity, connection, and communication. Like most folks my age, I started out on Facebook, long before it turned into the internet behemoth it is today. A few years later I joined Twitter, which quickly overtook Facebook as my favorite social media platform. When I started making videos and short films, I launched a YouTube channel. Then I moved onto Patreon, an innovative crowdfunding site that provides ongoing financial support to virtually every kind of artist and creator imaginable.

Social media is full of religiosity, but social media theology may sound like an oxymoron. Theology is all about the eternal and social media is all about the ephemeral, right? What does Christian theology have to do with cat videos? But theology isn't just what we believe about God. It's how we live with God and our neighbors and all creation. Social media is a significant part of life for more and more people around the world. As we become ever more connected to one another online, the question may become, not if we do theology on social media, but how we do theology on social media.

Not that it's easy. When I first joined Twitter, I wasn't sure if it was even possible to do good theology in 140 characters. But it's surprising how much you can say in a tweet. A 140 character limit may seem overly restrictive, but it forces you to communicate in creative, compelling, uncluttered ways. For instance, here's my attempt to say something about Jesus and politics in a single tweet:

> The politics of Jesus:
> Love enemies
> Serve the poor
> Welcome refugees
> Make peace, not war
> Do justice & love mercy
> Care for all God's creation

Of course, there's much more you can say about Jesus and politics. But there's not much more you can say in 140 characters. Here's another example. It's one thing to write a book about the loving, inclusive nature of God. It's another thing to write a tweet:

> God invites the uninvited
> welcomes the unwelcome
> includes the excluded
> forgives the unforgiven
> loves the unloved.
> That's what God is like.

I probably shouldn't have been surprised that it's possible to tweet good theology. After all, Jesus was masterful at crafting short, pithy, memorable statements. Just think about the Beatitudes: "Blessed are the poor. . . . Blessed are those who mourn. . . . Blessed are the meek . . ." Every one of the Beatitudes would fit in a tweet. The Beatitudes are the tweet-able Jesus. And Jesus' brief, brilliant statements aren't limited to the Beatitudes or the Sermon on the Mount.

Over time, my tweets evolved into Facebook posts, which developed into YouTube videos. The content remained the same, even while the form changed and morphed as it moved from one social media platform to another. Here's a Facebook post that generated a fair amount of controversy and conversation:

> If you hate Muslims,
> if you despise immigrants,
> if you slander refugees,
> if you oppress people of color,
> if you dehumanize women,
> if you exclude LGBTQ people,
> if you think violence cures violence,
> please don't tell people you follow Jesus.
> You'll ruin it for the rest of us.

Lots of people shared that post and even more people reacted to it. Not all of the reactions were positive either. Social media theology often comes with a cost. You get stoned by your enemies on Twitter and you get crucified by your friends on Facebook. But it's worth it. Again and again, social media allowed me to communicate in new ways and connect with new friends, both online and offline.

Social media even helped my wife Jenny and me start a new church. StoryHouse is an open, inclusive, progressive faith community in Jacksonville, FL. We believe the way of Jesus is a way of love, inclusion, generosity, peacemaking, and creativity. Since our church is rather progressive and our city is rather conservative, it was a challenge to gather an initial core team. Social media helped. Several of the members of that core team were people we originally connected with online. Folks who started out as Facebook friends or Twitter followers ended up helping us give birth to StoryHouse. Along the way, they became some of our closest friends.

These days much of my work involves making things and sharing them online. I tweet on Twitter, post on Facebook, create videos on YouTube, and interact with the friends and supporters on Patreon who make everything else possible. I'm always open to moving onto new social media platforms as well, but only if those platforms offer something new or different or challenging. For its part, StoryHouse has a Facebook page and a Twitter feed, along with its own website. Because I use social media for both my creative work and my work with StoryHouse, not just for news or entertainment, there isn't a wide chasm between my social media life and my real life. There's just life.

Even so, it's still vital for me to find ways to unplug and unwind. In a world that's becoming more and more interconnected and fast-paced by the day, we all need to take a break, take a Sabbath, and take care of ourselves and those around us. As Anne Lamott says, "Almost everything will work again if you unplug it for a few minutes, including you." So don't ever be afraid to take a social media Sabbath. It's good for your social media theology and it's good for your soul.

If you want to do theology on social media, the possibilities are endless. There are all kinds of opportunities to create new things, connect with new people, and communicate in new and compelling ways. Just keep these things in mind:

1. Brevity is beautiful. Keep it short, simple, and uncluttered. Less is almost always more.
2. Online jerks are just jerks. Be humble, patient, and empathetic. Tweet others as you would like to be tweeted.
3. Fun isn't a four-letter word. Work on your theology and play on your social media. You'll be glad you did.

———————————

Nathan Hamm is a storyteller, creative, social media theologian, and the founder of StoryHouse, a church for the rest of us. He makes things and shares them online. You can find his videos and stories on YouTube, Facebook, and Twitter. If you resonate with what he creates, you can support his work at patreon.com/NathanHamm.

MICHAEL HARDIN

Theology and Ethics

Jerry Garcia says about life, "what a long strange trip it's been." This is true of my journey with social media. From 2002-2012 my main form of communication was my website (Preaching Peace). I began a Facebook personal page sometime around 2009 (as I recall), and eventually we created a Facebook page for Preaching Peace. I also have a Twitter account and it will soon be coordinated with Facebook and the Preaching peace website, up until now Twitter has not been significant for me.

In March 2013, at my wife-business partner's suggestion, I endeavored to do something I was told by others could not be done, viz., use Facebook as a virtual classroom to teach theology. However, I soon discovered there is a niche market all over the planet, consisting of the Nones and the Dones, an audience that is literate, and appreciates the value of rational and empathetic discourse.

Between 2013 and 2016 offers a tale that this essay allows me to look back upon narrate for the first time. Using Facebook as a platform to 'teach theology' has morphed into a full time business [Preaching Peace a 501(c)3] soon to go from two employees (my wife and myself) to eight full time employees. Recounting the three major phases we have undergone as a small non-profit, in my annual report last year (July 31, 2016) I wrote to the Preaching Peace Board,

"The third phase runs from 2013 to the present. In March 2013 I ventured into the world of social media completely unsure of what to do or how to navigate it. It was a steep learning curve. Our audience swelled that first year and was composed primarily of charismatics who had either seen *Hellbound?* (www.hellboundthemovie.com) or had read *Stricken by God?* (Eerdmans, 2007) or *The Jesus Driven Life* (JDL Press, 2nd rev. ed. 2013) or who were seeking to learn about mimetic theory. By 2014 we had reached 1,000 Facebook friends and it was clear that the greatest need of these former charismatics was education and we were poised to meet that need!

In August of 2014 we began running our six-month Mentoring Groups on Facebook and also began to run Reading Groups. These were a huge success with over 650 people involved the first year . . . In addition to all this we have also developed a positive mimetic Mentoring process and we currently mentor some 20-25 persons weekly or monthly. All of these mentees are in a private Personal Mentoring Group I have on Facebook (around 570 persons). This Group has provided 100% of the speaking engagements we will participate in this next fiscal year as well as a many new monthly supporters and other donors."

In certain Native American cultures, spiders are perceived as 'networkers' (as weavers of webs); in the same way if used with discernment one can actually help persons create strong social networks that become the backbone for a 'market' and real needs thus analyzed and solutions found. I have formed almost the entirety of what is poised to become a multi-million dollar a year non-profit almost entirely from social net-working on Facebook.

Facebook, as a platform, encourages feedback but it does not necessarily encourage conversation, and while it does turn relationships into friendships, the geographical distances between such friends precludes any community. Of course Facebook has the option of forming a group around a common interest but almost all so-called 'theological' groups are rather narrow minded and provincial in their mentality and foci. I decided to form social networks around the reading of a common theological book and engaging one another in a (secret) group on Facebook. All of these groups developed sister/tandem 'Fellowship' groups where they could get personal, and over time, some 20 groups of my Facebook friends developed interest in exploring one another's journeys.

We took this idea one step further in 2015 by developing a Mentoring Group with a suggested $210 donation for the six month duration of the group. This donation went straight to the 'manager' of all my Facebook groups and he led them through J. Louis Martyn's commentary on *Galatians*, Henri Nouwen's *The Wounded Healer* and the edited *Common Prayer: A Liturgy for Ordinary Radicals* edited by Shane Claiborne et al. The pedagogical process was such a success that we ran three consecutive six-month Mentoring Groups. Perceiving the need for quality education and listening to the needs of these persons (and paying attention to the demographics), we developed The School of Peace Theology.

My personal Mentoring Group of 600+ persons has no one famous enough to write on Patheos (except for friends already writing on Patheos). They are moms and dads or grandparents, single, work-a-day world folks from all walks of life. They have had so many wonderful things to say to one another in the Facebook Mentoring Group I thought their contributions worthy of Patheos and so turned my Patheos blog into my 'community' blog, the only thing of its kind on Patheos where the voice-of-those-who-have-no-voice because they are not celebrities that attract advertising dollars, have a voice.

Of the current 4,000 Facebook friends on my personal page I would venture to say that between 2-3% are faculty in universities and seminaries, perhaps 5-7% are clergy, and the 90% would be educated laity or those willing and able to engage a learning process. By carefully vetting a) who was accepted as a 'friend' on Facebook and by further vetting whom I would invite to my Personal Mentoring Group I have been able to create 'safe space' for my friends to ask any question they wish and to gain a good foundation for the current state of affairs in numerous disciplines so they are better, more critical readers and thinkers.

I have also eschewed theological/moral litmus tests on social media. Start that stuff on my page and you will be blocked. I might add at this that I have 'Page Rules' which I post fairly regularly, my form of the 12 Commandments; violate these and you will be blocked. One of my rules is "Thou shalt not quote Scripture without exegesis." Social media is replete with Bible thumpers and if one wishes to remain sane unfortunately they must now be allowed in (although I have made exceptions). I do not accept friend requests without first examining a person's page and have criteria by which I accept or deny requests. This goes a long way toward alleviating the troll problem on the Internet.

The biggest surprise of all was turning virtual friendships into face to face real life encounters, meals and walks. It is a given for me now that wherever I go to speak, in the US or the UK, I meet Facebook friends. It has been an honor to meet so many beautiful people from virtually every walk of life. I recall a long weekend in Paris in 2014 with my British friend Rob Grayson, the beautiful hospitality I have experienced on three continents, so many walks and hikes with new face to face friends. This has been my greatest joy.

First, I have been able to use Facebook friends to book speaking tours. For example, last year's trip to the UK (eight locations) was totally book and promoted through Facebook. I stayed with Facebook friends, saving on hotel costs. Second, I use Facebook to promote books I publish to an audience I know will purchase them and recommend them to others. Our monthly book royalties have consistently been four figures each month and I attribute a high percentage of that to Facebook sharing. Third, Using Facebook to create learning groups opened the door for us to create an online educational experience that was more like an ancient forum.

I confess that I allowed myself to get swallowed up in Facebook for three years from 2013-summer of 2016. I wrote long theological posts, around 125-150 a year. I have published the posts from 2013 and 2014 in *What the Facebook?: Posts from the Edge of Christendom*, volumes 1 and 2 (JDL Press); Volume 3 (2015) is due out this year.

Learning to navigate Facebook emotionally was a learning curve. At first I had to learn all about trolls and how not to engage them. This also taught me about myself and forced me to deal with being defensive online. These reflections early on grounded me in my own skin so that whether liked or not, whether trolled or not, I did not invest a single emotional ounce in what actually happened on Facebook. In other words I separated the Facebook persona of who I was from my own internal self-perception so as not get caught up in the mimetic trap that social media is really all about (and why one of the first major investors in Facebook, Peter Thiel, did so because of its mimetic character!).

Know going in that social media is a jungle, a battlefield, often alien and hostile territory. Learn to be a duck and let all things, praise and shame, favor and disfavor roll off your back. Don't get caught up in the mimetic character of social media (or you will lose your mind). I advise the following:

1) Develop rules for engagement on your page and be prepared to block people who troll you.
2) By all means self-promote, but don't just promote yourself. Promote those in your sphere of influence.
3) Share only the truth as you know it and vet your news sources (satire sites can be very, very clever!)
4) Short pithy posts tend to be shared more than longer posts and nobody shares boring posts.
5) Be yourself and don't take anybody's, um, er, scatological comments personally. They don't know what they are doing.

Michael Hardin is the co-founder and Executive Director of Preaching Peace, co-founder of The School of Peace Theology and of Theology and Peace. He has edited or written ten books. His M.Div. (1988) is from North Park Seminary and Michael is almost finished with his PhD in theology at Charles Sturt University. His book The Jesus Driven Life _has been compared to Luther's 95 Theses and Bonhoeffer's_ Discipleship. _Michael is also a singer-songwriter. Hardin's websites include Preaching Peace (www.preachingpeace.com), The School of Peace Theology (www.theschoolofpeacetheology), The Peace of the Gospel (www.thepeaceofthegospel.com), and Making Peace (www.makingpeace.com). He is on Facebook waaaaay too much (Michael Hardin, Preaching Peace Nonprofit Lancaster) and you can follow him on Twitter, @peace_theology. Preaching Peace has a YouTube channel featuring Michael's teaching videos._

JOHN W. HAWTHORNE

Theology and Sociology

I rely heavily on Facebook and Twitter. When I write, I share my material on both platforms. With Facebook, I may share the material in multiple groups depending on the relevance of the topic. When I share information on Facebook, it's usually an article I found interesting and relevant to contemporary conversations about politics and/or religion. I stay away from click-bait or alarmist material. In my own writing, I'm often trying to shed a more nuanced light on contemporary issues. Usually I write because something is nagging me about the shape of coverage of a given topic and I have to add my two cents to keep my mind from dwelling on that thing.

My Twitter strategy is a little different. I use it to gauge what is going on in the broader world (through a somewhat limited lens given the 700 people I follow). When something is intriguing or useful, I will share. When there is an alternative viewpoint or additional data needed, I will often respond.

I started blogging about seven years ago but didn't seriously begin a social media presence until 2013. I was working on my book and knew that having an established platform was important to publishers. Having moved beyond that extrinsic motivation, I know engage because of the democratizing value of social media that Manuel Castells has explored. Social media provides access to a sociologist in a small Christian liberal arts institution in Michigan that I could never have had in previous platforms. I can engage scholars, people at think tanks, researchers, and opinion leaders. I hope this is valuable in sharing a thoughtful progressive evangelical voice into arenas where it was harder to access due to our segmented world.

I've been surprised at how the currency of a topic varies depending on what else is going on in the social media universe. There may be a topic I wish to engage but everybody is distracted by an awards show or an outrageous tweet or post made by some public figure. What I thought was valuable insight got drowned out in the sheer magnitude of activity.

On the other hand, I'm always surprised when people find something out of the archives that they found useful on a given day. It's not clear why some piece I wrote 4 years ago about Christian colleges is relevant this morning.

Yet another example: In February of 2016 I wrote a piece about evangelicals supporting Trump (in the primary). It was titled "Why Are Blonde Women Supporting Trump?" and was about using various demographic characteristics to stand in for other variables when there may be spurious relationships. Approaching the election and since the inauguration, that particular post is picking up a handful of views daily. I'm not sure what makes it still relevant but it keep showing up in searches.

I often use my own blog as a sandbox for exploring ideas. I wrote a series of pieces in March of 2015 on the nature of structural inequality as reflected in the NCAA basketball tournament pairings.

The use of time is the largest challenge to social media engagement. I estimate that I spend at least 2-3 hours per day checking on happenings on Facebook and Twitter. Being aware of what's out there is a legitimate part of my scholarship. It is usually a result of seeing a trend emerge and asking questions about it that prompts me to set aside another 2 hours to write a blog post.

To those considering using social media more, I recommend it be a discipline and not just a random activity. It requires the attention that scholars give to journals or books. It's a rapidly shifting opinion field so currency is more important than depth. Avoid overly strident positioning because it limits your reach. At the same time, being too safe doesn't motivate people to share your insights, which is where the real impact comes in.

John W. Hawthorne, Ph.D. is a sociologist at Spring Arbor University in Michigan. He has spent 35 years in Christian Higher Education as both a senior administrator and a faculty member. His specialties are in the sociology of religion, social inequal-

ity, and Christian Higher Education. He is the author of A First Step in a Much Larger World: The Christian University and Beyond, a book for freshmen entering Christian Colleges, published by Wipf and Stock in 2014. Hawthorne blogs regularly at www.johnwhawthorne.com under the title "Sociological Reflections". He is regularly on Twitter (@johnwhawthorne) and occasionally on LinkedIn.

CHRISTINE HELMER

Historical and Constructive Theology

There are two forms of social media that I use. The first is my academic website. I created this website (helmer.northwestern.edu) to add content to the basic information included on my departmental faculty page. Content is information about my courses and conferences as well as pdfs from published articles, relevant pages from volumes I have edited, such as the TOC and introductions, as well as published book chapters. I am not sure if this website is as effective in reaching potential readers as sites devoted to researchers, such as ResearchGate.

The second social media site is the massive open online course (MOOC) on "Luther and the West" that I developed in 2016 at Northwestern University. The MOOC is on the Coursera platform and is free to anyone with internet access. It launched on Oct. 3, 2016 and is projected to run as an on-demand course for three years. I often look at the site to see if there are any questions, concerns, or discussions. The most interesting discussion to date is the one prompted by the question, "How do people talk about religion in your part of the world?" In addition to giving me an idea of who is participating in the MOOC, this question gives me insight into the diversity of ways in which religion is addressed around the world.

The idea to produce a MOOC on Luther had been percolating in my mind for a number of years. I have spent more than twenty-five years studying Luther and his influence on many of the ideas that we regard as western values. I also knew that while Luther is a household name, the reception of his work has been limited to those identified as "Luther scholars" and Lutherans. My aim was to bring Luther into meaningful discussion by a broad global audience. The 500th commemoration of the Protestant reformation in 2017 was the perfect opportunity to produce the MOOC. The provost's office at Northwestern University awarded me a very generous grant that paid for the different parts of the MOOC's production, including the film crew and three weeks of filming during the hottest July weeks of 2016, the production and post-production team, and the advertising. I was privileged to work with a fabulous film and production team at Northwestern (the NUAMPS team). The entire team was committed to producing a work that aimed at educating an audience about Christianity in the west, its basic commitments and as well as its ambivalences.

I think that as educators of Christianity, one of the urgent questions for today is how to communicate scholarship in Christianity to a broader population. The academic study of Christianity at least in North America is located chiefly in university divinity schools and theological seminaries at the master's level. Confessionally connected colleges also have requirements in theology for undergraduates. Yet my concern is the relative lack of Christian studies in secular institutions of higher learning in addition to what I perceive to be the difficulties in translating academic resources in Christianity to a broader community. Social media thus is a powerful forum that might help to disseminate thoughtful scholarship done in the academy to people interested in deepening their knowledge of Christianity. *Homebrewed Christianity*, in my estimation, is exemplary in this regard. I designed the MOOC specifically for the aim of explaining Luther's basic ideas and how they shape the way we modern people think about the world. I focused on three ideas, namely the Bible, freedom, and the relations between religion and politics, and showed how these ideas were important in reception history. The section on Luther's Bible translation gave me the opportunity to discuss Luther's anti-Judaism in depth, while the section on freedom opened a discussion of the west's ambivalence on the topic with respect to the history of slavery in addition to Martin Luther King, Jr.'s theological ideas that informed the civil rights movement. For the third section on religion and politics, I was interested in showing how both are related in complex ways in contemporary decision-making, and I used Luther's excommunication by the pope and ban by the emperor in 1521 as foundational story.

The production of the MOOC, while one of the most wonderful experiences in my academic career, was also one of the most challenging. Particularly difficult was the compression of a vast amount of scholarly information into 4-6 minute lectures. The reason for this specific time frame was a social media study conducted at Northwestern University. The study concluded that 4-6 minutes is optimum for a video lecture. I had naively anticipated a simple conversion of my undergraduate lectures on "Luther and the West" to the MOOC format, but soon discovered that the MOOC genre is entirely different from a face-to-face real time lecture. Thus the script-writing phase took much longer than preparing a lecture or even writing an article. I finally settled on a format that began with a brief "hook" or story to catch the viewer's attention, the development of one idea with mention of one anecdote and a biblical reference, and ending with either a summary or a look forward to the subsequent lecture.

I think that the primary challenge of writing the scripts was not to reduce the content to bullet points. Learning in the humanities is different than the acquisition of information. I tried to develop the MOOC lectures as invitations to "think for yourself" while communicating basic information as well as showing how ideas can be analyzed from historical, cultural, theological, and philosophical perspectives. I am grateful to three students at Northwestern—Alex Gordon, Natalie Yeo, and Emily Blackman—and my husband Robert Orsi who edited, read, reread, and refined the scripts, up until the very last minute before filming.

One other surprise in the script-writing process was the checking of facts. Because my focus over many years of teaching Luther has been on ideas, I have tended to gloss over historical, biblical, and geographical facts. The MOOC format, as I discovered, is unforgiving with respect to erroneous facts, which if filmed, are permanent. Together with students and colleagues, I checked and double-checked facts. Hence my advice: always fact check because facts fade in one's memory!

The most important intellectual development I had while producing the MOOC concerned my commitment to articulating the ambivalences in Luther's thought and legacy. While I had envisioned the MOOC for the 500th celebration of the Protestant reformation, it became clear to me that his "reformation" ideas could not be responsibly discussed without demonstrating their difficult and insidious aspects.

Luther's anti-Judaism, evident in his earliest writings on the Psalms to the sermons he delivered just days before his death in 1546, had to be discussed as central to his biblical interpretation and theology. I used the lectures on Luther and the Bible to work out his anti-Judaism in relation to the Christian anti-Jewish idea of supersessionism. I also showed how the Nazis used the violent polemic in Luther's 1543 text, "On the Jews and their Lies" as propaganda for the November pogrom against Jews that the Nazis carried out on the eve of Luther's birthday, Nov. 9-10, 1938.

Luther's idea of freedom as articulated in the key reformation text from 1520, *The Freedom of a Christian*, also has an ambivalent reception history in the west. While famous philosophers, such as Kant and Hegel, carried out sophisticated analyses of freedom, the reality of many people over the past five hundred has been very different. I used the opportunity of the section on freedom to show that any philosophical discussion of the topic must include mention of the reality of slavery and oppression of African Americans, people of color, and women. This section includes an interpretation of Luther's idea of freedom from sin effected by Christ and Martin Luther King, Jr.'s understanding of freedom, civil rights, and the suffering (and even death) entailed by standing up for justice.

The question of time, or "work/life imbalance" as a feminist theologian once quipped, is my single deterrent to starting a Facebook and Twitter account. I also think that the capacity to concentrate on a subject matter long enough to get lost in it to write about it is compromised in this "age of distraction." Thus I am conflicted as to what I think might be the important benefits of being connected to a fast-paced world of online scholarship and the demands for the tiny bits of solitude that I can squeeze out of busy days for the quiet needed to think.

Finally, I recommend the following to scholars considering MOOCs:

1. A MOOC is a team effort, requiring editorial help, a film crew and production staff, and other professional assistance, such as copyright experts and people knowledgeable about images and maps. There is real joy in working together with other people on a single project.
2. A note to theologians: you can say what you need to say using half the words in ordinary language.
3. Check and double check the facts.

Christine Helmer, Ph.D. (Yale University) is a theologian who specializes in historical and constructive theology. She is the current holder of the Arthur E. Andersen Teaching and Research Professorship at Northwestern University in Evanston, Illinois, and is also Professor of German and Religious Studies. She was awarded an honorary doctorate in theology from the University of Helsinki in 2017. The author of The Trinity and Martin Luther *(Zabern 1999; reprint forthcoming with Lexham*

Press) and Theology and the End of Doctrine (*Westminster John Knox 2014), she is editor (and co-editor) of numerous books in the areas of Luther studies, Schleiermacher studies, biblical theology, and philosophical theology. She is also the main editor of the Christianity section of the* Encyclopedia of Bible and its Reception *(de Gruyter). See Dr. Helmer's website at helmer.northwestern.edu and her MOOC "Luther and the West" at www.coursera.org/learn/luther-and-the-west (or bit.ly /2ki9OFe) in addition to promotional videos at vimeo.com/198709510 and vimeo. com/183541655 and a podcast interview at homebrewedchristianity.com/2017/02 /06/luther-and-the-west-with-christine-helmer/ .*

ROBYN HENDERSON-ESPINOZA

Public Theology

I have historically used Facebook and Twitter, and a few years ago I began using Instagram. These three technologies shape my social media presence, and I post several times throughout the day.

After realizing that the work as a theologian / philosopher / social theorist needs to be able to translate theory and concerns to action, I began transitioning all of my posts to reflect my deep commitment to translation.

I am surprised to learn that folks engage at a deep level with Facebook and Twitter. Given the image-driven platform of Instagram, folks engage the images and also engage in whatever comments are left.

A lot of my work around bridging has come from public conversations through social media. I have been grateful that folks have engaged this concept with the real tangible questions that have offered.

I generally check social media throughout the day, but don't have dedicated time for social media. As someone who has several deadlines with their writing, I tend to make a mental note of touching in with social media, but not getting sucked in to social media, as so many folks complain about.

I would recommend to scholars considering using social media the following:

1. Figuring out how to translate in 140 (Twitter) is a helpful exercise, especially if you are teaching undergrads.
2. Make sure your handle is something that identifies you.
3. Try and keep your handle between social media platforms similar or related.

———————

Robyn Henderson-Espinoza, PhD is trained as a constructive philosophical theologian and serves as the public theologian in residence at Faith Matters Network, Nashville, TN. Robyn is a graduate of the Joint PhD Program at the University of Denver / Iliff School of Theology, and continues to learn the practice of translating theory and theology to action. Deeply involved in Movement work and committed to what they call 'activist theology,' they work hard to bridge the academy with social justice movements, in particular queer justice movements, racial justice, and immigrant rights work, among others. Committed to the politics of radical difference, Robyn seeks to ground their work in ongoing acts of bridging and finding a deep unity with those who enflesh the deepest differences in politics, theology, and ethics. Robyn is currently finishing a manuscript for Augsburg / Fortress Press on Activist Theology. See Henderson-Espinoza's website www.iRobyn.com for more information on their work and travel schedule. Robyn sends out a monthly newsletter called the Nomadic Activist Theologian. You can sign up for the newsletter on their website. Robyn is on Facebook at https://www.facebook.com/publictheologian/, Twitter at @iRobyn, and Instagram at @iRobyn. Robyn also uses Soundcloud to upload their public talks, sermons, and occasional conversations with other thinkers. You can find Robyn's feed at https://soundcloud.com/irobyn. Some of Robyn's videos are on YouTube.

WM. CURTIS HOLTZEN

Philosophical Theology

Regarding the worlds of social media and theology I have found that Twitter and Facebook are the platforms that work best for me. I use Twitter when I want to say something short, pithy, and provocative. Facebook is my go to when I have something of greater substance to offer or when I want the discussion.

I first become interested in social media to keep tabs on my daughter (Myspace first, then Facebook) but like many of my generation, soon found it was good for other things. I saw that many of my students were using it and so it became a good way to stay connected with them, especially post-graduation. My theological use of social media has certainly evolved over the last couple decades. Like many of us over forty years old my introduction to social media began in the 1990s with the free AOL disc and membership. I remember setting a timer so I would not go over my prepaid time in the chatrooms (were they called "channels"?) which was a common occurrence. These chatrooms and message boards were my go to for theological and philosophical chat and debate. These chatrooms brought home the reality that there is far more ideological chat than careful and thoughtful discussion "out there." The anonymity of chatrooms gave freedom without any need of restraint. In fact, I would from time to time argue anonymously for positions I thoroughly disagreed with simply to see the kinds of responses I could evoke.

I hope I can be forgiven for these youthful indiscretions. Eventually, chatrooms and message boards were replaced by Facebook. This meant my posts and chat had to be more careful, open-ended, inquiry over declarations. I could not make radical and inflammatory comments if my name was attached! Facebook has brought restraint, for me at least, I can't speak for others.

My use has moved on, though not entirely, from theological debate to the promotion of books, articles, and conferences. I should also add I have a "fan page" I created for the promotion of a retired theologian (Keith Ward) who was very instrumental in my development as a scholar. He does not have a Facebook page but was flattered when I asked if I could create one for the promotion of his work. I also have a Facebook page devoted to a book I edited and from time to time will invite friends to "like" the page as well as post quotes from the book. I have my own book coming out soon and look forward to seeing how to promote it and use it for discussion and education. While this may not count as "social media" over the last 15 years I have been involved in online college education. Since 2002 I have designed and taught online classes with students from all over the world.

I have been surprised by both positive and negative experiences I've had with social media. The positive is that there is great potential for affirmation and constructive critique. Not only for me to receive each of those but for me to give it. I have been delighted to find many of the authors I respect are on Facebook, Twitter, or have blogs with comments they actually read. I have made it a point that when I read a book or article I have found worthwhile that I find a way to let the author know. This has even led to the promotion of my own work. Roger Olson once spoke about his favorite philosopher, Keith Ward, in his blog. I left a comment letting Dr. Olson know I had edited a collection of Ward's essential writings. Well, it wasn't but a couple months later that Dr. Olson had mentioned this work in a blog. That casual comment has led to a few more book sales and the opportunity meet and speak with Dr. Olson.

I have also had opportunities to post thoughts that have generated constructive dialogue. The dialogue has often forced me to find better ways to articulate and explain ideas; ideas that seemed clear to me but, as I learned, were obviously held up by unspoken presuppositions. When social media is constructive, it is an energizing medium for refinement of ideas and mutual betterment.

While I've had many positive experiences with social media I am most surprised by how easily it is used to confirm our biases and create polarizing "us vs.

them" attitudes. And I would be lying if I said I have not been seduced by this temptation. Perhaps it is the anonymity or simply not having to see another person's face that brings out destructive offerings. When passionate posts and tweets are put out there, with the best of intentions, there is the tendency to stop thinking critically about it. One friend offered the explanation that once we put our ideas in "print," out there for all so see, it is that much more difficult to retract or refine your thinking once new ideas or facts have surfaced.

The other problem with social media is it is easy to silence critics. I understand the benefit of blocking those who simply harass or are "trolls" but there is the temptation to block or unfriend those who are genuinely seeking to help others think better. I was once part of a group that discussed all things Bible. A "discussion" came up about the literal existence of Satan. The tone of the discussion was that if one did not hold this belief they could not authentically be a Christian. I tried to show that this was a grave mistake by asking a series of questions like "what if someone holds that Jesus is the Christ and his death and resurrection is the means of personal salvation but this person fails to believe Satan is a real or literal person?" I was told that the person would still be damned because they did not hold all as the Bible authoritative and true. When I further asked "what if they came to see their belief about Satan was in error and came to affirm Satan was and is a real and literal person?" When I was told that the person would now be saved I tried to show that this was a very problematic stance since it made salvation rest on right beliefs about Satan more than beliefs about Jesus. I fully expected this was going to lead to a deeper discussion about the nature of essential and nonessential beliefs, but I was wrong. I was expelled from the group and access blocked. End of that discussion.

Ultimately, like many other narcotics, social media simply enhances our personalities. If we have a propensity for learning and encouragement we will find such opportunities. But if we have a propensity for confirmation bias or negativity we also have that platform.

Despite some of its problems social media for me has sparked some conceptual breakthroughs. Not necessarily great ideas or great projects, though I hope those will follow. Before the advent and my use of social media I was exposed to a much smaller group of thinkers. My theological discussions are limited to colleagues and friends, students, or church members. Social media however has uncovered a whole new facet of thinkers.

I belong to a few different theology groups on Facebook. In these groups people will post ideas, quotes, and questions. These are all good but it is the discussion that follows I find most interesting because it is here that I get to read the thoughts and see the thought processes of someone outside my denomination, outside my demographic, outside of SoCal, and sometimes outside of the country. Maybe most importantly, however, is that I can read and engage with those who are outside, often far outside, my assumptions and presuppositions. One example of this comes from a theology group I will pop into from time to time and follow the discussion. The topic centers on the doctrine of God but other issues certainly come up. What I have been surprised at is the predominant conservative thought of the group. Many members of the group hold very different ideas about the nature of scriptures, the use of metaphor, or the value of science than I do. Reading the thoughts of those in these groups has helped me better understand the thought processes of many who share a basic conclusion with me but arrive at that conclusion by very different means.

All this to say, some theological conclusions are branded "liberal" or "progressive" when there is a whole host of folk who have that same theological conclusion but arrive at it by very conservative or traditional means. This "discovery" has helped better understand that schools of theology are more hermeneutically diverse than first thought, and perhaps it is social media which allows for that.

I have often thought to myself, "I need to spend more time on social media." Well, maybe not quite like that, more like, "I need to spend more *quality* time on social media." Most often I spend my time reading posts or articles. Facebook and Twitter have become a reward that when I finish grading so many papers I will take a Facebook break. I would like to schedule or set aside time to work on social media, to devote time to the promotion of ideas and projects. That may have to wait.

I will end this essay with three recommendations to those considering using social media. My first is simple and obvious; do not post anything you might regret later. Some may have a tendency to post overly provocative ideas or statements. While these are great for conversation they may come back to bite. This practice is probably fine for many but for those of us working in non-tenured positions or at schools or churches with a legalistic constituency it might be best to error on the side of caution. For those who use social media but are looking for professor or pastor jobs may also wish to use caution since potential employers can easily look at your social media feeds.

Second, be selective in your responses. While you want everyone to feel like they are part of the conversation there are comments that are best left ignored. I have had people leave posts or make comments that are simply ridiculous and I have made the mistake of engaging. I soon learn, however, that these are not always people interested in reasonable conversation. Some ideas do not need to be legitimized by responding. Comments like "all evolutionary scientists are demon possessed" or something like that are best left alone. Let others engage if they see fit, but as the host of the discussion I would resist such engagement.

Finally, I would suggest that those using social media do more than promote their work or theology. I am far more apt to follow a theologian who talks about more than theology. I like to see comments about life and the day to day or pictures taken on vacation or a long hike. This helps me identify with the theologian or scholar when he or she is posting thoughts and ideas. Now of course one can go too far and share more than followers want to read, but overall I think it is good to do more than sell. The idea behind social media should be to invite others to share your journey. Advertising is fine, but invitation is much better.

———————

Wm. Curtis Holtzen, D.Th. is professor of philosophy and theology at Hope International University in Fullerton, CA. He is the co-editor of several books and has contributed essays for several others. Look for his book "The Faith of God" (IVP) in late 2018. Holtzen can be found on Facebook at "Curtis Holtzen" and on Twitter @CurtisHoltzen

ZACK HUNT

Public Theology

My adventures in social media theology began like so many other trips to the internet, as an act of procrastination. I was a youth pastor at the time and left Google Talk open on my desktop at work throughout the day. It kept me connected with a handful of fellow ministers I graduated from college with and afforded us all an easy distraction whenever we needed it. I mean, we were there for each other whenever a pastoral crisis arose or a deep theological question needed answering.

One of those fellow pastors and I often found ourselves sharing funny and sometimes cringe worthy Christian memes, videos, and stories we found during our digital travels. That sharing frequently sparked more serious conversations between the two of us and eventually we decided the world would be a better place if the rest of humanity could share in the hilarity and insights we enjoyed every day. So, we started a WordPress blog to host our findings and post our unrequested thoughts with the rest of planet Earth. We named our blog The American Jesus, both in honor of Stephen Prothero's eponymous tome which we both enjoyed and because the focus of the blog would be American Christianity.

Although, I now run the blog alone and have since dropped the American Jesus moniker, American Christianity—and all that comes with it—remains the primary focus of both my writing and activity on social media. While there have certainly been moments when I've considered stepping away from my social media activity, I've chosen to stay with it because I've found that social media affords me not only the ability to stay up to date on the constant comings and goings of American Christianity, it also offers me a platform from which to contribute to the ongoing conversations and events shaping the Church in America which I otherwise would not have.

When we first launched The American Jesus blog and to no one's surprise but our own, the world wasn't waiting with bated breath for our every post. As we quickly discovered, trying to create an online audience out of thin air is about as easy as getting Donald Trump to stay off of Twitter. We realized we needed something which would help us stick out in a crowd of untold millions all clamoring for the internet's attention. So, in the pursuit of building an audience we sought out a creative way to both garner attention, but also make a point about the subject matter our blog focused on, American Christianity.

The solution evolved from our love of sports. Having filled out more NCAA March Madness brackets than either of us would like to admit, we settled on the idea of a March Madness spinoff that would highlight the good, the bad, and the ugly of American Christianity by pitting current Christian pop culture topics, issues, and icons against one another in a bracket style tournament that would allow readers vote on the winner of each matchup until a champion was crowned. We called it American Jesus Madness.

The name was admittedly not the most eloquent, but the absurdity of our make-believe tournament was not without purpose. Satire has the ability to entertain while simultaneously forcing the reader to confront and, hopefully, think about serious issues whose problematic nature should be apparent, but may be difficult to see — or accept — due to one's presuppositions. A satirical make-believe tournament about American Christianity may, on the surface, appear to be little more than yet another excuse to procrastinate on the internet, but its disarming format allowed us to explore important issues in a way that was approachable for people who might otherwise prefer to ignore the tensions the various matchups highlighted. Over the course of its seven year existence, American Jesus Madness has demonstrated a consistent ability to spark important conversations by shining a light on both the absurd and serious problems plaguing the Church in the United States.

Obviously, a once a year burst of creativity is not enough to sustain a conversation, let alone build a social media platform. Any sort of effort towards sustained and productive online engagement, whether it be theological or something less divinely oriented, requires a great deal of time and dedication. You're competing—for lack of a better word—with countless other bloggers, writers, and everyday people with a computer and an opinion, not to mention an infinite amount of cat memes. It can feel overwhelming at times and without question it can become a major drain on your time, both your free moments and those moments when you're supposed to be working but can't focus because you've just *got* to put that anonymous troll in their place because no logical fallacy should ever go uncorrected!

Healthy, productive social media requires good time management skills every bit as much as it requires good content. Not only is it important to develop a schedule for yourself regarding when you will write, post, etc., it is equally or perhaps even more important to know when to walk away and when not to engage that random person who just stopped by the comment section of your latest blog post to let you know your ideas are the worst thing since the Final Solution.

Before writing your first blog post or sharing your first inspiring tweet, decide how much time you want to dedicate to your online platform and adjust your definition of success accordingly as the level of reader engagement will, most likely, vary greatly depending on how active you are online. If you only want to share something online once or twice a week, don't feel pressured to do more simply because there are others out there who post every day. If you do want to post every day, decide before you start sharing what that looks like: is it just a simple daily blog post or are you also cultivating content for readers across your social media platforms? In either case, create a realistic schedule based on the time you can actually devote to social media without sacrificing important commitments in your offline life. Deciding beforehand how often you will post on social media and sticking with it will not only create a consistent timeframe in which your readers know to expect new content, it will help create a healthy routine for you by ensuring you still have time to accomplish the important things in life like eating and practicing basic hygiene. Moreover, if your social media schedule is commiserate with the time you actually have to devote and you don't extend yourself beyond your predetermined posting schedule, that schedule will go a long way towards preventing digital burnout.

You should also decide ahead of time which social media platforms you want to use, that way when you do decide to start intentionally engaging online, you're ready to share your content across a variety of platforms instead of scrambling afterwards to figure out where you should be sharing and how to reach the people interested in what you have to say. As a blogger, my primary social media accounts are my blog, Facebook, and Twitter. I also use Instagram, but it serves more as a look into my personal life and interests for readers than it does a source of content for them to engage with. That said, use as many or as few social media accounts as you're comfortable with and understand how to use. The advice your parents gave you when you were young is just as relevant for social media as it was for middle school: don't feel pressured to use something you're not comfortable with or something that doesn't serve your readers just because all the cool kids are doing it. For example, a service like Snapchat may be all the rage at the moment, but if your focus is interpreting first-century apocryphal texts, it's unlikely a photo driven app like Snapchat will be of much help either building or engaging your audience. Be intentional about which social media platforms you use and how you use them. The more strategic you are with social media, the more effective you'll be reaching, engaging, and eventually building your audience.

As you contemplate dipping your toes in the turbulent, yet tempting waters of social media, allow me to welcome you by way of three pieces of advice I wish had been shared with me before I dove headfirst into blogging. The first and perhaps most important thing I can tell you may be obvious. If you don't have it already, it's best to develop thick skin before engaging on social media. Remember that comment I made earlier about people calling your work the worst thing since the Final Solution? That happened to me and, unfortunately, it's just the tip of the iceberg of ridiculousness you will inevitably encounter online. If you're not prepared for it and if you don't learn to laugh it off, it will quickly get under your skin and you'll find yourself saying or doing something online that you'll regret and nothing good every comes from doing regrettable things on the internet.

Second, in the academy there is a heavy emphasis on breaking new ground and to do that you often have to research and write about increasingly obscure subject matter. There is most certainly a place in the social media world for sharing obscure or little known information with a civilian audience. In fact, if you time it just right and are contributing to a popular conversation, it likely will be well received. But don't be afraid to write about things everyday people want to read and talk about. That is to say, don't be afraid to write about current events and connect those current events to your area of interest if at all possible.

Third, don't write for traffic. The siren's call of more and more blog hits and more and more Facebook shares can be hard to resist, especially when you see the undereducated and over-opinionated getting obscene amounts of attention online. You may feel immune to the sway of social media traffic measurements now, but I assure you, if you are invested even the slightest amount in whether or not anyone is listening to what you have to say online, the temptation to focus more on numbers than quality of content can become overwhelming for anyone.

Yes, a large social media following can seem like something of a measure of success, importance, and authority both online and off, but what the Church needs from you is quality content, not bragging rights.

Finally, at the risk of turning the end of this essay into an old-fashioned tent revival, allow me, if you would, to conclude with a brief testimony. After nearly a decade spent heavily engaged with the Christian blogosphere, I can attest to the great need the Church has for more trained theologians, biblical experts, and in-the-trenches pastors to join the online conversation. That's not to say those sorts of folks aren't already contributing, nor is it an outright dismissal of those contributing online who don't have the professional training of those in the academy, but ideas spread quickly and regardless of intent. As a result, lasting and catastrophic theological damage can be done to the life of the Church with just the flick of a finger. Whether intentionally or not, the internet has become a formative source of theology and practice for the people of God. The problem, of course, is that this digital discipleship is too often lacking in the structure, scholarship, or sometimes even orthodoxy that has defined healthy Christian discipleship for millennia. However, declaring internet use "anathema" is not an option, nor should it be. We have no choice but to embrace the digital age we live in. But to do that faithfully, the Church needs digital shepherds. The Church needs well-trained, articulate, creative, and engaged teachers and leaders who engage the people of God where they are—online. The Church needs you.

Zack Hunt is a graduate of Yale Divinity School, a youth ministry veteran, and an ordained elder in the Church of the Nazarene. His eponymous blog ZackHunt.net has been consistently ranked among the top Christian blogs on the Internet and his writing has appeared in a wide variety of places including Huffington Post, Christianity Today, Yahoo!, and Relevant Magazine. You can keep up with Zack by following him on Twitter (@zaackhunt), Facebook (Zack Hunt), or Instagram (@zaackhunt).

LARRY W. HURTADO

New Testament and Christian Origins

I have my own blog, and a Twitter account. The latter simply picks up my blog postings. Initially, I wanted to set up a blog site to be operated collectively by members of our Centre for the Study of Christian Origins. I didn't know how to go about this, so a colleague sat down and guided me through the process. As the learning exercise, I set up my own blog site. But it immediately "took off" and has continued to grow in readers. My colleagues in fact showed little interest in the CSCO blog site, so I've simply continued on with my own.

I view my blog site as a place where I share results of my scholarly investigations and reading with the wider public. It's a kind of "leaves from my workshop" thing. I try to make things as accessible as the subjects permit, but I don't "dumb down" things. In part, as there is so much "fake scholarship" (roughly = "fake news") out there, I see my blog site as a place where readers can go if they care to have comments from an expert in the field of Christian Origins.

I post notices of publications of others that I find noteworthy. These can include recently published books, but also journal articles. I also summarize my own projects as they appear, such as conference presentations, essays, and books. I provide a list of my own publications on the site, and also typically provide the pre-publications version of my own essays, with information on the published version. I also comment from time to time on issues that arise, such as the now-infamous "Jesus' wife" fragment that was subsequently proven to be a hoax. In all of this, my aim is primarily to offer to a wider public (which includes fellow scholars and students in the field, as well as many "general" readers) the fruits of my own work and that of others in the field of New Testament and the origins of Christianity.

I've been pleasantly surprised to see the number of interested readers and the wide range of countries. My blog site is read on an international scale far beyond any of my paper publications. But I've been unpleasantly surprised to see that there are also "trolls" and individuals with a "bee in their bonnet" who try to use every opportunity to intrude and push their crazy notions.

I write a blog posting when I've got something to say, and I remain silent when I don't. Most postings of a few hundred words at most require maybe 30 minutes to write. It's not a big demand on time. The larger demand on time can happen when you try to handle comments, particularly stupid ones!

I recommend the following to scholars considering using social media:

1. Develop a clear idea of what you're trying to accomplish. Is it a virtual bulletin board, or news postings about other sites (which means you'll have to keep up with other blog sites), or a place where you offer gleanings from your own work to the world?
2. Determine which social medium works best: blogging, Twitter, Facebook etc.?
3. Determine whether you're a scholar first, and a use of social media within reason, or vice versa.

Larry W. Hurtado (PhD, FRSE) is a scholar in New Testament and Christian Origins. He taught in Regent College (1975-1978), the University of Manitoba (1978-1996), and the University of Edinburgh (1996-2011). He is Emeritus Professor of New Testament Language, Literature & Theology, and lives in Edinburgh. He is the author of ten books, and over 120 essays in journals and multi-author works. He continues actively engaged in research in his field. Hurtado's blog (larryhurtado.wordpress.com) features his comments on issues and publications in the field of Christian Origins and related subjects. His Twitter feed (LarryWHurtado) features alerts to his blog postings.

DARREN IAMMARINO

Religious Studies

I use podcasts, Instagram, YouTube, LinkedIn and Facebook, with podcasts and Instagram being the most relevant to my classes. Aside from YouTube, it seems that the social media platforms utilized by most professors are not the same first picks used by their students. For example, I cannot think of too many — or any for that matter — professors who use Snapchat, Pinterest, Yik Yak etc. as a teaching tool.

My initial foray into social media and teaching began when I attempted to make some shorter video clips on a YouTube channel to use in conjunction with an online class I was creating. My hope was to stick to 10 minute videos or a microlecture format. The key with most social media seems to be to "micro" everything. Therefore, it seemed to me that curated, short videos could lead to greater retention of material compared to long, lecture style traditional format classes on a campus. The results were mixed and not quite what I had hoped for.

Like most things in life, success depends on how much effort and creativity you can put into a task. I found it exhausting attempting to create videos with any regularity and so after making about 8 videos, that approach fizzled out. There is another big reason I moved away from YouTube, but that will be described below in a subsequent question. In a perfect world where teachers can afford great equipment, high-end editing software and so forth, YouTube and microlecture videos still feels like a highly promising approach.

I continue to use social media, but not because I am creating new online courses. Since I currently only teach on campus, my social media needs and interests have shifted. For a couple of years at San Diego State University, I ran a religious explorations club and so the student officers of the club made use of Facebook for updates on all club activities and that was helpful, but never quite reached the threshold of members to generate sustained and lively dialogue. Currently, I use Instagram to post motivational and inspirational one-liner quotes. In the near future, I will be posting quotes from the sacred scriptures that we happen to be covering in the upcoming week . . . a simple fun way to generate interest. Additionally, I have toyed around with the idea of using Instagram to post an image or short video clip for an extra credit question on a test and then giving the students thirty minutes to see whose comment comes closest to the truth.

In the last few years some unexpected surprises have arisen while employing social media in the classroom. For example, there appear to be only three or four "useful" platforms out there in the following order of relevance: Podcasts, YouTube, Instagram, Twitter, and Facebook (for clubs only). The real surprise for me, which has blown me away concerns audio lessons or podcasts in a typical two or three-person conversational style. Although podcasts may not technically qualify as social media, they have tremendous advantages over all other approaches. Think about it like this . . . radio still exists! Furthermore, it is still a popular medium.

Radio has not died because it has the following four advantages over the visually-oriented social media apps: portability, repeatability, affordability, and sustainability. Can you watch a YouTube video while driving? I hope not! However, all of us can easily listen to a podcast playing through our car speakers. It may just turn out that this portability and repeatability make podcasts the least expensive and most direct way to increase grades and performance.

In my own experience, when I worked at San Diego State University with large lecture hall classes, I found that custom audio lessons I made with a colleague created a dramatic increase in retention of the material. Grades were up, and participation was up because people do not read the textbooks, but they will listen to a podcast and come with questions. How can a textbook that costs $120 compete with free or ridiculously inexpensive mp3 format audio files which are effectively: weightless, portable, endlessly repeatable, and sustainable for the environment? Short answer: they cannot. The other major surprise concerns the use of Instagram as an advertising tool on campus. However, this is best addressed by the next question.

Aside from the stunning success with podcasts mentioned above, there has been another concept that has worked well, but this time focusing on advertising via Instagram and Facebook. In the past two years, I have been given very tough classes and time slots where attendance has been historically low. I needed to find out a way to reach students in large numbers, assuming the conversion rate from any form of advertising would be below 1%. Putting up fliers on bulletin boards like the old days is not going to cut it if you need to generate a 30-50% increase in enrollment. This led me to turn to the key social media apps of the millennial generation: Instagram and Facebook.

The two problems that needed to be solved were: (1) what content/text should be on the post and (2) what image should be used to accompany the text? I stuck with a philosophy that has served me well in teaching, provocative/cryptic one-liner quotes. For example, I created one Instagram post that read as follows: Seek Prophets! Enroll in Huma 104 2:20 M W. The post was accompanied by Moses holding the 10 commandments in a rather Charlton Heston fashion. For another class, I created (borrowed!) the somewhat well-known text: When the student is ready, the teacher will appear. Enroll in Huma 106 T 6:35-9:30. The image I chose for this post was of a hooded Buddhist monk with his face mainly occluded.

The results from this approach have been a noticeable increase in attendance over the last year that I have been utilizing this method. For the spring semester of 2017, two of the three classes exceeded maximum enrollment; whereas, the third class saw a modest 20% increase in attendance. Granted, there are other factors that could also have affected these numbers and so this is more anecdotal than rigorously tested and controlled for other variables. Nevertheless, it seems at a minimum that posting these images to your college's Facebook and Instagram accounts ensures that it is seen by literally thousands to tens of thousands of students. Assuming that your college's Instagram account has 10,000 followers and with the further assumption that at least half of those are currently enrolled, then if you get half of one percent as a conversion to enrollment you are looking at 25 students which is almost certainly enough to ensure that all of your classes will "make."

On a separate, future oriented, and more speculative note, there is the issue of how augmented reality could radically alter the 21st century college campus. Augmented reality is when our view of the external environment is modified by a computer, which can enhance a live, real-world experience by providing additional video, graphics, and sound. The information is basically an overlay onto a real-world object and it uses GPS data or tags to know what data to display and where to display it.

Instead of guidance counselors stuck in the corner of a building divorced from the "real world issues," augmented reality can literally transform an entire building, open space on campus, a library, individual departments etc. into an up to date personal campus ambassador or assistant. The idea here is that a student uses their iPhone or smart device and aims it at a building or at certain parts of the library or at the front door of the philosophy department and they receive updated information about how to get a library card and check out a book, or what the new requirements are for the philosophy major and who to contact. Perhaps the student learns via their device that a beautiful open area on campus is used every Friday at 5 p.m. by the drama club and they can attend any performance they want . . . literally the possibilities are endless. In fact, to stick with the drama club example, the club literally could record a short performance and people walking by can "see" it only with their device, which will superimpose the performance onto a garden area on campus.

Sadly, I have felt pulled in too many directions by the mundane demands of life combined with teaching that I have not put together a proper cohesive social media strategy. Sometimes I see a problem and think about how social media can help, but I have let the memory of YouTube video creation and podcasts cloud my motivation. Videos and quality podcasts take a good amount of time and the level of commitment can just be too much. In the near future, it is my hope that I will return to the beginning of my career when I focused on creating content. The truth is that you need consistent and quality content to maintain people's interest and engagement with social media. It is not quality over quantity, it is the demand for quality and quantity.

The reality is that there needs to be new ways for professors to monetize their social media and possibly, *a social media sabbatical* to begin this project and allow the time to build it as a habit, to see its potential on all levels. Perhaps there is a general fear on the part of the universities that if they provided a sabbatical for social media, the professor may learn that they do not need the university that much anymore. My answer to question 6 addresses one hypothetical way in which professors could liberate themselves from their administrative overlords.

I see pros and cons to using social media. Let me conclude with a few:

Pro: Social media and tech literacy more generally, just may bring about a revolution in the way higher education is delivered. For the last one hundred years, we have been limited by the same model of higher education . . . you go to a four-year college, then you do a Master's or enter a Doctorate program for another 2-8 years. There is another option that could easily be adopted that would solve the problems of low pay for lecturers, as well as providing a radical new option for a continuing education post-college: *grad apprenticeships*. If professors marketed their research background and their areas of expertise on something resembling an Angie's List—basically a directory of curated education services—then a college grad could take a new direction separate from the brick and mortar Master's degree or Doctorate.

Imagine a student looking through this hypothetical directory and finding two or three professors that catch her eye due to their specific research and they reach out and pay a fee *that is set by the professors themselves*. Then an agreement is reached and via synchronous online teaching (e.g. Skype sessions) and asynchronous (e.g. podcasts, writing assignments, research projects, readings), a student is mentored. Once the professor deems that the mentee has reached a certain proficiency (e.g. via completion of a major project), they then write a letter of recommendation and issue a certificate, *which ties the mentees success to the name and reputation of the mentor*. As a potential employer, I may be more inclined to hire someone who went through this type of process rather than a Master's degree granted from a brick and mortar school . . . after all, if someone well known is willing to endorse them, then they probably have the education I expect them to have. Your name, your record becomes your brand. Brand loyalty can be fierce if you have a compelling backstory or mission statement to tell. Nothing builds brand loyalty more than social media platforms in the 21st century.

Con: You need to have a story or a purpose for using social media. I am not sure this is a con so much as a warning. Just being on Facebook or Twitter is meaningless and most people post meaningless things onto their accounts. As a professor, you probably have a lot to say, ha! Even still, it is more important how you say it and social media platforms are not going to automatically create interest just because you use a hashtag. Essentially, as a professor you have the potential to build a decent following and thus, you are basically building a brand: Dr. so and so. The trouble is that most brands have a short shelf life and a terrible business plan. So, my advice is plan it out and see if you really need social media to help achieve your goals. If not, then just do not do it, you will be wasting your time and other people's time as well.

Con: It can hurt your feelings. The last piece of advice I have here is that you need to remember that what you say will be heard and seen by many others and there are those who would prefer to troll your videos, tweets or whatever. Last year I came up with a short quote that seems to apply to social media . . . "Everyone wants to give their two cents, too bad it's rarely worth more than a half pence." Still, if you have a reactionary personality, especially a quick temper, then best to avoid a public, near permanent record of what you said and how you reacted. In the end, however, as long as you are sincere, then the right people will gravitate to your material and you will know that you are helping others, even if it is through nothing more than an inspirational quote on Instagram you post or a comment you leave on someone else's profile.

Darren Iammarino, Ph.D. is a process theologian and professor of humanities and religious studies at San Diego Mesa College where he teaches world religions, New Testament and Old Testament. Iammarino is also a back-to-back winner of the favorite faculty award at San Diego State University. His most recent book, Religion and Reality: An Exploration of Contemporary Metaphysical Systems, Theologies, and Religious Pluralism, *proposes a novel way of facilitating interreligious dialogue; it can be found on amazon. Iammarino's audio lessons/podcasts can be found on www.hybridedtech.com. He can also be reached on Instagram or Twitter at the following handle: @driammarino.*

THOMAS INGRAM

Public Theology

Engagement via social media carries with it benefits and burdens. The obvious benefit stems from its ability to enable connections beyond our everyday experience while providing us with a platform from which we can insert our perspective into the conversation. However, it is easy for us to fall prey to its always-on attraction by investing too much time to the detriment of our family, friends, and work. The challenge for me, and likely you as well, is to curate a presence on social media that adds value to those we are connected with while at the same time maintain the ability to be fully present.

I engage social media in primarily two ways. The first is intentional when I have something to post. The goal in this type of engagement is to get in and get out as deliberately as possible. The other is a more casual engagement, kind of like a trip down the hall to the water fountain and back. Now, every now and then, I might meet someone at the water fountain and have an extended conversation. But, I try to make these interactions the exception rather than the rule.

My friend and D.Min. mentor Leonard Sweet always seems to be on the leading edge or perhaps bleeding edge of trends, so with his encouragement, I made my first real venture into the world of social media via Facebook in 2009. Facebook provides me with as much of a social media footprint as I am currently interested in maintaining. It also enables conversations, which aligns with my communication goals.

Twitter, on the other hand, is more of a broadcast or re-broadcast platform rather than a conversational medium. Tweets seem to consist of someone announcing something or a re-post of something someone else announced. I feel the topics we discuss related to faith or the church need a relational exchange rather than a pronouncement of position and so my social media engagement via Twitter is limited.

For my social media based research, I use a crowdsourcing application from Ideascale.com. Ideascale's platform allows the generation and sharing of ideas between participating members of a group. These groups can be invitation-only, or open to the public. It is easy to use and makes possible a level of problem solving and interaction not available from other methodologies . . . in my view.

My first venture into social media based research happened quite accidentally. It began when I was finding it increasingly difficult to discuss faith or Christian topics with my non-Christian friends (likely you have experienced this as well). Simultaneously, I was sensing a methodology disconnect in that, while the Church was taking a more "seeker-friendly" approach to Sunday mornings, the reality was, those outside the faith wanted no part of it because they held a certain animosity toward both Christians and the Church.

Because of this, I did what probably anyone would have done (slight sarcasm); I created two websites where I asked non-Christians to submit ten things they did not like about Christianity or the Church. The site titles were a little harsh: tenthingsihateaboutchurch.com and tenthingsihateaboutchristianity.com but ten things I don't like about church just didn't seem as likely to inspire participation. During the six-month research period, the sites logged over 800 contributions from people all over the country.

While I was hoping the sites would encourage non-Christians to tell us what they didn't like so we could perhaps adjust our efforts, what happened was much more interesting: 86% of those who contributed self-identified as Christian. This was a "Houston, we have a problem" moment for me. The results of this research were the inspiration for my book *The New Normal: A Diagnosis the Church Can Live With.*

My next venture into social media based research, was a crowdsourcing project I worked on with Leonard Sweet. This project not only became the subject of my doctoral dissertation, but also provided the framework around which my newest book *The Book of Signs: A Crowdsourced Field Guide for Followers of Jesus* was written. In this research, we invited people via social media to help us answer the following question: What are the 100 words that make us Christian? Unfortunately, Len's schedule prevented his participation in co-authoring the book about the results of our research.

When we launched the Book of Signs crowdsourcing project, it was exciting to see people participate in the research and the high quality of their contributions. Participants could submit a topic/word, define it as they wished, and then vote for their favorites. This aggregation of results enabled a hierarchical listing of the contributions to emerge.

Early on in the research period, one word began to rise to the top of the pile: "hear." I approached this with some degree of skepticism thinking, more than likely, whoever submitted that word must have gotten their friends to join and vote for their submission . . . a rigging of the system if you will. However, throughout the research period it was not dislodged from its position of prominence; it remained #1.

When it came time for me to write reflections on each of the words, I viewed the #1 word "hear" as the great imposter. However, as I began to research what I could write about this particular word, I discovered the depth of relevance it held for the topic, in no small part due to Romans 10:17 NRSV "*faith comes by hearing, and hearing by the word of God.*"

If I had been tasked with picking the #1 word from the contributions, "hear" would not have been my choice. However, I think the crowd did the better job. And so, I am learning the crowd is capable of incredible insight if we are willing to give them an opportunity to be heard. At this point, I think the majority of my research and writing in the future will contain some component of crowdsourced inspiration and insight.

Social media, as we know, is a kind of stream. Posts flow down our news feed and unless we are willing to commit more time to it than we probably should . . . we miss things. But, every so often we happen upon Facebook at the right time and somehow, perhaps providentially, we stumble upon something we needed to see.

One of these times for me was when I saw a post from Peter Rollins announcing a road trip he was about to embark on across the country (with associated map) asking if anyone along the route wanted to host him for a speaking engagement. His route showed him passing a couple of hundred miles from where I live. I had never met Pete, but I decided to message him about the possibility of our hosting him for an event. We worked out the details.

I publicized the event via social media and asked others to share as much as possible without becoming annoying (maybe I got a little annoying . . . you would have to ask my "friends"). But, the event happened and we had about 150 people show up. This led to a second visit by Pete a few months later where he and I got to spend several days together.

Because of the connections and community generated by these events, I have now been able to host Chris Heuertz, A.J. Swoboda, and Tripp Fuller with more to come. And, as a bonus, several of those who came to that original Rollins event have become friends who gather together to dream and discuss how the Church might better engage our culture in the here and now.

There are a lot of ways in which we can engage social media. For me, social media is not the end game. Social media is the means through which we can make connections and build relationships that just might manifest in the real world if we are not content with just screen-to-screen connections. Who knows, we might just end up as friends.

I have heard it said: no matter where you are, most of the smartest people work for someone else. While this statement references the work environment, I think it reflects a truth about the global economy of ideas as well: the best ideas always seem to be just a little beyond our grasp. Our task as theologian/scholars is to figure out how we can more effectively access and then utilize those ideas and solutions for the Church. I like the idea of crowdsourcing as a means to this end for a couple of reasons. First, it has a way of enabling and encouraging unexpected solutions via the power of the crowd . . . the idea that we are smarter together than we are alone. And secondly, I am encouraged by the way in which this methodology seems to be supported by Paul's Body of Christ metaphor.

If I were to give any advice on social media use, this is what I'd say:

1) We hear a lot about building our platform these days. There is little doubt, a bigger platform can help us get our message out and possibly contribute to greater influence. However, I tend to take a different approach. I would suggest rather than putting our efforts into building a bigger platform, we should instead concentrate on doing the work and building relationships. I think those who do the work, if it is good work, will be rewarded with a bigger platform.

Now, this path I am proposing will likely take longer and be more difficult. But, if your work and/or ministry are worthy of a platform, I am confident a platform built by the Holy Spirit is more valuable and enduring that one resulting from a good search engine optimization algorithm.

2) One day after expressing frustration with the adversarial tone of many of the comments to my social media posts, a friend of mine gave me a piece of advice I thought was very insightful. Here is what they said. "Tom, these type of discussions are more for the audience than the participants." After a bit of reflection, I had to agree. Irrespective of how many "friends" or "followers" we have online, those participating in the discussion are typically a small number comparatively. We carry on these public discussions oftentimes seeming to make no progress with those directly engaged. However, as my friend so wisely suggested, we must always remember that these discussions have an audience . . . a silent audience . . . a silent audience who is watching and paying attention to not only what is said but also how it is said. I know this because from time to time I get a private message from someone with a comment related to the discussion. Or, if I am lucky, a private "thank-you" for my public position.

All of this to say, there are different levels of engagement on social media: engagement with those who participate and engagement with those who observe. Oftentimes I think our greatest contribution resides in the potential impact we have on the observers.

3) Our culture seems to be transitioning to an experience based culture. Words, lessons, and instructions have all diminished in value. Experience is where learning now resides. The value of the expert has also diminished since many if not most of life's questions can be answered via a hand-held portable device that connects us to the global information base. And so, how do we communicate the truth of Christ in this new world?

In my view, we need to move from *me* to *we*. We need to move from proclamation to participation as we transition from those who distribute discoveries to those who guide others into discoveries of their own. If we as theologians and scholars can adapt to this new participatory cultural terrain, I think no matter its twists and turns, good guides will always be valued and needed.

After many years in the creative and business sides of television and music production, Thomas Ingram now divides his time between research/writing and mentoring/coaching/encouraging others in their efforts to pursue God's purposes for their lives. He holds a MBA in Leadership and a Doctor of Ministry in Semiotics and Future Studies. He also engages in a little Creation Care as an active gardener and volunteer educator for the Tulsa County Master Gardeners. Connect with Tom Ingram via his website thomaseingram.com, Facebook at facebook.com /thomaseingram, email at tom.ingram@mac.com, or join his crowdsourcing projects at crowdsourcingtheology.com.

BRADLEY JERSAK

Practical Theology

t's interesting as a theologian to take a step back, to observe and analyze one's engagement on social media, especially when it emerged more instinctively than strategically. After all, isn't that what theologians do? The best theologians follow and describe where the winds are blowing rather trying to be wind turbines. When I pause, here is what I see.

I typically begin with the blogs I edit and where I write, and from there, add links, summaries and comments through Facebook, Twitter and sometimes Instagram. It seems I started at a point when my life was too peaceful and needed more drama, more anxiety, and more haters. So I launched into social media and *voila!* Now there's no shortage! But seriously, other than the blogs, I had previously dipped into social media and found engagement there discouraging and stressful. But as an author, I reluctantly took that stage again strictly for the purposes of marketing. Readers liked my accessibility for questions and of course, there's no greater favor you can do a vocational teacher than ask him a question. I found myself drawn into some good conversations and real relationships — I met solid people who I might not have met otherwise. And I began to follow others who nourished my soul — folks I now regard as my teachers and mentors. So I was drawn in . . . fruitful collaboration was happening in FB groups I was invited to and doors were opening to new ministry venues.

I still struggle with some of the thoughtless 'trolls' and petty arguments. So I avoid browsing the comment sections unless I get a notification that mentions my name, which is how people try to start conversations. But it's also meant giving myself permission to unfollow or unfriend folks more quickly such that after about a year, my newsfeed is a place of encouragement more than a stress-inducer. Some find this rude, and I recognize that it makes for an echo chamber of likeminded people. I'm fine with that. If I want to experience real controversy and critique, I find it healthier to face it with people I know.

Eventually, I was also asked to include social media engagement as part of a ministry contract, so on days when I get frustrated and am most inclined to unplug entirely, I remind myself that being there is part of an actual job.

Social media engagement has also surprised me on several fronts, but most especially on the personal level. First, there are those people I meet online who eventually become face-to-face friends. Or conversely, there are acquaintances I meet casually who end up staying in touch long-term via social media. The quality of these connections came as quite a happy shock considering how cynical I can be about the internet.

In fact, the different types of people who befriend me on social media are also surprising—people I wouldn't normally rub shoulders with where I live day-to-day, especially not by ideology. These range from military commanders (I'm a pacifist) to monks to Christian drag queens and angry atheists. Social media is an ironic place for me to start humanizing those I'd otherwise regard as radically other!

Another grand surprise came when I was writing a children's book *Jesus Showed Us!* It was written, illustrated, laid out and ready to go. However, my funds were tapped out and I couldn't afford the printing. My illustrator, Shari-Anne Vis, suggested I try crowdfunding. I thought if I could raise $5000, I would be able to print 1000 paperback copies. I gave it 60 days, but when the crowdfunding went to Facebook and Twitter, the full amount came through in just 24 hours! And it kept coming... I quickly calculated that if we raised $6500, we could go with hardcover, so I polled online whether donors thought I should continue taking donations. The response was a unanimous and overwhelming yes. In any case, people were happy to prepay for their own copies, so I thought, why not?

By the end of one week, $10,000 had rolled in and we were able to print 3000 copies, all through the kindness of my social media friends! Most of the donors have never met me, but I realized we had developed tremendous trust and good will through years of interaction through these media streams. I was so grateful for this help from a source that I wouldn't have considered on my own.

I'm sometimes told that I post and share too much content, which might give the false impression that I give tons of time to social media. The reality is that I have great difficulty juggling multiple jobs, writing deadlines, editing projects and marking papers. As for social media, I do all of that during breaks (not counting writing blogposts). For example, I might grade three essays, then grab a coffee and post something on Facebook while I take a breather. I especially like tweeting over supper. Just kidding. But I really do love live-tweeting other people's sermons or teachings.

Now imagine I'm at my desk all day for three days in a row, marking paper after paper, or editing pages and pages of someone's book or laying out a magazine — the need for little breaks is obvious in spite of the workload. I may end up posting something every few hours through that process. Unfortunately, that can overload other people's feeds or worse, they think I just sit around on social media all day long. The truth is, the busier I am, and the more I appear online. C'est la vie.

My advice for scholars using social media is the following:

First, ask yourself why you think you need to be there. If you already have sufficient venues for writing and teaching, and no marketing responsibilities, why bother? But if you want to extend your teaching to students or disciples beyond your current reach, give it a go.

Second, don't feel tempted or obligated to browse everything in your newsfeed. In fact, I would avoid going on at all without a purpose. If you aren't about to post something or to view a particular friend's posts, why are you checking in? That's where things get really time-consuming and problematic.

Third, avoid petty squabbles and take permission to unfollow, unfriend or block those who try to hook you. Your page is like your stage: you are not required to give anonymous people an open microphone in your classroom or pulpit, so establish similar boundaries for your page . . . note: *your* page.

Finally, be wary of how easily we forget that we're engaging real people with families and jobs and struggles. I'm alarmed at how quickly dehumanization occurs in the heat of a disagreement when we can't see live eyes or hear live voices or read non-verbal cues. I am a daily witness to how competing comments devolve into sub-Christian and sub-human behavior, including in myself (public apologies are necessary). I've discovered three keys to avoiding this if followed religiously: be kind, be kind, be kind.

Bradley Jersak, Ph.D. is an author, editor and teacher (after pastoring for 20 years). He is on core faculty at Westminster Theological Centre (UK) and adjunct at other schools. He teaches New Testament, Patristics and Christian Spirituality. Brad has written over a dozen books, ranging from Christian spirituality and theology to political science and even children's books. He is editor in chief of CWR magazine and blog and the Clarion Journal. He is also a tonsured reader in the Orthodox Church. See Jersak's website at www.bradjersak.com and his blogs at www.clarion-journal.com and www.christianity-without-the-religion.blogspot.ca. He is on Facebook at www.facebook.com/BradJersak (public) and www.facebook .com/bradley.jersak. You'll also find him on Twitter (@bradjersak), YouTube (Brad Jersak) and LinkedIn.

DAVID KYLE JOHNSON

Philosophy

have found using and appearing on social media, as a means by which to promote the usefulness and importance of philosophy to the general public, to be an extremely rewarding and worthwhile experience. It has not only enabled me to widely distribute my academic work, and publish other works not suited for classic academic outlets, but it also inspired my latest book, earned me an award for philosophic "public outreach," led to me working for The Great Courses, and gave me the opportunity to (successfully) convince Bill Nye (The Science Guy) to value philosophy.

How do I use social media? I regularly use Facebook and maintain two blogs for Psychology Today (Plato on Pop and A Logical Take.) I have also written for online philosophy magazines such as Scientia Salon, The Electric Agora, and The Ethics Centre. When I lecture publically for local organizations, I will (when available) post the lectures to a YouTube channel I maintain for the purpose. My lecture at Google, on my book Inception and Philosophy, has over 740,000 views and led to me being hired to do courses for The Great Courses.

I do use Twitter as well, just not that often; I find it difficult to say what is necessary with the limited number of characters. I use my own personal Facebook account to speak on political issues, but also have a professional "author" account on Facebook where I address matters more directly related to philosophy. Given the importance of having informed knowledgeable people involved in political discourse, however, I have recently considered moving more of my political posts to the author's page. (Writing this essay was one of the main motivating factors for this.)

What I find most satisfying is writing for my Psychology Today blogs, where I can reach a larger audience and take the time to make informed well-developed arguments. I began the *Plato on Pop* pop culture blog simply because I (and my colleague William Irwin) were invited (by *Psychology Today*) to write a blog on pop culture and philosophy (after the publication of our book *Introducing Philosophy Through Pop Culture*). We thought it would be a useful way to promote philosophy and the "pop culture and philosophy" movement. We still do.

I expanded to a separate blog (*A Logical Take*) because I felt I had helpful and useful things to say that were unrelated to pop culture. As one who teaches logic and critical thinking I have unique talents that can be used to debunk conspiracy theories, Facebook memes, bad reporting, fake news, lying politicians, etc. I now publish there when something happens in the public sphere about which I think I have something helpful or meaningful to say (if, of course, I have time to write something up).

I started my professional "author" Facebook and Twitter accounts as a way to promote the teaching work I do outside the class, most notably my courses for *The Great Courses: Exploring Metaphysics* and *The Big Questions of Philosophy*. (At a conference for such professors, this was encouraged.) I will spread news that my Great Courses "students" are interested in, post about something relevant to one of my lectures occurs, or share my work anytime I write a blog or publish a journal article or book.

Given my use of Facebook, one might wonder whether I ever engage in such things as Facebook "debates." Since using social media I have learned of the "back-fire effect"; confronting people with argument and evidence is less likely to persuade them and more likely to make them entrench in their previous beliefs. Therefore, to the extent that I ever engage in debate on social media, I never do it to persuade the person with whom I am debating. Instead, I do it to try to persuade those who might be observing the debate; I try to demonstrate to them that my position is more reasonable and well thought out (and that my opponent is irrational and/or misinformed).

I have also learned of research which strongly suggests that comment sections on articles most often serve to misinform readers; the article will be well researched and thought out, the comments with be un-researched and contain outright lies—but, upon reflection, the reader will not remember who said what.

Thus the comments can often "undo" any learning the article accomplished. To this end, I do not put a section for comments on any of my blogs or articles.

(I do not, by the way, consider this an infringement of free speech. The reader is still free to share my article, along with an argument against it—or just blog their response to my article themselves—and I would ever suggest they should be unable to do so. But free speech does not legally or morally require me to give uniformed dissenters a platform—which is exactly what a comments section does. For similar reasons, I have been known to block trolls on my Facebook page, once a debate with them has outlived its usefulness.)

My use of social media has not gone without recognition or satisfying reward. In 2011, I won an award (from the APA on public outreach for philosophy) for one of my first *Plato on Pop* blog entries (on IBM's WATSON winning Jeopardy!). (That, along with other articles, helped inform lectures I later gave for *The Great Courses*. I am now in the midst of preparing a philosophy and sci-fi course for *The Great Courses*—many ideas from the blog will likely be used.)

An open letter I wrote to Bill Nye (for *A Logical Take*) about philosophy led to me being featured in a (forthcoming) Bill Nye documentary, which then gave me a chance to meet him and then (successfully) persuade him of the value of philosophy. He even listened to my "Big Questions of Philosophy" course and emailed me saying that he is now a big fan of philosophy. I later learned that he went through the course guide book so many times that it fell apart and he had to get another copy. His new book is going to have a chapter on philosophy.

Through my use of social media I was also able to engage with some high school students in the U.K. Their teacher had them read my article in the journal *Think* on whether souls exist; I answered their questions via a blog entry on *A Logical Take*. I also once posted, on my blog, my answer to a question I put on my logic final. It was kind of a final lesson on how to use logic to effectively evaluate arguments.

I have also been able to use the blog to "publish" work that wasn't really appropriate for other platforms. For example, I wrote something on the Shroud of Turin for Schick's *How to Think about Weird Things* book, but it was unable to be used because of limited space. I ended up developing the piece and posting it on "A Logical Take." Similar endeavors led to much more. An Op-ed I wrote I 2009 for the Baltimore Sun (on whether parents should lie about Santa), not only drew a lot of attention, but ended up inspiring multiple blog posts, a course on Christmas, and then later my book "The Myths that Stole Christmas." This in turn led to me appearing on multiple podcasts (including *Point of Inquiry*), being featured in articles (in USA *Today*, *The Washington Post*, and *The Christian Science Monitor*) and five guest blogs for *The London School of Economics*.

I don't get near enough time to spend on the blog as I want. Given the election of Trump, I feel like I could spend all day every day, using logic to evaluate news and world events, and I've have something important to say everyday—but I just don't have the time. I usually just write and post something when I have a little down time. Occasionally, if something really strikes me, and the article just appears in my head without much extra effort, I'll just take the time to write it. As for Facebook and Twitter—again, I'll just post something when I have a little downtime. However, since the Trump presidency, I find myself spending more time with it.

If I were to give advice to scholars considering more use of social media, I'd give the following advice:

1) Don't let it take over your time.
2) Be selective in responding to the emails you will receive; that too could take up way too much of your time.
3) The world needs more educated people to speak out on matters of importance. Do so.

————————

David Kyle Johnson is an associate professor of philosophy at King's College in Wilkes-Barre, PA. He has done two courses for The Great Courses *(Exploring Metaphysics and* The Big Questions of Philosophy*), is the author of* The Myths that Stole Christmas, *and has published extensively for Wiley-Blackwell's Philosophy and Pop Culture series. He also was a winner of the 2011 American Philosophical Association Op-Ed Contest (for his Blog entry "Watson in Philosophical Jeopardy). You can find Dr. Johnson on Facebook at https://www.facebook.com /Dr.DavidKyleJohnson, and on Twitter (@Kyle8425). He also blogs for* Psychology Today *(Plato On Pop: https://www.psychologytoday.com/blog/plato-pop and A Logical Take: https://www.psychologytoday.com/blog/logical-take).*

CRAIG S. KEENER

New Testament

get the greatest response on my personal Facebook page, where I have 5000 friends and 1432 followers at the moment. (I feel badly for the followers because of the 5000-limit cap but I do not engage as much with the unlimited "book page" that a friend started for me, since it generates less interest.)

I do some serious things on Facebook (e.g., announcing when one of my new books comes out), but it is mostly personal and family events. It gets more interesting when I am lecturing in a different country and post the photo. Most days, though, I am just writing books. Facebook thus proves most useful in communicating something helpful for my readers when I have a new book to announce or, once in a while, also post a timely blog post (most recently on immigration).

Probably more pastorally fruitful is my blog site, craigkeener.com. I lack the tech savvy and the common sense of most bloggers to address trendy topics, but I hope that the time I do invest will be worth the positive outcome in readers'/viewers' lives. The first year, from August (when a friend started the site for me) until the end of December, I had just 6062 views. The second year it rose to 49,242; the third year, to 99,904; the fourth year, 132,828; the fifth year, 171,738, i.e., over 470 views per day. Last year (the sixth, 2016) it dropped back to 163,387, about 447 views per day; so far in 2017 it looks higher than the 2015 level (an average of 494 views per day). My own best day so far for view count in a day was 2414 views. At the moment I have 736 subscribers to my blog.

My blog usually includes three kinds of posts: Bible study material; videos of Bible lectures (some just a minute long, many an hour long); and silly cartoons about seminary life. The cartoons are to keep us from taking ourselves too seriously, but appear also because they are the posts that require by far the least amount of work! At the moment I run at least one of all three kinds of posts every week, though I can well imagine falling behind in the future, since I must also teach full-time, mentor doctoral students, and write academic books. Is it worth the time invested? I do not know, but I also lack the tech savvy to know how to reach a wider audience, whether I should choose a different site, etc.

Happily, some free resources on my blog site have proved more valuable. A free Bible interpretation manual there is available in several languages, and via a couple other websites the Spanish translation alone has now been downloaded well over 20,000 times.

I began the blog site to try to provide resources to a wider audience, including to believers in countries where they could not afford or have access to my academic writings. I do not have current stats about the countries viewing the blog because the friend who started the site and has administrator rights has been busy for a few years, but in 2013, when I had only about 60% the viewers as now, the visitors were from 185 countries. The largest number (37,888) were still from the U.S. (with 2899 from the U.K., 2172 from Canada, and 1864 from Australia), but other locations were also represented, including 1552 visitors from the Philippines, 1019 from South Africa, 892 from India, and 685 from Singapore. I am certain that the figures today would be more diverse; 2013 was before my ministry in Indonesia and India and before many contacts from Latin America.

I went on Facebook for two reasons. The first was to catch up with old friends with whom I had lost contact. The second was because a marketer from one of my publishers urged that this would promote the books that I write. (I write the books, after all, in hopes that people will read them.) Last year five of my books came out, and many readers also post pictures of the books on the Facebook page when they acquire them.

I cannot respond to all the comments and messages, but I have discovered that Facebook is sometimes a medium for personally encouraging people's faith. I have also been surprised by how many people view my posts on craigkeener.com, despite my lack of tech savvy or even full administrative rights to back up material on the site.

I have also been surprised by what gets the most likes and responses on

Facebook. Videos do not generate much engagement; even if they are just 30 seconds long, viewers apparently want to move through Facebook more quickly. Opinion posts generate more but usually not an abundance, except when someone makes a very controversial comment to which others respond. Photos with very brief comments can easily generate 400 likes, including announcements of a new book release, but especially photos with my family. (I am confident that my wife's extraordinary beauty has something to do with that.) But my prayer requests every few months generate more responses than anything else (except my birthday) — even without a photo. I am enormously grateful for that. When I was abruptly hospitalized about two years ago, the response to my wife's photo of me in the hospital was overwhelming. It amazed me how many Facebook friends really cared enough about me personally (or at least that I could keep writing books!) to comment and pray.

What has surprised me the most, however, is the diversity of engagement on Facebook. I have discovered that I have a much wider range of readers, denominationally and internationally, than I had guessed. That has made me feel all the worse that I am longer free to accept friend requests from readers. Nevertheless, I remain encouraged by the wide range of readers I do have.

On the list of priorities and thus time invested, social media is admittedly close to the bottom. This is partly because I am not sure about the impact compared with the impact of my books. Usually I engage Facebook on brief breaks from work or after I have finished my work for the day, often just before going to bed. (I recognize that it is probably better to disengage from the computer entirely before sleep, but pressing deadlines recently have kept me working on books most of the day.) Still, this is something that I do regularly, as I enjoy engaging with real people (and not just books) when I can.

In terms of creating blog posts and videos, often I wrote or filmed a number of these at once and then scheduled them to post over a long period of time. I write down the cartoons ideas when they come to me, usually when my brain is too fried to do anything else, but often draw the pictures for them four or five at a time over the course of an hour on my "day off."

Craig S. Keener (PhD, Duke University) is F. M. and Ada Thompson Professor of Biblical Studies at Asbury Theological Seminary. He is author of twenty books, five of which have won awards in Christianity Today; *more than seventy academic articles; several booklets; and more than one hundred fifty popular-level articles. One of his books,* The IVP Bible Background Commentary: New Testament, *now in a*

second edition, has sold more than half a million copies. Craig's website is http://
www.craigkeener.com/. Feel free to subscribe to it on the site, but also note the side-
bar that allows you to search various categories for devotionals/Bible studies on
various books of the Bible, videos, etc. Craig is on Facebook; there are several "Craig
Keener" Facebook persons but Craig's the one at Asbury Seminary. Googling "Craig S.
Keener" and Facebook will take you to the book page.

GRACE JI-SUN KIM

Constructive Theology

use the usual social media, Facebook, Twitter, LinkedIn and Instagram. Among
these, my primary platform is Facebook as it is the easiest means to share and
post my blogs, pictures and articles. Facebook, unlike Twitter, has no word limit
so I do not feel constrained when I post something. I also find that I have the most
interaction with friends and those following me on Facebook than any other form
of social media. Facebook is the easiest place to post pictures, blogs, announcements, videos and other information.

Since Facebook has become a primary platform for social media interaction, I
also began a public Facebook. This has become a good way for me to share my
work and make myself available as a scholar to and for the public.

Many scholars do not use Twitter as much as Facebook. For one reason or
another, Twitter isn't a big presence for us scholars. Many people use Twitter to
quickly disseminate thoughts and ideas. However, I am always cautious of writing
a tweet. Thus, much of my tweets are just to announce a book I wrote or a blog I
had just published. I realize I am not making full use of Twitter as it was created
to be, but I am open to using Twitter more frequently in the future as I gain more
confidence in my work and public presence.

One of the reasons for engaging in social media is to create a public presence
and to share my work with the general public outside the academy. This approach

helped me to reach out to those outside of the schools and help to make an impact on wider religious discourse.

My first book was published in 2002 and my next book came out in 2011. I have three children which made it almost impossible to sit and write. Hence, the reason for the large gap between the two books.

Originally I used social media to connect with readers of religious/spiritual books. I was excited when I finished the second book and wanted to get the word out to readers. The book is an attempt to present a global understanding of the Spirit and I wanted to reach people all over the world. I turned to social media to help advertise the book.

I had a good mentor who encouraged me to blog about the new book so that others will get to know about it. She said that the Episcopal Divinity School (EDS) would be able to host it on their blog site 99 Brattle. I started blogging in 2011 and haven't stopped. I kept blogging on EDS site but eventually I decided to create my own website to connect with readers.

I knew nothing about creating a website, but my nephew convinced me that it was simple to do. I gave it a try and now have a blogsite designed by me.

As I gained followers on my site I wanted to share my work to a broader audience. Facebook became a good platform to share my work.

We scholars tend to only speak to one another or a small circle of fellow scholars. It is usually a small group of 10 or so conversation partners that a scholar finds themselves communicating with. This is important as it informs and educates one another. But what good is it to the world when we are just talking to just one another? What we do must matter beyond our own circle of scholarly conversation partners, it must make an impact in the world we live in. The way we write and engage our scholarship in the social media can change the world for the better.

Social media will increase our conversation partners. It forces us to write more succinctly and simply without using "Ph.D. words and jargons". It pushes us to make our scholarship accessible and to the wider public. This is how I see social media. It is a powerful tool to use to change the world. This is how we need to engage the world and make a difference. We need something which will change us and make us stronger. The response from non-scholars on my work has been surprisingly good. Many have been challenged and formed by my work which is so rewarding to me. To know that my work is affecting people's lives and making changes in groups of people is more than I had imagined.

Social media has bigger platforms that can widen the audience and conversation partners that was not possible before social media came into play. It can be a powerful tool as it changes our thoughts. It distributes information quickly.

The reason today I continue to use Facebook is to share my work, but also to get a lot of news. It is also a place to see what other scholars in my area are engaged in. It is an easy way to keep up with people that you rarely or occasionally see. In addition, Facebook is also a good place to see what is trending in the news and in social media. It is good to be on top of things so that I can make my work relatable to the wider audience. I realize that I need to make sense to my teenage children and others and thus I feel social media helps to keep me relevant.

Another advantage of using Facebook is the various Facebook groups that you can be part of to engage in the conversations that you are interested in or would like to hear more about. Asian Americans have become an invisible minority and our voices are not being heard by the wider society. I am worried that Asian Americans do not get enough leverage in social matters as we are continuously pushed to the margins of society.

White dominant society sometimes views Asian Americans as "white" when it is convenient for them to think so and then people of color when it serves them better. We have been given names and titles such as 'honorary whites' and 'model minority' which does not help Asian Americans as marginalized groups within our society. Rather, what these terms end up doing is pitting Asian Americans against other people of color. It perpetuates a false narrative that if "blacks work as hard as Asian Americans, then they will succeed and live well". Or "if Hispanics just studied harder, then they will get in Ivy League schools". These are narratives perpetuated by terms such as 'model minority' and is very problematic.

Furthermore, terms such as "honorific whites" begin to eliminate Asian American's experiences of discrimination and racism as Asian Americans are viewed sometimes as "white". Asian Americans are constantly told that our experiences of racism were not racists as we are 'white' people. So out of convenience for white people, we are told that we are one group and then another group when it is not convenient for white people.

In such a context of racialization and discrimination, I appreciate Facebook groups such as "Asians NOW!" and "Progressive Asian American Christians." It is difficult for me to meet Asian American scholars and Christians who are passionate about social justice issues as I live in a small city with a small Asian American population. Therefore, these two Facebook groups have been an enriching experience and an important conversation partner for me.

Furthermore, social media has also slowly become another research platform for my work, in addition to the traditional journals and books where I glean information for my studies. Relevant information and articles on various topics are shared on Facebook and Twitter. They are now becoming resources for my writing and scholarship. This is something which I would have never imagined 10 years ago, but it is becoming the norm for many scholars who write for the public.

I have learned several things by engaging social media. I am coming to understand that social media is a powerful tool to educate and mold people's thoughts, ideas and views of the world. People around the globe are using social media to make news travel faster and to share important information about global issues affecting people in large masses. As scholars and theologians, it is important that we also enter this medium to challenge, form and transform the dialogue that is happening and occurring in our communities and areas of work.

What has surprised me is how social media can drain us and steal our time away. When I get bored I go into social media . . . and it can be a place where we waste a lot of time reading irrelevant posts and ideas. It is mind boggling to see how easily we can waste time and it is incredible how fast time flies when one enters social media.

Oftentimes, we are drawn in as we want to see what is trending on social media. I am still surprised at how fast information is shared. In February 2016, I wrote my TIME article on Chris Rock, Oscars and racism. This short piece started to explode on social media and soon Chris Rock was trending on Facebook. If you went to read the trending articles on Facebook, my TIME piece was there. It is amazing to me how quickly information gets posted, shared and read. Not only within my own community or country, but globally.

Social media has allowed several things to occur in my own life. When I was growing up, I was extremely shy, a bit more than normal. There were various reasons for that. First, being an immigrant, I couldn't speak English very well and was always self-conscious about myself . . . Secondly, due to my lack of practice in speaking out loud, I was a terrible public speaker. In grade 5, we had a public speaking assignment in school. Every grade 5 student had to do a 3-5 minute speech. We could use cue cards to help us but not to read from. As each child before me gave their speech, I was tormented by the fact that I had to go up soon. As my turn drew nearer, I started to sweat and tremble in my seat. My hands got all fidgety and my palms were sweaty. Finally it was my turn to give my speech. My hands were so sweaty that I could barely hold my cue cards and when I finished the cue cards were so damp they were illegible. My sweaty hands soaked right through them.

Going from being such a quiet child to now being a professor who teaches and gives public speeches has been a long journey. As I speak more and more, I gain more confidence and now have come to enjoy speaking. I think speaking is a good opportunity to share various thoughts and ideas that challenge the status quo or the dominant white male theology.

I am now trying more multimedia work such as podcasts and YouTube interviews. I find it an effective way to share my work. It is proving repeatedly to be a good platform from which to share my research, publications and my own activism.

There is a lot of activism present online. Petitions are formed and signed, videos of activist work are shared, ongoing ideas are shared and lots of information are being shared quickly and efficiently all over the world.

We do not have diverse voices in the mainstream religion, politics and society. We must have diverse voices. We need to hear voices especially of women of color and Asian American women. Social media provides such a platform for various voices to be heard and it is good that I can share my voice through such an open platform. Traditional channels owned and controlled by the dominant white society do not often provide an opportunity to share my different perspective. Social media does, so I continue to write, and produce podcast and YouTube interviews so that I can share my unique position and theological understandings.

A final thought about social media is a caution about the amount of time spent on social media. One needs to be able to protect one's time and analyze the efficiency of one's social media presence. One needs to be careful of not wasting too much time as people begin commenting on their work. I know of many friends who try to convince others of their position and continuously comment on posts.

Social media has become a necessary evil. It takes care and attention to manage one's website and social media platforms. It isn't a matter of just writing and posting, one should also check what others are doing. It is important to keep up with the media stream and see what is happening online to really engage with social media.

To stay relevant one needs to constantly evaluate one's social media presence. So, it is important to keep reading and rereading and analyzing one's work. If something isn't working out well, it needs to be redone in a more effective way.

First, be prepared to spend a lot more time than you had first anticipated. Social media can be a beast in that once you enter it, it leads to many doors and alleyways. Some will lead you to unexpected connections while others may lead you astray. It is important to stay focused and budget the time spent exploring what others are doing online.

Next, exercise discretion before posting things on social media, especially if it can land you in the hot seat. There have been many people who lost a job due to one Facebook post or tweet. So, we always should exercise caution before deciding to share something on social media. If it is going to be offensive in any way, we need to think twice before we post it. Is it worth offending people to make a single post?

Finally, be prepared to learn. There is so much information and learning tools on social media. (There is of course some useless information.) Social media can be a good learning playground to explore and expand one's thoughts and imagination. One can be seriously challenged by social media which can reshape one's religion and philosophy. It can even alter one's outlook and challenge one's perspective on life. For such life-altering events, we should enter social media with the understanding that we will learn and be challenged by it.

———————

Grace Ji-Sun Kim is an Associate Professor of Theology at Earlham School of Religion. She is the author or editor of 13 books most recently, Intercultural Ministry; Planetary Solidarity; Embracing the Other: Here I Am; Contemplations from the Heart; and The Grace of Sophia. *She is a co-editor for the Palgrave Macmillan Book Series,* "Asian Christianity in Diaspora". *She writes regularly for The Huffington Post, and have written for TIME, The Nation, and The Feminist Wire. See Kim's website,* Loving Life *at http://www.gracejisunkim.wordpress.com and follow her work there. You can also follow Kim on Twitter @gracejisunkim, Facebook https://www.facebook.com/gracejisunkim/ and Instagram https://www.instagram.com/gracejisunkim/ You can read her Huffington Posts at http://www.huffingtonpost.com/author/gjskim-440 Kim is also in LinkedIn, YouTube, Google+, and Pinterest.*

J. R. DANIEL KIRK

Biblical Theology

M y public online life began in the blogosphere. After several years blogging at the aptly named Shibboleth, I started hosting a blog on my own site and entitled it Storied Theology. I have blogged as often as daily at different stretches in my career, and now update on average once a week. I also record and produce a weekly podcast that offers commentary on the Revised Common Lectionary. I use Twitter and Facebook daily. On Facebook, I have both an author page and a personal page. Of all these platforms, Facebook tends to be the one that draws the most extensive conversations and engagements.

I began to blog because I wanted to have a platform for broadcasting some of my own ideas. I was involved in theological debates bubbling up in the denomination I was part of. I wanted to be able to bring my voice as a budding New Testament scholar to church conversations that tended to be populated by the voices of seminary-trained pastors or historical and systematic theologians.

As the blog developed, I kept blogging because I always felt that there was more to say. People in my church circles care about the Bible, so blogging about Bible, biblical studies, and theology was a good way to be a regular contributor to the lives of Christians whom I might not otherwise have contact with.

Getting into my teaching career, I found that hosting a regular blog became a way for my former students and other pastors to receive continuing theological education. I recall one student who sat through a whole class with me on "the cross in the New Testament." About a year, after he graduated I was teaching that class again and so was blogging about some of the core themes. He made a comment in response to one of my blog posts expressing the wonder of someone who has had their eyes opened to a new idea for the first time. It took a whole class *plus* reading my blog for a year before the ideas started to sink in.

That impulse to serve the church, especially through conversation with pastors and leaders, reflects what still animates the best of what I do: bringing high-quality New Testament scholarship into conversation with the life of the church. This is the driving force behind my weekly podcast. I figure that if I can influence how a couple thousand pastors preach on a Sunday morning that I am maximizing the impact of my training and productivity. When I was teaching regularly, six courses a year, it would take me six years to teach as many students as I had readers of my blog on a good day. That many people might never read an academic article I write. Social media is terrific for amplifying the popular impact of my scholarship.

My biggest surprise in my online engagements has been the extent to which professors expect social media engagements such as blogs to be in the same voice, tone, and scholarly caution that they want to see in technical scholarly writing. The fact that I write for normal people made my blogging suspect to seminary colleagues in ways that I was not anticipating. Even in seminaries, there is an academic snobbery that makes quickly dashed off blog posts somehow "beneath" the calling of a professor.

My second major research project, recently published as A *Man Attested by God*, had its genesis in a series of book reviews on my blog. After I had read and responded with no doubt exaggerated frustration to a few books on New Testament Christology over a short period of time one of my readers commented, "It looks like you've got your next book project." He was right.

Managing the time to blog and keep up with social media has become increasingly difficult. I used to try to blog daily on my own platform. I would sit down and write for about thirty minutes, find a picture that matched what I wanted to say, hit publish, and go. I would share the post on Facebook and Twitter, but that was it.

Now I am on a larger blog hosting platform. I am doing everything "right" in terms of ensuring that my pictures are the exact right size, writing slugs that will come up when the link is shared, sharing the posts on social media, scheduling posts about the blog, inserting page breaks to increase page clicks—it has become exhausting. So now I try to blog a couple days a week, but the extensive time suck has contributed to the falling away of my blog writing.

I try to contain my podcasting to one or two 90-minute blocks of time during the week. I use one of those to interview / record, and the other to produce the show and write the copy for the blog post that accompanies the audio.

In order to do these things while writing academic work, I tend to use the first hour or ninety minutes of my day to do the writing for my serious writing projects. If I do that every day then I make steady progress on my "real" work no matter what I manage to do or not do on my social media platforms.

If I were to recommend three things to scholars who are considering using social media, I'd say this:

First, I would discourage graduate students and professors early in their career from blogging. If you are saying interesting, relevant, provocative things then the positives of your growing platform and exposure will likely be overshadowed by the negatives of senior faculty and hiring committees not trusting your work. I had thought that the faculty was supportive of my blogging efforts. Then I heard of a senior colleague who said, "I don't trust a professor with groupies." That's when I realized that the medium itself was dicey.

Second, I would encourage folks at the front end of their careers to use Facebook for networking. There are lots of conversations around biblical and theological studies, and young scholars are often talking to each other in these venues. Those can be vital connections.

Third, always try to remember that a member of a hiring committee might be on the other side of any tweet, Facebook comment, or blog post that you write. This is extremely difficult to keep in mind. Acting in a professional manner of such a kind as people want to see when they are making decisions about your professional future is very hard to pull off.

J. R. Daniel Kirk (Ph.D., Duke University) does New Testament scholarship with a theological bent and an eye on the church. He is the author of three books: A Man Attested by God: The Human Jesus of the Synoptic Gospels, Jesus Have I Loved, but Paul?, *and* Unlocking Romans: Resurrection and the Justification of God. *Kirk is currently Pastoral Director for the Newbigin House of Studies in San Francisco. You can listen free to LectioCast, Daniel's weekly podcast, on iTunes, Stitcher, or wherever great podcasts are gathered. Follow him on Twitter @jrdkirk and on facebook.com/jrdkirk. His blog can be found by heading to StoriedTheololgy.com.*

ADAM KOTSKO

Philosophical Theology

I maintain a blog as well as a Facebook and Twitter account. For most of my online life, the blog was primary, but it was superseded by Twitter. More recently, I have shifted my primary usage to Facebook.

I already had an online presence before I even began graduate school. I maintained a website in high school and college, which I converted to a blog shortly after college graduation. I naturally discussed my academic interests there, but my focus was primarily on personal blogging. Only after I began my PhD did I shift focus to create a more strictly academic group blog (*An und für sich*) with other graduate students in the humanities.

When Facebook started to become a dominant force online, I was very reluctant to sign up, because I found the prospect of connecting with high school acquaintances and distant cousins very unappealing. One colleague of mine in graduate school continually pushed me to sign up for an account for "networking" purposes, and I initially signed up for Twitter (which was emerging as the "next big thing") in the hopes of getting her off my back. My network on Twitter was primarily academic, though I did not use it strictly for academic purposes. Instead, my focus was mostly on its entertainment value — the compressed format of Twitter has led to a culture of highly compressed multi-layer jokes. Ultimately, however, I was driven from Twitter when an ill-considered joke was decontextualized by a prominent right-wing website, leading to a campaign of systematic harassment that included phone calls to my institution demanding that I be fired.

In the wake of this experience, I finally signed up for Facebook, where I found that my graduate school colleague was correct — there is an incredibly rich network of academics who are strongly engaged with Facebook. The atmosphere is somewhat less entertaining, but more supportive overall. Facebook allows me to manage my privacy with greater flexibility, allowing me to connect with a wide range of people without exposing me to harassment from bad-faith interlocutors. Much more than my blog or Twitter, Facebook has connected me with academic opportunities like invitations to give lectures at other institutions (most notably an invitation that resulted in a trip to Australia) or to collaborate on publications. Facebook also provided a good forum to seek help and expertise from people in other fields and to talk through concepts and arguments in a safe and supportive environment.

My biggest discovery in my time online is that the political right has weaponized social media against academics that they view as too liberal or left wing. I do not want to go into detail about the specifics of my harassment experience, but they resulted from tweets that I had no reason to believe a wide audience would see. In one case, they were tweets I actually deleted within a few moments of posting, only to discover that someone had already taken a screenshot. In another, the remark that became such a focus of ire was directed at a single individual, and without special efforts, it would normally be visible only to people who followed both of us (a very small group in this case). I am forced to conclude that I was being somehow monitored to see if I would slip up in some way.

The machinery of right-wing harassment is extremely efficient, and it quickly reaches some very scary places. What began with a relatively mainstream conservative blog soon moved on to the so-called "alt-right" and ultimately to unapologetic Neo-Nazis who, believing me to be Jewish, hurled anti-Semitic abuse at me — including invitations to step into the gas chamber. As a privileged white straight man, I got off relatively easy. Campaigns against women, people of color, and sexual minorities are much more vicious and sustained. I was also fortunate to have the full support of my institution. Many academics have not been so lucky. Eager to avoid bad publicity, some schools have publicly disavowed or even disciplined academics in the face of right-wing harassment — a misguided approach that only emboldens enemies of academic freedom.

At the same time, I don't want to give the impression that it's all bad. I have been stunned by the generosity and support of fellow academics online. Social media has connected me with amazing people whom I would not otherwise have met. It is also often shocking how quickly and precisely social media can answer a question—many times, the answer is faster and much more reliable and nuanced than a Google search could uncover. For instance, once I asked why Debussy briefly changes keys in the middle of "Clare de Lune," and within minutes, I had three people rushing to give me a cogent and informative answer. And more broadly, I have learned that there is always someone up for a conversation about almost any topic, be it finer points of Greek grammar, questions of translation in Heidegger, the details of Christian doctrinal heresies, or the philosophical implications of *Buffy the Vampire Slayer*.

One of my most amazing social media experiences came shortly after I joined Facebook. I had just completed work on *The Prince of This World*, a study of the complex theological dynamics surrounding the devil in the Christian tradition and the ways they unexpectedly affect ostensibly secular political concepts in modernity. I had some sense that the ideas I was developing could be productively applied to contemporary neoliberal economics, and so I posted on Facebook, "Does anyone want to invite me to come give a talk on the devil and neoliberalism?"

My initial thought was that a speaking invitation would force me to flesh out the idea—but much to my surprise, one of the first responses came from an academic who wanted to invite me to speak in her department in Australia. Given the long flight involved, she recommended that I use her invitation as a starting place for a broader speaking tour, and with her help I was ultimately able to string together six speaking engagements in Australia and New Zealand. The discussions I had on that tour led me to revise my lecture into an article, which I am now planning to use as the basis for my next book. None of this—neither the opportunity to travel to a part of the world I may never have visited otherwise nor the new book project—would have happened without the connections I made on social media.

I think this story is emblematic of how academics should think of social media—with an emphasis on the "social" rather than the "media." It's about building connections that can develop into real-world encounters. It should supplement and amplify real-life connections, not replace them.

People sometimes ask how I make time for social media. This question always strikes me as strange, because it is part of my daily routine, so that it doesn't feel like it takes up much time. I browse social media over my morning coffee and normally make a couple posts or comments. I check in periodically throughout the day during downtime that I likely could not use productively in any case—the ten-minute break between classes, for instance, or the time spent waiting for the subway.

When I'm doing computer-based work (grading, writing, etc.), I normally have a browser window open and flip back and forth periodically. I know that for many people it can be a problematic distraction, but I actually find that it helps me to focus. If I have a stray thought unrelated to what I'm working on, posting a couple lines on social media helps to get it out of my head and turn back to the task.

If I were asked for advice, my first thought would be that *no* academic who is not already using Twitter should start now. Twitter has become a dangerous place, particularly for academics, and above all, for academics who are new to its peculiar culture. I still maintain a locked Twitter account, primarily to keep in contact with friends (and to keep up with the jokes), but I will never again take the risk of using a public account.

Facebook is a much better environment. It is amazingly dense with academics in all fields, and my experience tells me that you are not actually required to connect with high school lab partners and second cousins if you don't want to.

Adam Kotsko is Assistant Professor of Humanities at Shimer College, where he also serves as Associate Dean. He holds a PhD in Theology, Ethics, and Culture from the Chicago Theological Seminary, where he specialized in continental philosophy and the history of Christian thought. He is the author of several books on theology, philosophy, and cultural criticism, most recently The Prince of This World *(Stanford University Press). See Adam Kotsko's group blog, An und für sich (http://itself.blog). He is also an avid user of Facebook (Adam Kotsko) and Twitter (@adamkotsko); both accounts are private, but he is open to friend and follower requests.*

KWOK PUI-LAN

Theology and Spirituality

I was rather slow in adopting social media and did not have a smartphone till the fall of 2016! Since my workday usually consists of sitting in front of my computer for extended periods of time, I was reluctant to be connected to a mobile device so that people could reach me 24/7. My friends expressed disbelief when I told them I didn't have a smartphone. They wondered how I could manage without it, given my frequent travels and busy schedule. When I eventually decided to change to a smartphone, it was because I had found a monthly plan that was even cheaper than the pre-paid plan for my flip phone!

At first I did not even want to open a Facebook account because I thought it was time consuming. But an Asian and Asian American women's group I belonged to suggested it as a vehicle for us to connect with one another and post information. Friends in the group insisted that I open an account, and reluctantly, I did. I started to use Twitter too, thinking it would be a less time-consuming way to share information and catch up with friends. Now, I continue to use social media because it allows me to connect easily with colleagues from different periods of my life across several continents.

My social media use now extends to my writing as well. After I have published a new book, I announce it with a photo of the book cover on social media. When I have come across an interesting book, I promote it on Facebook and some of my friends would buy the book I recommended. My friends also share information about their publications on social media where I can consult some of the articles they recommend. Facebook enables me to reconnect with colleagues that I have lost touch with for some time. For example, I was able to invite a colleague to guest lecture in my class by leaving a message on her Facebook page. Although I have not opened an account on Academia.edu, I have accessed articles posted by other scholars on that site.

I began blogging in relation to my teaching. I asked students in my Spirituality course to create a blog and post their spiritual journals there in 2011. At the time I did not have a blog and in order to find out what the experience would be like, I started a blog myself. I have found writing a blog to be the easiest way to self-publish: I can write whatever I want and whenever I want to write it. I also enjoy reading comments readers leave on the blog. I used social media to share that I have written a blog post on "A Postcolonial Eucharist." It was amazing to discover less than 24 hours later, that the blog had more than 700 page views. Via social media, I can find out what is happening in different parts of the world in real time. For example, during the Occupy Central and Umbrella Movement in Hong Kong in 2014, my friends from Hong Kong posted updates and pictures as the movement evolved. I also found out from social media that South Korean President Park Geun-hye was removed from office, after the country's constitutional court upheld a parliamentary vote to impeach her. My Korean friends were elated and spread the news on social media upon learning the court's decision.

When Joerg Rieger and I wrote *Occupy Religion: Theology of the Multitude*, we decided that the book should build on the experience of people who have participated in the Occupy movement. In addition to interviewing students, friends, and clergy during our travels, we decided to use crowdsourcing on social media. We announced that we were writing the book and asked friends to recommend websites and people we should connect with. Through crowdsourcing, we found out information about the Occupy movement in Canada and in a few American cities. We also monitored postings about the movement around the world. Crowdsourcing was invaluable because the Occupy movement was still developing when we wrote the book in the spring of 2012. As the first theological book on the Occupy movement, *Occupy Religion* was published in the fall of 2012, only a year after the movement had begun.

Our research and lives have been so affected by the connectivity of social media. Does this constant connection to the Internet change our minds and ways of thinking? Nicholas Carr published a controversial article "Is Google Making Us Stupid" in *Atlantic Monthly* (July/August 2008). He has since expanded his argument in *The Shallows: What the Internet Is Doing to Our Brains*. He asked if spending a lot of time searching and surfing online would change our brains and make us less able to read and think deeply. This also includes surfing various social media platforms. His answer is yes, saying that many of us have lost the attention span needed to engage in deeper and complicated thoughts. Some of us can't even finish reading a long novel!

In "Overloaded Circuits: Why Smart People Underperform" published in *Harvard Business Review* in January 2005, Edward M. Hallowell argues that many people are suffering from attention deficit trait (ADT), a cultural trait that is distinguished from, but related to, attention deficit disorder (ADD). ADT springs from multitasking, data overload, and the increasingly fast speed of modern life. People with ADT have difficulties setting priorities, staying organized, and managing time. These symptoms can undermine the work of an otherwise gifted person.

I try to avoid developing ADT by minimizing multitasking and slowing down. In order to have a productive life for the long haul, I have to develop a good working habit. During the time of the day when I am most creative, I work on my research and writing projects, instead of answering emails and checking social media. I only check Facebook and other social media outlets when I have a break or when I feel tired in the evening. Sometimes I purposely leave my smartphone at home instead of carrying it with me to convince myself that I do not need to continuously connect to the Internet and social media. I found out exposure to blue light from tablets and mobile phones before bedtime affects the quality of my sleep. I try to read a book before going to bed and avoid using electronic devices, but I am not always successful in doing this.

Social media can be an easy and convenient way to connect with people and to organize in the future. We have seen this during the Occupy movement and the Women's March after Trump's inauguration. I hope people will continue to devise creative ways to use social media to effect social changes. Yet, using social media can also be addictive. After posting something, you want to see how many "likes" you receive and how many comments. In restaurants, I have seen people busy taking pictures of the dishes to post on social media, instead of enjoying each other's company. It is important not to let social media outlets take over our lives.

I was surprised to find out that while social media can help people feel connected, it might also cause stress and depression in some people. Seeing photos of friends on vacation or celebrating in a party might create the impression that your friends are enjoying their lives, while you might feel lonely and envious. It is important to remember that people post selective events on social media and not to compare ourselves socially to our peers based on a Snapchat moment.

During the season of Lent, I have seen some friends posting that they would give up the use of social media for a certain period of time. But we don't need to wait for Lent to do this. We can establish a Sabbath time, during which we can refrain from using social media and concentrate on cultivating relationships with people around us.

———————

Kwok Pui-lan is the William F. Cole Professor of Christian Theology and Spirituality, Emerita, at the Episcopal Divinity School in Cambridge, MA, and the 2011 President of the American Academy of Religion. Kwok has published extensively in Asian feminist theology, biblical interpretation, and postcolonial criticism. She was the recipient of the Award for Excellence in Teaching in 2009 from the American Academy of Religion and has written or edited twenty books in English and Chinese. Kwok uses Facebook (Kwok Pui Lan), Twitter (@KwokPuiLan), and writes a blog (kwok.puilan @blogspot.com). She also manages the website for Pacific, Asian, and North American Asian Women in Theology and Ministry (http://www.panaawtm.org/).

JASON LEPOJÄRVI

Constructive Theology

L ike most people, I suppose, I both love and hate using social media. I use Facebook and Twitter daily, and in that order. While I might be able to *post* on more than two platforms, I certainly could not *participate* meaningfully. Contributing meaningfully and reciprocally takes time. It requires both give and take, and everyone knows that it is of course far easier to give (post) than to take (learn).

The reason why I originally gravitated to social media was probably no different than that of anyone else. I wanted to connect with both *people* and *ideas*. This double-interest, so to speak — the love of people and the love of ideas — is still the main reason why I continue to use it. And I find that you need both loves. If you are not going anywhere, you cannot have travel companions. If you cannot have travel companions, what is the point of going in the first place? Some people reserve one social media for "personal" communication and another for "professional" communication. For good or ill, I find it difficult to separate the two.

I have discovered to my delight and horror that social media seems to bring out the best and worst in people, myself included. Every media and innovation has its corresponding virtues and vices, its strengths and weaknesses. As a general rule, I would say that the snappier the medium of communication, the *more* attention should be given to *courtesy* and *argument*. This might sound counterintuitive. But think about it. As essays are compressed into letters, and letters into emails, and emails into comments, and comments into tweets, and tweets into snaps — the more difficult it becomes to remain kind and clear. The first casualty is always either courtesy or argument. Sometimes both.

The most helpful breakthroughs or discoveries that emerge through using social media are, I find, nearly always *joint* pursuits. Someone posts a question. Soon "friends", in C. S. Lewis's sense of the word, chime in: people who find the question valuable even if they don't agree on the answer. I have made several discoveries through unhurried, civil, and lucid discussion on social media.

Here is just one example. I once remarked how J. R. R. Tolkien and C. S. Lewis seemed to view friendship love between women and men rather differently, and that the proof was in the pudding. This led to a wonderful conversation that lasted several days with ever more knowledgeable people chipping in. This took place a few years ago but I am still reaping its fruits in my thinking and teaching today. In fact, I have recently incorporated the theme into my course on the theology of love.

I mentioned above that I "hate" using social media. Perhaps I exaggerated. But the truth is that you simply have to develop your time-management skills. Otherwise you lose yourself; and what good is your life then? As a Protestant Christian, I discovered *virtue ethics* quite late in life. I must have been over twenty when I first learned about this "ancient" posture toward life — not just the moral life but intellectual life. What does this have to do with social media? Well, quite a lot, I now think. Moderation is nearly impossible without self-control and other virtues. These virtues help us to enjoy the good things in life be it food, drink, sex — or information, communication, time. Not having developed deep roots earlier it sometimes feels like an uphill battle. But there is probably no alternative. Fight or flight. One of the most helpful books has been *The Intellectual Life*, a classic by A. G. Sertillanges. Nearly a century old, it is packed with perennial wisdom. I return to it regularly to recalibrate my vision, purpose, intentions, and methods.

If I were to advise those considering using social media, I would begin by saying: Cultivate your virtues, cultivate your virtues, and — this is important — cultivate your virtues. Not just the obvious virtues like self-control and practical wisdom. But also virtues like courage and love. It might sounds surprising, but courage has an important role to play in managing your time and other obligations in relation to time spent on social media. It will give you the ability to say "no" to things as well as "yes". It will give you the ability to defend what you have found to be true and right.

Together with love, courage will empower and even compel you to support that friend, student, colleague, or stranger who is being "executed" online for the latest heresy in whatever discipline. Be kind, but be courageous. Your turn will come later.

———————

Jason Lepojärvi, Ph.D. is a Finnish-Canadian theologian, philosopher, and C. S. Lewis expert. His doctoral dissertation God is love, but love is not God *(2015) analyzed C. S. Lewis's theology of love. Lepojärvi is a former Junior Research Fellow in Theology at St. Benet's Hall, Oxford, and President of the Oxford C. S. Lewis Society. He currently lives in Vancouver, British Columbia, and has launched a postdoctoral research project on idolatry at Regent College. See Lepojärvi's websites, "Lewisiology" (in English) at lewisiology.com and "Rakkauden ammattilainen" (in Finnish) at rakkaudenammattilainen.fi. You can find him on Facebook (Jason Lepojärvi) and Twitter (@JasonLepojarvi), more often than not hosting a discussion or friendly debate on ethics, religion, philosophy, or politics.*

BEX LEWIS

Theology and Communications

These days I use many forms of social media, for different purposes, using some much more regularly than others. I remember being excited by Friends Reunited in 2001, being confused by Myspace back in 2005, and setting up a Facebook account at the end of 2006, and then not using it until I became a tour leader for Oak Hall in March 2007 because I couldn't work out its purpose. Several years later, the picture is very different, and I would regard myself as a 'digital resident' of many spaces (not a 'digital native', which is a term I'd contest!).

Facebook continues to be my most used platform, with over 2,000 'friends', although I would not say that all friendships are equal. Some are spoken to frequently, making use of private messaging and various group options as well as the more public discussions spaces, whilst for others, it's more like having a long-term address book in which someone comes to mind quite some time after I met someone. Some of those friends are ones that I've known well offline, whilst others I've never met outside of Facebook.

The other platform that I use most is Twitter, where I have over 10,900 followers, most of whom I follow back. This continues to be exceptionally useful, and currently irreplaceable, for connecting with people with similar interests, even if points of view may be very different, as we connect around keywords and hashtags.

My devices are full of apps, but the other social media apps I use with any regularity include Instagram (largely scenery, food, and quotes from books), YouTube (where I watch more than I produce), WordPress for blogging since 2009 (after travel-blogging in 2007-8), LinkedIn (for a professional profile), Slideshare (for sharing presentations) and Messenger and Whatsapp for more private conversations. I'm still struggling to get the hang of Snapchat and Reddit, one because I don't seem to have enough connections on it, the other because I haven't had time to play with it!

I first really engaged with 'the digital' in1997, when I 'built' my first website. I adapted the official paperwork from my PhD application, and saved my Word document as HTML, and I was live! I was looking to demonstrate what I was engaged in, seek answers for research on a topic of popular interest (second world war propaganda posters), and connect with interested parties (there were still a large number of people who would remember the war alive then, and I had a questionnaire ready to send out, although most replies came via newspaper postings)! Move forward a few years, I've learnt Dreamweaver, am building small sites for people, encouraging them to think about how to listen to their clients, create their own material, and keep 'current'. This was accompanied by a research project in 2001-2002 focused upon accessibility, usability, and how to create content for lecturers to use with students to consider how digital structures and actions changed the dynamic for content.

I'm more content orientated, particularly the question of 'why', and so I was really pleased once social media went mainstream at the beginning of 2009. I had just returned from global travels, needed a job, and started looking at digital roles. Digital seemed to be an expanding fields, I was openly able to go for job interviews, and that's when I realised the possibility of connecting with experts and interested 'others' in the field, and accessing the most up to date information. I find that I use different sites in different ways, with Twitter and Facebook (probably in that order), giving me the best scholarly content and conversations, partly because of the wide range of people using them, and the way that connections made either at conferences and events, or through acquaintances in common, leads to different conversations within a different environment.

With so many new connections, every day it's possible to learn something new on social media all the time, although with a strong eye on having to learn to spot fake news! I see part of my role to both myself, and encourage others, to highlight where sites such as Snopes have disproved stories. It's important to consider efforts that can be taken to leave the 'filter bubble', in which algorithms are all too keen to keep us, although I haven't gone as far as a friend, who caused consternation when she liked Donald Trump's Facebook page!

I've found social media really useful as a sounding board for potential ideas for conference papers, articles, and media interviews, crowdsourcing ideas which can be spread more widely—right now I've a very busy conversation going on Facebook about how to stop neighbouring cats pooing in my garden—of which the consensus appears to be dried citrus peel, coffee grounds, lion poo, or get your own cat (erm, I can just about keep my Pokémon alive!). I could Google it, but to be honest, there's so many 'quack' ideas, I want to know what has actually worked for people! There's a lot of useful information, and a lot of laughter there too—the best of social conversation, and I don't even have to be in the same geographical space!

I have really enjoyed seeing the potential for bottom-up opportunities provided by social media for the church. It's very easy to focus on the top-down projects that are done at a national level, and the ability to engage in a Facebook discussion with the Archbishop of Canterbury, or follow the Pope on Twitter is certainly something that's great and a new opportunity offered by the digital. It's often the small, experimental things in which one sees the most impact on a relational level—and I'm more interested in the 'social' of media, than of the 'media'! As a leader on Oak Hall holidays, I was expected to provide pastoral care on trips, and noted it was significant who spoke to me a lot on the trip, and it typically wasn't the same people who spoke to me via Facebook afterwards.

The disinhibition that's blamed so much for cyber-bullying really seems to give people an opportunity to speak up. As Bryony Taylor, a student of mine, wrote last year "People find it easy and more comfortable to ask questions about faith in a private space online . . . people on social media are directly contactable in a way that has not previously been so easy; paradoxically there is a distance offered by the online environment akin to the screen in the confessional box." I've also been interested to hear of case studies within churches where, for example, a Methodist church was next to a school, noted the parents waiting in the rain, invited them in for tea, toast, and warmth, which led to the formation of a group in which Facebook was integral in building relationships, and allowing questions and conversations, bringing a number of members to a point of faith, and, in time, membership of the church, even though the original intention hadn't been evangelism.

In some ways, it seems difficult to explain the power of social media on my everyday life, including my academic life, because I'm so embedded within it, that many things have just become 'normal'. If I need some ideas, some quotes, some suggestions of readings, I will just put a post up, and see what catches people's attention, but it goes much deeper than that! I always want to emphasise the importance of online/offline interactions, and how the lines between them have blurred more and more as the years have gone on. Potential collaborations start online, and lead to offline meet-ups, or a conversation starts offline, and the ideas continue flowing online. Sometimes they stay fully online, and that's fine too!

This has been noticeable in my last two jobs. I met the Director of CODEC via Twitter, went to an event at Durham University, and ended up running The Big Bible Project for five years, which developed into a project that brought together voices from the pew, the pulpit, and the academy to contemplate discipleship in a digital age. I met my current colleague at an event, and maintained contact via Facebook and Twitter. Observing my continued interest and passion for particular topics, and after my book *Raising Children in a Digital Age* was published, he started to suggest that I should apply for a job at Manchester Metropolitan University—and I am now in a role there.

Social media for me is all about the relationships that are built on the various platforms, about listening to others, about giving and taking, and about genuinely being interested in the conversations that I participate in, otherwise I wouldn't give it so much of my time. Within the (disputed) Myers-Briggs framework, I am an extreme extravert, so apparently then "regard anyone as a potential friend", for which social media is a great job, and a huge potential time suck! As those relationships are 'real', when I ask for information for a presentation or media, people don't seem to object, and this often gives a real 'voice' to what could otherwise present some quite dry theory. The most interesting thing that has happened is the media opportunities that typically come via social media, either from a radio station that already has me on the radar, or because I post a story about something that interests me, such as Pokémon Go. That particular topic led to being featured on a Radio 4 religion and belief programme about how churches, many of which are Pokestops, could use it as a tool for mission, a bridge for conversation, to take groups on walks, or as a topic within sermons.

As with anything, there's no exact right way to manage time, and sometimes I can see that I've spent 'too long' on social media, but this is usually symptomatic of being tired and wanting a bit of light relief from writing lectures, preparing writing, or especially marking! I often use social media as an incentive to engage with when certain work is completed, although at other times I use it as a work tool! Many of the people who I connect with are interested in the same research topics as I am, so it leads to interesting conversations, and potential collaborations. I have a friend who experimented in Lent with not picking up her phone until 9.30am, and found this set the day off right. I have also been involved in endless conversations with those giving up social media for Lent (generally because it is seen to be 'wasting time') along the lines of "are we saying that what happens online is not real, so you're just going to disconnect for Lent"?

Particularly for those who are housebound in some way, social media is a true lifeline, but also, I wouldn't spend all day stood next to someone's desk having a chat, so I don't spend all day on social media. Sometimes it's running all day in the background, and I flick backwards and forwards, especially if I'm looking for inspiration. If, however, I have some deep thinking or writing to do, I'm quite likely to turn it off—and sometimes will send a tweet of accountability saying "I won't be back until 1,000 words are written", or whatever target feels appropriate. It's certainly something that's of concern for managers, although if work is outputs driven, rather than presenteeism, it shouldn't cause a problem!

If asked, I'd give the following advice to those considering greater use of social media:

1) If you're not already familiar with it, take some time to get to know it and understand it. It took me three months before I saw any real value from Twitter conversations, and I felt like I was posting into the desert. As connections built up (quality, not quantity), then I started to see how give and take worked online, sharing my own findings and knowledge, as well as receiving helpful information from others. Social media has become a more commercialised space, but as you become comfortable online, you can use it more effectively. It's worth spending a little time each day to target interesting users, who may, or may not, follow you back, share content that is interesting, bearing in mind that you don't have to generate it all yourself, and it's not a journal article, so doesn't need to be as overworked. It's certainly not a magic bullet, any more than any other form of communication is, and it is about communication, not technology.

2) Have some idea what you are going to post about on social media. In my personal account, it's about what I'm interested in, and I tend not to over-curate, but I have a core of content that seems to be (now I need a moment to think), social media, faith, social justice, books I'm reading, DIY progress, activities I've been involved in, events I'm at, sermons I'm listening to, to discuss TV programmes, and I like to have fun! I find it a great place to let off steam, but as I'm always saying, there's a few cogs going around in my head before I post anything on social media (because it is at the same time

ephemeral and permanent) — do I mind God seeing it? My parents? Any children I know? Do I mind if it ends up on the front page of the newspaper, and will I defend what I've said five/ten years later, or demonstrate how I've changed my opinion? Can my worst enemy do something with what I've just posted — twist it, take my IP, or burgle my house? And — enjoy it!

3) I use social media quite a lot within teaching, as well as to connect with colleagues both within my team, and more widespread. Always use it as a solution to a problem, rather than a solution looking for a problem (unless you just want to experiment with it). Most teaching units have hashtags that students can tweet on, or look at extra stories that we've tweeted, public content can be placing on a blog rather than Moodle, collections of videos can be made on YouTube. I connect with students on public platforms such as Twitter, Facebook groups, or via LinkedIn, but not as Facebook friends (at least not until they've graduated).

There are so many opportunities within the digital environment, although the media loves to focus on the negative. As we become critical, constructive and confident inhabitants of it, we can contribute to it as a positive part of our lives.

———————

Bex Lewis trained as a mass communications historian. She is Senior Lecturer in Digital Marketing at Manchester Metropolitan University, and Visiting Research Fellow at St John's College, Durham University, with a particular interest in digital culture, and how this affects the third sector, especially faith organisations. She is Director of social media consultancy Digital Fingerprint, and author of Raising Children in a Digital Age: Enjoying the Best, Avoiding the Worst *(Lion Hudson, 2014) See Bex's institutional online profile at: http://bit.ly/drbexl-modb, and personal website at: http://drbexl.co.uk/. She can be found on most social media sites by searching for either "Bex Lewis" or @drbexl.*

TODD A. LITTLETON

Pastoral Theology

Len Sweet once described the differences between people in terms of cultural location as either an immigrants or natives. I am not considered native to digital or social media culture. When my youngest daughter was provided her first cell phone at 16, now 28, Text messaging was just taking off. When I would call her on her cell phone she may not respond. However, if I texted her I could expect a prompt reply. Admittedly this was infuriating as someone who grew up with landlines and knew what a bag phone was.

Eventually we negotiated communication and I learned the difference between what it meant to be a native to digital culture and the feeling of being out of place as an immigrant. My adaptation to social media came much quicker. Both of my daughters helped inform me and teach me the do's and don'ts of social media. They alerted me to what platforms teenagers used and how uncool it might be for me to dabble in those spaces. My assessment of digital/social media culture leaves me settled that my daughters would be considered 1.0. My grandsons will surely be 2.0 if not 3.0.

Once I learned the ropes of social media culture, I took up social media use and remained and remain alert to the various channels as they develop. I have social media accounts with Facebook, Twitter, Instagram, LinkedIn, Pinterest,

Snapchat and About Me. My primary tools include Facebook, Twitter and Instagram.

My initial aim to become involved online included the desire to write short theological reflections via a blog. Admittedly I hoped to engage others interested in theological subjects at the intersection of the examined life. When social media channels developed they became a logical means to share and promote these reflections. WordPress, my blogging platform, provides plugins to enhance the distribution of blog posts. Writers hope to be read, and often. Social media channels provide an inexpensive, if not free, way to promote thoughts and ideas.

Over time I have been working to distinguish how I use social media for personal and vocational projects. Facebook Pages, for instance allow a measure of separation between what you may put out that is personal and point to what is vocational or professional. And yes, sometimes these two spaces overlap.

Guy and I graduated from college together. We went our separate ways and had not communicated in any form for maybe twenty years. Guy found me on social media and read some of my writing. He reached out to me and we reconnected. We were both Religion majors and on track to serve in local churches. His course of study eventually led him to UC-Santa Barbara pursuing a PhD in philosophy. Themes and authors I was only discovering served a very central part of his studies. The interactions provided me a conversation partner to harness helpful ideas and avoid caricatures commonly offered by critics. The relationship has been invaluable as I moved toward an emphasis on pastoral theology in my thinking and writing. Guy traveled through Oklahoma earlier this year. He stopped over and our online reconnection became a real-time event after 30 years.

Using social media to spur conversation is not without its pitfalls. I have been surprised how easy it is for real-time friends to forget they know you. It is not uncommon for friends to engage your thoughts and speculations as if they were total strangers. The context of friendship is jettisoned for an internal need to right my ship. Social media does not often allow for a fully orbed explanation of an idea. I learned quickly these interactions may prove painful.

People rarely abide long blog posts. They appear more reticent to read a long Facebook post. On the other hand Twitter makes it necessary to be as succinct as possible when not linking to a longer form piece. Some are opting for threaded tweets, combining a series of tweets to produce in effect a long form tweet beyond the 140-character limit. These circumstances make clarity essential. More often than not it requires readers to give the benefit of the doubt while looking for explanation over against the more reflexive response to assume the worst.

My own experience has led me to be a bit more cautious when posting what

could easily be considered controversial. I now attempt to take the way my followers, regular followers, interpret words and phrases into account. It is a bit
burdensome but if these media are for communication, then I think we must take
up the hard work to be as understood as possible. Granted there are those who
seem bent on oppositional thinking no matter the subject.

On the other side, you never know who may be reading your post. Last summer I hastily jotted down ten lessons I learned from Facebook. I had been reading
shared articles and personal posts in the aftermath of a series of police related
shootings. Carl Raschke, a philosopher from whose articles and writings I have
learned, messaged me. He asked if I would turn that Facebook post into an article for the website, *Political Theology*. Talk about floored! I gladly accepted the
invitation.

Over time I discovered high quality podcasts via social media. Some of my
favorites provided interviews of authors, thinkers and practitioners I would not
otherwise know about. Recently I moved from a podcast dedicated to a brief
mashup of Scripture Texts from the Revised Common Lectionary to an interview-
based podcast targeting the pastor-theologian. The project is still in its first year
and I am still getting a rhythm down for the show.

The very opportunity to participate in this book project came, I think, from
my interview and interactions with Tom. His most recent book, *The Uncontrolling
Love of God*, provided for a great conversation as well as an opportunity to write
an essay for the book's dedicated website. Our interactions on social media have
proven beneficial to me as I continue to work through the content of his book.

Through social media I have been able to get to know the voices behind
my favorite podcast shows long before I met any of them in person. These
shows—Homebrewed Christianity, Crackers and Grape Juice and The Christian
Humanist—have also been great partners to help get the word out about my own
podcast. I know my own work would not be nearly as successful without them
using their social media channels to help spread the word.

Social media may steal too much time if you are not careful. I generally set
some personal guidelines as to when I check my channels. I am careful of how I
utilize notifications of activity—responses, shares, reposts, etc. Generally if I post
a new podcast episode accompanied by a blog post, I will schedule Tweets and
Facebook posts using an app like Hootsuite. These scheduled posts keep from
falling into the trap of stopping good work to promote or interact with those who
respond.

Here are three things I would recommend to scholars using social media.
First, be consistent. If you use social media to promote your blog or podcast or

other important ideas, decide the schedule best for you. If you post aggressively out of the gate but then slow to once a month, you risk losing your audience. *Second*, be responsive with charity. Our ideas are our babies. But, social media is unlike other forums to promote and share your work. Many may choose to hide behind the anonymity and lack of proximity to challenge, even ridicule. *Finally*, and this is for emphasis, be thick-skinned. Learn from your most ardent critics. Avoid defensiveness. How you respond publicly, in social media, will reveal something of your character. You will win more people with a soft answer than an incendiary retort.

Despite these suggestions that could be construed as cautions, social media provides imaginative and unlimited possibility to engage with others, their ideas, and to work out your own theological projects. I consider the benefit and resources made available via social media and digital culture to outweigh the occasional negative feedback.

Todd A. Littleton, D.Min, is a pastor with an interest in practical, public, theology. He has been pastor with Snow Hill Baptist Church, Tuttle, Oklahoma for nearly 23 years. He has written articles—offline and online—related to pastoral work and theology, among other subjects. See Littleton's website, Patheological at toddlittleton .net. Subscribe to Todd's podcast on iTunes—patheological: The Podcast for the Pastor- Theologian. Littleton is active on Facebook (Todd Littleton, talittleton), Twitter (@LittletonTodd and @patheological) and Instagram (doctodd). Occasionally you will find Todd on LinkedIn and Pinterest.

JAY MCDANIEL

Public Theology

I have created two websites in an emerging tradition that some might call "public humanities," or, perhaps better, "public liberal arts with a theological focus." I want to reach people who are religiously affiliated, religiously unaffiliated, and the vast majority who are somewhere in between. Toward this end I use Facebook groups as a platform for discussion, working closely with the process theologian/novelist Patricia Adams Farmer and her idea of taking process philosophy to the hearts and into the streets with Fat Soul Philosophy. My primary website is Jesus, Jazz, and Buddhism: Process Philosophy and Theology for a More Hospitable World: www.jesusjazzbuddhism.org. A companion site is Process Philosophy for Everyone: www.processphilosophy.org. The Facebook Groups are Process Philosophy for Everyone; Jesus, Jazz, and Buddhism; and Fat Soul Café.

I teach in a liberal arts college and many of my students are "spiritual but not religious." And I work in the summers in mainland China, where many more students and friends fall into the same category. I wanted to develop a platform that might speak to them at many levels, somehow linking "spirituality" with the whole of life: art, science, philosophy, food, music, culture, theology. China was the prompt. I was going to mainland China on a regular basis to teach process philosophy, in the context of which I was working with many internet-savvy young

Chinese in face-to-face settings. They lacked resources for continued study, particularly in applied process thinking.

I decided to develop a website with short articles which might serve their ends, and then realized that there were people in other nations — North America, Europe, the Middle East, and Africa — with similar interests. Most of the readers of the website live in the United States, but some live in England, Germany, France, Norway, Iran, and Rwanda. I wanted the pages to speak to the whole of life: art, music, science, philosophy, ecology, ethics, and daily life culture — because that's what was important to my Chinese friends and also my student friends. I realized that the pages needed to avoid jargon; that the essays needed to be relatively short and, where possible, inclusive of narrative; and that images and music were as important (sometimes even more important) than text. The webpage offered a way to do multi-media pages of this sort.

By virtue of my experience in China and also my experience as a classroom teacher, I was especially interested in reaching people who occupy a third space between fervent belief and fervent disbelief, single-minded affiliation and a rejection of all things religious. Many of my students are in this situation. I named it Jesus, Jazz, and Buddhism in order to elicit curiosity but also to make a point about religion. Jesus symbolizes the kind and compassionate heart who identifies with the poor and powerless; Jazz symbolizes diversity, spontaneity, and creativity; and Buddhism symbolizes a sense of interdependence, mutual becoming, and being present in the present moment.

Generally speaking the website explores a way of being religious that combines these qualities into a single way of living that can be internalized by people of all religions and people with no religion. My hope was that I could develop a companion platform that might provide opportunities for conversations about, and springing from, the articles. I turned to Facebook group pages toward this end. At the same time I began to recruit writers and artists from many walks of life to become 'columnists' for the site or to write occasional pieces. I have about forty writers of this sort. I intentionally avoid listing "credentials" of writers, because I want the spirit of the site to be deeply democratic and non-elitist.

I imagined, and still imagine, my readers to be spiritually-interested generalists. The pages of JJB are for believers, nonbelievers, and the vast majority who are somewhere in between. The genre of the articles is what some scholars call "ordinary theology" or "ordinary philosophy," meaning that it is theology from, by, and for people who are not in touch with more scholarly materials, and who are developing their theologies and philosophies amid the dynamics of everyday life.

I want to help them develop their philosophies and theologies by offering spring-boards for reflection and feeling.

I've had six happy surprises when using social media. The first is simply that there is a "market" for a website such as JJB. While the numbers are not stagger-ing, it averages 600 to 800 unique viewers a day. I feel that I am actually reaching people. A second is that the message "keep it short" and "tell stories" is right on target. People do not take the time, or will not make the time, to read long pieces. A third is that art and music, poetry and image, are as important as text in terms of reader response. A fourth is that a website like mine can play a small but im-portant role in world history. Through my website, I have been able to bring in progressive Muslims, one of whom now uses the site as a platform for articulating a vision of progressive Islamic theology in the process spirit. A fifth is that, in some ways, relatively "famous" people can be brought on board. By profiling mu-sicians, I have enlisted the interest of actual musicians, some of them a bit fa-mous, who are now part of the open and relational movement in their ways. I learn about the musicians from NPR, write a story on them, and then share the stories with their publicists. On occasion I get responses. The sixth is that the articles and images and poetry not only communicate ideas, they are a spring-board for ideas. Whitehead calls them "lures for feeling."

I once thought of theology as a text-based activity limited to scholars in uni-versities and intra-mural debates among them. I now realize that "theology" can and should emerge from the hearts and minds of ordinary people, that it need not be preoccupied with "answers" at the expense of hearty questioning, and that it can, but need not be, conjoined with religious affiliation.

Bricolage: the activity of gathering materials at hand from whatever sources are available is essential to digital culture. It can seem "chaotic" or "sloppy" to those who think in primarily literary terms, although in the arts — modern poetry, for example — it is commonplace. Witness the Wasteland by TS Eliot or the Cantos by Ezra Pound. In some ways the activity undercuts the assumption that good ideas must have clearly traceable sources from textual traditions and opens the door for improvisational creativity. For my part, as someone interested in theol-ogy, I am hoping that more and more theologians can accept, in others if not also in themselves, the spirit of bricolage. I think our times call for it. "Tradition" is in some ways being superseded by "affinity groups" of like-minded souls who are engaged in bricolage. It's jazz-like.

I spend an inordinate amount of time — probably too much — on the website. However, and importantly, I have learned to combine it with classroom teaching.

When I teach classes on world's religion, ecotheology, religion and popular music, etc., I create pages for the general public which can also be used (and are used) by students in the classroom. I have a student assistant whom I pay, who archives materials; and I have various friends around the US and in other parts of the world who write for me. Still it's a lot of time and energy. Fortunately, it's also fun and productive.

I need to take lessons from others. The only social media I now use are Facebook groups, and those are insufficient. But I do have advice for those of us trained in scholarly, text-based traditions. These traditions are, of course, very good. But if you are interested in communicating with ordinary people in ways that might make an actual difference in the world, and in fostering conversations among others, a conversion is required. You — we — need to get over the idea that "depth" occurs only in scholarly, text based discussions and accept a more multi-faceted epistemology: wherein we realize that "ideas" can be discerned through a variety of media and that ordinary people can have "good ideas" worth spreading. It also helps to appreciate multiple ways of knowing: verbal-linguistic, visual, musical, and emotional. Digital culture, in its way, sometimes problematic and sometimes promising, is effecting this conversion — like it or not. Bottom line? Go for it.

Jay McDaniel is a public theologian influenced by process theology. He teaches at Hendrix College in Conway, Arkansas; and also in mainland China in the summers, under the auspices of the Institute for Postmodern Development of China. He has written or edited 15 books. His interests are trans-religious theology, ecology, music, and interfaith dialogue. See McDaniel's websites: Jesus, Jazz, and Buddhism: Process Philosophy and Theology for a More Hospitable World (http://www.jesusjazzbuddhism .org/) and Process Philosophy for Everyone (http://www.processphilosophy.org/.) For the general philosophy and social vision underlying this work, see Fat Soul Manifesto (in Chinese and English): http://www.jesusjazzbuddhism.org/fat-soul -international-a-manifesto-in-english-and-chinese.html.

JAMES F. MCGRATH

Biblical Studies and Science Fiction

I have been blogging since November 2003, and my primary social media platform remains the blog. However, it has long been clear to me that, without Facebook and Twitter, my blog posts would not have the reach of circulation or the breadth of readership that they do. Relatively few people read a blog post, copy the URL, and mail it to someone that they know — although that certainly does happen! But much more frequently, if someone reads something, they will share it via a platform such as Facebook, for all their friends to see — or perhaps in a Facebook group for a set of individuals with shared views and/or interests.

I began blogging when it was still something relatively new — so new that I had to download a program, and then host the blog on my university web space, in order to blog. And so presumably I must have had at least one good reason! In fact, there were two major motivations for starting to blog. One was that it was an outlet for exploring my side interests, such as the intersection of religion and science fiction — hence the original name of the blog, which was "Exploring Our Matrix."

The other reason was to provide a venue for expressing my own religious opinions publicly. As often happens with those who study the Bible in depth and detail, I was originally motivated to undertake such studies by a rather conservative sort of personal faith. But those very studies challenged and transformed my thinking.

Often when one travels that route, starting in or passing through a venue that treats changing one's mind or learning new things as abandoning the "truth once for all delivered," it may require courage to speak honestly about one's convictions. The irony, of course, is that conservative Christianity teaches you to be prepared to go against the flow, and then is shocked when some realize that conservative Christianity itself presents a current that the Bible calls them to swim against.

In my case, however, the big challenge wasn't to speak freely in my church context. I had settled into a wonderfully welcoming and diverse community at Crooked Creek Baptist Church in Indianapolis by this stage, and so in some ways I was more concerned to speak publicly so that others might feel empowered and emboldened to do so. And I was not concerned, as those employed at conservative religious educational institutions typically need to be, about a possible loss of my job if I were not to hold the right theological views. No, the challenge in my university, since it is not religiously affiliated, was to find a suitable place to talk about my own faith, in ways that went beyond what I felt was appropriate in the classroom. A blog provides those opportunities. Unless you are already famous beyond the level of a typical assistant professor, initially no one is likely to be reading the blog, which can allow you to find your voice and become comfortable speaking publicly before anyone starts to engage you in conversation.

Any blogger who blogs frequently will have moments at which they wonder whether the investment of time is worthwhile. You can see statistics, and so know that people are visiting your site. But how many are really reading, and who are they? A small readership with influence might potentially be a more rewarding audience than a much larger one of a different sort. I didn't think about it that way, however, until I received an e-mail from a blog reader who had never commented on the blog before. He explained that he worked at NASA, and was seeking advice on resources to give to a relative who was a creationist of an anti-evolution sort. Up until that point, it had never occurred to me that anyone at NASA might be reading my blog!

Moments like that can encourage you to continue. Of course, if you are like me, you would probably write what you do anyway—indeed, for me blogging is like taking notes and keeping a journal, just doing so publicly where others can see it. But finding out even a little about who your readers are, and that what you write is proving meaningful and valuable to them, can provide much-needed encouragement at times when you wonder whether you might as well just be writing in a Word document for no one to read except for yourself.

Blogging has really proven to me to be something that breaks down the long-standing distinction between a big research-focused university and a smaller teaching-focused one. At the latter, one may lack colleagues (to say nothing of grad students!) who work on areas close enough to your own research projects to provide useful feedback, whether in a seminar setting or merely by commenting on written drafts. If one blogs, however, one can connect with other blogging scholars whose interests may be even closer to one's own than typically happens at a research university. Sharing of ideas happens on and between blogs, from floating a vague first inkling of a thought that occurred to you, to sharing and discussing a draft of an article or book chapter.

I have had lots of interactions that have benefitted research projects. It was fairly recently, however, that I had for the first time the experience of mentioning something that really was just a casual observation, a mere musing on an intriguing possibility, only to have the editor of an academic journal who reads my blog leave a comment, saying that he thought the idea deserved further exploration in an article, and if I pursued it further, I should submit it to that journal for consideration. I decided that I was indeed interested in pursuing the project, and the result was not merely an article that was accepted for publication subsequent to peer review, but also the experience I had not had in a long time of lying awake pondering the topic and jumping out of bed excitedly with ideas that I was eager to jot down. If you're curious, the article is about the intersection between the Gethsemane story in the Gospels and Philippians 2:8, and it is due to appear in the *Journal for the Study of the Historical Jesus* in the near future.

On the one hand, if one's blogging is related to and in service of one's professional work, then one need not feel guilty for spending *some* time engaging in conversation with other academics, sharing ideas and obtaining feedback, and promoting published work through social media. All of that is conducive to academic productivity, and in some cases is itself a form of scholarly activity. But that said, there certainly is a risk of not managing time and priorities well, and spending more time blogging than one should, and as a result spending less time doing other things that may deserve more time or more immediate attention. Realizing this, I have made it my habit of late to schedule posts several days or even a few weeks out, so that just once per day a post appears on my blog, unless something comes to my attention later in the day which I think deserves an immediate public comment. By approaching blogging in this way, I may have several days or even weeks in which the blog is sort of on autopilot. But a feature like autopilot, when used effectively, is conducive to the safety and effectiveness of the flight crew — and also for bloggers. If I am sharing a musical setting of a biblical text, or a meme that I made, there may be no reason that it needs to become a second post today, unless it relates to something that is trending news. If it can wait until tomorrow, then tomorrow when my daily blog post is already taken care of, I can focus on other things. This approach has been helpful in balancing blogging with other responsibilities.

The three things I would recommend to scholars considering using social media are the following:

1. Do it. Social media is a way of connecting with family and friends, with fellow academics, with students, and/or with the general public. And so whether what you need is a way to take your mind off of academic work, a way to participate in a wider scholarly community beyond your small institution, a way to collaborate on projects without physical proximity, a way to get students talking and reflecting beyond the classroom, or a means of disseminating your work to scholars and a wider audience, at least one of the above is a good reason to make use of social media. And if many or all of them are important to you, then avoiding social media will be counterproductive.

2. Use social media in ways that feel right, work for, and ultimately make sense to you. Some people are masters at the use of Twitter. For others, Facebook is a better outlet. For many, a combined presence across multiple platforms will be best. If sharing brief sentences and then getting back to work is what fits your personality and schedule, then focus on Twitter. If you want to review books, then a blog will be a much better choice than Twitter (although you can use the latter to spread the word about blog posts, potentially). Rather than tweeting or blogging because other people you know do it, find the outlet that works for you. It will be more satisfying to both you and your readers if you are a proficient tweeter than a frustrated, ineffective, and eventually lapsed pinterester.

3. Remember that social media are modes of communication, much as books, op-ed pieces, and TV documentaries are. They can convey valuable or worthless content. The quality depends on the one doing the writing, and not on the platform. Not all books are the same, after all. Some offer life-changing insights, while others offer dangerous drivel. Some blog posts contain absolutely worthless quackery, while others are the draft for what will eventually become an important book read all over the world. Don't let the snide remarks of skeptics deter you, if you are offering material that you and your readers find worthwhile, and you can tell from comments and/or stats that your work is being read. Focus on producing good content, at a length and frequency that works for you, and then also find ways to make it visible to others.

But be careful about that last step. There are people who e-mail their acquaintances every time they write a blog post. A better approach will be to give blog readers a means of subscribing by e-mail if they prefer to be notified of new posts that way. Some people will comment on every blog they know, linking to their new blog post which isn't at all relevant to the post they are leaving the comment on. Occasional sharing of links in the context of genuine interaction in comments will get you more readers and more genuine engagement than an attempt to spam the internet with what is essentially advertising. Blogs depend on advertising for generation of income, just as bloggers must engage in self-promotion (a form of advertising) if they are ever to connect with a readership. But we have all seen sites where the ads are so aggressive, distracting, and/or distasteful that it ultimately leads you not to read the content that you went there hoping to find. So be careful to approach the dissemination of your blogging (or your Twitter or Snapchat accounts) with the level of seriousness and professionalism that you want people to also associate with your content.

———————

James F. McGrath is the Clarence L. Goodwin Chair in New Testament Language and Literature, and Faculty Director of the Core Curriculum, at Butler University in Indianapolis, Indiana. McGrath has published books and articles on the New Testament, which is his main field, but also in other areas of interest such as religion and science fiction. He is also a published science fiction author. McGrath teaches an adult Sunday school class at Crooked Creek Baptist Church. See McGrath's blog ReligionProf at http://www.patheos.com/blogs/religionprof/ You can find him on Facebook, Twitter, YouTube, Pinterest, and Google+ by searching for that same user name, @ReligionProf. For those interested in his formal academic publications, his Academia.edu page will also be of interest, as will his SelectedWorks page (Butler University's institutional repository of digital copies of published material).

BRIAN D. MCLAREN

Public Theology

N ow in my early 60's, I suppose I've been an early adaptor to the digital world, but by no means a trailblazer. I began with a blog, then expanded to Facebook and Twitter. For a while, I also used Slideshare and YouTube. For longer articles, I still prefer my blog. It provided me a way to respond to questions (Q & R = Question and Response) personally, but by making responses public, their impact could broaden and I wouldn't have to keep answering the same questions repeatedly in a private email. The blog also provided a way to respond to individual notes (A Reader Writes) in a more public way.

I do not use a Facebook profile (personal page) but instead use a Page as a public figure. I have had a lot of trouble with Facebook, as "fake me" accounts arise every few months, with someone impersonating me, gathering friends, and then asking for money. Quite annoying. But my digital advisors tell me that they think Facebook is currently more important than my blog.

I have been surprised how much I enjoy Twitter. It is the line of social media I am most active on (because of its brevity), and the one I feel I am using because I am enjoying it (usually). One downside of Twitter is that hostile people can use my name/handle to garner attention for things I find offensive or counterproductive, and on a few occasions, I've considered dropping it. But it is currently my best way to connect quickly with a broad audience.

Originally, as an author, I used social media as a way to communicate between books and about my books. Gradually, as I began to see my role as a "public theologian," I sometimes felt that my social media work was as important as or more important than my published work. Now I feel that much of my work is movement building, and for this, social media is paramount.

I remember being in Cambodia and finding Cambodians with very limited English who depended on my blog for theological input. Similar responses have come from around the world, really.

On the other hand, just the other day a fellow who is active on social media said, "Oh, I haven't heard anything about you for years. I thought you retired or died or something," which says that people can get into their own channels of social media and be unaware of other whole realms of conversation.

Many of my speaking engagements have come through social media. Once, someone forwarded a sermon to me that had been posted online from a pastor in East London. He quoted one of my books. I sent him an email saying that I would be in London soon and would love to meet him for a cup of coffee. He replied that he lived, not in London, England, but in East London, South Africa, and that it would be a bit too far to come for a coffee! Eventually, though, he invited me to South Africa, from which a whole new set of relationships and conversations emerged.

I find that the same brain cells that get used in answering emails and posting on social media are the ones I use to write books. So if I'm active on social media, I'm not at my best for more professional writing. That means that I need to limit my social media work to an hour or two a day (or less) when I'm in the writing zone. When I'm researching, it is very valuable to post a question or ask for resources and have people from around the world respond.

If I were to give advice about social media to scholars, I'd recommend these three things:

1. Limit your social media time intentionally—both in quantity and in placement in your schedule. Say, "I'll do social media from 11-12 am," and stick to that.

2. Learn some of the "tricks of the trade" so you don't waste a lot of time. I found that spending 2 hours on a 1000 word piece often produced a lot less results than spending 20 minutes on a 150 word piece. I learned that posting at 7 am got a lot more attention than posting at 4 pm. I learned that sending out a short quote from a famous person often did more good than a long dissertation from me!

3. Find a way for people to contact you, but don't waste a lot of energy in comments sections responding to trolls. "Don't feed the trolls" is really good advice.

Brian D. McLaren is a former pastor and church planter. He now works as an author and activist, and serves on the board of Convergence (convergencus.org) and the Wild Goose Festival. His 15 books include A New Kind of Christian, A Generous Orthodoxy, *and* The Great Spiritual Migration. *He blogs at www.brianmclaren.net.*

PAUL LOUIS METZGER

Theology and Culture

blog, use Twitter, post at Facebook, and do videos and podcasts. The most common form is blogging. Occasionally, I will even talk to people in person!

If I recall correctly, I started blogging in 2012. I was invited to write regularly for the Christian Post. A bit later, the opportunity emerged to write for Patheos. I don't recall having written a single blog post prior to the first invitation. One of the main reasons why I chose to blog after being asked is that it provided greater access to the public here and abroad, including for those interested in theology, but who may not be in a position to attend college or seminary to study formally, or even purchase books. This is still a major reason why I blog. I am reminded of Martin Luther's conviction that the ploughman should be able to read and understand the Bible in his own language. While I write in English regardless of the venue, some venues are more accessible than others for today's "ploughman," such as with social media, like blogging.

The apparent or near anonymity of various forms of social media continues to stand out to me. The same goes for the seeming familiarity of connection with others. Take Facebook "friends," for example. I remember a prior seminary dean encouraging faculty to create Facebook accounts to develop exposure and more connections to students, alums, etc. I had never engaged Facebook prior to his recommendation. Soon after acclimating myself to this new form of connecting with people, a student reached out with a "friend" request. I gladly accepted. A few days later, we crossed paths on campus, but he did not acknowledge me when I said hello. And here I thought we were friends! In all honesty, while humorous now, at the time I was a bit shocked.

Social media and other forms of technology can give us a false sense of familiarity, even intimacy in some cases. Here I am reminded of the movie *Her*, where a man falls in love with the voice of his new operating system. While I have a relationship with Siri, we really need to see a counselor, as we frequently have trouble communicating with one another.

To return to the statement on anonymity, people do a lot of drive-by-shooting of comments at blog posts. As with road rage, due to the apparent safety, immunity and invincibility that comes with being surrounded by a car or truck's metal and glass, people can feel emboldened to lash out through social media, as they surf behind a computer monitor's plastic and glass. Some use alias monikers, perhaps so they can hide.

Social psychologist Jonathan Haidt shared during a TED Talk in November 2016 that one of the factors that add to the cultural divisions in America today is our demonization of one another through social media. While social media can bring us together in significant ways (one of my principle reasons for blogging), if we are not careful it can also lead us in the opposite direction — cultural fragmentation due to demonization and objectification.

Now while I try my best not to fan the flames of people's virtual anger, the fear I have for myself is that I can substitute social media presence/image for embodied presence and reality. So, whether or not people talk in booming ALL CAPS voices on social media channels, we should all make sure that we are in person what we are on the screen. Otherwise, when the screen shatters or we are exposed, we will need to take our cue from the Wizard of Oz and cry out, "Pay no attention to that man behind the curtain!"

Certainly, virtual presence and real presence can operate well together: I talk to my wife on the phone and email and text her, and we eat dinner face to face. But how often might we substitute the former for the latter, whether it is with family members, friends, or those entrusted to our care as teachers and thought leaders?

I am currently writing a social ethics text, and have found that being able to reflect upon the subject matter through blogging has helped me in my efforts to hone and develop further my thoughts in more inviting terms. As a diversity of people respond to my public musings on social ethics, it helps me get a better sense of how to articulate my particular Christian convictions more meaningfully and dialogically in our increasingly pluralistic culture.

Also, I wrote numerous blog posts from Japan during two research trips. As a result, it has provided increasing venues to produce more work toward the development of a global theology of culture. Along these same lines, such blogging led to one book project written from Japan years ago being published in 2015 with Patheos: *Evangelical Zen: A Christian's Spiritual Travels with a Buddhist Friend*, with a foreword and responses by the late Zen Buddhist Abbot, Kyogen Carlson. So, just like social media allows your work to get out to all kinds of internet outlets, it can also open up doors to more traditional outlets for publication.

Social media can take over one's life, especially if one is a bit wired toward compulsiveness. I need to guard myself from getting hooked to social traction and feedback. Sometimes I have to tell others that while I hope I can respond to their queries at Facebook, I might not be able to do so because of various responsibilities. This is hard for me. Sometimes I ask to get together with them instead, especially if the conversation is likely to become explosive online. All this takes time, but it is important if I wish to retain a human connection with others. I try and blog three times a week at my column at Patheos. Some of the writing I do there spills over into other domains. I always try to connect the dots between classroom instruction, conference creation, book projects, and blogging. In so doing, not only am I able to give people greater access to theological reflections beyond the classroom, but also I am making better use of my time in my calling and passion behind the lectern and desk as a teacher and writer of books.

If I were to give advice to scholars considering using social media, I'd say:

1. Develop thick skin and a soft heart. Everyone has an opinion, and many of them want you to know how much better their opinion is than yours. Try to keep in mind that there is a real person behind the critiques, and that they, too, have hurts and fears and longings for significance. Something I have learned from blogging is that certain people will either expect each blog post that you write on a subject to say everything that needs to be said on that topic, or they will find a way to misunderstand what you write, no matter how long or short, and no matter how clear you seek to state your case! Sometimes you just can't win, but stay at it, for you will find (perhaps when you least expect it) that God really touched someone through a particular piece you wrote. Those instances make all the frustration worth it.

2. Don't allow social media to replace face-to-face engagement, but use social media to complement it.

3. Don't allow the number of "likes" or "dislikes" to drive you, but rather your pursuit of love and truth for the sake of people. Similarly, don't allow peer

review and fear for tenure keep you locked up in the ivory tower. Otherwise, you/we might as well speak and write only in Latin; but what good will that do for the ploughman who can only speak and read in the common vernacular? We need to make sure we are bringing theology and philosophy into the country fields and city streets.

Paul Louis Metzger, Ph.D. is Professor of Theology & Culture at Multnomah University and Seminary, Portland, Oregon. He is also the Director of its Institute for Cultural Engagement: New Wine, New Wineskins. Metzger writes widely on theology, ethics, and culture. He is the author of numerous books and articles, and serves as Editor for Cultural Encounters: A Journal for the Theology of Culture. *He is a member of the Center of Theological Inquiry, Princeton. See Metzger's blog column — "Uncommon God, Common Good" (patheos.com/blogs/uncommongodcommongood/) and website — "The Works of Paul Louis Metzger" (http://paullouismetzger.com/). He can be found on Twitter (@paulouismetzger) and Facebook (facebook.com/paul .metzger). See also his institute's website (theologyofculture.com) and his journal's website (culturalencountersjournal.com). Because of the social nature/subject matter of this volume, Metzger was inspired to create his own YouTube channel — "Paul Louis Metzger" — to express his values more broadly and build more relational connections to people.*

JORY MICAH

Pastoral Theology

In terms of my social media platforms, Facebook, Twitter, Instagram, and YouTube. Facebook & Twitter are most primary. I began to use social media in order to build a following because I knew I was going to write a book. Publishers will not even begin to look at publishing your book if you do not have a large social media following. It took me about three years to build a following of over 40,000 people, between all social media platforms. I work hard at building my following every single day.

People are very cruel on social media, when they don't agree with your theology. I have had to deal with a lot of heartbreak, and have had to learn to have tougher skin. But, I have also built many great friendships and theological allies.

My entire ministry began from social media. Out of social media, I have been asked to speak nationally, I have been contacted by various publishers and followed by major Christian public figures. I owe a lot to social media; it got my entire career started.

I am not great at time management. I spend way too much time on social media, which is one reason I am so successful at it, but it also can give me stress, because I need to learn to step away more, relax, and have fun with family and friends. Now that I have built my base following, I am slowly learning to do that more. It is difficult, because to be successful on social media, you always have to be present and one of the first to respond to current events, but it is not worth giving up your whole life for. Like everything in life, it is learning to find a balance.

My advice to those considering using more social media is the following:

1. Don't be a snob on Twitter. Follow people back. Make friends with people. If you care about people, they will care about your work.
2. Be one of the first to respond to current events. Pay attention to current events in both the secular world and the Christian world and apply it to your work.
3. Learn balance. Don't let social media steal your soul. Block mean people. Disconnect sometimes and enjoy life with family and friends.
4. Treat others how you would want to be treated.

Jory Micah is native to Pittsburgh, PA, where she and her husband, Luke, are on a mission to reach millennials with the Gospel. She earned her BS in Church Ministries and her MA in Biblical Studies, with an emphasis on Christian Doctrine and Church History. Jory became a Christian feminist in graduate school and wrote her master's thesis on women in church leadership in the first two centuries of the early church, using the Bible as her primary source. Jory has been published with Relevant Magazine and Christians for Biblical Equality, and just completed her first book and is hopeful that it will be published in the near future. Jory was named a top female blogger in the Christian industry and has grown her blog to 40,000 views per month. She currently has over 9,700 followers on Facebook between her public personal page and her public ministry page, over 14,000 Twitter followers, and over 2,500 Instagram followers. Jory also travels and speaks to a national audience. Find Jory Micah at jorymicah.com, Twitter.com/jorymicah, facebook.com /BreakingTheGlassSteeple/, instagram.com/jorymicah/, youtube.com/user/joryryan

LISA MICHAELS

Theology and Ministry

From its inception, I have embraced the concept of social media as useful for teaching, training, and maintaining connections, but I didn't initially think it would become anything more than an occasional tool. Fast forwarding more than a decade, I'm a bit astonished at where this phenomenon has led me. Currently, the primary social media presence for which I am responsible includes blogging and Facebook. Over time, I have found that attempting to *manage* a large number of social media outlets makes it difficult to provide high quality material. However, limiting the number of platforms of which I have direct administrative control has actually served to increase the level of engagement with others, which came as a surprise to me. In recent days, I have been asked to contribute to a variety of blogs, podcasts, and YouTube interviews, which have functioned as opportunities to 'cross-pollinate' the social media presence of other theologians, philosophers, and scholars whose specific interests are diverse. I think this is a great way to increase the audiences of everyone involved and to shed light on a wide range of topics, many to which we would not be able to bring expert level knowledge or experience on our own. It seems that we can provide greater value in community, joining our various perspectives.

Although social media was initially a personal outlet for me, I sort of dabbled in using it for theological teaching, from the onset (and for me, that means Xanga and Myspace)! I specifically launched Flip Flops, Glitter, and Theology, though, in response to the request of a friend who desired an accessible blog for people who have not been theologically trained to make sense of overarching theological concepts. As academics, we often use big words, perhaps simply because we love language. Speaking for myself; I'm absolutely guilty of this. But it doesn't really matter how intelligent we are, or how vast our vocabularies have grown, if we have lost the ability to communicate basic ideas in common verbiage.

So, I began with the intent of blogging three times per week, using the following broad categories: Ministry Monday, Thursday Theology, and Sacramental Saturday. Originally, I had a small group of theological friends and colleagues who were also blogging regularly, and our plan was to intentionally engage in the kind of cross-pollination I mentioned above, but that has changed and shifted over time. Part of that, I think, has been the evolution of my content.

I had been blogging at FGT for just a few weeks when loyal readers from my personal blogging days began to ask for more narrative, and while my favorite pieces to write were (and still are) the research oriented, academic, explanatory essays; it was obvious that any article that included a real-life story was attracting a noticeably larger audience. Although I had absolutely no desire for this blog to be 'attractional' in nature, I did have to take a step back and ask myself if these were the kinds of anecdotes that people needed in order to make sense of theology. Honestly, I wanted the answer to be, "no." I was at a place in my life, education, career, family . . . just everything . . . where I no longer wanted to 'put myself out there' for public scrutiny, but I also realized people were desperate for accounts that allowed *them* to 'fit in.'

I started thinking about how important it is to find ourselves in God's story. Just stop to consider how many parables and metaphors are used in Scripture! And I realized that I not only needed to be willing to share my life, but I also needed to offer this platform to others who have a narrative to tell. So I did . . .

I'd like to make it clear, at this point, that my intent is still essentially the same. I want my theological work in the social media realm to be exceptionally accessible (even to the degree that I appear to be less of a scholar), because people matter, and we all need to find ways to relate to the study of God and the inherent practices that come from solid theological underpinnings. But (and I really mean this), if someone else wants to be the face of accessibility, I would be more than happy to hide out in a library, smelling old books and writing pieces that have more endnotes than content, someday!

As I stop to consider what has been surprising about using social media as a theological teaching tool; the thing that is most unexpected is that people are actually reading what I write! I hope that doesn't come across as false humility, because I'm serious. There are an incredible number of bloggers and pages that people could choose to follow, and I am often taken aback by the interest in my content.

I'm an introvert who loves the written word, so social media has leveled the playing field. Introverts come in as many different forms as there are people; so for me, being an introvert doesn't mean I don't have anything to say or that I am even somehow hesitant to say it. If you have any respect for indicators such as the Myer's Briggs assessment, I actually fall into a 'rare' personality category (less than 1% of the world's population) that may be described as an extroverted introvert, and more specifically as an advocate. I'll stand (sometimes strongly) for others, but I won't fight for a platform. Social media allows me to take my time to thoughtfully consider exactly what I would like to communicate and how it might best be conveyed. It allows me the necessary space to be contemplative and fastidious in my work. No one who follows me on social media is reading my 'first drafts.'

So, it continues to surprise me when I show up at conferences or meetings or even randomly on the sidewalk and learn that people take such an interest in what I share that they actually know both what my six year old thinks about the Eucharist and how much I like my peppermint bark coffee and cheesecake. These are glimpses into my life that I likely wouldn't have shared without social media platforms. The implications for communal theological discussions are, therefore, almost limitless.

But there are things about which to be cautious . . .

People have said things to me like, "You really wear your heart on your sleeve," or, "I feel as if I truly know you," and I'm floored when this happens. In all honesty, I am meticulous about every word I write, because the Internet is forever. I hope there is never a moment in which anyone thinks I am sharing so openly out of a sense of naivety or that I am unaware. If I have something (anything) to offer from my life that will allow someone else to understand God more perfectly and relate with God more deeply and redemptively, then it's my responsibility and honor to share it. The story is mine, but it is not mine alone. However, I don't tell everything (or even close to it).

Another thing is, other people are not always who they appear to be, online. Just as someone could mistakenly think they know me; at times, I have been sadly mistaken about other people due to their social media presence. We need to exercise care when we enter into relationships with others in a digital world.

However, let's not be overly cautious, because these relationships and interactions are important to opening additional opportunities. To illustrate, several writing projects that might be described as 'interesting' have emerged (or more accurately are *beginning* to emerge), because of the work on my blog. Included among these is some research on the sacraments and how we might embrace them and live more sacramentally, as Protestants.

Additionally, I am aiming to open the floor for charitable discussion among people who hold vastly different worldviews in the areas of religion, politics, and social action. What I'm finding is, the majority of basically decent people in the world (or at least *my* world) have a desire to stand for *something*, but we're living in intensely polarized times. Our personal narratives affect this to the extent that we don't always listen well. It is my hope to provide some space for gracious conversation, or even debate, which might help us all to recognize the good in one another and the deep personal desire to support and call attention to significant causes, even if the issues that matter most to me are not the same ones that stir the hearts of every friend or colleague. We tend to work against one another, but there is actually a lot of beauty in the fact that we have different interests and can, therefore, commit our resources to a multiplicity of redemptive tasks.

You'll have to stay tuned for more on this, but I am hoping to (soon) branch out into multiple interview formats that will allow for increased dialogue, participation, and collaborative effort.

With this in mind, social media has undoubtedly changed the landscape of social communication, as its name would suggest. There was a time when my children would say, "All of Mommy's friends live in the computer!" I think we're past that now, but there is something really important to be said of balancing time spent engaged in social media and time spent in face-to-face engagement. I want to be careful, however, not to relegate social media to something less than 'the real world.' We live in a different reality than we did twenty years ago. Social media is a legitimate means to relationship and certainly an excellent way in which to stay connected globally.

Considering this, time management is an essential part of my life. Realistically, there are usually not enough hours in the day to actually obliterate my 'to-do' list. I have to prioritize, and as far as social media goes, I have to think about whether or not the various tasks are related to work, ministry, or personal and relational well-being. If I'm working on a blog post or participating in an interview (Skype, Messenger, Email, etc.) that will lead to greater knowledge, perspective, or resourcing for theological education or ministry, then I'm using my time wisely. If I'm offering pastoral counseling or connecting with friends and family in meaningful ways, then I'm using my time wisely. If I've fallen down what I call 'the scroll hole,' and my eyes are glazed over as I 'like' memes and cringe at bad political posts, then I should probably be doing something more productive.

Also, I think it's reasonable for others to expect me to be fully present to them when we are meeting face to face. So, unless I have an exceptional reason; I don't even answer my phone or texts when I'm having a conversation with someone who deserves my full attention (and let's be clear . . . if I'm having a conversation with *anyone*, he or she deserves my full attention). The same rule applies to social media. If I looked at my phone every time there was a notification on Facebook, for example; I would *always* be looking at my phone. I would never get anything else done. So, for me, social media and my responsibilities therein are simply *a part* of what I do (and maybe who I am), and they have to fit into their proper places.

If I were giving advice to those considering using social media more, I'd say . . .

First, know your audience and speak their language consistently. If your average reader or listener is a graduate level educated philosopher or theologian, then you get to use big words. If your average reader or listener is a layperson who desperately wants to grapple with theology in terms he or she can understand, then you get to pull out a thesaurus to remind yourself of the common synonyms for the things you love to say. If you have any question about which way to go, start with something very simple. I can testify, from experience, that my average reader will not click through if I confess that I am posting an academic paper. So, if you do work outside your usual parameters from time to time, you might have to be willing to employ a catchy title, or click-bait, or a picture of a puppy.

Second, do not attempt to re-invent the wheel. There are many excellent social media outlets, already. If you have something new and different to offer, do it! However, if your work would fit well with something that is already established, try to find a way to get on board with the previously established work. Guest post for a blog or two. Do some podcast interviews. Contribute to Facebook groups that pique your interest and segue well with your expertise. Unless you have something quite unique to propose, these collaborative avenues will effect more change than individual efforts. And besides, it's really irritating when there are seventeen groups comprised of the same 80 people, because everybody wants to be the leader. Work well with others! As a side note to this, many people *think* they want to have an increased social media presence, but it's a lot of work (usually with very little tangible reward). There are countless endeavors that have been launched, only to be archived as obsolete after a post or two, an episode here or there. Those lone pieces might hold incredibly important truths that could be widely appreciated were they assimilated into a larger body of work. I repeat, work well with others!

Third, be more translucent than transparent. What I mean by this is that you should be absolutely honest in everything you write or say on social media platforms, but remember that these platforms usually offer you an opportunity to conscientiously edit. Put very plainly, do not air your dirty laundry or try to advance vendettas. If you're taking a very personal approach, speak from your own perspective. I probably take this further than most, but I do think it's OK to 'vomit' your feelings all over the place, if they are genuinely *your* feelings. Self-deprecating humor can go a long way toward establishing yourself as a real person who understands life apart from an ivory tower. Be careful to protect the identities of others, however, unless they have given express permission to share their stories — even others who don't fall into the 'protection of the innocent' category. Change names, change places, etc.

Social media is a powerful means that allows us to communicate and connect in ways that were once inconceivable. Even though this has become a regular part of my daily life, it's still mind-boggling at times! But when we embrace the dichotomous ability to be both vigilant and abandoned; the potential for learning and growth, in community, is endless.

———————

Lisa Michaels is a follower of Jesus, theology student, author, blogger, editor, educator, wife, mom, and aspiring peacemaker. She has a B.S.M. (business management) from Indiana Wesleyan University and an M.A. and M.Div. (both in theology/spiritual formation) from Northwest Nazarene University. In her spare time, L sings and dances with babies (AKA teaches early childhood music), plans outlandish vacations, drinks voluminous amounts of peppermint bark mocha (preferably at local coffee shops), and masquerades as Catholic, so she can participate in the Eucharist more often. She writes about theology, the sacraments, and ministry to the least of these at Flip Flops, Glitter, and Theology. She has also been featured on the podcast, "Voices in My Head," at, "A Plain Account" (a Wesleyan Lectionary Commentary), and at, "Uncontrolling Love" (essay responses to Tom Oord's book, The Uncontrolling Love of God). flipflopsglitterandtheology.com; facebook.com/flipflopsglitterandtheology; rickleejames.podbean.com (episode 198); aplainaccount.org; uncontrollinglove.com

ROGER HAYDON MITCHELL

Political Theology

I use WordPress, Twitter, Academia.edu, ResearchGate, Facebook, and LinkedIn. I'm not including Email or Text Messaging as although I try to use email collectively it is regarded as a distribution mechanism whereas social media is viewed as a collective mechanism. Text Messaging is regarded as social media but generally I only use it for friends and family. So in this chapter I am focusing on accepted social media platforms.

I began with WordPress in 2010 when my son, who is a Media and Education professional, got me started. WordPress, Twitter and Academia are primary for me, although Facebook is increasingly so. I use WordPress extensively, particularly when I'm actively involved in research and writing when I blog several times a month and engage with any comments. I blog less when pursuing the activism side of my work, because I don't blog lightly, often spending hours over wording. When involved in hands-on initiatives I don't have time for this. Then Twitter comes into its own, both as the means of maintaining the informal relational connections necessary to linking with like-minded activists but also as a way of subverting myself and hopefully those whose perspectives are partly other to mine and where we have some agreements but often hold counter cultural norms. Many people are surprised to find a Pentecostal Charismatic theologian a political activist, certainly not on what appears too many to be on the left of left on most matters! I think this maybe why I don't experience Twitter as an echo chamber.

When I discovered how to bleed my Twitter feed through my Facebook page the latter came alive as I connected with a whole new cohort of people who knew me of old. I was an evangelist and church planter for many years and then a postcolonial reconciler internationally before I became a theologian so there were plenty of old friends and acquaintances out there who began to find me online. Connecting my WordPress blog to Twitter means that every time I post, the title and link is automatically tweeted and this in turn bleeds through my Facebook page.

This has significantly boosted its impact and readership. I take friendship very seriously, seeing it as theologically foundational, so I do have serious reservations about Facebook's use of the word "friend." I have attempted to get round this somewhat spurious use of the word by having a disclaimer on my Facebook page where I explain that my primary social network presence is on Wordpress, Academia and Twitter and that if people ask to be my friend I take it to mean that they want to engage with my research, writing and activism on those platforms and to respond accordingly. If they comment on Facebook I ask their permission to cut and paste their comment onto my blog if appropriate.

I find Academia.edu really helpful as a means to keep up with others researching in a similar field. I keep the focus of my profile there quite specific so as not to be inundated with less than relevant papers. I like the way in which Academia provides an immediate impact by connecting papers to potential interested audiences. It is a way that lesser known theologians like me can have an occasional extraordinary impact that boosts the overall interest in our work. In this way you can unexpectedly and suddenly shoot into the top two percent of academics among the millions on the site. I'm not quite sure how this works, but two of my papers, my chapter "Authority Without Sovereignty" in *Towards a Kenotic Vision of Authority in the Catholic Church* and my contribution entitled *Thank God for Secularity* in the Nonreligion and Secularity Blog had me up there for several weeks.

I generally accept all requests from LinkedIn and occasionally look at recommended connections from the site and send out invitations to those I think might appreciate the contact. I'm not looking for a new job, although it is fun to contemplate what the site decides I'd be good at, but I find it a useful means of communication and get personal messages from time to time. It is a supplement to the direct messaging facility on Twitter.

I regard all knowledge as relational, but because my desire is to reposition the church for the world and not for itself I have deliberately located myself mainly outside known confessional institutions. Lancaster University Department of Politics, Philosophy and Religion where I am an honorary research fellow is known for the secular orientation of its Religious Studies. When I had my original interview for doctoral research in theology here some twelve years ago I was reminded by the then Head of the Religious Studies Department that they regarded Christianity only as a living memory. I think I replied that I was glad that they at least thought it a living one! In this situation social networking has been a wonderful innovation and discovery for me. While not an independent scholar, I have a particular sphere and field which is liminal to the mainstream within and without the confessional or secular contexts.

Social networking enables the disclosure of others on the same trajectory with whom I can begin to relate. I found this out as soon as I began experimenting with WordPress as a means to collaborative research and writing, particularly when linked to face to face friendships I had built up over the years and furthered through occasional theology weekends in our friary home in Silverdale on the Lancashire and Cumbria borders. Maintaining and extending this informal counter-political community remains a core ongoing purpose of my social networking.

For someone like me with a strong sense of stewardship to call and facilitate post-secular radicals outside the mainstream and into a new ecclesial expression and experience, social networking provides a constant hopeful opening to the future in the everyday. This fulfils and accentuates an experience I had in 1990 on an anniversary return to Fiji where I had worked as a pioneer together with the students of the Christian Fellowship at the University of the South Pacific and the International Fellowship of Evangelical students to bring into being a student movement across all the island nations of the South Pacific in the early nineteen-eighties. It was the year that Tim Berners-Lee invented the World Wide Web. As I stood at Korolevu on the Coral Coast as night fell I sensed the Holy Spirit saying to look up at the stars and down at the sand and in words reminiscent of God to Abraham, I heard "as innumerable as the sand and stars, so will the descendants of the World Wide Web be for the kingdom of God." As its incredible potential has since evolved I have never lost the sense of hope that vision brought me.

I was challenged to discover soon on in my engagement with social media how quickly it exposed my self-centredness. It offers a stage to show off without the immediate feedback that as a public speaker I was used to receiving and that had kept me relatively objective in my assessment of myself and my performance. I also discovered that I tend to have more interest in my own site than other people's, which is critical to admit, if true, as it means that playing to your own gallery can boost your ego without properly engaging with genuine research. This is probably true of many of us researchers and writers whether or not we engage with social media. We can be more concerned for our own self-promotion than promoting justice and overall wellbeing, even when such subjects are the focus of our work. Social networking has brought me up short and caused me to face this. With different people this tendency will have different expressions. But for me as a nine on the Enneagram, what other people think is important to my shadow self. Checking out how I appear to be doing in numbers of hits and followers can be alluring.

So social networking has raised visceral moral questions that have required personal discipline. The need to actively prefer the living presence and immediate relationships that embody the kingdom of God is something mature people would like to think comes automatically. It doesn't. I try to restrict social networking mainly to the category of work as I find this helps keep at bay the compulsion to check constantly who has been reading my posts. Another discipline is to spend time on the blogs of friends or colleagues even when they are not directly interacting with me. It is unlikely that we will interest others in what we have to say if we are only interested in reading and listening to what we have to say!

I have been fortunate that I have never been trolled and rarely received negative feedback online, despite a fairly eclectic approach to followers and networking (this is not an invitation to begin ganging up on me) so in my personal experience the internet has been a positive space in which to operate. So while social networking has challenged my own attitudes and motives, it has improved my assessment of the 'others out there.'

However, I do need to add a huge qualification to all this. There is another side to the internet that those of us experiencing its positive context cannot ignore. There are those who while excited by its potential have experienced its capacity for promoting toxic worldviews and anti-human behaviours at such a level that they find themselves recoiling from it. As already explained, I don't write without deliberate collaboration via social media. So yesterday I tweeted "Getting down to my chapter for a forthcoming book on social media for theologians and philosophers." Within minutes people began to comment on Facebook.

One comment came from my son Chris, an academy principal, who introduced me to social media. In the intervening years he has had seriously negative experiences of the dark side of the internet. He had this to say: "I started out as a fan boy of the anarchic potential of Web 2.0 . . . was later fascinated by the potential empowerment of social media including social journalism and 'collective intelligence'. My multimedia performance show and MA dissertation explored ideas of wisdom in crowds and opportunities for amateur culture to rival 'flat pack and shrink wrapped culture'. These ideas (Jenkins and Guantlett) still excite me . . . but I have also found, at personal cost, that these ideas tend to be academic luxuries.

I am increasingly inclined that social media may be a terrible swindle that reduces connected presence and generally contests listening or life compromise . . . the development of anti truth or post honesty is interesting as is bogus identity construction. As an educator, I am aware of no greater barrier to authentic learning currently and I have very substantive worries that Snapchat and Twitter have turned mobile phones into torture devices with addictive properties as savage as skunk for adolescent mental health."

It is not surprising that I take seriously the above heartfelt response from my first social media mentor and tutor who has hands on experience at the heart of the internet culture. While I'm more positive from my own personal experience and perspective, I can see that these may be to some extent "academic luxuries" when toxic behaviours are perpetrated and mainstream education is so adversely impacted. Yet I still feel hopeful about the positive potential of social media if through it we keep pouring love into the deep structures of the contemporary world.

I see the internet as one of the key redemptive gifts of the era with which to do that. I regard it as an access point to new political space and a means of connecting with what Tom Oord calls essential kenosis. Those familiar with my research will know that I trace the genealogy of peace through empire and show how it displaces the alternative narrative of peace through love. What I nickname "the sovereignty delusion" proves to be a virus that constantly seeks to eat up new locations wherever they arise. The space of the internet is no exception and vulnerable to this invasive ideology. I see this as an imperative for social networking, both to realise its potential and to come in an opposite spirit to those default influences that threaten to dominate it.

For more than a decade I have been part of a group of radical theologians, activists and friends who are attempting to expose the sovereignty delusion while pouring our lives into the love stream and who engage with social media on both fronts. This is no simple good versus bad, them and us, binary approach but an inclusive outpouring in the midst of the hegemony of empire. At the heart of this has been the development of an alternative definition of the kingdom of God, expressed in the newly made-up word 'kenarchy' which is gaining some modest traction among thinkers and activists for positive peace and a repositioned ecclesia. This has blossomed and seeded through the positive use of the internet.

The initial discussions about suitable words for the counterpolitical kingdom of God took place in the interface between blogs and face to face discussions at theology weekends at the friary here in Silverdale with, among others, my friends Stephen Rusk, Peter McKinney, Mike Love, Julie Tomlin Arram and my wife Sue before my friend and fellow blogger Andy Knox came up with the word. All of them contributed to the book *Discovering Kenarchy* which Julie and I co-edited and which was in part originally developed online. The interface with Martin Scott and his Perspectives blog and Andy Knox's reimaginingthefuture blog, among others, helped extend the scope of our thinking and networking. My original PhD thesis subsequently published as *Church, Gospel and Empire: How the Politics of Sovereignty Impregnated the West* benefited from online interaction and my subsequent book *The Fall of the Church* did so again.

All along the innovation and development of kenarchy has been progressed through tentative blogging and while the majority of surfers and viewers are not commenters, those who do comment tend to be other theologians or activists with significant ideas. I can confidently say that these comments have been sources of genuine collaboration. Several of these in the course of the early development of kenarchy made sure that we weren't just about words. Personal stories of oppression as women, concern for the environment and costly egalitarian love saw to it that theological theory was fully applied and hands-on.

Although most of the social networking involved in the development of kenarchy was written, mainly due to my lack of expertise and ease with video and podcasting, where we have used them they have been disproportionately helpful. The ecclesia video I posted on my blog in 2012 still gets watched most days. And more recently two Nomad podcasts have been popular. And while not social media in themselves the courses that I teach in the Richardson Institute here at Lancaster University and with the Westminster Theological Centre, both of which help carry kenarchy forward, contribute to the collaborative interface between teaching, activism and social media.

Self-employed, honorary, grandfatherly theologians like me have the advantage of not being under the same strictures of time that younger theologians juggling teaching timetables and childcare may experience. However, as I've already made clear, my conviction is that relationship and children are key to knowledge in general and theology in particular. So I find it helpful to intentionally and consciously remember that what Marshall McLuhan said back in the nineteen-sixties remains true. The medium is the message. So attention constantly divided between partners, children and social media devices gives the lie to love. I talk a lot about deep structures, a phrase I borrow from the activist linguist philosopher Noam Chomsky. I try to make sure that kenotic love is the deep structure of my life, not just the surface content of my written or spoken words. So first of all making sure that we think we have got the balance right and then listening to and taking on board the irritating cautions of loved ones who still think not, is the key!

Presence is a much used word these days, but I think it is an important one. My wife Sue sometimes informs me that I'm not very present even although I am bodily there! And of course being present in the room with friends and loved ones while engaged with a mobile phone or other social media device, is not really presence. But I think it works both ways, and a huge danger for social networking is the failure to be present there either. A really important factor in managing social media and other obligations is the issue of presence. Tweets, comments and posts that lack the heartfelt presence of the person are, for those of us wanting to pour love into the space of the internet, as devaluing to the recipients as the partner, teenager or parent who is present in the room but not to their loved ones.

Practically speaking, I do think it is helpful to decide on the primary platforms to engage with, and then attend to this front end of involvement and not worry too much about the rest. As I have indicated, for me this means attending to Twitter and WordPress. By attending I mean several times a day on Twitter with few exceptions, and Wordpress at least once a day. Allowing this to have a modest level of pressure about it is, I think, necessary for genuine engagement. Otherwise our online presence is less than real. This is where the interface with email and social media is key for me, as I receive notifications of new activity on Twitter, new followers on WordPress and comments on Facebook.

If I were to give advice to those considering more use of social media, I would begin with a plea for engagement and a recommendation for its benefits. I was a teenager in the sixties, I was educated before computers or the internet. So please, older theologians reading this who may have failed to engage with social networks, please do. I'm dyspraxic, maths phobic, and frankly not brilliant at science or DIY! But it only took me a day with a knowledgeable friend to move into the world of computers and laptops and once my son set me up on WordPress in 2010 I was away in a few minutes. After that getting up and running on Twitter took no time at all. So ask for help if you need it.

I recommend platforms like Hootsuite that make Twitter easy to use by enabling you to peruse various columns of tweets, such as your own feed, a general feed from those you follow, direct messages and mentions. You can detail particular subject matter or individuals that you are interested in. I also recommend aids like Commun.it which will do your thanking for you and keep tweets flowing when you are unable to retweet or construct your own. Klout is a helpful way of tracking and checking your influence, but it is important to check your motives! I have never paid for the professional upgrades on any of the platforms and always work with the free versions. I may not know what I'm missing of course, but the paid versions presumably facilitate social media for business, which I have personally no interest in using it for.

As a scholar I have found Academia.edu. invaluable. I could use it more than I do, but it works at many levels and positions me well on Google which is really helpful as a first or second port of call for people looking to find out more about me.

"Roger Haydon Mitchell Ph.D. is a political theologian and activist. He is an Honorary Research Fellow in the Department of Politics, Philosophy and Religious Studies at the University of Lancaster, where he is the External Partnership Coordinator for the Richardson Institute for Peace Studies. He is also on the faculty of the Westminster Theological Centre. He is the author or co-author of 7 books as well as various articles and papers." You can find Roger at https://rogerhaydonmitchell.wordpress.com/; on Twitter https://twitter.com/roghaydonmitch; on Academia.edu https://lancaster .academia.edu/RogerHaydonMitchell; on Facebook https://www.facebook.com /rogerhaydon.mitchell and on LinkedIn https://www.linkedin.com/in/roger-haydon -mitchell-38379752/

BRINT MONTGOMERY

Philosophy

A s a general opening remark, social media motivates me to write on topics that normally I would let pass unaddressed. I don't think I'm alone in this response. Some years ago, I saw a cartoon on the Internet which had a wife saying to her husband, now typing away on his computer, that it was late, and that he should therefore come to bed. The husband's reply was instructive: "No, I can't — somebody on the Internet is *wrong!*"

There is something about a direct encounter with the social media platform "other" — some disembodied mind presented as mere bloodless, virtualized text on a screen, one who dare holds either a contrary (or, worse, contradictory) position from your own. Action is demanded! This is especially true if you respect either their position in society (e.g., another educator) or their close personal relationship (e.g., a life-long personal friend). And if they are completely unknown to you, then a troll may very well appear (on either side of the debate) and set good manners aflame.

Like 1.23 billion other people on the planet who log on *daily* to Facebook,[1] I have a tiny bit of psychological addiction with that platform. If I happen to miss a day, it will kindly email me about interesting happenings. It's narrow A.I. is well tuned to know who I follow. So I always come back for more. But, surely I'm a free agent; so, I can quit anytime I want. The thing is, I rarely write anything on

Facebook. For me, it's mostly about cartoons, doofy vignette videos of real life, and snarking on friends and family. Fortunately, the political stuff just makes me hate the human race, so that's actually good news, or maybe fake news — either way, it makes it way easier to log off. No, it turns out my social media platform of choice (as opposed to "of addiction") is this: Quora.

Bertrand Russell once wrote a book called "Problems of Philosophy". It was about doctrines in epistemology and language, mostly. But Philosophy has a few new problems these days, and those decidedly are *not* about doctrines. In his review of the book, "Socrates Tenured: The Institutions of 21st-Century Philosophy"[2], Stephen Howard writes,

> "Philosophers are indulging in insular debates on narrow topics, writing
> only for their peers: the result of a natural-scientific academic model
> that encourages intense specialization . . . [T]he mainstream of philos-
> ophy is failing to engage with the major questions of our times. The
> debate over our technological modernity takes place in magazines
> and blogs, in what the authors call our 'latter-day Republic of Letters'.
> Insofar as academics are consulted for help with answers to contempo-
> rary societal challenges, it is scientists and economists who tend to be
> called upon."[3]

I'm pretty much in agreement with this observation. And I find it sad that Philosophy, which is a branch of the humanities, has lost what is supposed to be the advantage of that approach: the ability to make us feel a connection in the grand human experience both to those who have come before us and to our contemporaries.

I think Quora can help address this. Quora is a question-and-answer social media site where questions are asked, answered, edited and organized by its community of users, often giving algorithmic selection priority to those with explicit credentials and excellent entries. There are four reasons I write on Quora: out of empathy, for encouragement, as enlightenment competition, and for Socratic challenge.

Often people asked philosophical questions that I myself have asked in the past, so I can empathize with the irritation or confounding nature of the issue. Furthermore, such questions often come up for anyone, given enough life experience, so answering them alleviates (admittedly, in a very small way) a kind of dissonance that everyone has about philosophical matters.

Another reason I like writing on social media, and on Quora in particular, is that you can encourage others who took the time to write a good response, or make an insightful observation about some situation. There are so many trolls on the internet today, that it has become a serious challenge in artificial intelligence methods to filter the remarks of these kinds of people out. But I would think there should be equal effort in somehow encouraging and supporting those who are helpful and supportive of an online community. Often, we reap the advantage of reading their thoughts, but never take even a moment to just compliment them on their efforts. This was one of the genius moves that helped Facebook become so popular, the thumbs-up "like". But making an outright encouraging comment is even better. In the tiniest way, a justified, encouraging remark about someone's efforts to answer a question moves the world into a better state.

Although I'm not a very competitive person by nature, often when I write a response on Quora, I hope to be the highest ranked writer by views. Not so much because I'm trying to "get views" for the sake of popularity, but because I want my answer to be the best among other high quality contenders. As a rule, if I put a lot of time or thought into answering something, but someone else gets 2x or 5x more views than I did, I want to know what he or she saw that I didn't! (Or why theirs was the preferred answer, and mine wasn't.) Indeed, sometimes I've been schooled by other writers on what I missed. So there is a "fun" element of competition, but an "enlightenment" element too, the latter of which is far more important to me. And as compared to formal publication, most philosophy articles are read only by an ever shrinking handful of people. A sad fact is that only 10% of philosophy articles are ever even cited, this being the result of a severe and continuing drop-off over the last decade.[4] On Quora, in contrast, one can see dozens, then hundreds of readers instantly reading your answers within an hour or so of posting them. There are methods for upvoting and commenting on every post. Soon you can see the thousands which have perused your writing. It makes those few paragraphs you wrote totally seem worth your best efforts!

People sometimes reach for simplistic answers to very deep and subtle questions. This cheats others who might not recognize the inadequacy of such approaches, and who could be tempted to acquire and duplicate them in their own thinking. So, asking well-placed questions, sometimes with nose-tweaking Socratic rhetoric can get people to respond in a deeper way, thus letting them round-out their views with reasons. Virtually always, this allows hidden assumptions or background commitments to be brought to light. And a moment's reflection can show those to be quite crazy commitments. I've always felt that all the action is found in hidden assumptions and background commitments, so engaging others in social media has given me much to discover about other people in my digital circles.

One thing that did catch me off guard is how differences of social sub-cultures can easily affect how one is judged morally. I think scholars should always take this into consideration when using social media. I'll close with an anecdote here.

In one Quora post, I had described how I locate students who would make good Philosophy majors. I talked about how I would first meet them socially, then later likely spring on them a controversial philosophical conversation, sometimes disagreeing with them on what would seem like (rightly) settled issues. For example, sometimes I'll ask a question I'm confident they know the answer to, and then say something like, "Bah, that's a crazy view," knowing full well that it isn't. But I just want to see how they react. Do they immediately ask questions or start ranting? If so, what kind of questions do they ask? How do they handle cognitive dissonance when they are psychologically certain they are right, but when somebody is arguing against them—do they get angry; cave quickly for social nicety's sake, or try to inform and educate their interlocutor during the interchange?

As it turned out, I had an impassioned taxi driver inform me, in a comment to my post, that my approach was kind of cruel. "I would be hurt," she explained, "if someone whose opinion I respected told me my position on something was 'crazy.' And then to find out that the whole thing was some 'test' to see how I would react? Wow. You're lucky your jaw is intact! Professors have no business playing games with students. You can get your point across and get a feel for the personality you are dealing with some other way," she concluded.

Talk about getting my comeuppance! In response, I moved to explain how one can be kind about it, and that a debate is not an insult. That's what a "deep" person realizes, that the value of ideas is separate from the value of the person. That's a lesson which some find harder to learn than others. But it is essential for Philosophers doing their work in the discipline. What was her response? She turned off her fare light, and totally splashed me with water at the curb: "Well, good luck with that . . ."

———————

Brint Montgomery is professor of philosophy at Southern Nazarene University and serves as director for the Philosophy program in the School of Theology and Ministry, where he has taught for 21 years. After serving in both the Air Force (c. 1981) and the Army (c. 1985), he obtained a BA in Philosophy (1989) from Northwest Nazarene

University, and attended Nazarene Theological Seminary (M.Div., 1994). He then went on to Oklahoma University in Philosophy (MA, 1996) and Philosophy of Mind (Ph.D., 2003). He is an ordained elder in the Church of the Nazarene where he has worked in campus ministry. He was also a founding member and current review coordinator for the Wesleyan Philosophical Society. His academic writing has focused on Philosophy of Religion, and he has ongoing research interests in Philosophy of Mind, Logic, and Artificial Intelligence. Recently, he has co-edited Relational Theology: A Contemporary Introduction (*Point Loma Press*, 2012).

SOURCES

[1] "The Top 20 Valuable Facebook Statistics — Updated March 2017" *Zephoria Digital Marketing Website* (Accessed 3/14/2017)

< https://zephoria.com/top-15-valuable-facebook-statistics/ >

[2] Frodeman, Robert and Adam Briggle, Socrates Tenured: The Institutions of 21st-Century Philosophy (Collective Studies in Knowledge and Society), Rowman & Littlefield International (September 26, 2016)

[3] Howard, Stephen "Book Review: Socrates Tenured: The Institutions of 21st-Century Philosophy by Robert Frodeman and Adam Briggle" *The London School of Economics and Political Science Blogsite.* (Accessed 3/14/2017)

< xhttp://blogs.lse.ac.uk/lsereviewofbooks/2017/01/23/book-review-socrates-tenured-the-institutions-of-21st-century-philosophy-by-robert-frodeman-and-adam-briggle/ >

[4] Mizrahi, Moti "Too tight to cite (updated once more)" The Philosopher's Cocoon Website 11/11/2015 (Accessed 3/14/2017)

< http://philosopherscocoon.typepad.com/blog/2015/11/too-tight-to-cite-.html >

R. T. MULLINS

Philosophical Theology

I do not have many different social media platforms. This is intentional as I do not like to put too much of my life out there for the public to see. I only use Facebook and Academia. I primarily use Facebook. I upload my published papers on Academia. I do have several videos on YouTube, but I do not have my own YouTube channel.

During the first year of my PhD, someone mentioned Academia to me. It offered a free public profile for academics, and it put that page at the top of Google searches when someone looks you up. This is very important for people on the job market since potential employers sometimes do a quick Google search on you if you are a serious candidate. (I say "sometimes" because I have been in multiple interviews where it was not clear that the hiring committee had a clue who I am.) Academia also lets you post your published or unpublished work, and keeps track of who has found your page from around the world. It is interesting to see my Academia metrics after I speak at a conference, or the first day of class. The metrics will usually show a spike in page views from whatever city in which I am speaking or teaching.

As I continued in my PhD, I started to use Facebook a bit more to promote my scholarly interests. Facebook has always been for me a medium to keep in touch with family and friends. It still is, but now I can no longer get by as an academic without it. After a conference, I will usually get quite a few friend requests from people that I met at the conference. I had a research fellowship at the University of Notre Dame in 2013-2014. After Notre Dame published a list of the new re-search fellows that year, I received multiple friend requests and messages on Facebook from people wanting to follow my research. Now that my book is pub-lished, and my papers are being discussed in classrooms, I regularly get friend requests from people wanting to follow my research. I also get messages from people asking questions about my work.

Facebook has become one of the main ways that academics communicate with me. Most of the invitations that I receive to speak at conferences come via Facebook. As do many invitations to contribute a chapter to a new book, or an article to a special issue of a journal. So it would be very difficult for me to stop using Facebook at this point in my career.

Another aspect of my continued use of Facebook is for my students. Being connected to so many different academics on Facebook has a particular perk. Say a student has a question during class that I am not able to answer fully. I can mes-sage one of my many friends who specialize in that area, and get their take on the question. Then I am able to relay that information to my students. Students really enjoy hearing answers to their questions from the scholars that they are reading and discussing in class. It makes their coursework more personal because they have had some kind of contact with the scholars they are studying.

Multiple things on social media have surprised me. I shall note two that are more likely of interest for this book. One negative and one positive.

The negative thing that I have discovered is that philosophers and theolo-gians at top-notch universities can easily turn into children over controversial topics. When reading the comment section of any news article or video on YouTube, one will witness the most irrational conversations unfold. These con-versations are typically off the cuff insults, prejudiced statements, unanalyzed beliefs, unexamined false accusations of offense and prejudice, failures to stay on topic, moral grandstanding and virtue signaling, and so on. In general, it is some of the most epistemically and morally vicious conversations that one can witness. One would expect scholars to be better than this. One might think that philoso-phers and theologians would engage in the most sophisticated of conversations on social media. This does in fact happen, and happen often. However, I have witnessed philosophers and theologians quickly turn conversations into the aver-age comment section of a YouTube video.

I shall focus on one example, though I could give many. In 2016, the eminent Oxford philosopher, Richard Swinburne, gave a talk on Christian ethics at a regional meeting of the Society of Christian Philosophers. The conversation that ensued online after his talk was an absolute train wreck. The conversation quickly devolved into name-calling, insults, moral grandstanding, and other epistemically vicious behavior. It was quite shocking to watch the drama unfold. Professors at Ivy League schools spouted off some of the vilest comments, and then when asked to apologize, made their comments even more foul. It was surprising to witness that philosophers and theologians can be guilty of such irrational discourse. I have long known that scholars are not consistently rational in their thought processes and behavior, but this was an ugly reminder of that fact.

One of the positives of being connected to other academics on social media is that I know people all over the world. I often have to travel for speaking engagements, conferences, job interviews, and so on. Being single, this can sometimes be a lonely feeling. Yet social media has made my travels less lonely because I have people all around the world wanting to get together and show me their city. For example, on a recent trip to New York City, I had several friends excited to spend time with me after I announced that I would be coming to speak. On a trip to Scotland, a philosopher in Glasgow offered to get lunch and discuss epistemology. I have even been able to play host on a few occasions for other traveling academics. Whilst I was teaching at Cambridge, a professor from Calvin College told me that she was in town. So I took her to a local roller derby match. This sort of thing happens often. It is really nice to know that I have friends in just about every city I visit. And it is nice to know that I can return the favor by being a warm host to others.

I have never had a *major* breakthrough using social media; just minor epiphanies. I often have moments where I feel like I have developed an argument that is too good to be true. So I will message some friends on Facebook to run the argument past them, and get their feedback. Instant messaging can be useful for hashing out some ideas.

When I have an idea that I am mulling over in my head, I will often message my friend JT Turner to get his feedback. JT's feedback is always so helpful. For instance, my paper on panentheism contains a whole section that is not in the original draft. In the original version of the paper, I argued that there simply is no such thing as panentheism because the concept is far too vague to be meaningfully distinguished between theism and pantheism. I still think this is right, given the versions of panentheism that are currently on offer. However, JT reminded me of a previous conversation where I had come up with a way for panentheists to demarcate themselves from theism and pantheism. It is merely a view in logical space, and not a view that I am sure anyone has actually endorsed. So I was reluctant to add this into my paper. But JT developed some arguments as we discussed it, and eventually persuaded me that I needed to include this in my paper. So I went back to the drawing board, developed the ideas, ran them by JT, and created an entire new section of the paper.

The less activity one has on social media, the less interaction one will receive. If I am actively posting on Facebook, or messaging people, I will be on Facebook quite a bit. If I refrain from posting, I typically have less interaction.

Another great tip is to set your phone to silent, and place it face down so that you cannot see any flashing lights to indicate a new notification. Many smart phones will also allow you to prevent notifications from coming through for a period of time, or indefinitely. If you find yourself on social media too much, start utilizing these features on your phone.

Three things I would recommend to scholars considering using social media are the following:

1. Do your best to refrain from posting anything without thinking it through for a bit. You want to avoid posting in a rush, or when emotions are really heated. You will want to consider how others might read your post, and if it will have the outcome you are expecting.

2. Do not be overly political with your posts. There are many reasons for this, but I shall name only one. Unless you are a political scholar, you should not be quick to post things that are outside of your area of expertise. People who follow you are often subject to the "hallow effect." They will see you as a public intellectual, and assume that you know much more than you in fact do. So if you post something political, there is a good chance that people outside of the academy will place more epistemic weight on your ideas than they ought to. If you do post something political, make sure that you have really looked into the sources, the ideas, and the facts before posting. Also, post it with a humble attitude. Show a willingness to hear other viewpoints, and be open to correction when appropriate.

3. Do not shamelessly promote yourself. Social media is a great way to promote your work, but be careful about the way you do it. When I have a paper or book published, or a podcast interview with me is released, I will create one post about it. When someone writes a blog about me, or replies to published work, I will create one post about it. Loads of academics do this. However, I do not make my social media presence entirely about my academic work. Most of my social media presence is about other areas of my life. Most academics that I am aware of do this as well on social media.

But there are several who only post about their work *ad nauseam*. If every single post is about your new book, and why it is the most important book ever to be written in the world of theology, you are doing something wrong. You will start to look less like an academic, and more like your friend who is trying to get everyone to buy their new health and beauty products.

––––––––––––––

R.T. Mullins (PhD, University of St Andrews) is a research fellow and director of communications at the Logos Institute for Analytic and Exegetical Theology and the University of St Andrews. He has previously held research and teaching fellowships at the University of Notre Dame and the University of Cambridge. He specializes in philosophical theology, and has published in the areas of disability theology, the doctrine of God, philosophy of time, the Trinity, the Incarnation, evil, and personal identity over time. When not engaging in philosophical theology, he can often be found at a metal show.

JOHN C. O'KEEFE

Practical Theology

Back in the day [sometime around 2004/5], *Social Media* seemed like such a weird thing; granted, it still does, but *in the way back*, it seemed even stranger. Why would I want to be friends with someone I never met, would met, or could met? The whole idea of this thing we came to call Social Media was just strange, but to be honest with you, I soon found it to be rather exciting, and enlightening.

My very first jump into the shallow end of the Social Media pool was with *Myspace*; and like all of us on Myspace, my first friend was Tom. I had no idea who Tom was, with his white t-shirt, corny smile, sitting in front of a white board with some unreadable writing. I'm not sure even how I became friends with him, or why I wanted to be his friend, but there he was, big as life. But it was cool, I had a friend who didn't live across the street, or who I worked with.

It was not long after I started my Myspace account, I just could not deal with it any more. Besides being amazingly slow to load [*though that might have something to do with AOL Dial-up*], and at the time rather intrusive nature, it just did not meet my needs. What started out as fun, soon became an electronic *booty call*. Now, I never considered myself a prude, but I can't begin to tell you how many messages, and emails, I started to receive from women [*and a few guys*] of all ages, looking for just a one night stand. I'm realist enough to realize that the friends request I received from some of those beautiful young ladies, were actually over weight, middle aged men, sitting in their Mom's basement with their Pokémon posters, and dragon collection. I soon realized, Myspace was not cutting it for me, and if this was Social Media, I was out; besides, how many times can one actually view pictures of cleavage? So, I walked away from Myspace; but not Social Media — there was this new game on the block, and his name was *Facebook*.

At first, Facebook didn't seem any different from Myspace [*twin sons of different mothers*], with one big difference, it never seemed to have the *booty call* feel Myspace developed. Now, I didn't join Facebook right off the bat, I needed a detox period — besides, I was too busy with my Google, and Yahoo Chat Groups to worry about Social Media [*never connecting the dots, that those early groups gave birth to Social Media*]. As I went deeper, and deeper, into Facebook, and other Social Media sites, I soon found they had an amazing use — I could connect with people all over the place who actually wanted to read what I have to say — and that was a great shock.

Currently, I have accounts with Facebook, Google+, LinkedIn, Pinterest, Snapchat, Path, Periscope, and Twitter, to name a few. While I'm not active on all of them, I do use them all. Currently, I use Facebook, Instagram, Twitter, and Google+ the most; with Facebook being the primary. I also use smaller social media platforms, such as, *Nextdoor*. Nextdoor keeps me connected with happenings in my local area — events, issues, and other things that help me in my role as the Lead Pastor of a church. While I publish regularly on Patheos [*Progressive Christian Channel*] I find sharing thoughts on Social Media have helped expand my voice, and drive my Patheos Blog.

I started *ginkworld.net* back in 1999/2000 to give myself a place to shout, scream, rant, and rave. When I started ginkworld.net, there were two other sites dealing with what was call, at the time, *Postmodern Christianity*. There was ginkworld.net, *theooe.com*, and *next-wave.com* — each of us were dealing with how the church needed to change, could change, and how the church needed to evolve to reach a new generation. When I started to write, I wrote under the name *Punk Monkey* most of the time — he was a rather angry little bugger with a major chip on his shoulder [*I'm not saying much has changed*]. As ginkworld.net was growing, things changed quickly, Social Media came about, and changed the way I strived to reach those wanting to hear my voice.

I started using Social Media as an extension of my writing, and sharing my voice. It may sound silly, but I divide my Social Media presence between myself as an author [Author's Page, Groups Pages] and my personal life [Personal page]. Those who friend me on my personal page [about 3,900 friends] see only personal stuff — you know, cute little catchy sayings, cat videos, what I had for lunch, and talking dog videos. I seldom link my writings to my personal page, because I want people to head over to my Author's Page [about 1,000 people follow], my Book Page [The Naked Jesus—about 7,500 followers], or one of the pages I started, or am an Admin on [all total, there is a reach of about 240,000 people].

At first, Social Media was a way of keeping connected with friends and family member; and it was great for that particular reason. I found it to be amazingly simple to remember birthdays, and other special days [*I have a form of dyslexia that, along with other things, does not allow my mind to record dates*]. Once I published my first book [*Boneyard; Creatives Will Change The Way We Lead in The Church*] I found that people actually wanted to hear my views on the changing church; they wanted to hear my views on theological issues facing the church in this crazy time. People kept asking me to publish more on Social Media, so I did, and do. But it was not until I published by fourth book [*The Naked Jesus; A Journey Out of Christianity, and Into Christ*] where I saw the power, and benefit of Social Media on my writing, and sharing my voice. I am always amazed when people share [sometimes thousands, but mostly hundreds of time] what I post with others. I soon realized that I could reach people, those hurt by church, those abused by church I could have never reached without social media.

My biggest surprise in using social media was, people actually wanted to hear my voice, and have conversations about points I made. I was surprised at the push back from some, and how others opened my eyes to points I had not thought of before.

When I first started using Social Media, I would receive emails, messages, and text from people expressing how what I was writing changed their lives, and to be honest with you, that freaked me out, big time. Others would tell me how excited they were that I put into words, what they were feeling, and unable to express until they read an article I wrote. Others would tell me, in no uncertain terms, that I was evil, and that I would fry in hell for what I wrote, and what I was sharing. To be honest with you, those that said I was the devil incarnate, were the voices that kept me focused. I figured, if I was pissing off that many people *in the church*, I was on to something. Which brings me to another big surprise; dialog can open people's eyes.

I'm not sure of the article, but I will never forget Richard. He wrote me daily, sometimes three and four times a day, telling me how wrong I was on many points [*I started to think that Richard didn't have much to do with his life, because we would pick apart my articles like a surgeon*]. Most of my friends told me to block him, I just couldn't. There was something in his personal messages to me that seemed like he was searching for something to hold on to.

Richard was very conservative [no surprise on my end], and that is putting it mildly. He fought me on every topic; if I said I used a PC, he would tell me that PC's were the devils tool, and I had better get a Mac before I died, because using a PC was a sure sign I was not right with the Divine; If I said use a MAC, he would tell me the same thing about a PC. Over the years, Richard started to change his tune. He was still conservative [my desire is not to change a person's theology], he started to see other points of view. He started to open-up in conversations, and share personal things that caused him pain in his life. Over time, he came to understand where others were in their faith journey. He came to understand that different people, could be at different places along the *Christian spectrum*, he may not have agreed with where they were, but he softened his heart enough to actually have conversations with others, in a loving way.

I strive to see how each post does after I post them. One breakthrough came when I looked at the insights over a month period of time. The biggest breakthrough for me came when I noticed those articles I wrote, the ones I hand crafted, nurtured, groomed, nuanced, rubbed in all the right places, and I knew where going to kick-ass, and take names, fall flat. Those I wrote on the fly, and even had some horrid spelling mistakes, went *virialish*. It said to me, just speak from the heart—don't get too heady. Let's be honest, who cares what the original Greek has to say, people want to know how things are now, today.

For example, I remember posting a meme about Starbuck's coffee cup being red—and how many were upset that it did not have a Christmas Theme. Off the top of my head I don't remember what I wrote, but it was something like "You are concerned with a red cup not being Christian, But nothing when it comes to poverty, hunger, war, violence, and more." It was done quickly, had no article connected to it, and that meme was viewed over a million times, and added 3,000 people to The Naked Jesus Facebook Page in just a week—it blew me away. It had over a million views, and was shared almost 45,000 times.

I have found, just writing as I think, plain, simply, and direct, while focusing on love, sharing grace, sharing my views on how the church has missed the mark, or how the church gets lost in the silly, seem to get across to those who follow my pages, or are involved in groups I started. This leads me to another breakthrough: People just want you to be you.

This breakthrough came when I realized people are not seeking out great theology, in one denominational style, or another. In fact, if you belong to a denomination spewing the company line can be very dangerous to those outside the church looking in. If, and you can pick your own example, your denomination is standing boldly on the wrong side of history, and you do not question that stance, people will just walk away from your conversation. People, those inside the church, and those outside the church, want an honest, open, transparent dialog on issues — not the company line. Granted, this can be hard for some — I know, within my denominational tradition I am considered the "red-headed stepchild."

To be honest, I don't think I have mastered the balance when it comes to my time on social media. In our home, I have had to make some guidelines I need to live by:

First, no electronic at the dinner table — none, nope, never, nada — Now, that is not something always accomplished, but we keep each other honest to the task at hand. If I bring my cell phone to the table, Shellene looks at me, with the eyes only a loving wife can use, and I remove the phone to my desk.

Second, I try to live by the reality that when Shellene and I are home, I am not on the computer — with Social Media. I might be working on a lesson outline, but I'm not on Social Media.

Third, I set aside one day a week to write articles for social media. Throughout the week, I keep notes on what I want to say, and I take Fridays to do the writing. I'm off from the church on Fridays, and Shellene is at work — so, it just makes sense to use Fridays.

This is hard, because people are looking for timely information, based on current happenings. But we have to remember, with a 24 hour a day news cycle nothing is ever truly timely, and current changes all the time.

The first thing I would recommend to those considering using social media is to be active. If you are posting, make sure you have a voice in the community. For example, don't join a group simply to post in that group — join, build relationships, get to know people, let them hear your voice — than post links to things you wrote, or what them to see. One of the biggest mistakes people make is to not being involved in the groups they belong. Also, don't join a group where you differ from the theological reality of the group. For example, don't join the Facebook group Progressive Christianity if all you desire to do is tell them how wrong they are, or you keep posting things that flow against the group as a whole. There are plenty of groups out there who share your views, and would love to hear your voice — pick gatherings where you can actually be heard, and not tagged as a troll.

Second, post like crazy. I have found that people who want to hear your voice, what to hear your voice. Also, share the voices of others — even those you disagree with. By sharing other voices, you are saying, "I may not agree with this, but found their points rather interesting.

Third, this is important — don't get discouraged. I have seen more people walk away from Social Media because they did not get to 10,000 followers in a month.

The Naked Jesus Facebook page has been hovering around 7,300 for months — No sooner do I think it will break the 7,300 mark, I see I have lost people liking my page — this happens. I could have posted something that ticked them off, or they could have like the page a year ago, thinking it was one thing and realized it was something else — It does not bug me. Because the people who are reading what I wrote, want to hear it. If you keep thinking in terms of the number of likes you have, it will break your heart, and discourage you quickly.

———————

John C. O'Keefe is an author, a trouble maker, a questioner, a doubter, a lover, but mostly he is the kind of guy that loves the church so much, he is screaming for it to change, and shed its old ways. John has written four books, the latest is The Naked Jesus; A Journey Out of Christianity and Into Christ. *He is currently working on his fifth book,* FORGIVE; Learning to Live With The 'F-Word,' *which should be released in later 2017.*

STEPHEN OKEY

Systematic Theology

I remember joining Friendster my senior year of college. Nothing else online was like it: a way to build and maintain friendship networks online that discouraged the anonymity that had been such a part of my previous online experience. It also helped that, facing graduation, it offered a way for my friends (and especially acquaintances) a way to stay in touch after we left school. Friendster was quickly supplanted by Facebook, which I began using in divinity school, shortly after it launched. It has remained my primary and most consistent social networking platform since.

Since about 2010, though, I've been most engaged with Twitter. The key to this shift for me has been coming to understand my own distinction between public and private personae. Facebook remains the place where I engage with family and friends, where I share personal photos, and where I wish others happy birthday. Twitter, on the other hand, is the place where I most interact with other scholars and colleagues, engage with my students, and respond to significant events or news stories. My Twitter feed is public and accessible while my Facebook profile is private and hidden. There is assuredly some overlap between the two—some of my closest friends are also colleagues—but I seek to carve out different spaces online the same way I do in the rest of my life. And, for those places where there is overlap, I typically use Instagram (in part because it easily shares to both platforms).

Additionally, I write for the blog Daily Theology (http://dailytheology.org). It's a collaborative blog whose contributors seek to make the ideas and insights of theology accessible to the everyday lives of its readers. In terms of working out my thoughts in a more developed manner, the blog is often the first place I go to share my work. It has become a really positive place of communal conversation.

Seeing a distinction between my public and private personae online was driven by the start of my undergraduate teaching career. I first began using social media professionally in order to engage my undergraduate students. I was in the final years of writing my dissertation, and it was right around when Twitter was popular among traditional age college students. While I had my own feed, I created a separate one for our course, thinking this would be an effective way to reach students without feeling as though I was compelling them to follow *me*. My plan was that the feed would be a source of interesting links relevant to the course, a way to engage in digital office hours, and a forum for treating students to hints about upcoming quizzes in class.

This was also spurred in part by the early adopter mentality I inherited from my mother. I grew up with computers in the house, learned to code before middle school, and was among the early people on the local online bulletin boards. When it came to social media, I hoped I might be an early adopter of this technology and its potential for improving my teaching. One semester in a general education theology course I taught, I checked Twitter the night before their midterm. Rather than emailing me, a student had tweeted a question about infinite regress in St. Thomas Aquinas' five proofs for the existence of God. This led to a surprisingly productive back and forth about how his arguments worked, and I was pleased at how that improved her performance on the test the next day. Admittedly experiences like this are rare, but they give me hope for continuing with social media in my pedagogy.

As far as scholarship and networking go, the value of social media was only realized later. When some friends of mine and I started Daily Theology, it afforded a greater level of visibility for me within my discipline. I found that when I would go to conferences, people already knew who I was. I received more followers on Twitter and more friend requests on Facebook. As the technology improved, I noticed the possibilities for conversation improved as well (although so too did the possibilities for snark and venom).

My professional participation in social media still engages students and colleagues. I include my Twitter handle on every syllabus along with a hashtag specific to each course. I make arrangements to see friends, and to meet new people, via Twitter and Facebook before conferences (and, once I'm there, I often participate in live-tweeting certain sessions). At its core, most (but not all) of the value comes from building both weak and strong ties in my larger theological networks.

Interestingly, a research project that I am currently working on is both about social media and came about because of my participation in social media. It focuses on how social media participates in and shapes the reception of magisterial teaching in the Catholic Church. The particular focus is on how Pope Francis' Twitter feeds have affected reception of his teachings, especially the encyclical *Laudato Si*. When that text was released, it was accompanied by extensive tweeting from his accounts. These tweets suggested key quotations and essential ideas that Francis wanted his readers to grab onto. Analysis of more than 60 tweets from the days surrounding the release reveal a savvy and intentional social media strategy that was designed to accompany — and to amplify — the release.

These efforts have helped to make Francis' teaching more accessible to his followers. It has created a platform for responding to his work, both positively and negatively. Moreover, it has provided the impetus for a lot of discussion among lay Catholics about the significance of the encyclical, whether that be on the scientific questions of climate change or the interpretation of dominion and stewardship in scripture. Yet in making teaching (and the teacher) more accessible, there are also concerns about whether the means of social communication risk de-contextualizing magisterial teaching. There's the risk that anything the Pope says (or tweets) will be viewed as having the same level of authority as any other document from the Vatican. The teaching could become flattened, giving the faithful a deeply flawed understanding of the relative importance of different teachings. In this way, the structure of the technology, and the modes of thinking that can encourage, can profoundly shape our understanding.

I came to this question in part through my engagement with other scholars on Twitter. I've actively followed the Pope on Twitter since the @Pontifex account debuted, and I had previously written a critique of the social media strategy of Pope Benedict XVI. The paper I'm working on is part of a conference panel where all three of us first me each other through Twitter. Without my time spent on social media, I may not have met my interlocutors for this research, and I certainly would not have come upon the topic in question.

Even with its benefits, social networking also brings significant challenges. As obvious as it might seem in retrospect, I've been struck by how demographics play a role in one's engagement with social media. Behemoth networks like

Facebook are not actually universal, and so for a few years none of my students were on it, and then a few years later they all were. The same is true for Twitter, Instagram, Yik Yak, and other platforms. I notice this especially with respect to age, but it's not even generational: one or two years of difference in age can have dramatic effects on which networks one actively participates in.

This has been important for me in terms of thinking about the "echo chamber" argument about social media. Many cultural commentators claim that our feeds simply reflect our own preferences, and thus we don't have genuinely new encounters or read articles that might meaningfully challenge us. Cultivating a diversity of sources and a diversity of conversations requires conscious intentionality; it's not the default of the platforms. Thus if I engage with people in largely the same demographic groups that I'm a part of, and if I only use the platforms that fit these demographics, there is a real risk of becoming trapped in that echo chamber.

Time management can also be a significant challenge. It can be easy to lose oneself in scrolling, scrolling, scrolling through one's feeds with mindless abandon. It's also possible to be drawn into a conversation via social network and become sidetracked from one's other goals.

One thing that helps me is that I usually use the Pomodoro technique for managing my time in general. This approach breaks time into 25 minute work chunks followed by 5 minute breaks. When I am working on an essay or something for my classes, I try to fit small amounts of social networking into those breaks. However, because I also manage multiple accounts (one for my university department, one for the blog I write for), sometimes I need to set aside more sustained focus. In those times, I dedicate one or two 25 minute blocks in a day to this work. I try to be disciplined and not let these periods bleed over into one another, and that helps a great deal.

A second thing that is important for me is developing good virtues in terms of engaging technology. After my wife and I had been dating for about a year, we realized that we each had habits of going to our phones whenever we were just a little bit bored or distracted. If these moments didn't sync up, the other would often feel slighted. So we formulated rules fairly early on about our mutual phone use (largely built around asking the other for permission if there was good reason). With social media, I recently came to recognize that having Facebook on my phone presented an easy temptation to get lost online for extended periods of time in a way that neither Twitter on my phone nor Facebook on my laptop did. So in this case, deleting the app made for a great improvement.

Three things I would recommend to those considering more use of social media are:

1. Decide if and how to distinguish your professional/public persona from your private one. For some, this distinction is unnecessary or even burdensome. For others, it helps to have a sense that certain platforms have certain uses. I've been grateful to keep my public persona primarily on Twitter and my private primarily on Facebook. It has shaped what I share in each place, which in turn has generally improved the kinds of conversations I participate in on each network.

2. Seek out the conversations you are interested in and can contribute to. Sometimes these are narrow in time (the few days surrounding a conference), and sometimes these are public or private groups where people share links and discuss. Participating can certainly help introduce you to new ideas or issues you were not yet aware of, but even more so it can introduce you to the people who are tuned in to your common interests. For me, some of the individuals I have met through these means have become valued collaborators.

3. Keep the logic of the technology in mind in order to improve how you inhabit its spaces. I think it's always worthwhile to recognize that what is said online is an odd combination of disposable and permanent. Disposable because it takes so little effort to send a comment out into the ether, but permanent because it will always be there. Similarly, it's always possible that something you intend to be part of a small conversation will get out of your control. So just as you let your yes mean yes, so too let your status update be a true reflection of yourself.

Overall, as someone who came of age with the internet, I certainly remember life before many of its conveniences and perils, but I also remember the excitement of new developments and innovations. From my 6th grade science teacher showing us how to get onto county-wide bulletin boards through dial-up to my high school self's quest to craft the most clever away message for AOL Instant Messenger, even now up to finding the right hashtags to put on a Tweet or Instagram photo, I've been struck by how each new technology develops its own grammar and logic. Social networking can be a real boon not only for our personal lives, but also for our teaching and our research. The key, I think, is to figure out how to navigate its structures virtuously and with purpose.

Stephen Okey is an Assistant Professor in the Department of Philosophy, Theology, and Religion at Saint Leo University. He is the author of A Theology of Conversation: An Introduction to David Tracy (Liturgical Press, forthcoming), as well as both scholarly and popular articles. He serves as the Treasurer of the College Theology Society. You can find Stephen Okey at his website, stephenokey.com. He writes for the collaborative Daily Theology blog (dailytheology.org), where he also hosts a podcast featuring interviews with theologians. He is active on Twitter (@stephenokey) and Instagram (@stephenokey), and occasionally he signs into LinkedIn.

KEEGAN OSINSKI

Sacramental and Liturgical Theology

I have accounts on just about every social media platform there is—Facebook, Twitter, Instagram, LinkedIn, certainly. But also Tumblr, Goodreads, Snapchat, Pinterest, Ello, Peach, Influenster, and probably a couple of others I've forgotten about. Primarily, for my work (and life in general) I rely on Twitter and Facebook.

My use of social media for professional, academic reasons has evolved with my own personal involvement in the professional academic sphere. I joined Facebook and Twitter in 2007 and 2008, respectively, while I was in undergrad, and using the platforms to form and foster professional relationships has been a natural extension of my regular use as more of my life has become focused on academic work. The goal is making connections—and not in a skeezy, self-serving, corporate "networking" kind of way, but in such a way that your annual conference feels more like a family reunion or summer camp. I use social media to find my people, my guild, the people who have navigated these academic waters before me and who navigate it alongside me now. As long as social media remains a place to create and engage in these communities, I'll continue using it.

One thing they teach you in library school is that when people have an information need, they will ask their immediate social networks for help before they consult an expert. I've discovered that with social media, your immediate social networks can *include* experts—of all kinds. Real research, knowledge-sharing,

337

and scholarly communication are not only happening at conferences, in class-rooms, and in academic journals. They're happening on social media all the time.

Every single one of my publications is due in some way to social media. In 2013 I attended my first conference. I had submitted a paper proposal, it was accepted, and a few weeks later I was on a plane, headed to a gathering without knowing a soul. I had connected with a few other presenters on Twitter before-hand, and two of these new friends suggested I fly into Kansas City and they'd pick me up at the airport, and we'd drive the three hours to Springfield. I was broke, and funding the trip myself, so of course I got into a car with a couple of strangers from the internet. As the conference started, I had about 100 Twitter followers; by the end of it that number had almost doubled. I'd met scholars, PhD students, and ministers, who were either at the conference or following its hashtag on Twitter, all of whom were working on exciting projects that I never could have known about or kept up with had we not connected. The conference itself was great, but the real magic was in keeping in touch afterward. Because of these connections and our continued relationships, I've given a paper on a panel with a well-known philosopher, written a piece in a journal of practical theology, had a chapter in a book alongside some big-name theologians, and published my first peer-reviewed article. I've co-written papers, co-facilitated discussion groups, and co-organized events, all with people "from the internet."

I was in a job interview once, where a portion of my presentation had been about engaging students and their research needs on social media, since that's where they are and where they're asking questions. Someone raised their hand and asked, somewhat incredulously, "So, are you just always on Twitter?" Much to their dismay, I think, I answered, "Well, yes!" Part of this is undoubtedly due to being a Millennial, on the cutting evolutionary edge as we morph into a bionic post-human species, but social media is simply part of my every-day. I don't often think of it as a discrete task or obligation, rather just part of my daily life—I make coffee, I check Twitter. I take the dogs out, I check Facebook. During the work day, checking social media is in the same rotation as checking email.

I do want to emphasize that this constant checking is indeed checking. It's not the mindless scroll or the detailed catch-up that do have their place now and then. A typical check is to attend to any notifications (I keep all sound and pop-up notifications off, because I like to be in control of when I check my social media), see if any important or interesting news has broken, and move on. It takes all of 30 seconds.

Of course, there are days where social media becomes more time-consuming than others, like that afternoon those llamas got loose in Arizona, or in the days after the Presidential election, or when a conservative think tank has published a blog about your work and every social media check includes notifications of people calling you a messenger of Satan, but for the most part social media can be seamlessly integrated into daily work without being too much of a burden or a distraction.

I would recommend the following to those considering using social media more:

1. Be yourself. A lot of people like to talk about "professionalism," and I know several people who actually have "professional" and "personal" accounts on social media, but I don't buy that. Compartmentalizing your life, even on social media, leads to a kind of inauthenticity that precludes quality relationships. And relationships are what social media is about. I have plenty of "professional" contacts on Twitter — professors, recommenders, editors, supervisors — and they see my smart takes on current events; but they also see my selfies with my dog. And that's OK! Because all of that is who I am, and in seeing all of that, they're getting to know me, for real.

2. Engage. Social media is a two-way street. If you're online just to push out content and talk about yourself, you're missing the point. Ask questions. Answer your @ replies. Tell people what you think of their posts. Conversation is key.

3. Have a sense of humor. Yes, important, valuable, and serious work can and does get done on social media, but let's be real: The internet is about jokes. Even "professional" social media should be as fun as it is productive — more happy hour than faculty meeting.

Keegan Osinski is a librarian and scholar of philosophy and theology. Her primary research areas include sacramental and liturgical theology, continental philosophy, and queer and gender studies, and she is also interested in facilitating knowledge-sharing between scholars and clergy in new and creative ways. Keegan's landing page is at keeganosinski.com, and you can find her on Twitter using the handle @keegzzz.

ALEXANDER PRUSS

Philosophy

My primary social media platform is my blog, hosted by Blogger. I occasionally, but very rarely, look at other blogs. I have in the past posted on some group blogs. I use no other social media platforms for philosophical purposes right now. (I frequent some online forums and more rarely Facebook groups in connections with hobby interests.) But when I was writing the first draft of my infinity book, I had the full text available in a GitHub repository, committing revisions to it as I made them, and inviting comments from any readers. I guess GitHub counts as a social media platform of sorts. I removed the draft, though, when I started shopping it out to publishers.

In connection with my philosophical interests, I was asked to join the Right Reason blog. I put that off until I got tenure, and then joined it, and wrote a number of posts. The blog shut down, but I wanted to keep on writing stuff, so I started my own blog.

Before I had a blog, I would make notes on a PDA when I had a philosophical or theological idea that struck me. Now that I have my own blog, it is my primary notebook for philosophical ideas — but it's open to the public, in keeping with my general attraction to openness and transparency. Some of the ideas I write down I eventually transform into papers (I sometimes browse the blog to see if there are any publishable ideas).

Once I blog an idea, I can (and often do) forget it. Now I can always search for it (and sometimes do).

I have been surprised to discover that more people read my blog posts than attend conference talks, read articles by me, or are in my classes. So I've come to realize that to a significant degree this is my main way of spreading ideas.

Almost all the material in my current book project on infinity was first tried out on my blog. A layman on the other side of the world regularly gave me comments on technical blog posts on infinity and formal epistemology, comments whose scholarly quality was cutting edge (if he wanted to, I think he could be a really good professional epistemologist). This is someone I wouldn't have reached without my blog, and my current book project on paradoxes of infinity has benefited greatly. The comments continued when I started posting the manuscript-in-progress on GitHub; I would commit a chapter; he would give me superb comments; I would revise in light of comments; sometimes this would repeat in a number of iterations.

Writing on my blog is thinking. It is how I do almost all my philosophical research. I rarely if ever now publish anything that wasn't sketched on my blog first. I have almost no ideas, good or bad, that I don't blog.

Alexander Pruss is Professor of Philosophy at Baylor University. He works in metaphysics, philosophy of religion, applied ethics, formal epistemology and philosophy of mathematics. His first book was _The Principle of Sufficient Reason: A Reassessment_ (Cambridge, 2006). His last completed book is _Necessary Existence_, co-authored with Joshua Rasmussen (Oxford, forthcoming). He has a PhD in philosophy from the University of Pittsburgh and a PhD in mathematics from the University of British Columbia. Find his blog at http://alexanderpruss.blogspot.com

JANEL APPS RAMSEY

Pastoral Theology

S ocial media is a significant part of my daily life. While I primarily use Facebook, I am also active on Twitter, Instagram, and Pinterest. I also have several websites/blogs.

Facebook is the platform I use the most because I feel it reaches the widest audience. Facebook is also where I have my largest community. It is quite versatile; allowing space for discussion, room for links to resources, and privacy under certain settings. It is the easiest way to form and maintain a community for a particular group, like a church or a small group, in which people can interact and build relationship.

While Facebook is a great tool, it also has limits. When using Facebook, I often see things I like and they affirm my view — because that's the way the algorithm works. I see less of what I don't like and can hide things that irritate me. In that way, Facebook does not reflect the outside world. To impact the world, we have to engage with ideas we like and ones we don't like. This means it becomes my responsibility purposefully to keep my input wide, and making sure that what I share represents multiple points of view.

Beyond personal interactions, I started using social media to address difficult issues in the church. Specifically to highlight perspectives regarding women in ministry and to address issues around faith transitions. By using Facebook for these purposes, I can show people that they are not alone and that many people have similar experiences. I also like to explore social justice issues and share articles highlighting how the church deals with issues in different ways.

More recently, while I continue to use social media in these ways, my posts have changed. Since the election of 2016, I have changed the focus of my posts; increasing the number of times I point out things like issues of privilege, gender discrimination, racial discrimination, and inequality. Even if the people reading my feed think like me, there is purpose in encouraging each other to continue to #resist tyranny and evil while speaking truth into the world. We are called to defend the oppressed. And one way I do that is with social media.

Social media is complex and surprising. The way information spreads and the interactions you have with people online can be unpredictable. Sometimes articles you publish or share just fall flat, and other times people share content that didn't seem as valuable as other posts. It's often hard to gauge what will spread and what won't.

I am also surprised by the depth of friendships I have been able to cultivate in the online world. People often think those are "fake friendships", but I would argue that I feel very connected to some of the people I've met online. I make sure to meet them in person when I have the opportunity, and I care about their lives and the things they are going through. I feel like I make meaningful connections in online spaces that enhance my offline life, not detract from it.

I also like how I can interact with people that are better known. It is a privilege to get to ask them honest questions and get honest answers. To have them interact with me about their faith journey and reflect on my own experience is encouraging. To get to take a selfie with them is cool too. I appreciate their willingness to engage with me.

One downside to social media is the rampant sexism. Whether through blatant insult, subtle jabs, or microaggressions, the internet is not friendly to women. In fact, I have hesitated to be more involved online with people I don't know because of the stories I read about how women are treated. When well known, highly successful women have to pull back from being present online, it makes me afraid to be present online. Rape threats, name calling, and even death threats are regular occurrences for women when they keep speaking and participating in online life. That is scary.

One thing I have learned more about through my interaction with social media is the idea of unconscious bias. Not only did learning about this help me understand more about how the world works, but it also helped me understand some of my own journey better. When applying this information to faith journeys and interactions with systems (the Church), things that made no sense, start to become clearer.

Once I started sharing and writing about this interaction, people responded and wanted to learn more. Part of my Wounds of the Church project is to help shed light on why some of the things that happen in a faith journey happen the way they do. For example, being able to recognize and own the idea that failure is not always the fault of the individual can help people reconcile their understanding of a situation and the way things turned out. Acknowledging that certain systems, institutions, and churches are doing things without reflecting critically on why they do them, (and that this can cause harm,) often helps people move on.

Talking about this on social media triggered Facebook to tell me about an event involving bias and privilege that was taking place in my city. Because of that, I was able to attend this event and make some new connections. That opportunity may open the door for continued education on the topic. Thanks Facebook!

While social media has many benefits, it also has its pitfalls. Sometimes it's hard to keep track of how long I'm on social media. Blog posts can take hours, when I really need them to take *an* hour. It is easy to get lost in this other world that is always so accessible.

Recently, I heard someone talk about it as if our reality or our consciousness gets relocated into another place when we're in the midst of social media. That resonates with my experience. My consciousness, and maybe even some of my molecules or electrons, resonates with the place or person I'm engaged with at the time. It's easy to lose a sense of place and time when I'm really immersed online. I've contemplated different ways to track my social media use or ways to interrupt it, but then I get caught up in doing research or hearing the stories of people who experience the same thing, and forget what I was supposed to be doing.

One thing I have done is turn off some of my notifications. I didn't realize I could shut off the notifications that go to the home screen on my phone. Now I have it set up so that only a few apps can do that. If I miss something on one of the other social media channels, either a real person will reach out or I'll never know what I missed. It has definitely helped reduce my social media anxiety.

When it comes to using social media in conjunction with the academy, I'd start by encouraging others to get out there and engage with people. Now, you don't have to do everything all at once or all the time. However, you should be sharing your work and spreading new ideas. If you find Facebook to be overwhelming or distracting, don't use it. Or, have a professional page only and find a trusted student to post something occasionally.

Twitter is easy but limited. You have to start following people and then your audience will grow. You will want to be able to link to content so that you can say more than 140 characters.

While Instagram and Pinterest might seem weird for academic work, they also allow you to reach a different generation and group of people. Pictures don't have to be directly related to a topic, though they can be. It is also simple to use a tool like Canva or other "meme" type apps to add a quote to a picture and share it on social media. An interesting quote might be the thing that draws someone new to your work.

It's also important to recognize that some people love this stuff, and can live and breathe social media. While at the same time, other people wish computers didn't exist, or at least were not invasively tied to everything going on in life. Finding your own rhythm and tolerances is important. Framing it up as a way to engage new people in the dialog and to expose people to ideas they might not normally think about it is also a helpful lens. Posting in multiple places helps different types of users find your work.

I am thankful for my friend @_danielrosado who taught me how to tweet. I had never engaged much with Twitter. He patiently walked me through how he uses it at conferences and how he engages with theologians that are doing work that interests him. He is a pro at using social media to learn more about theology and to grow in his ever-widening faith. If you're not sure how to get started, reach out to someone that's already doing it and I bet they'll have you online in no time.

———————————

Janel Apps Ramsey, M.A.T.S., is a pastor, theologian, and feminist. She is the Co-Director of Brew Theology and the pastor of Evensong Community. She served for 20 years in the Church of the Nazarene in a wide variety of roles. She has taught and preached to all age levels throughout her career. Brew Theology is collective of groups that discuss theological/social/political issues. Evensong Community is a house church for people reorienting in their faith. You can visit Janel's websites at www.womenandchurch.com and www.woundsofthechurch.com. She is also responsible for the www.brewtheology.org website. You can find her at Janel Apps Ramsey on Facebook (where she posts daily). You can find her at @jlaramsey on Twitter, Pinterest, and Instagram. She is also on Google+ and LinkedIn periodically. She also writes for the Emerging Voices Blog on Patheos.

TRAVIS REED AND STEVE FROST

Theology and Communications

W e're going to assume we met at a conference, where all the good stuff happens over a burger and beers after the main sessions. In our mind, that's where we are, having burgers and beers. Cigars may or may not be involved. We've been sharing souls whilst partaking of said burgers and beers, when, in the course of conversation, we've meandered around to these questions . . .

Travis: Best case scenario [waves away cigar smoke] you'd be doing this in relationship. We're a visual culture, it's how people know and understand their world. We're moving into that, not away from it. So the main thing is a) moving images b) on the interwebs. That's the gist of it.

Steve: A long time ago Marshall McLuhan said "The medium is the message." If the message of the incarnation was that God isn't an idea but a person, then video, which pulls words off of the page and places them in the mouths of living breathing incarnate people, is one of the most appropriate vehicles to convey this message of cosmic relationality.

Travis: The Work Of The People is hosted on a website. It's that simple and unsexy. Once The Work Of The People got going Facebook came along. It proved to be a place where: a) people were hanging out b) we could share videos and c) have conversations about them. So we went there too.

Travis: Everyone is a theologian! People are hungry to figure out how to be themselves!

Steve: Communities, when they gather together and are in conversation with each other, make manifest a local and specific theology, a communal theology. You might have heard of the African word *ubuntu*, it means *I am what I am because of who we all are.* The theological version of ubuntu is something like: we are our understanding of God to each other.

Travis: What's needed is spaces for people to speak freely, to work out their faith in fear and trembling. Walter Brueggeman says church should be the last honest place on the block. But mostly it's not. It's really hard to do this kind of communal theology, to work out your faith in traditional faith communities.

Steve: They mostly follow a one-to-many broadcast of intellectual information, rather than a conversational format in which theology can be lived out, discovered, wrestled free in sadness, joy, pain and celebration.

Travis: An online community can hold safe space in which to begin to speak, to begin to question, to begin to wrestle. Video makes being part of the community accessible. It pulls theology out of the ivory tower and makes it livable. The future of publishing and learning is online. Not just because of the cost. It's because you can stay rooted in soil and work out your theology as a practitioner while learning. There's real time feedback.

Steve: It's not that it's the only way to learn, or even the best. But it is a way to learn. There's an obvious tension, because most of the theologians Travis films are supported by traditional schools and seminaries.

Travis: The possibilities of the online model are in contrast to pulling people out of the soil of relationship, to then disseminate top down information, to then send them out (in debt) and wonder why that's not sustainable.

Steve: The online community can be a place of trust, where people can ask questions and seek their own growth.

Travis: The sad truth is, in their own Christian communities people are often shamed for asking questions and wanting to grow.

Travis: Connection! Communion! Friendship! Influence! Feedback! Growth! Because the resource wasn't created as a tool for aseptic use in a clinical environment, but to be soil for growth and change in real lives, the response hasn't been thank you for this tool. The response has been . . .

Steve: . . . real connection, deep communion, lasting friendships, positive influence, welcome feedback, personal growth.

Travis: The more we connect and grow the more we're surprised by the depths of our need to dismantle our own privilege . . .

Steve: . . . our own defenses, our own self-at-the-center-ness

Travis: It's been a sustaining communion for me and the people who are part of the tribe. We've been at the table together through this connection of creating videos and then learning and growing through those videos. Sometimes that becomes literally being at the table together. People say, "Hey we're in Houston, can we come over" and they're in my back yard sharing a BBQ. Speaking and questioning freely has sustained them for another day, which sustains me for another day. That mutual sustaining starts online, in a safe place, then it gets carried to local soil, local contexts. TWOTP has grown because it's self-sustaining that way, it has influence because people trust it. Belief isn't about right thinking it's about trust.

Steve: By speaking freely about this ancient story that we love and doubt and laugh and weep over, we help each other trust each other. Our trusting each other helps us trust the story, because we **are** the story too. That's the story, that we have a place in the story! By speaking freely about it, we find our place in it.

Travis: There's a deep trust of something that's not just a product that's been effectively disseminated through a social media platform. There's an aliveness to this thing that's shared online, that builds trust. The aliveness comes before the platform.

Travis: The Work Of The People worked! The thing I started worked! And it continues to work! It didn't have to do with the technology, it had to do with relationship. Being online let people relate to this content on equal terms, it allowed them to breathe and ask questions openly. It allowed them to dance with theologians.

Steve: At the core of that isn't that it was online, it's how we relate to each other. It took the safety of an online community for people to start the dance.

Travis: In a top down patriarchal structure where faith can feel like it's being orchestrated by middle management, there isn't room to dance. [Knocks over an empty mug while making a dancing gesture] There isn't room for working out faith in doubt and messiness, but that's what's needed for people to grow. The Work Of The People itself, all the content, everything about it was cultivated, not manufactured. You can't duct tape fruit to the tree. There's a lot that didn't work. There's a lot of death. There are a lot of resources online that are cleverer, so it's not about that. It's about sticking with it, sticking with the truth of it.

Steve: Soil is layers and layers and layers of dead things. Cultivation is in The Work Of The People's DNA. That's why people know they can go there to cultivate their faith, to cultivate their growth. They know they can get their fingers dirty and dance because that's the process that brought The Work Of The People into being. You can't *manufacture* a Resource for Cultivation™ and expect people to believe it or to trust it. You have to cultivate a resource for cultivation.

Travis: It's not the Wild West where anything goes. I curate and create an ethos. But everything about the ethos speaks to open dialogue. I leave the mistakes in the videos on purpose, because real life has mistakes, so we aren't going to censor or shut down mistakes.

Steve: Our visual culture knows how to filter for bullshit. [Steve, being Canadian, apologized for swearing] It also knows how to read those cues, those tacit, subtle, unspoken things that say "this is what we're about, we're about open dialogue." People pick up on Travis' non-verbalized visual cues, not necessarily consciously because we're so good at decoding this stuff, but they pick it up, they know it's genuine, and they know it's safe.

Steve to Travis: I can just image someone missing the point of everything we've been saying and firing off a memo the media team: "Moving forward, we're leaving in mistakes."

Travis: For heaven's sake don't do that. Go have lunch with the media team and be vulnerable broken human beings together. Then go make a video about that.

Travis: If it's causing me to be not in relationship it's maybe not good. For instance there are ambiguities to this question, which came via email. I can start making assumptions about the question's assumptions. Is it a tactical question that views social media as a disembodied tool? i.e. "How much social media is enough to execute?" Or is it a question that's concerned for my well-being? "How do you stay genuinely connected?" It makes me want to sit down and have a conversation about it. So, that's kind of how I manage my time on social media.

I don't know, for instance, I wouldn't use inhuman automated marketing to efficiently talk about human vulnerability. I embrace the inefficiencies of navigating the many ways I can connect with people in today's world and trust my spirit to guide me on a case by case basis toward genuine presence.

Travis: [takes a swig of beer] Memorize! Execute! Just kidding. Make a video. Put in online. Send it to your friends. Have them send it to their friends. Let them speak freely. Let that inform your thinking. Let your thinking inform them. Just kidding, but not really. That's all TWOTP did. How about this? As much as you can, stay at 30,000ft with the whys, not at 5 ft. with the hows. Publishing, education and spiritual formation aren't changing, they've already changed.

Steve: The nature of work itself is changing, for everyone. It's scary, but it presents opportunities for people who want to — or need to — ask why. You can ask why, send it to your friends, let them speak freely and both be informed by the relational interaction. Isn't that legitimate learning?

Travis: When I think about the ability to do a digital epistle or a digital pamphlet, I think there's a lot of possibility there to publish in a way that is direct and immediate and allows for a rootedness in relationship. It allows for a dialogue of sorts, in interaction with a tribe.

Steve: You can still find ways to bring peer review into it, for sure to bring an editor into it without having to be constrained by traditional publishing models. On the fly pamphleteering could bring some weight and substantiveness to the kind of ethereal and dissolving nature of so much of what we read digitally. It could bring a bit of thoughtful prose to a world of leveraged sound bites.

Travis: It's scriptural in the sense of just writing letters to people. It can have this immediate influence that helps shape a lasting influence. It's not just about you and your ideas, it's about something larger that happens in lived lives. That's sort of obvious, and it's why people publish books, to help people live lives. But the time lines and disconnection that happens in traditional publishing tends to isolate people in silos of ideas. The influence isn't "People listen to what I say." The influence is in good theological wrestling getting into the soil of tribes right away, affecting the theological soil of lived communities in an ongoing immediate way. It takes work and sticking with it to get it going, to find the tribe, find the soil, but once that dialogue is going there isn't a whole lot of structure or resources needed to have a lot of impact. You don't have to leave the wilderness for the safety of structures, to then bring what you have back to the wilderness. You can create a kind of oasis in the wilderness that provides nourishment and refreshment while at the same time retaining the immediacy of visceral dialogue with the realities of the wilderness.

Travis Reed is a filmmaker and the founder of The Work of the People: www.the-workfothepeople.com Steve Frost is an artist, author and community organizer. He is Executive Director of Tasai, a Vancouver based cross-cultural artist collective making better cities though art. He offers Art Based Leadership Development to leaders in organizational contexts for the development of Sustainable Creativity. www.tasai.ca steve@tasai.ca

MONTE LEE RICE

Missional Theology

My primary social media platform is Facebook, which I daily use. At a secondary level, I use my monteleerice.wordpress.com blog, which automatically links new postings to my LinkedIn and Twitter accounts. While I find Facebook most advantageous as a social *cum* professional network platform, I utilise my WordPress, LinkedIn and Academia.edu accounts for providing online my professional documents (Curricular Vitae, Ministry Profile), as well as public access to some of my published and unpublished writings. However, at the root of these accounts, is my Box.com account. For that is where I first store documents like my CV, which Box.com feeds to these other accounts.

In relation to my scholarly interests, I first began using social media in 2006. I still find it helpful towards these aims. The story for me thus began in April 2006. I was on the pastoral staff of a large Anglican church. But that month things ended badly. So 2006 was a traumatic year for my wife and me. As the years passed, I realized in hindsight that 2006 marked the beginning of a long "sabbatical" from that kind of formal ministry employment and leadership role. Hence, I embarked on what some spiritual and vocational-ministry formation models refer to refer to as, "*isolation processing.*"

Yet that same year and for the first time ever, I started a blog; the one that I still manage as, monteleerice.wordpress.com. I did so because I thought it might prove professionally helpful if I established an online presence. So I began up-loading my developed Christian education courses, such as my favourite topics like, "Gifts of the Spirit," "Moving in the Spirit," and most dramatically, "Our Need for a Fresh Baptism in the Holy Spirit." Then in April 2007, I received an anony-mous question to my blog. The question was, "*What is your understanding be-tween Lucan, Johannine, and Pauline Spirit-baptism?*"

Time has now shown that that question, became a life turning point. The question affectively drew me to its themes. I knew it recalled the older Pentecostal scholarship issues. But I wrestled with how these conversations had moved for-ward in ways that was all new to me. Moreover, my time within the Anglican tra-dition moved me theologically forward, with a broader ecumenical outlook and reading of Scripture.

I spent several weeks reflecting on how I might best reply. But a year went by and I found myself amassing endless typed paragraphs with no seeming conclu-sion. Years later it reminded me of Ezekiel's encounter of the Spirit: "I sat there among them, *stunned*, for seven days." In 2007, I read Walter Brueggemann's book, *The Prophetic Imagination* (Fortress Press, 2001). That marked another turning point. For it inspired me with at last a main theme that began structuring those amassed paragraphs into several blog postings I titled, "Spirit-Baptism and the Prophetic Imagination."

Then through my observing my wife's new involvement with Facebook, in 2008 I set up an account. This soon proved highly fruitful. At least it felt so, given the satisfaction I felt from the experiences of "friending," and giving and receiving "likes" for published postings. For these reasons, I began spending less time with my blog, as Facebook became more part of daily lifestyle.

Beginning that same year, three practices fostered a more scholarly purpose towards, and outcome from my new Facebook involvement. First, was that I began posting book quotes and brief reviews or reflections from books I was reading. Second, these postings occasionally generated discussions or comments, which led to an expanding "friend" list, increasingly with people either interested in or involved in Pentecostal scholarship. Steadily, my "friend" list began comprising more established (and less notably known) Pentecostal scholars, doctoral stu-dents engaged in Pentecostal studies, or anyone with some interest in these kinds of postings and discussions.

Finally, the greatest catalyst towards a scholarly use of Facebook came about in late 2011. That was when Indonesian Pentecostal scholar Ekaputra Tupamahu, now a PhD student at Vanderbilt University, initiated the idea and invited me to join him in creating a new Facebook group, *Pentecostal Theology Worldwide*. Our globally diverse membership now comprises 8,300 members representing every continent. I believe we have effectively achieved part of our stated purpose statement, which is to, "Promote on an inclusive globalised platform, the art of shared theological reflection between grass-roots / ministry practitioners and voices and communities more directly linked with formal / interdisciplinary theologising."

We were especially encouraged by Anglican New Testament/hermeneutics scholar Anthony Thiselton's reference to our group in his 2013 book, *The Holy Spirit: In Biblical Teaching, through the Centuries, and Today* (Eerdmans). Thiselton cited many of our group's grassroots discussions as an example of growing Pentecostal "self-criticism," which he argues, illustrates the ongoing maturation of Pentecostal tradition as a theological tradition.

I suppose I have been pleasantly surprised to discover the much good I have reaped through using social media since 2006. Let me try to summarise three broad good things I have found through social media usage. Much I what I will say here would reflect what I have written in my other answers within this chapter. First, I have found social media, specifically in the form of Facebook, an invaluable aid towards generating broader levels of theological reflection and understanding. I have observed this emerging largely through its capacity towards fostering community conversation on a given thread, even if contributors have little or no previously no personal familiarity with one another.

Second, social media, and again primarily in the form of Facebook, has proved to be an effective and life direction-setting, networking tool. I am right now in the process of formally beginning a non-residential PhD programme in Pentecostal theology through the Center for Pentecostal and Charismatic Studies of Bangor University (Wales, UK). What broadly fostered this journey were several consecutively attended conferences and presentations at the Society for Pentecostal Studies. Yet, what initially initiated (and has continuously aided) that involvement plus encouraged and advised guidance towards PhD studies, were several strategic Facebook contacts. I am particularly thinking of one Facebook contact made in 2010. That contact, who is a well-known Pentecostal theologian, had in so many ways consistently done his best to prod and advise me within this journey. So looking back, that is an important thing I have discovered and experienced through using social media.

So to further elaborate, Facebook has over these years consistently effected a number of highly instrumental friendships or connections that have significantly aided this journey. While these contacts have comprised varied friendship levels or length of engaged relationship and sustained conversation, I can recall quite a number of individuals, each living and representing different contexts around the world, who in diverse ways have aided my path forward, and more importantly, have enriched my life. I hope in some way, I have enriched theirs as well. Just to reiterate the tangible role that social media has played within my life, I should moreover stress that these networks have literally enabled several trips across the world. There have also been Facebook friends who have graciously granted me hospitality in some of these travels. These have made me very thankful, to both them and God. Of course, I must mention that social media has also catalysed deeper family involvement within and perhaps fostered from these described endeavours. Therefore, in my opinion, social media has functioned in ways that not only illustrates the global Body of Christ as a global network, but moreover as a globally net-working community.

I believe my early Facebook usage initiated a unique way of communicating theological reflection at the grassroots level; namely, through *verse*. Prior to 2010, my postings were largely in paragraph form, which I published through the Facebook "notes" application. I originally did so because at that time, Facebook imposed a very limited character limit for regular postings. Yet I noticed that regular postings were more likely than "notes" to receive "likes." I suppose largely motivated by the "like" experience, I changed my Facebook writing style. More specifically, I strove to conceptualise thoughts in "tweet" form, using fewer characters as possible.

In March 2010, another factor funded this change. That month I read Evelyn Underhill's classic, *Practical Mysticism*. She suggested practices for perceiving God sacramentally present throughout daily life. Underhill moreover steered me towards a more meditative approach to Scripture reading, especially as I was becoming more familiar with the ancient practice of Scripture reading called *Lectio Divina*, or "sacred reading." Hence, I began posting meditative postings I that conceptualised through these approaches, as best I understood them.

The practice has roughly proceeded like this. I reflect on some theme that catches my attention from a book reading, a prayer, sermon, or song heard, or other kind of liturgical text. Then I express it through a proverbial or poetic genre, with the aim of making a Facebook posting (earlier on, working within its limited character allowance). I thus got in the practice of articulating these "meditations" as brief couplets— often through utilising something of a poetic genre. I want to suggest that we may define these postings as a form of a very ancient form of theologising; namely, *oral theologising*. Following is an example I especially like:

There's wonder in grey clouds
That works heaven below
Where the still voice
Speaks promise
To wombs
Hushed

But waiting.

Eventually, I applied this brief verse-shaped writing style to other kinds of postings involving a more theological or scholarly content or source. An example might be to paraphrase a theme from a scholarly work, or application from such, into a verse-structured couplet. Or I might express a theological or doctrinal concept that I have been thinking about, into a couplet. Following is an example, inspired from reading a theological work dealing with issues of *migrancy*, coupled with reflection on 1 Peter 1:1; 2:11:

Windblown migrants
Like refugees exiled
To fields across
The earth.

Like their Lord
Living at the margins
Crossing boundaries
Overturning fields of power

Planting seeds for a just world.

In 2014 I was reading the writings of Jewish philosopher Emmanuel Lévinas. In his reading of the Torah, God is wholly other than us, but we see a "trace" of Him in our neighbour's "face." He also suggested that the Torah's fourfold descriptive, "the poor, the stranger, the widow, and the orphan," signifies both human otherness and God's otherness, who summons us to hospitality with people radically different from us. That year I was also reading Anglican theologian David F. Ford's writings, who also drawing on Lévinas' work, describes salvation as a transforming journey, as we live before God revealed in the "face" of Jesus (1 Cor. 3:18).

Following are some postings that emerged from those reflections. Note that the third post comprises the title from C. S. Lewis' work, *Till We Have Faces.*

> The stranger, widow, and orphan
> The poor, blind, and lame
> The mute and deaf
> The bottom tier
> Small people
> God.

> At the margins we stand
> On holy ground
> Before God's
> Face.

> At the burning bush
> God commands us
> To the other's feet
> Before us

> Till we have faces.

> Here I am
> Brother and Sister
> Before Your face I stand
> Trembling but hoping
> That we together
> May build a world
> Where love reigns.

Following is a prayer and verse, I once formed, weaving together some ancient prayers to the Holy Spirit:

> Come Holy Spirit
> Lord, Giver of Life:
> Fill what is empty
> Birth what is lacking
> Heal what is wounded.

Holy Spirit comes
With thundering cloudbursts
Amongst nations dividing gifts
Pulling down the mighty
Raising up the needy
Turning the world
Upside down

Rightside up
Healing creation
Making all things new!

For some years up to this present time, I often daily wonder how well I am managing my time spent on social media in the form of Facebook. For several reasons I wonder. First, I have long recognised what psychology studies show us; that social media use produces an awful lot of pleasurable feelings. So much that it becomes a powerfully addictive practice. Hence, I also recognise that I often struggle with disciplining my Facebook involvement. Examples include late night access rather than going to sleep, or when I should be focusing on other immediate tasks or agendas before me. Another honest example is checking the "likes" or comments of postings I make.

Fortunately, I believe do a far better job at avoiding online access when I am bodily present in conversations with people. As my 27 August 2014 Facebook posting reads:

Before the face of one another
We stand before God
On holy ground.

This post again reflects my reflections on Lévinas's writings. So to reiterate his message: in the "face" of those immediately before us, God summons us to welcoming actions of hospitality. In a small way, this theme has helped provide some control over my social media use. So oftentimes, when I am with people in casual conversations, I even go so far as to put my hand-phone on flight mode, so that as long I feel appropriate, I will not even receive any phone calls.

When it comes to social media, I first suggest, work through its bane, and help shape its boon. Yes, in its present form, social media evokes toxic behaviours such as online addiction and the emotionally taxing experience of having been "trolled" (e.g., the experience of encountering emotionally harsh and discordant online behaviour). Over the past year, we have especially witnessed social media's toxic power with the emerging proliferation of the fake news" problem coupled with the displacing of authority from mainstream news media. Nonetheless, I strongly believe that social media even more comprises, great promise towards fostering human community, locally and globally, in manners congruent with the Christian vision of human community.

I remember some years ago, when Reformed Evangelical philosopher James K. A. Smith announced he was closing down his Facebook account because he felt it was a toxic self-forming practice. Smith has written much about everyday cultural practices that for better or worse form us. He suggests we consider all such practices as *liturgical* practices, in the sense that they affectively form our habits, desires, and ultimate aims. Yet while I appreciated and still appreciate his grounds for doing so, recognising that daily use of social media is a life "forming" practice, I also believe his posture is short-sighted. For I suspect that as time goes on, the human-IT interface will inevitability deepen, and social media is something on the way to that. Moreover, I suppose that contemporary social media will morph as new technologies and technological practices emerge. Hence, contrary to Smith, I do not believe we can or should refrain from social media. For in some way it is pointing forward to the future of human communication, even if the present technology eventually morphs into newer technologies and social media practices. So our better response is to continually reflect on how we may best foster social media practices and the technology itself towards the moral curve of new creation. I believe we should also do so, recognising within it an important "seed of the gospel": namely, the human thirst for community.

I would secondly encourage scholars who are considering using social media, to recognise that by doing so, they are in a very tangible way, fostering powerful bridges between grassroots Christian life and theological or higher Christian scholarship. They are therefore also fostering the emergence, practice, and fruit of grassroots theology and theologising. Consequently and finally, I would suggest that considering scholars be social media friendly: go ahead and "friend" all kinds of people! For by doing so, you really are touching the world; and who knows? You just might make someone one's day— even across the planet!

Monte Lee Rice is an American who has lived abroad as a missionary in Southeast Asia and Africa since 1989, primarily in Singapore where is based he with his wife Jee Fong. He has served in numerous roles within churches and Bible colleges. He has published scholarly essays and has presented several papers at the annual meeting for the Society for Pentecostal Studies. He earned his M.Div. (summa cum laude) degree in theology from Asia Pacific Theological Seminary, Philippines (2002). He is scheduled to begin in April 2017, the MPhil/PhD programme with The Centre of Pentecostal and Charismatic Studies through Bangor University (Wales, UK). See Rice's blog, Monte Lee Rice (monteleerice.wordpress.com), which is linked to his LinkedIn (sg.linkedin.com/in/monterice) and Twitter (@monteleerice) accounts. He also has a second blog (pentechorus.wordpress.com) that functions mainly as an archive for some of his earlier uploaded documents. Rice is also on Academia.edu (academia.edu/MonteRice), and is an avid Facebook user (Monte Lee Rice) user.

SARAH LANE RITCHIE

Science and Religion

'm continually fascinated by the way various social media platforms operate as "mini-cultures." Each platform has its own unique tone, flavor, and rules of engagement. Engaging with a platform is not unlike immersing yourself in a new language. Because of this, I find that I need to limit the platforms I engage with; I don't have the mental space to do justice to all of them. So, I focus on those that are the most 1) enjoyable, 2) popular amongst others I want to connect with, and 3) amenable to substantive communication.

Currently, I am active on Facebook, Twitter, Academia.edu, and various blogs that I write for. I use each of these platforms for different purposes; what "works" on Facebook may not work on Twitter! Facebook is certainly my primary social media platform, and this is largely because its advent onto the world stage coincided with my freshman year in college. In other words, there was never a time when my academic and social media lives were not intersecting. This is an important point, actually: at least for me, my personal, professional, and academic lives have always intermingled.

Facebook has been a big part of that; I am "friends" with people from all walks of life, and who are connected to me for various reasons. Professors, childhood friends, colleagues, friends, academics who I'm drawn to for one reason or another, and various people who are interested in what I do (but whom I've never met in "real life")—all of these show up on my Facebook feed. I realize that many academics prefer to keep their professional and private lives distinct, but that's never been a satisfying option for me. Facebook has allowed me to engage in a holistic way with others in my field, and connect my academic life to the wider world in a personable way.

I came of age just as Facebook was becoming "the" social media platform. I began using social media because that was simply how communication happened amongst my friends. As my academic career progressed, the line between "friend" and "colleague" became very fuzzy indeed—and I've always been fine with that. Thus, as my research interests became more clearly defined, I began to articulate them very naturally on Facebook. I began to share my research interests via Facebook posts and discussions, and became "friends" with others in my field. So while my social media usage began as a way to connect with peers, it evolved as I evolved. I continue to use Facebook for both personal and scholarly interests, and have become quite comfortable with the intermingling of my various "selves."

I have also expanded my social media usage; for example, I now do quite a bit of blogging, and this is focused almost exclusively on my research interests. And of course, blogging exists in a dynamic relationship with Facebook and Twitter—everything I write gets posted on Facebook and tweeted on Twitter. Blogging, for me, is a much more focused and intentional form of social media. While I use Facebook primarily as a way to connect and interact with people, blogging is a way for me to say something very specific. While blogging often leads to interaction and connection, it begins as something of a one-way conversation: I articulate all my thoughts on a particular topic and send it out into the ether, hoping something sticks.

To be honest, I was quite happy just sticking with Facebook for my social media needs, until I was approached about blogging on science and religion. Once I started blogging, other individuals and groups began contacting me, inviting me to collaborate on similar projects. I love this aspect of blogging! It has allowed me to communicate my research and ideas to very different groups of people, in a way that wouldn't have happened on Facebook or Twitter.

I'm continually surprised (and thrilled!) that social media has led to so many "real life" connections with people I would never have met otherwise. For example, I recently participated in a writing project, in which I was asked to write about the intersection of my research and my own personal story of losing (and regaining) faith. This was hard to write! As an academic, I am used to writing very analytically and in a scholarly manner. Connecting my research to my own story was a challenging and surprisingly vulnerable experience—and certainly not one I would have had in a strictly academic context. After the blog was published, however, I was surprised at how many people (many of them strangers) contacted me. These were people experiencing similar faith crises as I had, and who wanted to talk to someone about this process. Some of the resulting conversations have been very meaningful indeed — I no longer put much credence in the charge that social media prevents us from having real relationships! In my experience, just the opposite is true.

Social media has proven to be immensely helpful over and over again, often in small ways. For example, I was recently designing a new course on science and religion. We were really struggling with the title — it needed to be catchy and exciting, but also scholarly and straightforward. So, I posted all our options on Facebook and had a vote — we got loads of great feedback, and ultimately selected a good title with no problems.

On a larger scale, I've had many experiences of one interaction on social media spawning an entirely different project. For example, I once participated in a series of blog posts on divine action, which was a fairly academic endeavour. That project, however, led to an entirely different project exploring the implications of science and religion in youth ministry. These were extremely different projects, but tightly connected to each other — the blog series made me visible to the youth ministry organization. Again, it's all about the connections that you would never even think to make without social media.

Like most millennials, my iPhone is basically an extension of my body, and many of my social interactions happen on Facebook throughout the day. My husband and I often joke about how we have only talked on the phone to each other three or four times in our entire relationship. Almost all of our communication throughout the day occurs over Facebook's messaging feature! I think the difficulty with social media and time management is that social media is not always a poor use of time.

It's actually necessary to be on social media for academic interests, and much of normal communication with family, friends, and colleagues occurs on social media. Moreover, social media is a primary news source for me (particularly Twitter). The challenge, then, is for me to be honest with myself about social media usage. I'm a master at procrastination — mostly by getting detailed political or theological conversations on Facebook when, yes, I should be writing.

If I were giving advice to those thinking about using social media more, I would first suggest deciding which forms of social media are going to be your focus. You can't do it all! I primarily use Facebook, engage more passively with Twitter, and occasionally blog. But this is a very individual choice — many of my colleagues prefer to use Twitter, and cultivate a sort of Twitter persona that is distinct from their personal lives. In any case, I'd suggest just choosing one or two platforms and getting to know them well.

Second, I don't think it's realistic to try to completely separate your professional "self" from your personal "self." Life and work, particularly in academia, are hopelessly intermingled — work is part of your personal life, and your personal life happens (at least partially) while you're working. So, I don't find it necessary to separate my social media accounts — my friends, colleagues, and family all co-exist (mostly) happily on my Facebook page. In fact, I'd make the argument that it's important for academics to be sharing their research lives with friends and loved ones.

Third, if at all possible, figure out a way to prevent passive engagement with social media from taking over your life. It's one thing to be actively engaging with someone on Facebook about a paper you just wrote, but it's a different thing altogether to spend two hours absently scrolling through Twitter. This doesn't mean absently scrolling through Twitter is bad — but I've found it best to limit it to my bus ride home (for example).

Sarah Lane Ritchie is a doctoral student in Science & Religion at the University of Edinburgh, and postdoctoral Research Fellow in Science & Theology at the University of St Andrews. She also holds a M.Div. from Princeton Theological Seminary, and is actively engaged in theological leadership for the Church of Scotland. Sarah is a guest contributor for BioLogos (http://biologos.org/author/sarah-lane-ritchie) and an active user on Facebook and Twitter (@slaneritchie). She can also be found on Academia.edu (https://st-andrews.academia.edu/SarahLaneRitchie).

RICHARD ROHR

Practical Theology

I am honored that my daily meditations are sent as a daily blog to 260,000 people. Thankfully, staff do occasional tweets for me, and the same goes for Facebook. I do not keep up with these social media platform myself.

About five years ago, my staff started gathering meditations from my books and conferences. We use them in our social media posts. Now, they are perhaps more influential on a daily basis than my book or my CDs!

I was surprised to learn that social media sharpened up the formulation of my own ideas. It prompted me to be clearer and more succinct. With regard to my audience, the daily inbox notes were short and to the point. And this seems to have had great effect. At least that's what I hear from people who write to me or meet me at various events.

Because of the sheer amount of positive feedback and interest I received from the short daily mediations posted on social media, I gained the courage and confidence to put them in a larger book form. Social media played an instrument role in all of this.

Social media has radically increased my daily need to respond to email and do phone or magazine interviews. Perhaps social media makes it too easy for people to have access to me. They want me to write or do an interview for their blogs, magazines, Skype calls, etc. Thankfully, all of this coincided with my retirement four years ago at the age of seventy four! I could never have done this much work on social media from home, because I was on the road for so many years.

If I were to give advice to those considering social media, I'd begin with what I find is so positive: Social media gets a person's message out into the world, especially to Millennials. But the person using social media needs to be ready for lots of requests for his or her time and energy! And this brings in no income whatsoever! Of course, no payment is not a problem for me, because I'm a Franciscan. But for most people it would be a real problem. Most of the time there is not even an offer for compensation, maybe because people presume that I'm honored to be on their show. And, of course, the host is getting my message out. While this is true . . . , well, this is something to consider!

––––––––––––––

Fr. Richard Rohr is a globally recognized ecumenical teacher bearing witness to the universal awakening within Christian mysticism and the Perennial Tradition. He is a Franciscan priest of the New Mexico Province and founder of the Center for Action and Contemplation (CAC) in Albuquerque, New Mexico. Rohr's teaching is grounded in the Franciscan alternative orthodoxy—practices of contemplation and self-emptying, expressing itself in radical compassion, particularly for the socially marginalized. He is the author of numerous books, including Everything Belongs, Adam's Return, The Naked Now, Breathing Under Water, Falling Upward, Immortal Diamond, Eager to Love: The Alternative Way of Francis of Assisi *and* The Divine Dance: The Trinity and Your Transformation *(with Mike Morrell). Rohr is academic Dean of the Living School for Action and Contemplation.* @RichardRohrOFM

JONATHAN RUSSELL

Philosophical Theology

I was a latecomer to social media. I spent years in a band that used social media for marketing purposes, but never felt the desire to have my own, self-operated profiles. I believe it was my friends Stephen Keating and Tripp Fuller (the later of surely is featured somewhere in this volume) that convinced me at an academic conference about five or so years ago that as a practicing social media Luddite I was basically missing out on the daily pooling of ideas and good times that were happening on Twitter. I think the stimulation and enjoyment of being around so many interesting friends in that academic context — the immediacy and volume of the contact right there, "live" — easily translated into the pitch that Twitter, in a way, could function as the same kind of curated, intellectually stimulating environment. So I joined.

Ultimately, after a couple of years on Twitter, I realized it was not the medium for me. The steady growing flow of followers and great networking connections aside, after some feedback from others close to me, I got the sense that it was not the healthiest format for me. I found some of my character flaws (my tendencies toward being arrogantly argumentative and reactive among them) to be somewhat exacerbated in the Twitterverse — and people liked it and shared it . . . So, I left Twitter and joined the slightly less constitutively sound bitten (as well as less fresh and cool) medium of Facebook.

Facebook became (and remains) my only active social media outlet. Unlike many of my friends and generational peers, it was all new to me as of four or so years ago. What I enjoyed about it was the ability to have more long-form engagement. It felt like it had at least the potential to be more than a sound bite venue of exchange.

I began using social media to connect and dialogue with other friends, scholars, and activists, with which I would not otherwise have the regular opportunity to engage with. As a then graduate student (which I just can't seem to shake all the way off yet) it was a fun way to befriend and follow scholars and activists I was learning from. In the same sense, I was able to generate a wide pool of similarly and, in some cases, quite disparately minded "friends" across the philosophy, religion, and social activism communities.

In this sense, I see Facebook as a kind of *translation table* between otherwise disparate groups. By this I don't mean that I use it, for example, to get philosophers talking to religion scholars (though I do like with this happens), but rather as a translation table where the intersection of theory and "praxis" (that is to say, the action of seeking to transform a world) can be engaged in ways that apply the scholarly to current events and otherwise non-scholarly contexts.

Now, I immediately want to qualify and break down this kind of binary I've set up. It always reeks of a paternalistic air of trying to translate the high-minded stuff of theory for those "other" folks. I mean nothing of this sort, but rather that I see Facebook as a place to stage engagements between ideas and the current social and political contexts, which helps me bring the academic and scholarly worlds I'm interested in into conversation with the present in ways that I hope draws others in, or at least captures an analysis that's excites them, is helpful, or makes them want to say, "Actually no. It's like this!" In this sense, while I do use Facebook to connect with other scholars, get feedback on projects I'm working on and the like, I primarily use it as a context in which to drum up engagement and analysis of the socio-cultural and political present. As a simultaneous social services practitioner (working as a chaplain and social justice advocate on Skid Row in Downtown LA) and scholar of religion and philosophy, I like to use Facebook as a venue to let those two forms of life meld and clash with the present.

I think very differently than I used to. As Facebook often brings together many periods of our lives through the people it reconnects us with, all those present ways of thinking, identities, interests, and aspirations are constantly "fed" to me alongside my and others' past lives and thought worlds. It's an appreciably humbling kind of experience. Even the reminders of where I was at last year or the year before helps me constantly see that my present has not always been so, and my thoughts and feelings will very likely morph over and over as I move forward.

It's not terribly difficult to curate a generally charitable environment (even when you're regularly talking about religion and politics!) without simply only having "friends" that agree with you. I do maintain a relatively private social media community—my posts and most of my info is only visible to approved friends. I will occasionally, when something is particularly relevant, such as an op-ed piece I've written or a pithy post that people ask me to make public, make a post public and shareable, which creates an interesting contrast in terms of the voices you might see chiming in.

For example, I once wrote a post critiquing the "blue lives matter" hashtag as illegitimate in the way that it associated state authority and a job with the conditions of black life and, let's just say, it drew a lot of "interestingly" heated engagement from non-friends. Sadly, most of it was vitriol without much thoughtful reasoning. I guess it evinced the different criteria by which people carve out their sphere of "friends." I think I got put on a left wing watch website for that post. I don't think that's great for my scholarly career prospects if the current political climate continues as it is, but at least my "friends" will know who I really am.

My partner (my wife Noel) once gave me the great advice of thinking in terms aiming to post *at most* one post at day if any. I think this really helps me to spend less time scrolling, trolling, and posting my own stream of consciousness thought and knee jerk reactions (which I, of course, still collapse into from time to time), but it helps me think in terms of not being that person that is just flooding feeds with every thought that comes to mind.

If I were to give advice to those considering greater use of social media, I'd say . . .

1) Think of social media as a translation table.
2) Do not just peddle your work over and over (its tiring and annoying), but takes in the sphere of influence you find yourself in to prod your community toward deep engagement with the present for the sake of change.
3) Do not ask people to share your stuff. Just write good stuff that demands to be shared.

Jonathan Russell is scholar of philosophy and religion that holds a Master's degree in theological studies and is a PhD student in the Philosophy of Religion and Theology program at Claremont Graduate University. He is an adjunct professor of philosophy and religion and Chaffey College and contributing fellow and the USC Center for Religion and Civic Culture. Facebook: *www.facebook.com/jonnie.russell.5*

KATHERINE G. SCHMIDT

Theology and Media

S ocial media is an important aspect of my life as a teacher-scholar. I currently use Facebook, Twitter, Instagram, and Snapchat. Facebook and
Instagram are my primary forms of social media, with Twitter close behind.
I use Snapchat frequently, but not as frequently as the others. I think there may
be some interesting possibilities for utilizing Snapchat as a teacher, and I hope to
explore these in the near future.

As an educator, Twitter is primary. I have a separate Twitter account for my
courses, and I've used Instagram for my courses in the past. I find Twitter's infrastructure to be particularly suited to teaching. It helps that I can integrate my
Twitter feed into our learning management system so that students who are not
on Twitter can still see my tweets. It provides a way for me to engage with students in another way, and to suggest means for integrating ideas from my courses
into their lives as citizens and cultural actors.

As I think about the current technological moment, I have found it helpful to
think about people as digital immigrants, first generation digital immigrants, or
digital natives. I fall into the second category, meaning that social media use was
not as much of a conscious choice as it may be for older scholars and teachers.
However, I am not technically a digital native — being old enough to remember a
time before internet-mediated communication — which means that it is more of a

choice for me than it may be for my students. As a teacher, I find social media to be an important aspect of my teaching life for at least two reasons: 1) I have to maintain a presence in social media to be connected to the worlds of politics and pop culture, both of which are incredibly important for my courses; 2) I maintain a social media presence in conjunction with my course to make important connections for my students and expand the boundaries of my classroom.

My scholarship focuses on the theological implications of technology and digital culture, so my social media use is intimately connected to my writing and professional life. I have a growing interest in the ways in which social media operates in moments of death and birth in people's lives. I am currently mulling over the replacement of baby books and other artifacts of child-rearing by digital artifacts like publicly or semi-publicly shared photos. I am also intrigued by the online candor of individuals and communities during loss. As a scholar of religion, these moments intrigue me greatly, and I am always resistant to over-simplified and all-too-common explanations of digital culture, which usually take the form of critiquing narcissism or materialism.

On a personal level, I have been surprised at the role of social media in my long-distance friendships. I have maintained and fostered relationships with people over many years primarily through the platform of Facebook. However, because this social phenomenon has grown up concurrently and thus gradually with my cohort, it is only a "surprise" upon reflection such as this.

Because my scholarship centers on digital culture, it's hard to point to any project or scholarly idea that has NOT come from my use of social media. By way of example, a recent publication of mine focuses on the role of social media and identity construction for millennials, specifically during weekend activities that have effectively replaced religious services.

I connect with scholars in many different disciplines via Facebook and Twitter, which always inspires me to think more deeply about particular issues. A recent conversation with a poetry professor friend of mine, for instance, inspired one of my latest projects on Chick Tracts and media. Ongoing conversations with friends on Facebook (including shared images and videos) also inspired another project on what I'm calling PBS theology, which provides a theological reading of Mister Rogers, Sesame Street, and Bob Ross. Social media is now my primary space for scholarly collaboration and personal inspiration. It is where I think and begin writing about ideas that will later become formal projects. I would be hard-pressed to think of any of my projects that do not owe something to social media.

It is impossible explain my daily life in terms of "not using social media" and "using social media." This is due in large part to the fact that I engage social media on my phone. It travels with me everywhere, and is ready to facilitate my social media use at any given moment. The only two times I can think about as being strictly "non-social media" time are when I'm teaching and when I'm at mass. However, I do post stories about both of those events directly after. For example, if my priest gives an exceptional homily, I will post about it on Twitter (linked to my Facebook) as I walk home from mass. My time and obligations are suffused with social media. It is now the primary space of social life; I cannot really see it as separate in the way this question seems to imply.

The first thing I would recommend to those considering greater use of social media is to pick one platform only. Sign up for it and just "lurk," a term meaning to read and observe online without engaging others and making your presence known. The second thing I would recommend is to make a choice as to whether or not you want or need separate accounts for your personal and professional lives. I know scholars on both sides of this choice, so it's really up to the person. And third, and more importantly, do not force it. This is especially important if you're trying to integrate social media into your teaching. Students can smell inauthenticity from miles away. If you just don't "get" social media, be honest about it and go slowly. A colleague and dear friend of mine calls this the danger of the "tragically hip." None of us wants to be there.

_____

Katherine G. Schmidt, Ph.D. is an Assistant Professor of Theology and Religious Studies at Molloy College in Long Island, New York. She received her B.A. in theology from Mount St. Mary's University (Emmitsburg) in 2007, her M.A. in theological studies from the University of Dayton in 2010, and her Ph.D. in theology from the University of Dayton in 2016. Her research interests include American Catholicism, and religion and culture. Specifically, her work focuses on the intersection of religion and technology/media. Schmidt is an active Facebook user (Katherine Schmidt) and Twitter user, and can be found @schmidt_kg and @profkschmitty.

LEA F. SCHWEITZ

Science and Religion

As a way to begin, I have focused my launch through a blog/website and Facebook. I have been experimenting with Flickr, Instagram, Pinterest, and Twitter, but the learning curve and the cost/benefit (in terms of time investment) have kept my status at "lurker" rather than active user.

The next phase for me is to commit to a regular, active Facebook strategy and then, to build a platform for visual content, especially photography. Both are to complement my blog/website, which continues to be the virtual center of gravity for my theology of urban nature project.

Professionally, I began using social media out of my administrative work; it became clear that the Zygon Center for Religion and Science needed an online presence as part of our outreach strategy. From that, I have seen the possibilities for building communities through these platforms and for curating, credible content. From there, I began experimenting with it for my own scholarship.

I have two sons with wildly different temperaments. For instance, when we go swimming, one takes a running jump and leaps in, while the other cautiously, slowly creeps down the stairs, one at a time, into the water. Temperamentally, I tend to be a creeper rather than a leaper so when I was getting into social media scholarship, I looked for resources to help me think through how to approach this new adventure before jumping in. I was — and continue to be — surprised at the volume of "how to" information, and the relative absence of theological reflection about why.

I have also been surprised at the persistent suspicion about the form as a medium for high-quality scholarship. It is a suspicion seems to issue from particular understandings about power and authority in the production of knowledge and from assumptions about the divide between scholarship and activism. Intellectual activism? Public intellectual? Each of these continues to raise eyebrows.

And, then, add the gendered component, as well. Mama-scholar? This raises eyebrows, too. I can't even count the number of times I have been talking about my social media scholarship and watched the seed of suspicion grow. At some point, I say, "It's not really a mommy-blog. Yes, stories about my children may appear, but that's not what it's about."

Part of the reason that I am so excited about social media scholarship is the ways in which it can be public, personal, and activist; I have been surprised to discover the need to continually articulate that this can be a form of scholarship.

One of the conceptual breakthroughs has been through the use of aesthetic forms to communicate ideas and arguments. As a visual learner/thinker, I am enchanted with words, but images are the way my brain works best. Social media scholarship allows space for images to sit next to sentences. As a result, the unfolding of my arguments has been a better mapping of my actual research methods. This has been particularly important for my current scholarship.

This project aims to intervene in the phenomena described as the "extinction of experience." In a nutshell, the claim is that in American contexts, people are increasingly distanced from experiences of nature. Whether it is children in classrooms focused on test-based achievement, the decline of farming families, rapid urbanization, or fears of West Nile or Lyme diseases — all of these are factors contributing to the extinction of experiences of nature.

Through a combination of story, natural history, and philosophy of nature, my scholarship is trying to bring readers an immersion experience to overcome the extinction of experiences of nature and provide frameworks for these experiences to be meaningful. Pursuing this scholarship through social media allows me to share a wider range of stories and voices and to bring images and aesthetic experiences to bear on the ideas.

Conceptually, this has opened up new categories for my scholarship. Most recently, vibrancy is becoming increasingly important as an ambiguous, but ethically and aesthetically powerful conceptual framework.

Managing my time in relation to other obligations continues to be the Achilles heel in my workload; it is the key, missing ingredient. To date, I have not managed a consistent application of my social media strategy because of the time commitment. That said, there are some things I plan to try for the next season.

In particular, I would like to get out in front of content development. Rather than always feeling behind and under a deadline to get the next post out, I am going to try to schedule regular blocks of time to develop blocks of content, rather than the more ad-hoc, piecemeal approach I've been laboring under. With a more strategic editorial calendar, the hope is that I can also take advantage of the synchronicities that occur between say, my work-travel, my teaching, and my everyday living.

The scholars who seem to be most effectively using social media have made it a fluent, working, everyday language. Because this is still a growing edge, I need to be intentional about working ahead and also actively looking for opportunities to share content so that I recognize it as it comes up.

For instance, I attended the fantastic 2017 Wild Things Conference on urban nature in the greater Chicagoland area. This would have been a great place from which to share content. However, that didn't occur to me until I was on my way home from the conference. The goal is to see this as an opportunity beforehand rather than afterwards.

If I were to recommend three things to scholars considering greater use of social media, I'd say . . .

1. Focus. From everything I've read and from my own experience, the place to start is with one platform, maybe two. It isn't necessary to try to be everywhere all at once.
2. Not all scholarship needs or benefits from a social media angle. The first step is one of discernment. You should ask, "Is this the right route for my scholarship?" The answer will likely need to take into account an honest assessment of institutional buy-in (and about how to narrate your decision even if there is institutional buy-in), professional goals, research trajectories, and whether the sacrifice of time and creative energy is worth it.
3. Post consistently; complete your profiles; and, prioritize interaction and engagement alongside great content.

Lea F. Schweitz, Ph.D. is a scholar, teacher, and nature-mama. She teaches the Lutheran School of Theology at Chicago and directs the Zygon Center for Religion and Science, which engages questions, encourages creativity and explores connec-

tions in religion and science. She is an emerging thought leader in religion and science and an award-winning teacher. Currently, she is writing a book that claims and reimagines urban nature as a place for theological reflection and spiritual formation. Follow Schweitz on Facebook (Lea Schweitz) or on Twitter (@LeaSchweitz). Join her flock of nature lovers on Facebook @WildSparrows or by signing up for the newsletter at the project website: www.wildsparrows.com. Follow the Zygon Center for Religion and Science on Facebook @ZygonCenter or find us online at: www.zygoncenter.org.

J. AARON SIMMONS

Philosophy

Social media is increasingly a broad idea that speaks to one's online "public" presence. The virtual community/audience that results is interesting in its constitution (i.e., it crosses many traditional communal, discursive, and disciplinary lines), its goals (i.e., it is not united by a particular set of commitments or professional aims), and its temporal duration (i.e., not everyone who finds my work on social media will continue to engage with it for more than one or two brief sessions). Accordingly, being intentional about one's social media activities is not as straightforward as it might seem. It is not simply a matter of deciding how to present oneself, but instead trying to find a way to be oneself in relation to this complex "public" such that you can speak coherently while also speaking to where your readers find themselves. This is hard work, but it is essential to being a scholar not just "in," but "for" the 21st Century.

That said, I primarily use Facebook for my social media engagement. Although I like the idea of Twitter, I see it primarily as a place to advertise what I have done elsewhere (new essays in print, etc.). And, I admit that Instagram, Snapchat, and other similar sites seem a bit resistant to conversation from the outset. Alternatively, Facebook allows for conversations to happen (sometimes in near real time) in a format that does allow for one's ideas to receive at least a bit more development. As a philosopher, it is important that what I say is not only able to be backed up by reasons, but also that I provide at least some indication of what those reasons actually are. Accordingly, Facebook, as well as blogs and online formats such as open access journals, etc., are more my speed because they allow for more than merely discursive hand waving.

Nonetheless, it is important not to be too tempted to confuse Facebook (or any social media format for that matter), with a formal philosophy journal. I like to think of social media as ultimately serving three primary functions: (1) Expanding one's audience through information distribution — let's term this *the marketing function*. (2) Developing one's relationships with other professionals in the philosophical (or more broadly, academic) community — let's term this *the networking function*. (3) Testing out and getting feedback on one's early ideas about a particular topic, especially when that topic intersects with matters of broader social concern — let's term this *the critical function*. These three functions are not at odds with each other, but rather are overlapping and mutually reinforcing.

I should say, here, that even though it is not social media, properly speaking, I think that a robust commitment to open access publication is an important component of my online public presence. When I publish in an open access journal, say, I am able immediately to make that research available to all of my social media followers. This is important for lots of reasons, but in particular I appreciate that many of my academic friends on Facebook, for example, are not at institutions that provide access to much of the academic research held behind paywalls. Additionally, independent scholars or contingent faculty who don't have any institutional access to material are often cut out of the philosophical conversation. This is a moral failure in which we are *all* implicated (both regarding the situation facing such scholars without full employment, but also that those scholars are further marginalized due to the cost required to be able to stay current in the literature). When we expand our social media engagement and our public scholarly persona outward, we should quickly realize that our scholarship ought to be viewed as a kind of moral statement. Sure, it is important to publish in the top journals in one's field, but it is also important for top scholars to publish in journals that allow more scholars to become involved in that field — open access and online formats enable our work to become a matter of social activism.

I was a fairly late adopter in the social media game. I actually first got involved when I heard of my sister's (K. Merinda Simmons) great success in using a Facebook group for one of her religious studies courses at The University of Alabama. She told me about how easily her students took to the medium as a productive site for continuing the class conversations in ways that were free to reflect the students' own interests and tastes. So, for example, some students might link to a movie clip, a song, or an article that connected to things discussed in class. What was especially exciting about her experience, I think, was that other scholars around the world started joining the group and participating in the conversations that soon far outreached the bounds of the course material and yet allowed my sister's students to be in dialogue with the major players in the field that they were studying.

After hearing about her experience, I immediately joined Facebook, Twitter, and other outlets in order to see if social media could be a pedagogical tool in productive ways for my own courses. I have to admit that my own experience on this front has been mixed. My classes never took to the Facebook groups like I hoped, but I have come to see that it is extremely important for my students (many of whom are Facebook friends of mine) to see me interact not only with other scholars on social media, but as a public intellectual who tries to live out the things that I teach every day.

I continue to use social media because it is now seamlessly interwoven into how I understand myself as a scholar. It is simply part of what it means to take responsibility for one's own scholarly identity in a digital age. Here the marketing, the networking, and the critical functions of social media all come together such that I am actively meeting new people working in the field, while making my work available to people who might otherwise not discover it, and all the time attempting to foster discourse more broadly about those topics and questions with which I am primarily engaged.

Perhaps the most surprising thing to me (other than how shockingly unreflective some academics can be when they are speaking off the cuff!) is that I have repeatedly benefited from the substantive conversations that have developed via social media. Let me give just a couple examples of this. I once saw a friend of mine in religious studies post something about a recent essay that had appeared in the *Journal of the American Academy of Religion* (JAAR). I considered his comment to be problematic on a number of fronts and was disappointed to see that there was a long thread of comments basically reinforcing the "obviousness" of a view that I considered to be in need of a rather substantive argumentative defense. Well, I noted something to this effect in a comment and this then led to a robust back and forth with a variety of scholars (some I that knew and some that I did not). In the end, a different scholar who had been reading the thread reached out to me and some of the other participants in the discussion there on Facebook and asked us if we would be willing to convert our Facebook conversation into a published symposium in the journal that he edited. That symposium ended up including some very impressive essays and would never have happened had it not been due to a few random comments on Facebook.

As just one other example, I once posted an essay on the blog that I co-host called "Philosophy Goes to Church" that received a significant amount of attention and even though I tried very hard to encourage folks to post their comments over at the blog, the vast majority decided to engage each other on my Facebook thread where I linked to the essay. The disagreement was robust, the reasons were profound, the conversation was deep, and it eventually led to several other essays that got posted on the blog. I was proud to be able to foster such discourse simply but clicking "Share" on the blog post.

In addition to the published symposium on the JAAR essay that I mentioned earlier, there have been many productive results from my social media engagement that would not have occurred otherwise. Let me just list a few.

- The "Philosophy Goes to Church" blog was entirely created as a response to a very extended series of comments on a Facebook thread in which I had initially posted about something problematic that my (then) pastor said about Kierkegaard (I eventually got asked to leave the church in part due to my Facebook post, sigh). The energy with which so many people engaged in that discussion led me to see the need for a site devoted to allowing academics and pastors to think together — and the blog was born.
- Several friends of mine have made random comments about something they were currently thinking about and I was able to follow up with them individually and find ways not only to support their ideas, but in some cases also provide publication venues for them.
- My own commitment to doing philosophy of religion that is globally aware and critically engaged with other disciplines doing important research in religion (especially critical religious theory, sociology of religion, and cognitive science) is largely a result of having so many friends on Facebook that work in these fields. Frequently I say something that gets challenged by those people from their respective disciplines (again, the critical function on display here). This has allowed my own interlocutors to be far more wide-ranging than simply those who are likely to read a particular journal in which I might publish. As a result, what I end up publishing is itself far more wide-ranging.

Social media activities do not come without potential costs, however. Managing my time is made difficult by having a research agenda that would be considered heavy for faculty at most graduate institutions (even though I am at a teaching-focused and student-intensive liberal arts college), having a 7-year-old son (who feels the need to play soccer, basketball, and tennis, and do cub scouts), fostering a joyful marriage, being active in my church and local community, and serving on my HOA board, etc. So, it is important not to view social media activities as an "add-on" to an already busy professional and personal life. Accordingly, my social media engagement is not something that I find to be a significant time management issue because I have always approached it as merely part of how I already manage my time as an academic in a digital age. We have to be our own press agents (marketing function), we have to make and develop professional relationships (networking function), and we have to stay at the top of our game and keep our skills as sharp as possible as philosophers (critical function). So, social media helps me to do the things that I have to do. It is not an additional time drain, but simply part of the general time commitments that my professional life demands.

Now, I should say that where the time can get away from me on social media is when I have had to intervene and make sure to manage the conversations occurring on my Facebook feed, for example. As just one instance where significantly more time was required than I had planned, consider the following. I recently posted something on Facebook and made a general comment about the political significance of it that quite specifically reflected my generally progressive political leanings. Well, a non-academic friend of mine shared my post and it immediately received numerous comments from her own friends. One of those comments was from a police officer who did not share my political orientation (to put it mildly). He dismissed my claim with apparent outrage that anyone could even say such a thing (and threw in a good dash of "if this is what our kids are learning in college these days, then our country's moral foundations are being eroded"). So, I decided to respond to his comment, which led to a reply from him, which led to a rejoinder from me, which then brought about another reply, and so on. For several hours, I did nothing but try to participate in this conversation because I felt that if I did not do so that I was giving in to his suggestion that liberal academics are out of touch and no longer care about real education. Ultimately, these Facebook comments eventually turned into a series of private emails between us, which took even more time.

Although this took a good deal of time, it was worth it and eventually he not only apologized for being dismissive, but changed his initial views in several key respects. Not only that, however, but I also learned how better to nuance my own view so that I could try to avoid such angry responses from people in the future. He helped me to see that what I took to be clear was ripe for misunderstanding by those starting with different political assumptions. This engagement was mutually beneficial, but definitely time consuming. Yet, as all good philosophers know, when we start doing things too quickly our work suffers. Taking our time is part of what philosophical life demands and so, to be involved on social media, we need to be prepared to take our time if we want to do it right.

As something of a conclusion, then, let me offer two suggestions to scholars considering greater use of social media:

First, be prepared to be surprised, and often taken aback, by what other scholars say when they are not being reflectively self-aware. Although I try very hard to understand myself first and foremost as a scholar when I engage on social media (even though I do still cheer for the FSU Seminoles, and occasionally post links to extremely good heavy metal and conscious rap that I think others should also discover), many of my academic friends seem to abandon their professional identity and so post things that are either so ideologically extreme or so personally intimate that it can sometimes cause a critical reassessment of my prior impression of that person.

Second, be very intentional about how much you want the different areas of your life to intersect on social media. For example, I grew up in Evangelical Christian communities and went to a Christian college so many of my friends from those periods of my life remain quite conservative and religious. Yet, many of my academic friends are neither religious nor conservative. When these different groups sometimes interact with each other on my Facebook feeds, say, rhetorical and emotional fireworks often result. Now, as for me, I think that a robust democratic society requires that we all overcome our own narrowly circumscribed communities of discourse and so I have chosen not to post things only for some friends, or to restrict how the conversations develop, or to have different profiles (academic and personal, say). As I see it, if anyone should be capable of reasoned discourse with various positions and viewpoints, academics (and especially philosophers) should. So, although I often get frustrated with the views being defended by some of my non-academic friends, say, I am more often frustrated with the dismissiveness from some of my academic friends engaging those views.

I have decided that my social media presence will be something of a test case for the possibility of rigorous debate within overlapping communities that represent a wide variety of intellectual backgrounds, academic training, and political orientations. This is sometimes very difficult to maintain and it can take an enormous amount of time to wade in to the debates that develop in order to ensure that they don't get out of hand and continue to be defined by reason-giving and hermeneutic charity. Yet, this is important work and usually worth the time.

———————

J. Aaron Simmons is an Associate Professor of Philosophy at Furman University in Greenville, South Carolina. He is the author or editor of numerous books including God and the Other *(Indiana University Press), and (with Bruce Benson)* The New Phenomenology *(Bloomsbury). He is on the executive committee of the Society for Continental Philosophy and Theology and has served in official capacities for the American Academy of Religion, the Society of Christian Philosophers, and the South Carolina Philosophical Society. See Simmons's personal website and blog at www .jaaronsimmons.wordpress.com and also the blog he co-hosts entitled "Philosophy Goes to Church" (www.philosophygoestochurch.wordpress.com). Simmons can be found on Facebook (J Aaron Simmons) and also on Twitter (@jaaronsimmons).*

ATLE OTTESEN SØVIK

Systematic Theology

acebook is where I spend most time, read and publish stuff. I record movies and publish them at YouTube and I publish papers at academia.edu, but I do not find academia.edu optimal, so I hope to have a personal webpage ready soon. That will make it easier to sort different material into categories.

Some years ago when I was still not at Facebook and academia.edu, my colleague Liv Ingeborg Lied made the following point: Before, you could wait for the journals, read the articles, and write a response. Now people publish their ideas online long before the article appears, and when the article gets published, the discussion is already over. Researchers want to be the first to know what's new and the first to respond, and then you have to get involved online.

She was right. For example, I have recently read a pre-proof article published at a personal webpage as accepted and forthcoming. Now I have almost finished a response article and the first article has not even been published yet.

An additional reason why I continue to use social media, is that I get updated on so many different areas. Since I do interdisciplinary work, this is very useful. It can be new articles, new findings or discoveries, controversial news etc., like for example a discovered gospel, a controversial healing, a discovery in physics or neuroscience, yet another boy who has visited heaven, etc. I get interviewed quite often by Christian newspapers and find that in most cases I know the topic they want to interview me on and have comments to give, since some Facebook-friends have already posted something on it and discussed it.

A third reason is that other researchers contact me after having found stuff I have written online. It goes the other way as well — when I look for people to collaborate with on a larger project, it is easier to get contact with people who have webpages with their stuff published there, so I can get an impression of their work before I decide whether to make contact.

A fourth reason for being at social media is that I am alerted of more interesting debates and talks than I would otherwise have been aware of. I also announce my own future talks, which makes the attendance greater.

I have seen that more and more people also publish work in progress inviting comments and get useful response from others. Research have found that those who publish the most are the ones that have the most readers who offer comments before publishing. I hope to publish more work in progress in the future, and have done so to a small degree at academia.edu.

I love it when people give lectures on new books and publish it online. I listen to it while I do the dishes, and get oriented in new and relevant books. For my last two books, I have published online 30 minutes lectures about the contents of the book. I published an expensive book on free will which few will read, but I recorded a lecture on it, published on YouTube and a link on Facebook. After a couple of days a few hundred people had already seen it. My most seen video on YouTube has been seen over 13 000 times. Different papers I have published at academia.edu have been downloaded more than 1000 times. We want to publish, but we also want to be read, so for unknown scholars like me, social media is an excellent way of spreading ideas.

I have been surprised to see lately in online debates that people have asked each other what they mean on this and that, and as response they quote something that I have published online. I have never seen my *books* quoted in such online debates, so again it demonstrates how much further your ideas can reach if you make them accessible online.

I have discovered that publishers are more and more interested in whether prospective authors are active on social media. It is then very helpful to have something to show your publisher in order to increase the chances of having your next book published.

Some Facebook friends started to discuss a provoking critique that was made by an atheist criticizing cosmological arguments for the existence of God. I joined the discussion first at Facebook, and then published a critique at the same webpage where the atheist had first published. We discussed back and forth, and the people running the webpage asked us to have a debate that they could record and put on their webpage. After this, a professor of philosophy joined the debate, and I started discussing with him, and again the webpage owners filmed a new debate with us. The debate had now stirred up so many new ideas that I turned it into an article, now under review.

I am too busy at work to spend time on social media, but in the afternoon and evenings, I spend time on social media depending on what else I have to do. I see that I am still a lot less active on social media than many others. After all, it is just a few years ago that I joined Facebook.

If you want to get your ideas spread, social media will be more and more important. If you want to get updated on the newest research and join the discussions, social media will be more and more important. If you want to get your books published, social media will be more and more important. It seems to me that it will not be long before all academics must use social media.

Atle Ottesen Søvik is Professor of systematic theology at MF Norwegian School of Theology in Oslo, Norway. He has published books on the problem of evil; the problem of free will; the existence of God; Christianity and evolution and more. He is married and has three children.

Find Søvik on Facebook, Academia.edu: mf.academia.edu/AtleOttesenSøvik, and YouTube: Search for "Atle Ottesen Søvik" or "MF Norwegian school of theology"

JIM STUMP

Science and Religion

work full-time for BioLogos, the science and faith organization founded by Francis Collins. BioLogos began as an online organization. Collins had written *The Language of God* in 2006, and received lots of follow-up questions from readers. He assembled a team of scientists, theologians, and philosophers to write out answers to frequently asked questions, and these were posted online in 2009 at biologos.org. This section of our website still generates the most traffic to our site, but we now publish a blog on the website as well. In fall of 2015 we separated this into a collection of blogs, and one of those is under my name. I write several posts per month, and host several more posts per month by guest authors. We advertise all of our blog posts through Facebook and Twitter on our official BioLogos accounts, and I use my personal Facebook account for both personal and professional posts. I also have personal Twitter and Instagram accounts, but I've never quite gotten into the flow of using them consistently.

I started writing a personal blog back in 2007, when just about everyone was trying their hand at blogging. At that time I had written a few journal articles, but had not yet started writing books. Among other more mundane topics (like movies and the Boston Red Sox), I used the blog to talk about my professional interests in accessible ways. Many of my students and former students were interested in this relatively new medium, and I thought it might be fun to explore this mode of communication (and I even wrote a series of blogs about the philosophy of blogging). I never garnered a huge following, but it became a discipline of sorts for me to write consistently. It was a way of thinking more carefully and systematically about things in the news, or books I was reading, or other random thoughts I had.

When I started working for BioLogos in 2013 and blogging there, I discontinued my personal blog. That has changed some of my blogging style. My reasons for writing are similar, but now it is my job as well. So there are additional considerations, like promotion of the mission of the organization and consistency with its tone and content guidelines. My blogposts are now more polished pieces and are reviewed by a couple of other people before publishing. The topics I write about are also narrower and less whimsical than when I wrote on my personal blog.

Whether on a personal platform or for an organization, one of the chief benefits I see to blogging is that it promotes a reflective lifestyle. I don't think my experience is unique that writing something to be seen by others forces me to think more carefully about it. In fact, writing helps me decide what I think about something. It just isn't the case that I work out in my mind what I want to say first, and then write it down. The process of writing, with all its fits and starts and ample use of the backspace key, is literally the working out what I think. For many years I kept a journal that accomplished some of this too, but the public aspect of a blog forces it further, since there is the additional consideration of how an audience will respond.

The audience of a blog brings another set of concerns, though, that may not be as positive: readership is very easily quantifiable and that can become the metric that drives everything. Especially now as I blog for my job (or look for guest bloggers), we think about increases our traffic and attracting more viewers. We can't help but ask for any given post, "How many viewers will a post like this probably get?" And if that is the only thing we ask, it would drastically skew our content, because controversy brings eyeballs. It's very easy to let that dictate (or at least be a significant factor in) the kinds of things you publish. But it is not always the case that higher page views will achieve the goals you have for blogging.

Another virtue of blogging for an organization is the ease with which collaborative projects can be done. There have been numerous times on the BioLogos blog that we have brought together scholars for various projects. Social media lends itself to interaction with each other and promotion of ideas outside of the usual academic channels. We've had good success in attracting top scholars on particular topics related to our mission. Posting one of these each day over the course of a week generates interest in the series, and it is much more immediate than the traditional publishing outlets for that sort of thing.

But just like consideration of the audience has pros and cons, so too does the immediacy of social media. Most of my social media time is related to my job, so I'm able to use normal work hours for it. But there is an aspect of social media that can become quite consuming. Because social media has such instant feedback in terms of "likes" and "comments", it can be very addictive to monitor responses to what you've written. With traditional off-line media, it is gratifying to see your work mentioned or cited, but that happens only over months or years. With social media, the day a new post "drops", it is hard not to check in all day long to see what kind of response it is getting.

Because the blogging world is so crowded, it is difficult for someone who does not have a national platform to break into social media and get much of a following beyond family and friends. So first, I'd suggest joining a network of bloggers that has some built in audience. It's very easy to set up a joint blog, and if there are several authors who consistently post, the personal networks of all of them will more easily generate a critical mass of readership than any one of them on their own.

Secondly, success in blogging comes through maintaining consistency in writing. The short attention span of social media rewards those who generate new content on a regular basis. For scholars especially, that kind of writing can be a challenge, as they have typically been trained to write longer pieces with substantial research behind them. As with most things, you can get better at this kind of writing by practice. I'd suggest writing at least two blogposts per week to develop the consistency. And these should not replace research and other more academic writing. The blogposts I like best are the "tip of the iceberg" posts, where it is apparent that the author has a substantial body of research "below the surface" of the blog, and we're seeing the part that is fit for layperson consumption.

Finally, to succeed in the world of social media, you must participate in the social media of other people. If you want to start a Twitter following, you begin by following other people. If you want to blog, get involved in the blogs of others. Comment on their blogs and link to their blogs on your own posts. Social media is incredibly self-referential. It is not realistic to think you can just start putting out content and people will find and follow you if you're not involved in larger conversations that take place in the medium. Of course everyone knows that the interactions on the web can degenerate quickly into name calling. But at its best, participation in online communities can be a rewarding experience for learning from others and testing out your own ideas.

_____

Jim Stump was professionally trained as a philosopher. He worked for 17 years at Bethel College (Indiana) where he taught, established the philosophy program, and for five of those years served as the chief academic officer. He began working for BioLogos part-time in 2013 and then moved to full-time there in August of 2015. As Senior Editor, he oversees the development of new content and curates existing content for both the website and print materials. As time permits, and when the Spirit moves, he writes blogposts at Faith and Science Seeking Understanding (though he prefers the Latin title, fides et scientia quaerens intellectum). He has authored or edited several books under "J.B. Stump" (which is also how you can find him on Facebook), including How I Changed My Mind About Evolution *(IVP 2016),* Science and Christianity: An Introduction to the Issues *(Blackwell 2017), and the forthcoming* Four Views on Creation, Evolution, and Intelligent Design *(Zondervan, fall 2017).*

LEONARD SWEET

Missional Theology

My primary social media platforms are Facebook and Twitter. I have other accounts, but what I call my Twitter twitch and my Facebook hook are my main platforms. I was born BC (Before Cells) when text was a noun not a verb, and when contacts were lenses not connections. My kids are born AC (After Cells). So it's been an adjustment, but I've intentionally cultivated a diverse, well-brewed community from every nation, every ideology, every politics, and every religion, which makes for some interesting conversations.

For me it's all about the participation, which is why I encourage disagreement with me and only delete posts that promote party politics. Those who interact with me and each other on social media become a smart community, and make me smarter. Everything I post is made better by those who participate in that posting, showing me things I never thought of, finding new and better ways of saying what I was trying to say. I am a better scholar, writer, and disciple of Jesus because of social media.

I was shamed into social media by some Gen-X geeks who compiled a list of theologians who should be on Twitter and weren't. I was one, and spoke to one of the list-makers to give me three good reasons why I should be involved in social media after I gave him three good reasons why I shouldn't. After he made his first case that Twitter was the new village green, the new global commons, he had me.

And as a historian I began to remember all those historical examples of people like Robert Raikes (1736-1811) versus James Fenimore Cooper (1789-1851) and their reaction to the new media of their day. Raikes was an Anglican newspaper magnate who used the cutting edge technology to campaign for prison reform and invented the Sunday school as a means of bringing literacy to the streets believing that unemployment and ignorance was a major cause of crime. Cooper on the other hand was a novelist who hated this new media called "newspapers." He called it "a species of luxury which like the gallows, comes in only as society advances to the corrupt condition, or which, if it happen to precede it a little, is very certain to conduct it there."

I plunged into what I now call TGIF culture (Twitter, Google, Instagram, Facebook), and have never looked back. I even dedicated Viral (2.0), my book on the future of the church and social media and how the church can be "in" but not "of" the world (nor "out of it") to that person who called me out. My first chapter was a "Theology of Twitter" based on that conversation with him where I argued that the only question was not "Would Jesus Tweet" but "How Would Jesus Tweet?" Social media should never become a substitute for living, or an escape from living, but a resource for living. I wish I had more time to harness the full potential of social media and put it into play for the kingdom.

I was surprised to discover several things about social media. I'll list a few:

a) Media is not a zero sum game. The "migration" to social media away from print and television has been less an exodus than an expansion. People are buying more books than ever, and TV is still USAmerica's campfire. In fact, this is the golden age of television in terms of creative programming and captured audiences.

b) The assumption that people of faith or even "intellectuals" are capable of rational discussion is a problematic one. Many are now specialists in insult fests and razor-blade religion. Social media has turned many critics into crusaders.

c) A Facebook culture needs more facetime and mealtime not less. Barriers fall in face-to-face laughing and looking in each other's eyes generally. But nothing builds bonds more than facetime at mealtime.

d) Social media has made me more sensitive to the power of images for good or ill. I have a problem with snuff videos, whether they come from ISIS or battle documentaries or from mobiles capturing images of people being killed on the streets. "Whatsoever things are true, honest, just, pure, lovely, good report . . . think on these things" (Phil.4:8). This is one reason why I steer clear of politicizing my social media posts, which can become a vortex into a death spiral of negativity and ugliness. When I am asked, often in an accusatory way, why I refuse to post myself, and why I delete posts from others on my timeline, on politics, I give this one sentence answer: God did not promise to send us politicians who would save us and bring us "nearer, nearer, nearer precious Lord" . . .

e) I have surprised myself at how I can be more interested in Facebook "likes" and Amazon stars and Twitter retweets than in the peer reviews and critical commentaries of academic colleagues.

I used my social media for a couple of "crowdsourcing" projects. One of which was to solicit nominations for my "Bad Habits of Jesus" (2016) book with the promise of publication of some of their selections in the book. This proved so successful that the book boasts an appendix with many of my Facebook community featured.

I use technology pastorally—as my online parish. If the pope can use Twitter to shepherd the Catholic Church, I can set a daily table for my parishioners with food and drink. I also post notes from my reading on my feeds that normally would just nest in my greenhouse, which means I can daily in the glasshouse of my friends "break bread with the dead" (W. H. Auden). I practice disciplined prayer rituals for my social media community, which includes not just the 40,000 who follow me on Twitter, but my 5000 "Friends" and the 15,000+ "Followers" on Facebook, each one of whom has been prayed over when they sign up to follow my timeline. I answer all messages within twelve hours, and am constantly being sent prayer requests that I integrate into my prayer life. Social media has become for me, not just a mode of knowing, but a way of learning.

If I were to recommend three things to scholars considering greater use of social media, I'll say . . .

1) Every age and every media form is equidistant from eternity. As many positives as there are to social media, there are many negatives that can detour and derail your scholarly agendas, not to mention depress the spirit. For example, Twitter culture only swallows what can easily be regurgitated, and fosters bulimic intellectual appetites for gorging to a point beyond satiety. Then it sticks fingers down the throat and throws up all over everyone.

2) Not too long ago, authors were maimed if people didn't like what they said. Ears were cropped, noses nubbed, fingers cut off by critics. Those days are

back with a vengeance. Scot McKnight calls it "crowdpounding." You can handle both the criticism and the praise provided you don't inhale either.

3) The blessing of the Internet is that it contains everything. The curse of the Internet is that it contains everything. The need for curators of information, and platforms you can trust, is greater than ever before. Social media is my best illustration of why pastors ought to invite better preachers to speak when they're on vacation, not inferior ones. When someone shares something on their timeline I have written, or when I share something from someone else on my timeline, the person who brokers the insight or information is thanked and credited as if they were the source of the quote. Broker and curate the best to people, and it makes you look good even though your only role was to pass it on.

————————

Leonard Sweet is a historian, theologian, and semiotician. From 2000 to 2017 he occupied the E. Stanley Jones Professorship at Drew University, where he continues to mentor doctoral students while serving as Distinguished Visiting Professor at George Fox University and Visiting Distinguished Professor at Tabor College. He has written or edited 60 plus books, published over 1500 sermons, and is an ordained elder in the United Methodist Church. See Sweet's personal website, leonardsweet. com, and his newly released story lectionary preachthestory.com where you can access weekly homiletic resources some of which are free and some subscriber based. Sweet contributes two sermons a week to preachthestory as well as daily posts to @LenSweet (Twitter), Leonard Sweet (Facebook) and less frequently LinkedIn, YouTube, Google+

JON PAUL SYDNOR

Public Theology

teach World Religions at Emmanuel College in Boston and serve as theologian-in-residence at Grace Community Boston where my wife, Rev. Abigail A. Henrich is pastor. To promote Grace on social media Abby and I currently use Buffer, which allows us to post to multiple platforms simultaneously. Buffer will forward any post to Facebook, Instagram, Snapchat, Pinterest, etc., allowing us to reach our audience no matter their preferred platform. Of these forms, the primary one is Facebook, since we have been on it the longest, most of our participants use it, and it has more capabilities than some other platforms.

We also have a webpage through Weebly. Although Weebly has a free teaser-ware edition, we pay an annual fee to use certain tools that are important to us, and for increased memory storage. From the perspective of process theology, our internet outreach is dipolar. The webpage is our unchanging character, but Facebook et al are the timely way that our unchanging character interacts with the world.

As an academic, I believe in the Enlightenment. I believe that sound reasoning about valid facts produces the most informed debates, the best decisions, and the most desired outcomes. Academic institutions are the preservers of the Enlightenment in American society. As an integral part of civil society, we must participate in civic discourse. Social media are one way that I attempt to express my academic insights in popular culture. Recently, I taught a course on Muslim-

Christian relations. My students and I discovered that toddlers with handguns kill more Americans than Islamist militants; that on average, Americans think our country is 17% Muslim when it's really about 1% Muslim; and that Muslim-Americans are tremendously more likely to be the victims of hate crimes than to commit any crimes. I shared all of these facts on social media, often creating my own memes in order to do so.

I am also an ordained Minister of Word and Sacrament in the Presbyterian Church (USA). Currently, my ordained ministry is to stimulate spiritual conserva-tion for our small, progressive, emergent Christian gathering—Grace Community Boston. As a pastor, I want to share Jesus' message of inclusive love with a world torn by fear, hatred, and division. America needs Jesus' healing words of faith and strident injunctions of justice. One way to reach culture generally, especially seekers and the unchurched, is through social media. While Grace does not pros-elytize generally, we do want people to be aware of the progressive Christian option—that you can be faithful, rational, inclusive, activist, gay, prayerful, curi-ous, lesbian, prophetic, scientific, and worshipful. Fundamentalists have harmed so many people, some of whom believe that rejection by fundamentalists really means rejection by God. We at Grace want to assure them that God has loved them all along. Even if some Christians have hurt them, Christ cherishes them, and maybe they can feel their sacred worth through our community.

Some posts go haywire and some posts go nowhere, but we can never predict what will happen. We create visually compelling memes with essential wisdom, and only a few people respond to them. We create a simple meme on the spur of the moment with a throwaway line, and it gets a huge response. Go figure.

That being said, we have been surprised to discover how important our pro-gressive Christian memes are to a large number of people that we didn't even know were following us. We occasionally hear from friends, friends of friends, acquaintances, and strangers—non-Christian, post-Christian, agnostic, atheist, Buddhist, Hindu, Jewish, et al—who derive some spiritual benefit from our posts. They feel included and inspired, even though they do not share our label "Progressive Christian". We are pleased by this affirmation, since we see our com-munity as centered but unboundaried, focused on Jesus but open to all. We are pleased to be more than local. The Holy Spirit cannot be contained by categories or labels, and the thirst for meaning lies in every human heart.

Theologically, we have noticed that many people doubt their faithfulness be-cause they cannot subscribe to doctrines that fundamentalists insist are essen-tial. Others doubt their faithfulness because they are progressive, inclusive, and open-minded, and believe that Christian faith and openness to the world are exclusive. In order to alleviate these concerns, Abby and I created a meme series entitled: "What you don't have to believe to be a Christian." This series assured people that they can follow Jesus and still support gay marriage, reject nationalism, embrace evolution, practice science, respect other religions, struggle for equality between men and women, and more.

The response to this series of memes was huge. People who had been straddling the fence of faith and progress, with one foot in each camp, all of a sudden realized that they were standing in one camp, the camp of progressive faith. People felt drawn to Christ but hesitant due to the association of Christ with conservatism in popular culture. Now, they know that they can be Christian *because* they practice a universal ethic, not *despite* that fact.

For an academic, social media has to play an ancillary role to the essential business of scholarly research and writing. But, whenever I come across a particularly insightful quote, timely scriptural passage, or relevant theological idea, I want to share that with the world, beyond the bounds of academia. I do so by creating a meme and posting it to our social media sites. In this way, at least, some helpful scholarly work can make its way out of the ivory tower and into the public consciousness.

I would recommend the following to those considering greater use of social media:

1. Don't let your academic voice affect your social media voice. Instead, let your social media voice affect your academic voice. Much of what academics write is stilted prose. There's no need to use a long word when a short one will do just as well. My work on social media has changed my writing; I try to use more German than Latin, my average number of syllables per word has declined, sentence and paragraph length have both shortened. This change has improved my quality of writing without (I hope) compromising the depth and originality of the ideas.

2. Be timely. If you have a thought on a topic in the daily news, then you have to get it out immediately. You can't let your thoughts gel on a subject of immediate interest. It will be old in 24 hours.

3. Synthesize words and images. Human beings are visual *and* language-based learners, so memes that synthesize vision and language will make the most powerful impression.

4. Persevere in hope. You're doing more good than you know.

Rev. Jon Paul Sydnor, PhD teaches World Religions at Emmanuel College in Boston. He also serves as theologian-in-residence at Grace Community Boston where his wife, Rev. Abigail A. Henrich, is pastor. Jon Paul is the author of Rāmānuja and Schleiermacher: Toward a Constructive Comparative Theology. *He has also authored numerous articles on Hinduism, Christianity, and interreligious relations, and he has a blog on* The Daily Kos. *When not thinking really hard, Jon Paul loves to spend time with his family, especially when that time involves camping, soccer, chess, or Indian food. Feel free to follow Jon Paul's progressive Christian projects on the internet at http://gracecommunityboston.weebly.com/, or on Facebook at https://www.facebook.com/gccboston/.*

EDWIN WOODRUFF TAIT

Historical Theology

At this point, Facebook is my primary form of social media. I also have a blog which I use for longer, more substantive communication, sharing the posts on FB with privacy settings on "public." I comment from time to time on Patheos and other blog comment forums. I have been very active in the past on the "Catholic Answers" discussion forum, but only post there occasionally at this point. I Tweet rarely, since I find the space limitations of Twitter too confining and the medium as a whole not conducive to substantive discussion.

I began posting on Internet forums shortly after I went to Duke as a Ph.D. student in 1995. I was studying the Reformation, partly in order to sort out what I myself believed. I was therefore drawn to Catholic Protestant discussion forums, and often spent far too much time there to the detriment of my "official" studies. This continues to be a problem. I often get distracted by a Facebook conversation and put far more time and energy into it than it warrants, which gets in the way of other projects that are more valuable in the long term. For instance, in the past few days I have become involved in a lengthy and rather acrimonious argument with some Catholic online acquaintances, which ironically got in the way of my writing these reflections on effective online communication. I am probably less an example of an effective communicator (though I have had my moments of effectiveness) than an example of someone who has made nearly every mistake possible in this area and can warn others not to follow my horrible example.

Nonetheless, I continue to use social media. I continue to find in it unparalleled opportunities for engaging in conversations that are of intellectual interest to me, with people outside my immediate circle of "real-life" acquaintances and outside the bubble of academic specialization. After twenty years of inquiry I am now more confident of my conclusions and view social media less as a way of hashing out my own views and more as a way of persuading others. (It has always, of course, been both of these things, and will continue to be.) That has led me to reflect more deeply than I additionally did on what kinds of online communication are likely to be persuasive, and to attempt to limit my participation in unprofitable discussions (though I continue to get sucked into all kinds of arguments just because they push my buttons).

I am continually surprised by the quality of conversations possible online and by the fascinating people who engage in online religious discussion. While the Internet does indeed offer a haven to cranks and fanatics of all descriptions, one also meets extremely thoughtful people online whom one would probably never encounter otherwise. There are a lot of people who don't have advanced degrees in religious subjects but who read widely and think deeply on these matters. Intellectual inquiry is alive and well in our culture. And frankly, even conversation with the cranks and fanatics is often more interesting, at least to me, than yet another round of shop-talk and career-centered posturing with fellow academics. This is not to say that fellow academics don't have many interesting things to say, but that it's refreshing to have forums for discussion, whether with academics or non-academics, in which career is irrelevant.

Connected to this is a more disconcerting surprise — the uselessness of credentials per se in academic discussion. It's hard not to expect a certain amount of deference, especially when talking about matters directly related to my subject. And of course people who agree with you already are happy to have a person with an advanced degree on their side. But those who disagree will almost invariably see any reference to academic credentials as an expression of snooty arrogance and an admission that your view can't stand on its own merits. For instance, in the above-mentioned recent Facebook conversation, the person I was arguing with suggested, in a rather patronizing tone, that I wasn't paying enough attention to the historical context of Pope Leo X's defense of burning heretics at the stake. I responded, unwisely, that I had a Ph.D. in the church history of that very period, my point being that even if I was wrong, I wasn't likely to be wrong because of a failure to look at the question in its historical context. I was instantly attacked for this piece of arrogance by several different people, one of whom commented, rather oddly, that citing one's credentials automatically made one the "Janos Slynt" in any conversation. (Janos Slynt is an obnoxious and treacherous character in the "Game of Thrones" fantasy series — I'm not sure why he was particularly relevant.)

Another example, not involving me, is the exchange some months ago between the eminent classical historian Mary Beard and a right-wing British businessman and lobbyist who had claimed that immigration caused the fall of Rome. Beard said that it was much more complex than that and suggested, quite modestly, that she had written a few books on the subject. Academics, of course, saw this as a definitive put-down of an ignorant person. But Beard would have been more persuasive to non-academics if she had provided a brief summary of her own view. She did not do so for the legitimate reason that she didn't see Twitter as an appropriate forum for a substantive discussion of the fall of Rome. But if academics are going to engage on social media at all, they need to be willing to condense and popularize difficult ideas rather than expecting non-academics either to accept claims of authority or read lengthy works of scholarship.

For the most part, social media has been helpful to me because of its role in clarifying ideas I had gained from other sources and giving me foils against which to develop my own beliefs. But on a number of occasions I've learned about important sources through online discussions. For instance, the Catholic apologist Dave Armstrong (http://www.patheos.com/blogs/davearmstrong/) brought to my attention a letter from Philip Melanchthon to Johannes Brenz clearly distinguishing the Lutheran view of justification from Augustine's, and admitting that the Lutherans cited Augustine as an authority against "the Papists" even though they didn't really hold to his soteriology. This has become an extremely important document for my own thinking on the subject. Armstrong's interest in Catholic apologetics and his acquaintance with "outdated" works of Catholic polemical scholarship (in this case Hartmann Grisar's biography of Luther) brought to light a document that I had never seen discussed in conventional academic circles. (Since then, my friend David Fink came across the document independently and discussed it in a conference paper.)

In respect to managing my time, I am an example largely of what *not* to do, although many of my issues in this regard were an expression of my frustration with academia and my spiritual and theological restlessness. I have often used social media as a way of scratching certain theological itches, particularly having to do with Catholicism. I spent six years as an assistant professor at Huntington University, in an atmosphere not particularly conducive to academic freedom, particularly with regard to the expression of theological ideas in non-specialist contexts. John Sanders told me, from his own hard experience, that I would be OK at Huntington as long as I didn't get published in *Christianity Today*. I largely allowed my blog to lapse during those years, but I did participate heavily in the "Catholic Answers" discussion forum under the alias "Contarini." This often detracted both from my teaching effectiveness and from the limited time I had available for scholarly writing, but in retrospect it was a safety valve allowing me to engage with issues I cared about more freely than I could do in the classroom or in publication under my own name.

Since losing my job, I have had less time for academic work as a whole, but more freedom in how to structure that time, and I have made progress in incorporating the use of social media into my calling as an "independent scholar." But I still have a long way to go.

To fellow scholars considering social media, I first say to accept the egalitarian nature of social media, which can be frustrating at times, but also exciting and liberating. Don't expect deference to your credentials. Be willing to substantiate claims as clearly as possible, and courteously expect others to do so. It is common in Internet discussions for people who don't have solid support for their positions to make a claim and then ask other people to "do the work" to disprove the claim. I routinely object to this and insist that the burden of proof rests on the person who makes the claim. On one occasion, a friend and fellow academic argued that I was being unreasonable, because as a Biblical scholar he might sometimes make claims based on years of research into a subject and ask non-academics to do their own study to confirm what he was saying. The problem with this is that on the Internet no one is a "professor"—everyone is equal. Your authority is only as good as your arguments and evidence. Since no one will listen to you simply because of credentials, you must both accept and insist upon a level playing field.

Secondly (at the risk of being obvious), engage ideas rather than attacking people. This is more difficult than it sounds, because Internet discussion has a well-known tendency to become acrimonious. The instant nature of social media, combined with the fact that you are interacting with words on a screen rather than a visible, breathing human being, make it fatally easy to behave nastily. And no matter who begins the cycle of recrimination, it takes on a life of its own. I've seen lengthy discussions devoted to just who was misinterpreting whom or who had failed to substantiate their arguments or who had insulted whom most severely.

The only remedy is to get out of the cycle yourself as soon as you see it starting. Don't apologize unless you can do so without reserve, because an apology that includes some explanation of how you were provoked will just continue the cycle. Apologize without qualification for anything you have said that was clearly wrong or uncharitable. Other than that, simply redirect the conversation by making a substantive point. Don't berate the other person for not doing so. Lead by example. I have seen apparently hopeless conversations take a positive turn simply by refusing to get sucked into the cycle of recrimination. But it's not to my credit that I had to learn this the hard way, and that I still often fail to follow my own advice. Possibly no one else needs to be instructed on so obvious a point.

Finally, related to the previous point, have faith in the potential of the medium, if you are going to use it at all. Don't treat it as a form of "slumming" or a trivial waste of time. That becomes self-fulfilling. We are living in an information explosion comparable, as many have pointed out, to that caused by the invention of the printing press. Academics are positioned to lead the way in forging substantive, respectful modes of discourse amid this bewildering proliferation of "new media," holding up standards of truth and courtesy amid a welter of ideological bluster and macho bullying. But in order to do so, we must unlearn the habits of privilege and treat the media we are using with respect. We must always remember that we are communicating with real human beings, created and loved by God, and that professional dignity and the thrill of winning an argument are both trivial compared to the dignity and glory of these children of God, equally flawed with ourselves, with whom we have the honor to communicate.

———————

Edwin Woodruff Tait, Ph.D., is an independent scholar, organist, homeschooling parent, and homesteader living in Richmond, Kentucky. He is an adjunct professor of church history (online) for Asbury Theological Seminary and a contributing editor of Christian History Magazine. He also writes on occasion for In Trust. See Tait's blog at stewedrabbit.blogspot.com. He is a frequent Facebook user and occasionally tweets as @Amandil3. His contributions to the "Catholic Answers" discussion forum may be found at forums.catholic.com under the alias Contarini.

JONATHAN Y. TAN

Worship, Music, and Pastoral Ministry

I n my essay, "Ministry Meets Social Networking: Connecting with the Digital Natives" (*New Theology Review*), I made the case that social media has to become part of pastoral ministry, or the church will find itself increasingly marginalized in the lives of digital natives. I followed this up with my discussion of doing mission in cyberspace and using social media among the youth and millennials of Asia as I explored new frontiers of mission in my book, *Christian Mission among the Peoples of Asia*. At the same time, I would have to concede that this is easier said than done, if I were asked what I myself am doing, that could be used as examples for others.

I have a Twitter account and blogs on blogger, a YouTube account, as well as a professional (as distinct from a separate personal) Facebook page, plus a professional website on my own domain. I originally created the academic blog, *All Things Religion & Ethics* (https://allthingsreligion.blogspot.com/) for my students and courses that I taught. On this blog, which unfortunately, I have not found time to update more recently I highlight current developments in the intersections of religion, ethics, and society, as well as popular movements and spiritual practices from around the world that are not often well reported in North American news media. My other academic blog, *Academic Research Resources* (https://academicresearchresources.blogspot.com/), which unfortunately has fallen victim to time constraints on my part, represents my endeavors to provide useful academic resources for research to my own students and other interested scholars and students. Both of these blogs originated as my attempt to address the lack of research skills that I discern among my students, who usually rely on google and taking the first ten searches on the landing page as starting point for research, without any critical analysis or discernment on the quality and depth of the content in those first ten links. Even though I have not updated these two blogs with new links, I do get the occasional emails or messages from former students or members of the public alerting me to new links to add to existing entries.

Insofar as I would like to say that I practice what I write in my article and book chapter as indicated above, I find myself struggling, amidst my commitments to my teaching and service commitments, as well as my ongoing scholarship and research projects, to find time to update my blog pages and end up using Twitter to lurk and read, rather than post my thoughts. As such, I find myself defaulting to YouTube and Facebook as my primary social media platforms. I post regularly recordings of my church music engagements as a music minister to my YouTube account, and I share thoughts, post responses, and every now and then, write an extended note on a theological or ethical issue on my professional Facebook page. For my upper division classes (e.g., honors or upper division seminars), my students are also friends on my professional Facebook page and participation in various Facebook groups on topics germane to the seminar is part of the assessment for the seminar. I find that using getting students involved in Facebook groups that are relevant to the subject matter of the seminar increases attention and exposes students to a broader world beyond the written word in books and articles that I assign as part of the weekly seminar readings.

While I know of scholars who keep their Facebook accounts separate from their students, and I myself practiced this policy for many years, I came to realize over time that Facebook is far more useful than blogs and Twitter in that there is such a diverse and pluralistic range of Facebook groups—open, closed, and secret—that students can participate in through my introduction. Feedback from students range from how much they learn from other viewpoints and that there is a whole world out that discussing these issues that they didn't know had existed, as they use Facebook, Instagram, snapchat, and other social media platforms primarily for personal networking. I think students have great curiosity on social media, and it behooves us to guide them to relevant groups, get them admitted into closed or secret groups that are discussing issues pertinent to the course, and help them understand and appreciate the diversity, nuances, and range of opinions on social media, so that they learn how to make informed decisions and good choices through the hermeneutics of suspicion.

Besides being a theologian and academic, I am also a liturgy geek and professional church musician who lives and breathes all things liturgical and musical. My earliest social media presence is my YouTube account (https://www.youtube.com/user/ProfessorJTan), where I have, and continue to upload video recordings of liturgical music making in the various churches that I serve as a church musician. Complementing my Church Music YouTube channel is my World Christian Music blog, *Cantus Mundi* (https://cantusmundi.blogspot.com/), which I created at about the same time I created my YouTube channel where I showcase Christian music from around the world. I have not been able to update *Cantus Mundi* as frequently as I like, but I hope to devote more time in the future to highlight noteworthy indigenous global Christian music that reveal the depths of the diversity and plurality of World Christianities that are, thanks to migration, taking root in North America too. Over the years, I have received feedback and messages from visitors to *Cantus Mundi* who have found the examples most helpful, either for their personal devotion or interest, or church music planning in their own congregations.

To scholars who are looking to use social media, as I discussed in my article and book above, social media is here to stay and social media is to today's generation the way the circular letter was to Paul's outreach to early Christian communities and print was to Luther's generation during the Reformation.

First, if one is able to spare the time, blogging and tweeting are good ways of reaching out to a broader audience, as Savo Heleta's article in the March 8, 2016 issue *The Conversation*, "Academics can change the world — if they stop talking only to their peers" puts it ever so eloquently.

Second, academics should consider dipping their toes into social media, e.g., create an Instagram account to document one's research visually, making video clips and posting them on YouTube or Vimeo, and joining in the discussions in various groups on Facebook.

Finally, I would recommend that academics not shy from incorporating social media in class, using YouTube, Vimeo, Instagram, Facebook, and other social media platforms as may be appropriate to the course. Students need guidance on how to navigate social media and as they get most of their news from social media, academics could play an important role in shaping how students understand and interact with social media platforms using a specific course as starting point.

Do our students appreciate my social media activity? I think most do, even if they do not tell us directly. Every now and then, I get feedback in student evaluations. Here are two evaluations, taken verbatim from student evaluations I received, which capture succinctly why academics should consider social media as a form of pedagogical outreach to their students:

Evaluation #1

As for the youtubeYouTube videos and blog postings, I find your teaching method to be revolutionary- and I think that your method is how students that follow me will learn on a daily basis. You are the first professor that has integrated the Internet into learning at this level. My generation lives on the Internet, and it's awesome that this course entered my world, the Internet. My peers and I communicate via Internet all the time, and it's great to me that a professor has recognized it.

Evaluation #2

I have a confession to make: without school or work or SAC or some other project heavy on my back, I quickly become dead bored. What can I say; -twiddling is just not for me! So, after rearranging my sock drawer, I took to cleaning out My Favorites, and rediscovered your website from last semester's Islam course. After looking over your site, I was reminded of how devoted you are to your students: your website is unparalleled by any other professor I've seen at [university name redacted], and you update it so frequently (your blog has so much depth) and so far in advance (I really should have sabotaged my grades this last semester, if for no other reason than to take your Confucianism and Daoism class). It's a real dream boat of academia for Millennials, I think!

These two evaluations, which I have drawn from the many teaching evaluations that I have received over the years, serve to inspire me to try to find time for social media as part of my pedagogy to Millennials. To the extent that we can utilize social media to teach best practices in using online resources, we would be able to prepare our students to go out into the real world with the ability to discern between facts vis-à-vis the "alternative" garbage that are put out by websites and other social media sites of dubious value.

Jonathan Y. Tan, PhD is theologian, church musician, and a scholar of religions who is interested in interdisciplinary approaches to studying and understanding religions and their impact on human societies. He is the Archbishop Paul J. Hallinan

Professor of Catholic Studies at Case Western Reserve University and also affili-
ated faculty in the Ethnic Studies and Asian Studies programs there, as well as Co-
Chair of the American Academy of Religion's World Christianity Group. He has
written 2 books, edited 3 books, and authored 80 articles and essays on various
topics. Visit Tan's professional website at www.jonathantan.org, YouTube chan-
nel at https://www.youtube.com/user/ProfessorJTan, and find him on Twitter:
@ProfessorJTan and Facebook: Jonathan Y. Tan. Tan's social media blogs include
Cantus Mundi *(https://cantusmundi.blogspot.com/),* All Things Religion & Ethics
(https://allthingsreligion.blogspot.com/), and Academic Research Resources *(https://*
academicresearchresources.blogspot.com/).

KEVIN TIMPE

Philosophy

My use of social media has changed pretty substantially over the past decade. Back in the mid to late 2000s, I read, commented on, and regularly contributed to a number of blogs. The Garden of Forking Paths (and then the Flickers of Freedom blog that replaced it) for free will and agency and Prosblogion for philosophy of religion were a great resources for me early on my career. And I'm currently an administrator for the Discrimination and Disadvantage blog, where Shelley Tremain has a particularly wonderful series of interviews with disabled philosophers called Dialogues on Disability.

But in the past five years or so, Facebook has replaced blogs for the overwhelming majority of online philosophy interaction for me. The quantity and quality of discussion that goes on there has increased, and I've seen threads cited in papers as well as articles in the general media engaging philosophical issues. I use Twitter, but not very much; I find it a lot less conducive to discussion and substantive interaction. It's primarily a way of sharing links and trying to provoke our current POTUS toward another of his meltdowns. I technically have an Instagram account but I think have only used it thrice. I use Pinterest, but only to organize links and videos that I use in my classes.

I initially only used Facebook for personal purposes — keeping up with friends, sharing pictures with family in other parts of the country, etc. . . . I tried fairly hard for a number of years to keep my professional life and my personal life (as it plays out on social media) separate. But I'm very glad that that proved to be too difficult and didn't last long as a policy.

These two aspects of my life are now very interconnected. At nearly every conference I go to, I'll meet someone in person that I've known for a long time on Facebook. I've been asked to contribute to a number of scholarly volumes by people that I know via social media, and a few speaking invitations have come that way as well.

Perhaps I shouldn't be, but I have been surprised a number of times to meet others via social media and find that they're incredibly kind and supportive of my scholarship. And I know friends that have had FB discussions turn into scholarly publications, which I think is fascinating. A few of these have led to invitations to contribute to edited volumes or into co-authored projects. Though perhaps technically not social media, the shared folders function of Dropbox also makes co-authoring with colleagues at other universities significantly easier.

In addition to the kinds of connections and opportunities mentioned above, social media can also be a very useful professional tool in other ways. It's great to be able to talk with scholars in other parts of the country or the world. And while this could also be done via email, if it's done on Facebook or Twitter then it can also be done in a way that allows others to join in. It is, in some ways, like having a conversation in the hotel lobby at a large philosophy conference—except others can join in the discussion when they're done teaching.

Perhaps the most important use of social media that I've been involved in is a group that aids philosophers around the world with their scholarship. My previous university had very poor access to scholarly journals, both in print and online. Interlibrary loan would usually be able to get me what I wanted, but it would often take 2-3 days. I have a lot of friends that work at research universities, which have much better online access to journals. So for a number of years, I'd post a link to an article that I needed with a request for one of my friends with better library access to send a copy of that article my way. Voila—my very own interlibrary loan network that saved the university library staff from having to be the go-between. Eventually I noticed that a few of my friends would do similar things.

So just over three years ago while I was giving a final exam in one of my classes, I made a closed FB group for just this purpose. Rather than asking your ILL staff to get a journal article, members of the group can post a link to an article or book chapter they're looking for and their email address. Another member of the group with access to that resource can then send you a copy via email. The group currently has about 6500 members from across the world. My guess is that other disciplines would benefit from having similar groups. Maybe they already have something similar. If anyone wants to find out more about the group, they're welcome to contact me (via social media, of course, but email will work too).

When it comes to social media use, I admit to managing my time very poorly. We have three small kids and I love the flexibility of the academic life. I'm writing the present answer, for example, in the lobby of my kids' school after serving on playground duty, utilizing an hour or two before picking them up at the end of the day. But the ability to be present thanks to the job's flexibility means that I do a lot of work after they go to bed at night. And that kind of flexibility doesn't always interact nicely with the ease and short-term dopamine kick of social media.

When I'm working really hard on a writing project or trying to make a deadline, I'll often close out FB to focus. But most of the time I'm on my computer, it's open in a tab. (I just flipped over and interacted with four philosophers from around the country on a post about reading Harry Potter to my 6 year old daughter; but now I'm back. See, you didn't even notice that I was gone.) I'm bad at boundaries and balance, both in general and in particular with regard to Facebook. Saying I've figured out moderation on social media is about like saying I've figured out how to moderate my caffeine intake. I'm not even close to an exemplar.

As I've become more involved in disability advocacy and activism in the past few years, I've also seen the ways that social media makes such organization and action easier. While a decade ago I might know the philosophical work of someone elsewhere in the country or world, I likely wouldn't have known that they were the parent of a disabled child or that they had useful advice on how to more effectively advocate for individuals with disabilities. So the porousness of the personal and the professional has been really useful for some of my non-academic or non-professional pursuits.

Finally, I find that many people on Facebook don't manage their privacy settings well. I often share less with administrators than I do with colleagues. I have separate posting lists for family, for academics, and for close friends that I use for certain kinds of posts. Furthermore, the default setting for almost all my posts prevents people that I don't know from reading my posts. (Of course, one should also be aware that every post, no matter the security setting, can be screen-captured. So *always* be careful.)

Also, I recommend to scholars that they find out how to utilize the opportunities that social media makes possible to your advantage, but in a way that suits your personality. I don't recommend that everyone follow the same norms that I follow. (Some days, I don't even recommend that I follow the norms that I, as a matter of fact, follow.)

Finally, let me request more Dr. Horrible memes and references on social media! And if you have any good Spotify playlists for tear-inducing acoustic covers or Mongolian folk music, please send them my way.

———————

Kevin Timpe presently holds the William Harry Jellema Chair in Christian Philosophy at Calvin College. His scholarly writing focuses primarily on the metaphysics of free will and agency, virtue ethics, issues in the philosophy of religion, and the philosophy of disability. He and his wife also started a disability advocacy company, 22 Advocacy. Timpe's professional webpage, with links to much of his scholarship, can be found at www.kevintimpe.com. He can also be found easily on Facebook (though his privacy settings are usually pretty high) and sometimes on Twitter (@the_Timpest). He's still trying to figure out how to delete his academia.edu account and laments that it is a former philosophy that is responsible for such a pariah.

PHILIP TOWNE

Intercultural Theology

utilize Facebook, Twitter some (mainly when I'm at conferences), Instagram, LinkedIn, and Pinterest. I have also used a couple blogging platforms, most recently Tumblr, but don't currently write a blog. Facebook is my primary platform for use, as I keep in touch with many people through it.

I have used Facebook in two key ways in my own research and interests. First, to connect with specific communities. I have connected with several communities of people studying similar things to me or with similar interests. Academic areas such as Media, Religion and Culture or Intercultural Studies and Missiology are groups I keep up with and learn from. I also stay connected to various ministry groups that relate to what I teach.

The second way I have used it is to conduct research. For my dissertation that was recently completed, I constructed an ethnography on a particular community. Some of this was gleaned through Facebook and the community's blog usage. Using the tools of digital ethnography, using Facebook was a very strategic and intentional way to research. It also allowed me to become part of the specific community in another way, which has opened doors for me for further research.

Somewhat related, I also was an Internet Pastor for a couple years on staff at a large church. During this time, we attempted to utilize the internet to "reach" and minister to people. We had some degree of success, but difficulty came when there were other voices that challenged what was said in a Sunday service. All of the sudden, when we opened up a process where voices could express their opinions back to the church, not everyone was happy with this, and soon things like open forums for discussion were shut down. This was quite a learning experience on the power of the internet, and while this was a bit before more modern internet ministries, this opened my eyes to the kinds of challenges that were ahead as technology and faith came in tension with each other.

Part of my research (mentioned in the previous question) was related to how members of the community were pursuing spirituality in both their face-to-face and mediated contexts. I was quite surprised how open many of the members of the community were to discussing things of a spiritual nature. Many were quite open to sharing. I also found that their usage of social media was a key way that they were exploring things of a spiritual nature. We often imagine people seeking out a church or religious community when they have spiritual questions of some sort, but I found that most of those studied would rather seek out spiritual answers through either their community or online. So, in contrast to the perception that is often had that social media users are only putting their best foot forward and not being authentic, I found that when given the right chance and in a safe place, people actually desire to explore spiritual things online.

Another thing I have been surprised to see is the way in which we can easily be insular on social media. While we theoretically have more opportunity to hear various voices, often the algorithms built into platforms feed us information that confirms our own bias. We have to be intentional about seeking out alternative voices. Related to this, when there are debates, people seem much more willing to "unfriend" someone over it, which thus further continues this cycle of us only seeing things that agree with us. Certainly this is a generality, but as we use a platform like Facebook, we have to continually be careful that our confirmation bias doesn't creep forward slowly and isolate us from those with different perspectives.

Again going back to my own research project, one thing I had initially expected was for technology and social media to be a driving factor in changing the way people related to faith. However, what I found is that it was not a driving factor with whom I studied, but it was an essential factor for enabling this community itself. So, while Facebook didn't change the way they looked at spirituality, it did enable the community to be the community it is, and the community is experiencing spirituality outside of an organized religious context.

To further explain, what I mean by this is that the community itself does not get together in a face-to-face meeting regularly. Some of the members see each other regularly while others do not. But, there are a couple secret Facebook pages that we all use to keep in touch with each other during times we don't see each other. Almost daily there are numerous messages being put forth through these groups, alongside their individual Facebook pages. This social media usage enables the community to be who they are and without it, I do not believe they could exist in quite the same way. So, while social media is not the driving factor, it is an essential enabling one and one that extends their community online.

Personally, I have seasons and cycles of social media use. I don't use Twitter unless I am at academic conferences, because I find it very useful to follow certain discussions and hashtags while attending them. I don't use LinkedIn much, unless I need to network on a business level with a specific person or group. Pinterest is primarily used for home DIY projects (which is something my wife and I love doing). Facebook seems to be what I use the most, followed by Instagram. Since I am part of an arts community, many of them use Instagram to show art. My daughters also talked me into it because they use it to share pictures and poetry online, so I can keep up with them this way.

For me then, I tend to be fairly pragmatic with my use. I used to spend much more time on Facebook browsing, but recently (and partly due to the very divisive recent election season) I have stayed off unless I need something specific. I have even limited my mobile usage, removing the Facebook app from my phone. This has also helped me to be less distracted while I was finishing up my doctoral dissertation.

Peripherally related, I use an app that does Pomodoro timings when I am writing or doing other tasks. This really helps keep me on track by managing my time spent doing certain tasks in 25 minute increments.

If I were giving advice to others about social media, I'd first say that I am a big fan of openness and being genuine on social media. It can be easy to paint an ideal picture of yourself online, but I believe people see through this. Be who you are in real life.

Second, and this relates to the first, is I advocate people to mix business and pleasure. As a scholar you may promote what you are doing through social media, but don't allow this to be the only thing you share. Share things that you are interested in and be an interesting person. On my Facebook page one could find pictures of me playing in a band with skeleton face paint on, pictures of my family on vacation or swimming in the pool, DIY projects we are working on, articles posted about non-academic subjects I'm interested in or learning about, as well as other academic related posts. If we are one-dimensional that doesn't make us very interesting people, so why would people (outside of our specialized guild) be interested in our scholarship?

Finally, participate in what others are doing. Don't just do your own thing, but comment on other's posts, be a part of groups, and participate. This in itself helps promote what you are doing, but it also further helps build relationships with people, which I believe is very important.

———————

Philip Towne, PhD is Assistant Professor of Ministry and Intercultural Studies at Hope International University and Director of the School of Advanced Leadership Training. He previously served as a pastor for over a decade in Oregon, Idaho and California. He also loves art, music, DIY projects and his family. Find Towne on Facebook, Twitter, LinkedIn, and other platforms.

ALEXIS JAMES WAGGONER

Public Theology

came to use social media to enhance my ministry and my reach in reverse order: I worked in social media marketing prior to going to seminary and transitioning to full-time ministry. So social media was already a crucial part of how I understood content creation and marketing. That said, while I use social media to promote what I write and to help get the word out about my latest endeavors, the biggest benefit of social media in my ministry and writing is the connections I've made through it.

In terms of marketing my work, interacting with followers, and engaging people I admire, sometimes I feel I do the bare minimum! I am impressed how some people are so prolific — both in their writing and in their social media activity. I'm doing well if I can publish one blog post per week and push that out via social media — which I do via my personal social networks.

Something I learned when I worked in social media marketing that holds true on the ministry and theology side of things is people respond better to you as a person, than perhaps to a "brand." I've tried to run social media for my blog (The Acropolis Project) but I don't get near as much engagement there as I do when I'm posting under my personal Twitter, Facebook, and Instagram.

To that end, I use my personal Twitter, Facebook, and Instagram to publicize when I've written a new post or developed other content. I also send out my posts via my email list. On all these fronts, I have predominately allowed my reach and following to grow naturally and haven't put much additional effort or resources into growing the numbers. I experimented a bit with Twitter and Facebook ads to get my message to a wider audience and this is something that can have interesting benefits, but I haven't explored it to its fullest potential.

I know that nowadays publishers, event bookers, and others who may look to hire me are interested in follower numbers—for good or ill. Those of us in ministry may find that antithetical to the authenticity of our message and community but I understand that it's also a gauge by which I may be judged.

But more-so than garnering a large following or engaging in prolific tweeting, I have found the potential for connection and community via social media—when used well!—to be the most beneficial and encouraging. I am a part of several Facebook groups related to my areas of interest. These are great places to feel supported in your work, and to also pick others' brains.

Through these and other methods of outreach, I have made such wonderful connections using social media. One of my favorite stories is how I connected with someone who is now a cherished friend. She is also a minister and had moved to Nashville around the same time I did. I found her through her guest post on a site I was also featured on, and randomly reached out to her. We ended up meeting in person, really connecting, and we have now worked on multiple projects together including a published Bible study and a women's conference. She is an inspiration to my work as a woman in ministry.

I did something similar with a woman who ran the local chapter of the American Academy of Religion a couple years ago. I found her work online and just wanted to connect. She was gracious enough to meet with me, and—through a series of events—connected me to the Dean of Religion at the university where she teaches, and I am now an adjunct professor there!

On the flip side, I have been contacted through my website and email list by people who need support, or advice, or have questions about the work I do. As a chaplain in the Air Force Reserves I get contacted from time to time by other women who are interested in pursuing military chaplaincy but don't know of anyone else to reach out to (female military chaplains are few and far between!). In these instances I am thrilled to share my experience and expertise with people who may eventually become my colleagues. Some of those chance encounters have developed into relationships where I hope I'm able to provide some support and insight to what people are going through, based on a common experience that we wouldn't know we shared if not for the internet!

I am currently exploring how to use social media and other online tools to expand the reach of the work I do as a minister of adult education. When I teach classes, I impact a relatively small percentage of the people in my church, and an even smaller percentage of the faith community. I am looking for ways to make my content available through our church website in a format that goes beyond a one-way flow of information. This is the struggle of any online learning experience, but I hope to provide meaningful variations of the classes I teach to people that can't attend in person.

For my first foray into this experiment, I wrote daily Lenten devotionals made available via email to church members. Each brief devotional included simple, tangible practices for deepening faith over the 40 days of Lent. I accompanied this with a weekly class where we discussed each week's theme — an effort to meld on-demand online content with transformative community-building.

In this capacity, I see social media and online pursuits as *part of* my ministerial endeavor, not a distraction from it. Yet, it's admittedly easy to get sucked into a Facebook debate or the latest Twitter controversy when utilizing these tools. The biggest thing for me when it comes to managing my time on social media is keep my purpose front-and-center. As I've outlined above, I find social platforms most helpful as I seek to support others in the faith community, find support for my own endeavors, and integrate online learning into my religious education work. When I spend time on social media to these ends, it doesn't feel like a time suck and can actually be life-giving. But when I let myself get distracted by the noise — and there is a *lot* of noise! — I lag behind my goals and end up feeling drained and overwhelmed.

On a practical note, I've found it extremely helpful to turn off notifications from all social platforms! This is especially necessary when I need to buckle down and get some writing done. I don't have any social media or email notifications set up on my phone, and when I really need to write, I either go somewhere without Wi-Fi so I'm not distracted, or I turn my Wi-Fi off so I at least have to think twice before I get back online.

That's why I'm impressed by those with a seemingly constant social media presence. For my own practice, I find it works best if I manage social media and email in concerted chunks. I don't check any email, social media, news, etc. till later in the morning, after I've prayed, meditated, exercised, had breakfast with my husband and daughter, and gotten my daughter off to pre-school; in other words: after I've given my energy to the truly important things!

My overall suggestion to those considering how they should use social media in their work and ministry is to think of how it could enhance what you're already doing, rather than trying to build a strategy from scratch. Sure, there might be some value in utilizing a number of platforms but if you don't really understand them or aren't inspired by the connections there, it's not going to be sustainable. Find a platform or a strategy that is engaging for you, supports the work you're currently doing, and build on that.

Speaking as someone who used to work full-time in the social media world, I know first-hand how easy it is to let it *become* the focus of your work, rather than using social media in service of your work. To guard against this, it's helpful to know what you want to use social media for. Some people clearly see social communities as the frontline of their ministry and are able to spend large amounts of time on these platforms. If that's not the case for you, decide how social media can work for you and your calling and set boundaries and priorities to make this a reality.

Alexis James Waggoner is a theologian and educator. She is an adjunct professor at Belmont University and a minister with the Christian Church (Disciples of Christ). Her organization, The Acropolis Project (http://theacropolisproject.com) is dedicated to raising the bar of education in communities of faith. She is also a chaplain in the Air Force Reserves. She has a M.Div. from Union Theological Seminary in New York, a husband of 13 years, and a baby named Junia. Alexis creates curriculum, writes, and pontificates at http://theacropolisproject.com. Find her on Facebook: https://www.facebook.com/alexisinthecity and Twitter @alexisjwaggoner

NATHANAEL WELCH

Theology and Disability

I use Facebook, Twitter, Instagram, YouTube, and have a personal WordPress blog. I primarily use my blog to host content, Facebook to spark conversations around a topic, YouTube to share videos of lectures or webinars, and Twitter and Instagram to direct people to those blog posts, videos, or discussions.

There are two main reasons: first, the issues I address in my work remain largely hidden or ignored in the public sphere. So part of my reason for using social media was to raise awareness about these topics by introducing them to the places where public discussions naturally happen. Second, connected to the first, I use social media to help me understand the best ways to raise awareness about my interests. Seeing how people respond or engage a particular topic is helpful in understanding what approach to take, how to introduce a topic, or where there is a misconception I can shed light on.

I continue to use social media as a way to work out my ideas in public. Because of the immediate feedback that social media allows, I can better judge if an approach to a topic I am taking is something that resonates with others or not. There is a danger in only making content that appeals to everyone, but I want to be clear that this is not my goal. Part of my goal in this public outworking of my ideas is to find the best way to explain an idea, not simply to find what ideas people are already drawn to.

People, myself included, rarely use social media to learn something new. They usually use it as justification for continuing to hold the beliefs they already have. This makes trying to pursue open and respectful dialogue difficult, because they necessarily means that the people taking part must be willing to hear something they disagree with. I believe this is the single greatest challenge to using social media as a means for philosophical or religious dialogue.

It is possible, however, to have open and respectful dialogue on social media. But to do so requires no small amount of humility. I find that modelling the behavior that we expect from those that engage with our material to be the best approach. It is very easy, and all too tempting, to escalate because of ignorance or name-calling. But if we want to reach new people, and not just preach to the choir, then we must be willing to engage with those who disagree with us, and do so in a respectful and humble manner.

After sharing an article with a very strong political position, I had some tense conversation on Facebook with someone who disagreed with the article. However, I soon found out that this person didn't read the article, but was instead reacting to the headline. After further discussion, it was clear that this person was not interested in reading the article, but wanted to continue to tell me why I was wrong. This, in my experience, is the most challenging situation. One the one hand, I want to have a rational conversation about the content of the article, but, on the other, it is easy to forget how doing so (disengaged, rational reflection) is not only difficult for some, but can be seen as a threat. It didn't matter what the content of the article was, because it was perceived as a threat to their very being. In those instances it is incredibly important to remain humble and resist the urge to escalate the situation, that is, if your goal is open dialogue. Navigating these experiences has proved to be the most challenging lesson in social media for me personally.

A new project I am looking forward to was inspired by interactions on social media. This summer, a number of cities across the country agreed to host ArtWalks for people with disabilities. I have been hosting them in the LA area for the past year and was looking to expand the project. After seeing some other inspiring projects online, I decided to try and travel to each city and capture each ArtWalk event, like an ArtWalk road trip, with the ultimate goal of creating a book with stories and photos from each city. I want to highlight individuals that participate, collect their story, and compile it in a book to share and hopefully fund future ArtWalk projects for people with disabilities. The idea for this project was really generated from interaction and conversation with others doing similar projects online.

It is really easy to get sucked into social media and waste time. Often, the value it adds to my work is negated by its ability to distract me indefinitely. This is why I think it is really important to not just set aside time to work on social media, but to prioritize your goals and obligations.

At the beginning of every week I write out what I need to get done every day. This is sort of a "best case scenario" exercise. It rarely works out that I accomplish everything I wanted to in the time frame I set out. But, the act of thinking through what you *need* to accomplish in the week, and every day, helps to see the big picture and prevent me from getting lost in the weeds, or cat videos.

In addition to prioritizing what work needs to get done, I find it helpful to figure out how much energy or effort something will take me to complete. For example, responding to emails is not something that is difficult for me to do, and therefore it doesn't take a lot of energy for me to do nor do I procrastinate doing it (I know this is very stressful for a lot of people). However, what is very stressful for me is listening through podcast interviews, pulling out quotes to share, and writing show notes for each episode. This is something that, because it takes a lot of energy or effort for me to complete, I tend to put off as long as possible. Knowing this is really important when making my schedule and prioritizing tasks.

I recommend the following to those considering using social media more:

1. Know your audience. Who do you want to reach? Who is your intended audience? Why should they care about what you're saying? All of these are really important questions to ask *before* you begin writing/recording a single word. Everything else hinges on knowing this and keeping it top-of-mind at all times. Not just for tone or word choices, but for content as well. A good question to ask after you've finished: am I assuming too much, or, not enough?

2. Be consistent. Whether you podcast, blog, or have a video series, inconsistency kills. Posting a blog post once every two months is hardly enough to be effective, although, posting one every day might be a bit much. It isn't an exact science, and finding your sweet spot will take some trial and error, but it is well worth it. Your audience will respond better if they know they can expect to see or hear something at regular intervals.

3. Be controversial.* Take a stand on whatever the issue or topic is. I think too often people are afraid to take a side because they don't want to lose their audience. But there are two important things to remember: people love to tell you they disagree with you, and taking a position will help with #1. First, if someone disagrees with what you say, that is a good thing! They

are more likely to share your content and spark conversation around it. The nail that sticks out gets hammered down, and with so many people competing for attention, taking a strong position might mean getting hammered down, but it also means that you will stick out. Second, losing some of your audience is actually a good thing. Unless you are the Pope, you probably aren't trying to reach everyone. Being slightly controversial will help you find (and keep!) those people who are in your "tribe" and will help promote your work and stick with you.

*An important part of this is making sure your content isn't controversial for controversy's sake: it needs to be high quality content, otherwise you will lose your audience and not in a good way. All of this is to say, don't be afraid to ruffle some feathers. Making everyone happy is just another way of saying making nobody happy.

––––––––––––––

Nathanael Welch is a student at the Hatchery in Los Angeles, where he is studying theology, disability studies, and social entrepreneurship, and Media Guru for the Homebrewed Christianity Podcast. A former musician and music theorist, he spends most of his time developing a new type of community for people with and without disabilities that utilizes art and photography in the hope of cultivating transforming encounters. Learn more about the ArtWalk project at www.differentunited.com or follow his personal blog about theology and disability at www.nathanaelwelch.com. Follow him on Twitter, Facebook, and Instagram @nathanlovestrees for occasional rants, disruptive thoughts, and pictures of trees.

KURT WILLEMS

Pastoral Theology

t all started with a blog. Actually, it started with a conversation with a close friend. He informed me, back in 2008, that his dad (a smart man that we both admire) started to write down his thoughts on a medium called "BlogSpot." Blogging, apparently, is what all the smart and/or cool people with something to say are doing. After figuring out what a blog was all about, I realized that I was already about 5-10 years behind the cool curve in the Christian blogosphere: but that didn't stop me.

I started a blog. I wrote one thing. Maybe two. Then I posted a video of Kobe jumping over a car. Then I forgot. Neglected. Had little use for . . . my blog.

Eventually (after a couple of years), as new questions arose, I logged back into the blog. One of the first things I had to wrestle with was the discovering of something called "theistic evolution." Over time, the blog became a primary way I deconstructed and reconstructed my faith.

With the blog came Facebook. After Myspace basically spaced itself out of relevance, I began experimenting with Facebook as a tool for engagement. Another friend suggested that if I wanted more folks to engage with me as I blogged, that I should utilize Facebook to do two things: 1) find like-minded people who would enjoy the sorts of issues I was wrestling with in my writing journey; 2) promote my articles to my friends list on Facebook. The idea was genius!

I took his feedback and came up with a plan. I went to newly created "fan pages" that I admired (like N.T. Wright, Rob Bell, Shane Claiborne, etc.) and clicked on a button that showed you all of the profiles of people who "liked" these pages also. Of course, this option is no longer available as Facebook continues to tighten up the reigns, but back then it was easy. I'd send 20-30 people messages each day inviting them to add me as a friend for dialogue. I told them my intentions, and many (not all) were into the idea. This began my so-called "social media" following. But in all honesty, it was more like an exciting web of acquaintances (and some who I sincerely would call "friend") spanning from Malaysia to the UK — and many places in-between.

Eventually I adopted Twitter, to expand my networking capabilities. I didn't know much about Twitter strategy at that time, but along the way learned that Twitter etiquette involves following back those who follow you (as long as they aren't perceived as spam or stalkers). Then, someone that I connected with on Twitter shared with me a tool that helps you automatically follow people who have similar interests (like I had done on Facebook), and my Twitter experiment grew. Over time thousands of followers connected on this medium through a combination of strategy and thought-provoking tweets.

And then there is that blog. As my network grew, so did my blog. After a bit of church drama over the content of my blog (perhaps too innovative theologically for my context), I shut down the blog for a season. But when it became clear that I would be transitioning into a new season of ministry, I relaunched my site — The Pangea Blog — and then it happened: my big break.

In May of 2011 Osama Bin Laden was killed. *And now you are wondering: how was that your "big break?" What an odd thing to claim.* Agreed, but hear me out. As I drove home from a seminary class that evening, I heard several stories of cheering in the streets. I was greeted at home by these images being highlighted on CNN. And shoot — when I first heard the news I was a bit excited: until I paused. Reflected on my values. Prayed. And realized that there was something deeply disturbing about dancing the streets over the death of any human being. So I wrote about it. And that night, the article got shared. And shared. And shared. And suddenly, I had a legitimate online platform. That month, *Patheos.com* recruited me to blog on their website. What started out as a sarcastic suggestion from a friend had turned into an online community of people wrestling with church, theology, and culture.

In the following few years I blogged my brains out. Then, we started preparing to plant a church. Relocated 1k miles with a 3-month-old and eventually planted a church here in Seattle. While I continue to blog as I'm able, the medium that I've fallen in love with is podcasting. In March of 2016 I launched *The Paulcast: A Podcast All about the Apostle Paul*. It allows me to stay engaged in content creation without the added time that it takes me to put thoughts to paper.

My entire social media journey has been a scholarly quest of sorts. Not all my content is "scholarly" in bent, but it certainly is a dominant theme. Before my "big break" into the Christian blogging scene, I began to copy/paste sections of seminary papers into my blog to create articles. Seminary gave me the content that I could regurgitate (sometimes word-for-word) into the blog. Over time I found myself learning in such a way that my joy is often translating theological concepts in ways that regular folks connect with. I am pastor after all.

After relocating with my wonderful family to Seattle, we soon realized that while my main passion was pastoral, a close second is academics. We discerned that both loves integrate well into my calling and vocation, so I entered a second master's program, this time focusing on Paul within his historical context. After a couple of years, I realized that my online community might enjoy some of what I engage in as I study the Apostle. So, somewhat on a whim I started The Paulcast.

What this has done is kept me rooted in my scholarly interests and opened up doors to meet many leading experts in the field of New Testament studies. Bringing scholarship to a general audience is now the driving force of my social media presence. Of course, this means that I still get to apply such content in pastoral ways — often connecting dots to cultural realities that we face in the real world. This is the primary reason social media is part of my regular life, outside of my personal friendships and promoting our faith community: Pangea Church.

Two things come to mind as I reflect upon what has surprised me with the ongoing work of writing and podcasting. First, it is amazing to look back at older articles that I wrote — about things such as nonviolence, the end times, or nationalism — to see many negative commenters who have now become friends. I can think of a few folks who eventually "converted" to my way of thinking on an issue. Sometimes, I get follow-up comments on my blog from such people who say things like: "I can't believe I reacted that way to this article 5 years ago. Thinks have changed!" This has been more than surprising. Having an influence in the lives of folks I have yet to meet in person: this is a gift and responsibility — one that I do not take lightly.

Secondly, it has surprised me to find how many people are hungry for thoughtful theological content that intersects with real life. Sure, it is also fun to speculate about this or that theory — but what makes all the difference for people seems to be how a particular concept helps us see God or the early church more clearly. As these pictures become sharper, so also does our vision for what God

might do in the world today. In the same vein, I also been honored on several occasions when former Christians or atheists have gone out of their way to note
that it is the vision of Jesus that I promote that they would most easily endorse if
they had faith. That is the greatest complement I've ever been given through social media interactions over the years. People are hungry for better narratives for
understanding reality. Rooted theology can provide this like nothing else can.

When I graduated from seminary, I used my blog to crowd-source for my final
project. I was doing research on Genesis 1-3 with the presupposition that biolog-
ical evolution was compatible with biblical Christianity. On a blog post, I collected
stories from burnt-out evangelicals, atheists, agnostics, and even a few over-
zealous fundamentalists. These stories about how many had walked away from
the church due to an anti-scientific posture gave credence to the thesis of my
paper. I integrated many of the stories that were submitted into the application
portion of my research.

I am mostly terrible at managing my time when it comes to social media. As
my responsibilities beyond blogging (and now podcasting) have increased, it is
social media that usually suffers most. I think becoming more of a morning person is the only way to solve this dilemma. We shall see. As of right now I spend
about 5-10 hours per week on all things pertaining to social media, including writing and podcast creation.

If I could offer three bits of advice to scholars considering using social media, in short, they would be: 1) do it yesterday, 2) ask for help, and 3) make it a
priority.

The reason that I think scholars (and here, I have in mind theologians / biblical scholars specifically) should engage in social media is that I know of many
great teachers who should be teaching in larger classrooms. In other words, I
know of wonderful professors who have important things to say about God and
the world but who rarely take their innovation outside of academic conferences,
books, and classrooms. The scholars that I know of who have taken to social media are influencing important conversations that will have a permanent impact on
the church in the West. I am so grateful to many of these great thinkers who continue to make their content accessible in bite-sized chunks, for those of us who
cannot always read every book or article. Not only so, but these scholars often
find themselves able to engage in important cultural issues in a way that social
media shapes, that would not usually happen without a blog or podcast. I think
this makes for better scholars and a better church.

Entering the social media fray can be daunting. It takes a lot of help at first
and a little bit of luck. But it is worth it. Established scholars already have built in

credibility. What they often lack, in my experience, is the drive or "know how" in a web 2.0 world. But, and here I'm thinking of seminary professors (for instance), it is highly likely that you have a student currently or a former student who engages heavily in social media. And if not a student, some other bloggers have likely engaged some of your material. These are shoulders to tap. Also, when it doubt: Google social media questions and watch YouTube videos.

Finally, I hope that such scholars will make social media a priority. Utilizing this medium wrongly is dehumanizing, to say the least. There are downfalls to social media, some of which involve potential addictions to devices, content, and mindless scrolling. Checking "stats" can create anxiety. Getting the "numbers" up is hard. But even after noting the downfalls of social media on us personally, when kept in check it is possible to make it a priority in heathy ways. Build it into your daily workflow. See it as a part of your job. And then move on to the next task. As it becomes a priority (without become consuming), the anxieties will eventually work themselves out. And, even if only a few people read what you are doing with your scholarship online: adding some diverse voices to a conversation you are passionate about will add value to your research.

Kurt Willems (M.Div., Fresno Pacific) is the founding pastor of Pangea Church — "A church that follows in the way of Jesus, to inspire others in the way of love," which is located in Seattle. He is also the curator of The Paulcast: A Podcast All About the Apostle Paul, which has been featured on iTunes as "new and noteworthy." Kurt's written work is available at The Pangea Blog (hosted by Patheos.com), which has been ranked in the Top Christian Ministry Blogs by ChurchRelevance.com. Kurt is a graduate student at the University of Washington focusing on early Christianity, Greco-Roman Religions, and Classical Languages. See Willems' podcast, The Paulcast: A Podcast All about the Apostle Paul, at Paulcast.org (on iTunes and Google). His Patheos blog and other online sites can be found at KurtWillems.com. Follow him on Facebook (/KurtWillems) and Twitter (@KurtWillems). Pangea Church in Seattle is accessible at SeattlePangea.com where you can find links to the church's sermon podcast feed (on iTunes and Google) and videos (YouTube.com/SeattlePangea)."

AMOS YONG

Intercultural (Not Digitally Adept) Theology

A s an elder member of the so-called Generation X (I was born in 1965), I
have lived through the emergence of the household computer and now am
being forced to adapt rapidly amidst the i-age. Yet I also completed graduate school in the 1990s so that I much prefer to read physical books and browse
e-books only if I absolutely have to. All in all, I would consider myself technologi-
cally challenged, a relative neophyte far from a social media pro. I am not sure
that my habits, or profile, will change much. The following provides some indication — perhaps apologetic justification — of why.

It's not that I avoid social media and telecommunicative platforms altogether,
but I am a rather selective user. I wax and wane on Facebook; there are periods
when I have checked FB multiple times during the day or when I have scrolled
down looking not just for updates but for news. Then there have been periods
when I have logged in perhaps once or twice a day, and spent little time on it. I
always announce my new books — authored or edited — on FB, however, and
sometimes (much more rarely) will log in some notes of what I am reading. I do try
to promote scholarly events that I organize through the FB venue (part of my job
at Fuller Seminary is to organize the School of Intercultural Studies annual missiology lectureship), even as I also on occasion deploy its messaging system to

communicate with scholars if I cannot locate or identify an email address (my preferred form of scholarly interaction).

Other than FB, I periodically write reviews on Amazon books. Every once in a blue moon, I upload materials on my Academia.edu account. In the past I have blogged a bit, particularly during a time when I worked as a higher administrator (dean of a major seminary). I have Twitter and Instagram accounts but I do not work either venue. In my current position at Fuller Theological Seminary, the School of Intercultural Studies within which I work has a social media specialist who maintains our presence on the internet, and sometimes, I am featured in what is pushed out in these venues.

I am not sure when I started on Facebook, and after spending a few minutes seeing if I could easily identify my starting date or month, I gave up. My guess, in conversation with my wife, is that this happened sometime before 2010, perhaps as early as 2007. At that time, I entered the FB world in order to connect with friends from earlier in life that I had lost contact with but figured out could be found in that domain. Not too long after that, I began to get friend requests from those who had read my books or heard me give a lecture here or there, but did not know me in person. At one point a few years ago, I posted this note that appears on my page in the bio section: "If you friend-request me & we either have not met before or maybe met once at a conference somewhere, please include a note introducing yourself—thanks!"

As the number of friends I had continued to grow (it is a bit over 4,100 as of the time of writing: early February 2017), it dawned on me that I was being "followed" by those interested in my ideas. While I have always posted and continue to push material of interest to family and friends, it was then that I decided to assume a more scholarly and professional posture on FB.

This term (winter 2017), I am teaching an online graduate class in which, for the first time, I have provided students with the options to develop a social media final project rather than write a standard research paper. The results will not be clear until later but I suspect that I will avail myself more of social media possibilities in my teaching in the future. Graduate theological education is an increasingly online endeavor and this means the centralization rather than marginalization of social media.

What have I been surprised to discover or learn when using social media? The obvious confirmation is its capacity to expand one's networks. To be sure, this includes one's social network but for me as a theologian, also one's scholarly network. I have travelled abroad perhaps once or twice a year for the last ten plus years, so social mediation has facilitated developing and nurturing scholarly connections trans-nationally and trans-continentally. For instance, in one instance, a colleague in Europe asked if I would be willing to support his research and writing. I worked with him to develop a GoFundMe account and found a way to introduce his project to a number of scholarly networks.

On a less positive front: social media can be and is addicting, so we have to be constantly alert to its seductions. Keeping up with one's friends, maintaining one's networks, staying "in-the-know" about the world can be and is exhausting. Last year (2016), the presidential campaign in the United States was one that held me in its grip. I found myself on Facebook less and less interested in my friends and more and more focused on news articles about what was happening. I had to begin discerning which sources were so partisan and which were less untrustworthy. In the wake of the inauguration of the new president, it seems that the news he generates will not abate anytime soon. I am now wanting to disengage from what otherwise can be suffocating. To preserve my sanity, I am in a waning period of social media engagement. On the other hand, some might think that now is the time of resistance, and one way to do that is certainly through the social media platform. Perhaps I will be more politically active going forward.

My work as a Pentecostal theologian has been motivated in large part by a felt sense of vocation: that I have been privileged to have been a part of the first generation of Pentecostal theologians, effectively, and that we therefore are obligated to press forward in confidence but yet at a level of excellence. As my career has unfolded, I have received more and more writing and speaking invitations. It dawned on me a few years ago that my blogs could be selectively cobbled together and re-presented (and reworked as needed) as cohesive essays or articles. Already three or four pieces have emerged in this fashion with others in the pipeline awaiting appropriate occasions. Herein then was an unexpected benefit: effort put into one social media venue has paid dividends in other arenas.

As already intimated, I have long been driven by a sense of call as a Pentecostal scholar and theologian. One way in which this calling is worked out is in discerning important topics that merit explicit Pentecostal attention and engagement. So for instance, while I began in theology of religions (and have, since publishing my doctoral dissertation, also written four other books on that topic), I have expanded since to discuss theological method, theology of disability, political theology, theology and science, missiology, hermeneutics, and homiletics (so far), each from a Pentecostal perspective. But here is the catch: responsible scholarship and theological work requires research so that whenever one might speak into a new arena, one has to do original research and learn a new discourse—historic and contemporary—so as to be able speak intelligently into this new milieu. However this means, in effect, that I have had to write a new PhD thesis, in terms of getting on top of the literature, debates, issues, etc., every time I have turned my theological attention in a new direction. This can be and is exhausting. And the reality means that I have to work hard to do the research and writing that I do, and therefore do not have time for other (more leisurely) activities.

This is in part why I have not spent as much effort on social media as I might have. I already spend a lot of time on my computer (writing this reflection, for instance), and thus am less inspired to remain for more minutes or hours engaging in social media activities. As a husband, father, and in the last year plus also a grandfather, I have interpersonal commitments that take priority over further "computer time." I might want to take as much advantage of what social media affords as a scholar, but these aspirations are secondary to me when considered against the realities that constitute my personal and professional life.

To be sure, that means that I am not spending much time promoting my work compared to my colleagues. I have friends that are very active on Facebook, blog sites, Twitter, etc., lifting up their latest book, for instance. I know from my publishers that a more active social media presence translates into more books sold. Perhaps one day in my retirement I might wish I had invested more time during these years in promotion of my publications and ideas (I hope I do not regret this!). I am in this regard a bibliophile: I love books (I read them a lot) but I do not spend much time in the digital world generating interest in my published work.

So what would I recommend to my friends and others considering using social media? Millennials are inevitably going to be more at home in the digital sphere and they will find their way. For me, three considerations come to mind. First, set some goals about what one hopes to accomplish online. Second, establish a framework for achieving these objectives, alert to the constraints of your own life situation and context. Finally, be attentive to how social mediation might be disruptive of other important dimensions of life: one's work commitments, one's personal relationships, and one's spiritual practices, for instance. Beyond that, for me as a Christian theologian, one can only go where one senses the Spirit leading—so come Holy Spirit, even in the internetosphere: Facebook, Twitter, Instagram and our Global Reflections Blog.

———————

Amos Yong, PhD, is Professor of Theology & Mission at Fuller Theological Seminary, and director of its Center for Missiological Research. He has authored or edited over forty books, as well as serves as co-editor for four scholarly book series. He is past president for the Society for Pentecostal Studies and carries ministerial credentials with the Assemblies of God.

Index

About Me, 276

Academia, 4, 24, 59, 85, 91, 104, 109, 121, 143, 144, 179, 262, 305-06, 312, 319, 353, 363, 389-90, 440

Academic Freedom, 34, 185, 258, 407

Acropolis Project, 425

Activism, 2, 115, 251, 305-06, 310, 341, 370, 378, 382, 419

Algorithm, 105-07, 271, 314, 343, 422

Amazon, 59, 80, 83, 228, 399, 440

American Academy of Religion, 62, 119, 185, 264, 283, 287, 415, 426

American Values, 163

Analytic Theology, 92

Armstrong, Dave, 407

Artwalk, 430

Asana, 9, 179

Asian Americans, 249, 261, 415

Atheism, 76, 111, 135-36, 157, 326, 390, 402, 436

Author Page, 59, 81, 253

Barton, David, 82, 156

Beck, Richard, 24, 31

Becker, Ernest, 32

Beliefnet, 4

Bell, Rob, 148, 434

Biblical Studies Online, 101, 151

Biblical Studies Online, 99-101, 151

Biblical Theology, 99, 161, 165, 179, 253

BioLogos, 104, 158, 366, 393-96

Blogging, references found in nearly every essay

Blogosphere, 65, 110, 253, 433

Books and Culture, 157

Branding, 3, 8, 17, 34, 64, 73, 227, 425

Brueggemann, Walter, 108, 348, 354

Brexit, 100, 110, 152

Buddhism, 125, 225, 279, 295, 402

Buffer, 180, 401

Bullying, 126, 130, 132, 171, 271, 409

Campbell, Douglas, 32

Canva, 346

Castells, Manuel, 197

Center for the Study of Christian Origins, 221-22

Center for Theology and Public Life, 185

Chomsky, Noam, 311

Christian Post, 293

Citizen Theology, 27

Clayton, Philip, 80, 83

Clickbait, 26, 197, 303

Cobb, John B. Jr., 148

Collins, Francis, 156, 393

Commonplaces, 92

Communications, 64, 171-73, 269, 347

Constructive Theology, 147, 201, 247, 265

Coursera, 201

Crossan, John Dominic, 152

Crowdsource, 3, 106, 230-31, 436

Cursor_, 24-29

Daily Theology, 332

Dawkins, Richard, 110, 157

Digital Culture, 45-48, 173, 274, 275-78, 281-82, 374

Disability, 53-57, 417-419, 429-31, 441

Discovery Institute, 158

Driscoll, Mark, 54

Eastern Orthodox, 32, 111

Eliot, T S, 281

Erickson, Erik, 171

Ethics, 59, 146, 173, 183, 191, 208, 294, 411

Evans, Rachel Held, 158

Facebook, references found in nearly every essay

Farmer, Patricia Adams, 129-32, 279

Fat Soul, 131-33, 279

Fea, John, 82

Feminism, 39, 130, 204, 252, 264, 298, 346

Flipped Classroom, 9

FourSquare, 139

Fuller Studios, 92

Fuller, Tripp, 83, 147-49, 232, 369

Galbraith, Deane, 100, 151-54

Garcia, Jerry, 191

Generation X, 91, 397, 439

GitHub, 341-42

Goodreads, 80, 337

Google, 49, 53, 60, 80, 82, 83, 104, 109, 137, 161, 179, 215, 239, 262, 312, 319, 326, 398

Grayson, Rob, 193

Haidt, Jonathan, 294

Ham, Ken, 156-57

Heim, Mark, 32

Heresy, 78, 87, 267

Hinduism, 402

Historical Theology, 13, 79, 201, 405,

History of Christianity, 13, 95

Homebrewed Christianity, 92, 147-49, 202, 277

Hootsuite, 81, 277, 311

Huffington Post, 20, 69, 158, 252

Instagram, 7, 10, 26, 75, 85, 139-40, 143-46, 175, 183, 207-08, 217, 223-28, 270, 275, 297,

326, 332-35, 343, 346, 373, 377, 381, 398, 401, 412-13, 421-25, 429, 442

Intercultural Theology, 252, 421-23, 439-41

Interdisciplinary, 25, 32, 46, 66, 355, 389, 414

International Society of Science and Religion, 62

IPhone, 145, 226, 365

Jesus, 78, 81, 102, 149, 152, 156,162, 169-72, 188, 192, 211, 215-16, 222, 230, 236, 255, 285, 304, 327-30, 357, 397-99, 402-03, 436

JesusJazzBuddhism, 20, 125, 279-82

Jews/Judaism, 20-22, 106, 154, 203-05, 258, 357

John Templeton Foundation, 59, 70, 94

Kenarchy, 309-10

Lamott, Anne, 190

Latinx Studies, 115-120

Lectionary, 125, 176, 253, 277, 304, 400

Levinas, Emmanuel, 357-59

Lewis, C S, 24, 52, 70, 266, 267, 358

LinkedIn, 8, 10, 49, 51, 53, 85, 91, 121, 151, 223, 247, 270, 274-75, 305-06, 337, 353

Liturgy, 337-39, 360, 413

Loomer, Bernard, 131

Luther, Martin, 201-04, 293

McDaniel, Jay, 131, 279-82

McKnight, Scot, 81, 166, 400

McLuhan, Marshall, 1-3, 310, 347

Medium Stories, 109, 175-76

Meme, 46, 133, 215, 240, 303, 402-03, 420

Mendeley, 179

Merritt, Jonathan, 184

Microblogging, 139-40

Millennials, 91, 298, 365, 368, 374, 411, 414, 442

Ministry, 3, 14-15, 37-39, 81-82, 86-88, 175, 232, 235-36, 252, 264, 299, 343, 353-55, 365, 402, 411-14, 421, 425-28, 434

Missional, 14, 75, 88, 353-58, 397-99, 411, 421, 439-42

Moltmann, Jürgen, 148

MOOC, 4, 201-04

Moodle, 49, 161, 274

Moyes, JoJo, 54

Muslim, 15, 106, 111, 189, 281, 401-02

Myspace, 27, 103, 209, 269, 300, 325-26, 433

Naznet, 95, 157

Network for New Media, Religion, and Digital Culture Studies, 46

Networking, 3, 7, 45, 121-22, 130, 143, 255, 257, 307-11, 331-35, 337, 355, 369, 382, 383, 385, 411-12

New Testament, 136, 180-81, 221, 243, 253, 287, 435

Nextdoor, 326

Noll, Mark, 156

Nomad, 310

Nones, Dones, 191

Nouwen, Henri, 52, 193

Nye, Bill, 239, 241

Occupy Movement, 262-63

Ochs, Peter, 106

Olson, Roger, 210

Online Books, 24, 154

Online Church, 170-72

Online Education, 2, 4, 8-10, 162, 194, 201-204, 224

Online Journal, 4, 23-28

Onscript, 92

Oord, Alexa, 4

Oord, Andee, 4

Oord, Thomas Jay, 1-4, 51, 130, 147, 309

Open Access Theology Journal, 31

Orsi, Robert, 203

Palmer, Amanda, 107

Panentheism, 321

Pastoral Theology, 7, 275, 297, 243, 433

Patheos, 4, 78, 125-27, 135, 193, 293, 295,
    326, 346, 405, 434

Patreon, 187-189

Paulcast, 435

Peer Review, 27, 28, 31, 65, 80-81, 84, 96,
    117-18, 148, 185, 285, 338, 351

Pentecostalism, 14-16, 53, 111, 148, 178, 305,
    354-55, 361, 441-443

Periscope, 139, 147, 326

Philosophical Theology, 209, 257, 319, 369

Philosophy, 109, 113, 132, 135, 225, 239, 279,
    313, 341, 342, 381, 417

Pinterest, 8, 10, 109, 223, 343, 346, 377, 401,
    417, 421-23

Piper, John, 54

Podcast, 3, 20, 92, 101, 118, 139-41, 147-49,
    161, 223-27, 251, 253-55, 277, 310, 431-32,
    435-36

Political Theology, 24, 277, 305-09, 441

Pomodoro System, 111-112, 334, 423

Pope Benedict, 333

Pope Francis, 333

Postcolonial, 37, 39, 121-23, 262-64, 306

Pound, Ezra, 281

Practical Theology, 49, 125, 129, 139, 235,
    325, 367

Preaching Peace, 191-92

Prince, Joseph, 54

Process and Faith, 125

Progressive, 25, 37, 39, 125-26, 130, 189,
    198, 212, 249, 281, 326, 329, 385,
    402-404

Prosblogion, 110, 417

Prothero, Stephen, 215

Psychology, 31-34, 239-40

Public Theology, 75, 121, 143, 207, 215, 229,
    279, 289, 401, 425

PubPub, 27-29

Quora, 4, 109, 314-16

Rabbinic Studies, 19

Rand, Ayn, 156

Raschke, Carl, 277

Reddit, 109, 270

Rieger, Joerg, 262

Relegere, 151-52

Religious News Service, 183

Religious Studies, 69, 151, 223

Researchgate, 4, 59, 109, 143, 201, 305

Retweat, 10, 60, 63, 66-67, 312, 399

Rollins, Peter, 231-32

Russell, Bertrand, 314

Ryan, Paul, 156

Sacramental Theology, 302, 337-39, 356

Sanders, Bernie, 156

Sanders, Fred, 93

Sanders, John, 408

Science and Religion, 59, 62, 69, 155, 283,
    353, 363, 377

Science Fiction, 283-85

Second Life, 27, 49, 170-71

Sertillanges, A G, 266

Skype, 227, 302, 367

Slack, 9, 179

SlideShare, 289

Smith, James K A, 360

Snapchat, 104, 139, 218, 223, 263, 270, 276, 287, 337, 373, 381, 412

Snarky, 71, 173, 314, 332

Social Scholarship, 3

Society of Biblical Literature, 166

Society of Christian Ethics, 119, 183

Society of Christian Philosophers, 321, 387

Sociology, 197-98, 384

Socrates, 49, 314

Spirituality, 13, 52, 125, 143, 261-64, 279, 422

Story House, 189

Sweet, Leonard, 50-51, 229-230, 275, 397-400

Swinburne, Richard, 320

Swoboda, A J, 232

Systematic Theology, 29, 41, 65, 91, 175, 331, 389

TGIF Culture, 398

The Work of the People, 347-50

Theological Education, 85, 95, 161, 302, 427

Theology and Culture, 24, 293

Theology and Media, 103, 169, 187, 373

Theology and Technology, 37

Theology Beer Camp, 48

Thiselton, Anthony, 355

Thomas, Kevin, 4,

Tolkien, J R R, 266

Transhumanism, 61-63

Tremain, Shelley, 417

Trolls, 3, 67, 76, 102, 122, 193-94, 211, 217, 222, 227, 236, 241, 291, 308, 313, 315, 329, 360, 371

Trump, Donald, 109, 155-56, 163, 198, 216, 242, 263, 271

Tumblr, 109, 143, 337, 421

Tupamahu, Ekaputra, 354

Turner, J T, 321-22

Twitter Seminary, 66

Twitter, references found in nearly every essay

Underhill, Evelyn, 356

Unplug, 3, 50, 184, 190, 236,

Vlog, 144-46

Wabash Center, 162

Ward, Keith, 210

Webinar, 3, 429

Weebly, 401

Wesley, John, 14, 51

Whatsapp, 41, 270

Whitehead, Alfred North, 62, 281

Wipf and Stock, 96, 199

Womanism, 39

WordPress, 9, 53, 95, 99, 135, 165, 215, 270, 276, 305-07, 311, 353, 429

Worship, 82, 140, 162, 411-14

YouTube, 3, 49, 53, 93, 116, 118, 129, 143-44, 184, 187, 189, 223-26, 239, 251, 274, 296, 319-20, 389-90, 411-14, 429

Zacharias, Ravi, 156

Zoom, 49, 161

Zuckerberg, Mark, 96, 122

Zygon Center for Religion and Science, 377-379

Made in the USA
Lexington, KY
07 September 2017